Why Do You Need This New Edition?

If you're wondering why you should buy this new edition of *Wordsmith: A Guide to Paragraphs and Short Essays*, Fifth Edition, here are six good reasons!

1. **Build Confidence and Creativity with Informal Writing Assignments.** Each of the writing modes chapters (Chapters 7, 8, and 9) contains new impromptu writing assignments called *Small Scrawls*. Designed to be completed in one sitting, *Small Scrawls* will help you become quicker and more fluid in your writing.

2. **Recognize Formal and Informal Situations and Write Appropriately for Both.** When you speak, you naturally shift between formal and informal language, depending on the situation. Chapter 25, Word Choice, has been updated to help you fine tune that skill and to recognize categories of word choice that are generally not appropriate for college writing, such as slang, text-speak, and more.

3. **Write Persuasively.** Arguing effectively and writing persuasively are essential skills not only for college writing but also for the writing you will do in your career and throughout your life. This edition of *Wordsmith* includes an updated section on argument in Chapter 9, Examining Logical Connections.

4. **Explore New Topics in Two New Readings.** The readings section has been updated with two new essays on hot topics in today's culture.

5. **Enjoy Reading Your Textbook.** A conversational tone and real-world examples make reading and completing your assignments less tedious. Concise instruction tells you what you need to know in a straightforward manner, making it easier for you to absorb even the most challenging lessons. New exercises, visuals, and chapter openers throughout the text bring the material to life and add humor to the text.

6. **Master Chapter Content with Chapter Goals and Integrated MyWritingLab Prompts.** Each chapter in Wordsmith now opens with a chapter goal and ties in to the most powerful online writing tool on the planet, Pearson's MyWritingLab (www.mywritinglab.com). Now you can truly grasp chapter content and test your understanding of that content with MyWritingLab in a more meaningful way.

PEARSON

ANNOTATED INSTRUCTOR'S EDITION

Wordsmith

A Guide to Paragraphs and Short Essays

Fifth Edition

Pamela Arlov

Macon State College

PEARSON

Boston   Columbus   Indianapolis   New York   San Francisco   Upper Saddle River
Amsterdam   Cape Town   Dubai   London   Madrid   Milan   Munich   Paris   Montreal   Toronto
Delhi   Mexico City   Sao Paulo   Sydney   Hong Kong   Seoul   Singapore   Taipei   Tokyo

Senior Acquisitions Editor: Matthew Wright
Development Editor: Erin Reilly
Marketing Manager: Kurt Massey
Supplements Editor: Amanda Dykstra
Media Project Manager: Rob St. Laurent
Associate Managing Editor: Bayani Mendoza de Leon
Production/Project Manager: Raegan Keida Heerema

Project Coordination, Text Design, and Electronic Page Makeup: Laserwords
Cover Designer/Manager: Nancy Danahy
Manufacturing Manager: Mary Ann Gloriande
Printer/Binder: Edwards Brothers
Cover Printer: Lehigh-Phoenix Color/Hagerstown

To my husband, Nick, with all my love.

This book was set in 10.5/12.5 Palatino.

Credits and acknowledgments borrowed from other sources and reproduced, with permission, in this textbook appear on page 519.

10 9 8 7 6 5 4 3 2 1—EB—14 13 12 11

www.pearsonhighered.com

Student ISBN-13: 978-0-205-06023-8
ISBN 10:   0-205-06023-4
Annotated Instructor's Edition ISBN-13: 978-0-205-24437-9
ISBN-10:   0-205-24437-8

Contents

v

Chapter 9   Examining Logical Connections: Comparison-Contrast, Cause-Effect, and Argument   141

Chapter 10   Writing an Essay   172

Chapter 11   Writing Summary Reports   194

PART 2 Grammar   220

Chapter 12   Verbs and Subjects   220

Chapter 13   Subject–Verb Agreement   238

Chapter 14   Verb Shifts   252

Chapter 15   Coordination and Subordination   267

List of Readings by Rhetorical Mode

List of Readings by Subject

Preface

Thank you for choosing *Wordsmith: A Guide to Paragraphs and Short Essays* as your textbook. Whether you are teaching from this text or learning from it, it is my hope that you will enjoy its simplicity. Writing itself is a remarkably complex process that incorporates the personality and experience of each writer and each reader. It also requires adherence to agreed-upon rules of grammar, punctuation, and form. Therefore, I have tried to make this book simple in its structure, straightforward in its language and presentation, and easy to use for both instructors and students.

Updates to the Fifth Edition

Several changes have been made in the fifth edition of *Wordsmith: A Guide to Paragraphs and Short Essays*:

- Each chapter is now preceded by new learning goals to help students and instructors alike see what the chapter is intended to accomplish before they begin work in it.

- In response to requests for more informal writing assignments, each of the writing modes chapters (Chapters 7, 8, and 9) now contains several impromptu writing assignments called *Small Scrawls*. These assignments, intended to be completed in one sitting, inspire students' confidence and creativity as well as help them become quicker and more fluid in their writing.

- The section on argument in Chapter 9, Examining Logical Connections, has been strengthened with new coverage of ethos, pathos, and logos and identifying flawed arguments.

- Because so many instructors and students find MyWritingLab to be an invaluable supplement, MyWritingLab prompts have been added throughout the text to help instructors and students easily access additional course materials.

- Chapter 25, Word Choice, has been updated with a new section on eliminating the more informal constructions spawned by texting and the Internet.

- The Readings section has been updated with two new essays. Catherine Rampell's "A Generation of Slackers? Not So Much" explores the generation gap and contributions of the millennial generation now coming of age. Ann Bancroft's " How's the Day Treating You? Your Teller Wants to Know" looks at the issue of forced courtesy in our culture.

- An annotated instructor's edition is available with answers for most exercises in the text.

- There is little throughout the fifth edition that has not been re-examined and revised. For example, the coverage of APA style has been updated to meet the 2009 guidelines, new content on keeping thesis points parallel has been included in Chapter 3, and many new images and exercises have been added throughout the text.

Features of *Wordsmith: A Guide to Paragraphs and Short Essays*

- The three-part layout allows the freedom to mix and match the writing chapters, grammar chapters, and readings.

- A structured yet flexible approach to writing encourages clarity and creativity.

- A direct, conversational, student-friendly approach is used throughout.

- Lighthearted chapter openings promote a positive and playful approach to learning.

Part 1 Composition

Part 1, "Composition," takes the paragraph as its primary focus but provides an extensive chapter (Chapter 10) on the five-paragraph essay and a chapter (Chapter 11) on the summary report. The book begins with an overview of the writing process (Chapter 1), followed by a chapter on prewriting (Chapter 2). Planning and drafting, the next two steps in the writing process, are discussed in Chapters 3, 4, and 5. Chapter 6 deals with revising and proofreading.

Chapters 7, 8, and 9 present methods of development. I have sacrificed some flexibility by grouping the methods, so let me explain why. The first reason is philosophical. I believe it is more realistic to group the modes since they are seldom used in isolation in "real-world" writing. Modes with a similar purpose are grouped together, and the optional "Mixed Methods" assignments at the end of the chapter show how the modes can be used together in a single piece of writing. The second reason for grouping modes is more practical. I have found that, no matter how hard I try, it is not possible to cover nine rhetorical modes in one term. Grouping them allows me to assign a chapter containing three modes and then deal with only one or two in depth. If all three rhetorical modes chapters are assigned, students are exposed to all nine modes even if they practice only a few.

Part 2 Grammar

Part 2, "Grammar," can be used in a variety of ways: with direct in-class instruction, in a lab setting, as a supplement, or for independent study. Part 2 also works well for instructors who want to address more difficult grammar topics in class while assigning easier material or review material for independent study.

In the grammar chapters, explanations are clear, and each topic is taken one skill at a time, with numerous practice exercises for each skill. At the end of each chapter are review exercises in increasing order of difficulty, ending with a paragraph-length editing exercise.

Part 3 Readings

Part 3, "Readings," offers essays written by professional writers. In any craft, the works of accomplished artisans can inspire the apprentice. These essays model writing at its best: entertaining, challenging, and thought provoking. Each reading is followed by a comprehension exercise that includes questions about content, questions about the writer's techniques, and related topics for discussion and writing. Diversity in authorship, subject matter, and rhetorical method is emphasized.

Instructor Resources

Annotated Instructor's Edition. The AIE is a replica of the student text that includes the answers to the exercises. ISBN: 0-205-24437-8.

Instructor's Resource Manual. The Instructor's Resource Manual contains additional sample syllabi, a student answer key, and two chapter tests for each of the 29 chapters in the text. For each chapter, there is one short answer and one multiple-choice test for instructors to choose from. There is also a grammar pre-test and post-test. Additional chapter-specific assignments and teaching tips provided by Pamela Arlov are included as well. The Instructors Resource Manual is available for download at Pearson's Instructor Resource Center, which can be accessed by going to www.pearsonhighered.com. ISBN: 0-205-23556-5.

PowerPoint Presentation. A presentation for each chapter, which is structured around the chapter learning goals, can be downloaded at Pearson's Instructor Resource Center. You can use these presentations as is or edit them to suit your lecturing style.

Student Resources

MyWritingLab: Where Better Practice Makes Better Writers
www.mywritinglab.com

How do you improve your writing skills? MyWritingLab is an online learning system that provides better writing practice through diagnostic assessment and progressive exercises. With this better practice model, students develop the skills needed to become better writers.

- *Diagnostic Testing:* MyWritingLab's diagnostic test comprehensively assesses student skills in grammar. Students are given an individualized learning path based on the diagnostic's results, identifying the modules in areas where they most need help.

- *Progressive Learning:* The heart of MyWritingLab is the progressive learning that takes place as students review media and complete the various exercises within each topic. Students move from literal comprehension, to critical understanding, to the ability to demonstrate a skill in their own writing. This progression of critical thinking, not available in any other online resource, enables students to truly master the skills and concepts they need to become successful writers.

- *Online Gradebook:* All student work in MyWritingLab is captured in the Online Gradebook. Students can monitor their own progress through reports detailing scores on all of the exercises in the course. It also shows which topics students have mastered. Instructors have detailed reports, such as class summaries, that track the progress of their entire class and show individual student detail, as well as topical views and alerts.

- *EText:* The *Wordsmith* etext is accessed through MyWritingLab. Students now have the etext at their fingertips while completing the various exercises and activities within MyWritingLab. Students can highlight important material in the etext, tab areas they want to refer to again, and add notes to any section for reflection and/or further study throughout the semester.

MyWritingLab access codes can be packaged with the text. To order, please use ISBN: 0-205-87998-5.

For a complete list of additional supplements to package with the text, including dictionaries, a thesaurus, a grammar or editing workbook, and readers, contact your Pearson sales representative, or visit us at www.pearsonhighered.com.

Acknowledgments

I could not have written this book without the help, support, and collaboration of a great many people. I owe thanks to all the staff at Pearson, particularly Matthew Wright, Senior Acquisitions Editor, who is a joy to work with and who has given me some great opportunities; and Erin E. Reilly, Development Editor, who has done so much for this edition of the book that I cannot imagine how I ever did the previous editions without her. I owe a debt of gratitude to Raegan Heerema, Project Manager; Bayani Mendoza de Leon, Associate Managing Editor; Kurt Massey, Marketing Manager; and Eric Stano, Editor in Chief. I also thank the always cheerful, never ruffled Bruce Hobart, Production Coordinator at Laserwords Maine; Rohini Herbert, copy editor par excellence; Maxine Barber, proofreader; and Pam Bliss, cold reader.

Also, I thank the reviewers, whose comments helped shape the most recent edition of the *Wordsmith* series: Sharon Rinkiewicz, Broward College and Jean Sherrod, Pitt Community College.

I also thank Nick Arlov, my dear husband, for his love and support, and for the sacrifices he made so many years ago so that I could attend college. I will always be grateful.

Pamela Arlov
Macon State College

CHAPTER 1

The Writing Process

> **Chapter Goal:** Develop an understanding of the writing process and write a clear, organized paragraph.

Your ideas may seem scattered, disorganized, jumbled, and downright messy, but the writing process can help you funnel them and shape them into real

W
R
I
T
I
N
G

Writing is not a single act, but a process composed of several steps. As with most processes—swinging a baseball bat, playing the clarinet, or surfing the Internet—it is sometimes easier to do than to analyze. When people try to analyze how they write, their descriptions of the process are uniquely their own. Yet from a sea of individual accounts, the same steps emerge.

Focus on the Writing Process: Completing the Steps

Admittedly, the "Sorry we're open" sign in the photograph is probably the product of someone's slightly warped sense of humor. But as it brings a smile to your face, it may also serve as a reminder of the need to proofread carefully.

Often, the temptation to let prewriting, revision, or proofreading slide is hard to resist. But every step contributes to the final product. Taking time to complete all the steps in the writing process can be your personal form of quality control.

Reflect on It

1. Write down a process that you do that requires several steps.
2. List the steps in the order in which you do them.
3. Analyze the process. Is it a flexible process, like the writing process, that allows you to go back to a previous step if you need to? Or is it a process more like cooking, which does not allow you to add an egg once the cake is in the oven?
4. Finally, think about the importance of each step in your process. What would happen if you left out a step?

One writer, Antonio, describes the process this way:

Well, first, I need time to think. If I have a while before the paper is due, I never start right away. Some people might call it procrastination, but it works for me. After the ideas have had time to percolate, I sit at the computer and just start writing. I just let my ideas flow, good or bad. If that doesn't work, sometimes I try a more organized approach, jotting down an outline. It's all a part of finding my focus. Then, once I know what I want to say, I just write. I am a slow writer because I try to get it right the first time. But I never do. If I look at it the next day, I see where the holes are—where I've left out details. I'm bad about that. So my second draft is always better than my first. When I'm finished, I check to make sure my commas are in the right place and my grammar is okay. Then I'm ready to turn it in.

The Writing Process

mywritinglab
Visit MyWriting Lab for additional practice with the writing process.

Though everyone approaches writing a little differently, most people follow a process similar to the one just described. The writer in the example above may not be aware of it, but he is following all of the steps in the **writing process:** prewriting, planning, drafting, revising, and proofreading.

Prewriting

"... first, I need time to think."

Prewriting covers a range of activity from casually thinking about your topic to going through a prewriting exercise to get your thoughts on paper. You will probably find yourself doing some form of prewriting throughout the writing process. When you are sitting at a traffic light and the perfect example to illustrate your point pops into your head, you are prewriting. When you realize that your paragraph isn't working the way you wanted and you stop to list ideas or figure out another approach, you are returning to the prewriting stage. Prewriting is thinking, and the more thought you put into your paper, the stronger it will be.

Planning

"It's all a part of finding my focus."

Careful and thoughtful **planning** makes a paragraph easier for you to write and easier for your readers to read. Your plan may include a topic sentence—your statement of the main idea. Because it states the main idea, the topic sentence forms the cornerstone of your paragraph. Besides a topic sentence, your planning will probably include an informal outline. An outline can be as simple as a list of the points you will develop in a paragraph. Don't be afraid that planning will waste your time. Careful planning—or lack of it—always shows in the final draft.

Drafting

"I just write."

Sometimes **drafting** is a quick process, with ideas flowing faster than you can get them down on paper. At other times, the process is slow and difficult. Your thoughts grind to a standstill, and you become frustrated, thinking you have nothing to say. If you get stuck during the drafting process, don't quit in frustration. The creative process is still at work. What is happening to you happens to all writers. Write through the problem, or, if necessary, return to the planning or prewriting stage.

As you draft your paper, you should not worry about grammar, spelling, or punctuation. Stopping to look up a comma rule will only distract you. Concentrate on ideas and save the proofreading for later.

Revising

"I see where the holes are."

In its Latin roots, the word *revising* means "seeing again." **Revising** is difficult because it is hard to see your work through the eyes of a reader. Writers often see what they *meant* to say rather than what they really said. Sometimes they take for granted background knowledge that the reader may not have. Because of these difficulties, it helps to put your draft aside for a day or so before trying to revise it. With twenty-four hours between writing and revising, you will see your paper more clearly. It is also helpful to ask someone else to look at your work—a friend, classmate, or relative. Ask the person to focus on the *content* of your paper rather than on grammar, spelling, or punctuation. Ask which ideas are clear and which ones need more explanation. Ask how well your examples illustrate your points. A reader's comments can help you see your paper in a new light.

One word of advice—if you don't know how to use a computer, learn. Writing multiple drafts is much easier on a computer. Once you learn to write on a computer, the paragraphs, essays, term papers, and reports you will write in college will look much less intimidating.

Proofreading

"I check to make sure my commas are in the right place and my grammar is okay."

Proofreading is the final polish that you put on your paragraph. When you proofread, consider such things as grammar, spelling, and word choice. Replace vague words with specific words. Take out words that are not carrying their weight. Look at connections, making sure ideas flow smoothly from one sentence to the next. Because the stages of the writing process overlap, you have probably done some minor proofreading along the way. Before the final proofreading, set your paragraph aside for a while. Then proofread it once more to give it the luster of a finished piece.

An Important Point

If you go through the writing process expecting the steps to fall in order, like the steps involved in changing the oil in your car, you may think the process is not working. However, writing a paragraph is not a sequential process. It is a repetitive process, more like driving a car than changing its oil.

If you take a two-hundred-mile trip, the steps you follow might be described as "Turn on the ignition. Put the car in drive. Accelerate. Brake. Put the car in park. Turn off the ignition." Yet it is not that simple. During a two-hundred-mile drive, you repeat each step not once but several times, and you may even stop for rest or fuel.

Writing a paragraph works in the same way. You may list the steps as "prewrite, plan, draft, revise, proofread," but it is not that simple. You may change the order of the sentences as you write the first draft or correct a spelling mistake as you revise. Sometimes you repeat a step several times. You may even stop for rest or fuel, just as you do when you drive. Eventually, both processes will get you where you want to go.

EXERCISE 1   **THE WRITING PROCESS**

Answer the following questions to review your knowledge of the writing process.

1. The five steps in the writing process are ___prewriting___ , ___planning___ , ___drafting___ , ___revising___ , and ___proofreading___ .

2. The "thinking step" in the writing process is called ___prewriting___ .

3. The part of the writing process that involves correcting grammar and punctuation is called ___proofreading___ .

4. Major changes would most likely be made during the ___revising___ step in the writing process.

5. True or false? The steps in the writing process often overlap. ___True___

The Writing Process: Stephanie's Paragraph

The next section follows the development of one writer's paragraph from start to finish. In writing her paragraph, Stephanie went through several forms of prewriting, made two different outlines, conferred with members of her writing group and her instructor, and wrote two rough drafts. (Only the first of the two drafts is shown here because the final draft reflects all of the changes Stephanie made.) Before turning in her final draft, Stephanie also proofread the paragraph once from top to bottom and twice from bottom to top. Then she asked a member of her writing group to look over the final draft for any mistakes she might have overlooked.

The steps that Stephanie goes through are the steps that you will take as you learn the writing process. You will also share some of her frustrations. But, like Stephanie, you will find that what seems difficult at first is attainable, one step at a time.

Stephanie's Assignment

Stephanie's instructor handed out a list of three paragraph topics. Stephanie chose to write on this one: "Write about a piece of music or art that has a message for you. Don't just describe the piece of music or art; tell your reader how it affected you."

Stephanie's instructor suggested that the students prewrite, then make an outline. Earlier, the class had been divided into writing groups of four or five people who would help one another during the term. The instructor suggested that the writing groups meet to discuss each student's outline. Then, students would write rough drafts and bring them to individual writing conferences with the instructor.

Stephanie's Prewriting

In class, Stephanie did a form of prewriting called *freewriting*. (For more information on freewriting and other forms of prewriting, see Chapter 2.) In this prewriting, Stephanie did not worry about grammar or spelling, but focused on gathering ideas. Stephanie's prewriting is reproduced here without correction.

> I remember the day my art class went to an exhibit at the museum and I saw a piece of art—I don't know what to call it. Not a painting or a drawing, but something the artist had put together. Built. I was trailing behind the class and something just pulled me over into the corner where it was. It was just me and that piece of art, and when I lifted the curtain—Wow! I was so knocked out. I remember my art teacher used to talk about what art meant, and I never understood until that day. I felt all sorts of emotion. I think I'll go over to the Tubman this weekend and see if it's still there.

Later, Stephanie visited the museum and took the following notes:

"Beauty Standard" by Ce Scott

Black frame, masks placed at top & bottom. Each side has female figure tied at ankles, wrist, and eyes with golden cord. They have bodies like models—thin & beautiful. Masks are just blank—no real features. Frame has tiny words repeated over and over "dark brown eyes big full lips flat wide nose." Velvet curtain—very mysterious hangs there. Golden tassels hang down. "Mirror" embroidered on. Card says "Lift the curtain to see the image by which each of us should be judged."

Stephanie's Rough Draft

Ce Scott's artwork *Beauty Standard* is a piece of art with a message. It hangs in the Tubman African American Museum. It has a black frame decorated with female figures bound at the wrists, ankles, and eyes with golden cord. They have bodies like models, thin and beautiful. At the center of the frame is a black velvet curtain embroidered with the word "Mirror." On the frame, in small writing are the words "dark brown eyes big full lips flat wide nose." A card beside the work invites the viewer to lift the cloth and see "the image by which each of us should be judged." Underneath is a mirror—not the one held up by society, but one that reflects the image of whoever looked into it. The message is that the only beauty standard you need to meet is your own.

Stephanie's Writing Group Meets

Next, Stephanie met with her writing group. A transcript of the portion of the session dealing with Stephanie's prewriting and rough draft appears below.

Transcript: Writing Group Session, Monday, September 7

Eddie:	Okay, who's the first victim? Tran?
Tran:	I don't want to go first. Stephanie?
Stephanie:	I may as well. I think I need major help. (Stephanie passes out copies of her prewriting and rough draft, and the group reads silently.)
Tran:	I like it. You have good grammar and spelling.
Stephanie:	You're just saying that because I got you off the hook. You didn't have to go first. (Laughter.)
Kelly:	I like it, too. But your prewriting is really different from the rough draft.
Stephanie:	Yeah, the prewriting doesn't have much detail. I had to go back to the museum to look at the piece again because I had forgotten a lot.
Eddie:	Yes, but I like the prewriting. I can tell you were really excited about the painting.
Stephanie:	It's not a painting. I'm not sure what you'd call it.

Eddie:	Whatever. But in the prewriting, I can tell it really had an effect on you. In the rough draft, the excitement disappears. It's just a description.
Kelly:	Eddie is right. I mean, it's a good description, but it needs more of you in it.
Stephanie:	Yeah, I see what you mean.
Tran:	I chose the same topic, except I'm doing my paragraph on music. Anyway, I remember that the assignment said to tell how the music or art affected you.
Stephanie:	That's right! I do need to put more of my reaction in there somehow. But won't that make it too long?
Kelly:	Well, you heard what Dr. Pettis said. Plenty of support.
Stephanie:	Okay, guys. Thanks. You've been a big help. Anything else?
Tran:	Yeah. Will you help me with my grammar? (Laughter.)

Stephanie's Final Draft

Stephanie wrote a second rough draft. Then, she met with her instructor for a conference before writing her final draft. Stephanie's final draft appears below.

Beauty Standard

I always thought of art as something to hang on a wall, never as something that had a message for me. Then last fall, at the Tubman African American Museum, I saw a piece of art called *Beauty Standard* by Ce Scott. It had a black frame decorated with female figures bound at the wrists, ankles, and eyes with golden cord. At the center of the frame hung a black velvet curtain embroidered with the word "Mirror." A card beside the work invited the viewer to lift the cloth and see "the image by which each of us should be judged." On the frame, in small writing, were the words "dark brown eyes big full lips flat wide nose." The words made me think of the sixties slogan, "Black is beautiful." It was a statement of pride and at the same time a demand to be included. At the time, society's beauty standard was a white one. Even though ideas of beauty now include different races, so many people are still left out—the old, those who are overweight, and even those who are just average. Suddenly, I felt angry and a little afraid to lift the velvet curtain. I looked at the bound female figures and understood that society binds me, too. Hesitantly, I lifted the curtain. My own face, skeptical and a bit defiant, looked back at me. It *was* a mirror—not the one held up by society, but one that reflected the image of whoever looked into it. As clearly as if she were in the room, the artist was telling me, "The only beauty standard you need to meet is your own."

Stephanie's Approach to Writing—and Yours

Stephanie's final draft is the product of many hours' thought and work, and it is at least partly a result of her willingness to listen to the advice and comments of others.

Writing is a process of trial and error, and sometimes it feels like mostly error. Even experienced writers often find writing difficult, often wonder if they have anything worthwhile to say or the ability to say it. If you fear writing, even if you dislike it, you are not alone. But writing is a skill that improves with practice, and if you give it serious effort, you will amaze yourself. The following list, "Five Quick Takes on Writing," may help you put the task of writing in perspective.

Five Quick Takes on Writing

1. Take it a step at a time. Writing is often a slow process, and it always requires thought.
2. Take it seriously. The ability to write clearly and well will benefit you academically, professionally, and personally throughout your life.
3. Take it easy. Don't expect yourself to be perfect.
4. Take it to the limit. Stretch the limits of your imagination. Refuse to limit yourself by labeling yourself a poor writer.
5. Take it with you. Writing is a vital part of the real world. Make it a part of your life.

Group Exercise 1   The Ideal Conditions for Writing

In a group of three or four, discuss the ideal conditions for writing. Think about questions such as these: What tools do you enjoy working with? Do you write best with music in the background or in absolute silence? Do you like having others around, or do you prefer to be alone? Do you need coffee or snacks when you write? Do you need room to pace, or do you think best seated in front of a desk or computer? After each group member has contributed to the discussion, jot down the differences and similarities that exist among members of your group. Have a spokesperson report your group's findings to the rest of the class.

Writing for Right-Brained Writers

This section is for those of you who rebel at the idea of a step-by-step approach such as the one described in this chapter and outlined in the writing assignment at the chapter's end. Although prewriting, planning, drafting, revising, and proofreading are identifiable steps in the writing process, there's no law that says everyone has to approach them in exactly the same way.

For some people, a step-by-step approach does not come naturally. These people have a thinking style that is most often called "right-brained" or "holistic." The human brain is divided into halves, or hemispheres, and most people are wired to rely heavily on the left hemisphere—the half that is responsible for logical, sequential, step-by-step thinking. Some people, however, rely more heavily on the right half of the brain, the part that is responsible for seeing the whole, for thinking in images, and for flashes of insight.

The following questions may help you decide if you are a right-brained thinker.

1. If you were asked to analyze how you write, would your answer be "I don't know. I just do it"?

2. When you are required to turn in an outline, do you usually complete it *after* you have written the paper?

3. If you were asked to describe your usual prewriting technique, would you say, "I never prewrite"?

4. Do you often arrive at the right answer to math problems without following the steps?

5. Do you have a hard time getting detail into your writing?

6. Are you a "big-picture person" rather than a "detail person"?

If you answered "yes" to three or more of the questions above, you may have been seen as a rebel because you don't always follow a step-by-step, conventional approach to your work. But chances are, whatever other characteristics you possess, you are also a right-brained writer.

Right-brained people are often intuitive, seeing the big picture before others do. They have a strong creative streak. They sometimes grasp ideas easily without knowing why or understanding how. But unlike their persistent, list-making, left-brained brothers and sisters, right-brained people often have trouble with the details. Planning isn't in their natures, and they tend not to have systems or specific steps to rely on. Whatever the task is, they "just do it."

If you are right-brained, does that mean that the methods in this text can't work for you? No. They *will* work. But you may have to work at them a bit harder. Give them a chance. Don't count them out until you have had enough experience with them to determine whether they work for you or not.

There are other strategies you can use, too. Unlike more conventional methods, the following tips were crafted with you in mind. These ideas may give you the extra boost you need to harness your creativity and let your right-brained way of thinking work for you, not against you. If your thinking style is left-brained, read on anyway. There may be something here that you can use along with the logical, step-by-step approach that works so well for you.

Tips for Right-Brained Writers

✎ **Find your most creative time and use it for writing.** Some people find that they are at their best in the mornings. Others find that their creative juices begin to flow around 9:00 or 10:00 P.M. Writing will be easier if you schedule it to coincide with your natural period of creativity.

✎ **Use your rough draft as your prewriting.** Since you think in terms of the whole, you may find it easier to do a rough draft than to prewrite. Consider your rough draft a form of prewriting, to be extensively revised before you turn it in.

✎ **Give your brain an assignment.** When you have writing to do, let your right brain work on it while you are doing other things. At the beginning of the day, for instance, look over the assignment for a few minutes. Then come back to it in the evening and reap the benefits of having worked on the topic subconsciously. Or think about your topic before you go to sleep at night, then write in the morning. This technique can work not only in prewriting but also in revising.

✎ **Realize that doing the grunt work is a necessary evil.** Right-brained people are less likely to put in the time it takes to master the basics because doing so may be tedious and boring to them. They are also less likely to plan. But even the most brilliantly creative people need self-discipline. It's a hard lesson to learn, but mastering the basics is essential to creative work. Singers spend endless time on breath control and scales. Artists learn anatomy and basic drawing techniques. It is those efforts that set them free to do their best work. The payoff in mastering the basics is that once you have learned them, you can forget about them. They will be second nature. The same goes for planning. Once you have made a plan, you are free to do the creative work. Doing the grunt work now always pays off in more freedom later.

✎ **Make a commitment to writing.** Many professional writers are right-brained and face the same resistance that you do. Invariably, they say that the only way they can maintain the extended effort it takes to write books, plays, or novels is to have a routine and to write every day.

WRITING ASSIGNMENT 1   Writing and You

Write a paragraph describing your attitudes toward writing. Use the following steps.

Step 1: Prewrite. Jot down a few of the words that come to mind when you think of writing. Think of any significant experiences that have shaped your attitude toward writing. Consider your writing habits. Are you organized? Do you procrastinate?

Step 2: Plan. Look over your prewriting. Try to sum up your attitude toward writing in a single word or phrase, and then construct an opening sentence for your paragraph using that word or phrase. Use one of the following sentences, filling in the blank with your word or phrase, or construct your own sentence.

My attitude toward writing is _____

_____

When I think about writing, I feel _____

_____

My feelings about writing have always been _____

_____

Once you have constructed an opening sentence, decide how to organize your paragraph. A couple of possibilities are listed below.

1.   Take a historical approach, describing the influences that have shaped your writing. Use chronological (time) order.

2.   Try a step-by-step approach, describing what you do and how you feel as you go through a writing assignment.

Complete the planning stage by making an outline that briefly lists the points you plan to make in support of your opening sentence.

Step 3: Draft. Write out a rough draft of your paragraph. Focus on expressing your ideas rather than on grammar and punctuation.

Step 4: Revise. Read over your rough draft. Have you left out anything important? Is each idea clearly expressed? Does the paragraph flow smoothly? Is the sequence of ideas logical and effective? If possible, ask a classmate to look over your rough draft with the same questions in mind. Then revise your paragraph, incorporating any necessary changes.

Step 5: Proofread. Check your paragraph for mistakes in spelling, grammar, or punctuation. Look at each sentence individually. Then proofread once more. You have now completed all the steps in the writing process.

mywritinglab   For support in meeting this chapter's goal, log in to **www.mywritinglab.com** and select **The Writing Process**.

CHAPTER 2

Preparing to Write

Chapter Goal: Use prewriting strategies to become a more efficient writer.

Just say

NO

to

~~Arachnophobia~~

WRITER'S BLOCK.

Many people suffer from arachnophobia—fear of spiders. Some people also develop a fear called "writer's block" when they are confronted with a blank sheet of paper or a blank computer screen. They fear that they will not be able to think of anything to say, or that if they do find something to say, it will be wrong. Writer's block happens to almost everyone at one time or another. It is not an indication of poor writing ability. In fact, writers who get writer's block are usually those who care about how they present themselves.

One of the best defenses against this kind of fear is prewriting. Prewriting is a playful "safety zone" that you can enter without fear. In prewriting, your purpose is to generate ideas, not to judge them, so you can't go wrong. Even if you don't have writer's block, prewriting can give your writing a jump-start.

Focus on Preparing to Write: Gathering the Ingredients

When a chef devises a new recipe, she goes through several steps. She collects the ingredients, assembles her tools, and prepares the dish, often changing—or revising—the recipe as she cooks. Although all the steps in cooking are important if the dish is to be successful, thinking it through beforehand is also essential for success.

Prewriting before an essay is much the same: You need to think about what ideas or "ingredients" you need to properly address the topic. Only when you have those ideas in place can you come up with just the right recipe for the essay you wish to write. So think of the prewriting stage as that stage where you consider and write down every idea you want to cover in your essay. Of course, just like a chef preparing a dish, you can cut or add ingredients or change amounts as needed to make your essay a success.

Reflect on It

Aside from cooking, think about other things you do in life that have a "prewriting" stage. Describe those things and explain how they are similar to or different from the prewriting stage of an essay.

✍ Prewriting

mywritinglab

Visit MyWriting Lab for additional practice prewriting.

Prewriting is the first step in the writing process. It is the act of sorting out your thoughts on a topic and finding out what you have to say about it. Depending on the assignment you are given, prewriting may also include narrowing your topic to a manageable size. Prewriting begins the moment you receive an assignment. Quietly, in the background, part of your mind begins to gather information. However, it usually takes a bit of effort to bring that information to the surface. The prewriting methods in this chapter can jump-start the writing process by helping you collect your thoughts on a topic and get them on paper.

✍ Prewriting Methods

The aim of all **prewriting methods** is the same: to help you get ideas on paper. At this point in the writing process, it is not the quality of ideas that counts, but the quantity.

When you are ready to prewrite, sit at the computer or in a comfortable spot with pen and paper. Relax your mind and body, and remind yourself that prewriting is a playful exercise of the imagination and that it is okay to write down anything that comes to mind. As for the part of your mind that automatically jumps in to criticize what you think and say, give it some time off. Your purpose in prewriting is to put down every thought on your topic, no matter how ridiculous it seems. Later, you can discard what is not usable.

Some of the methods may feel awkward at first. But try them all. One will be right for you.

Brainstorming

mywritinglab

Visit MyWriting Lab for additional practice brainstorming.

Brainstorming, a listing technique, is one of the easiest prewriting techniques. To brainstorm, take a few minutes to list whatever comes to mind on your topic. Your purpose is not to censor or come up with the "right" items for your list, but to generate ideas.

Example of Brainstorming

Here's how one writer, James, approached a brainstorming exercise on the topic "Describe a favorite holiday memory."

Last 4th of July—family reunion
Lake Sinclair
plenty of food
Aunt Mil's fried chicken
baked beans
over 100 relatives
Mo's girlfriend!
saw Grandaddy Bennett for the last time
checkered paper tablecloths
ants
kids running and screaming
fireworks over lake—color and noise
Tim stretched out in back seat asleep on the way home

When James looked at his prewriting, he was not sure he could use it all, but he knew he had captured some of the vivid images and important memories from his Fourth of July family reunion.

| EXERCISE 1 | **BRAINSTORMING** |

Brainstorm on one of the following topics; then see if you have an idea for a possible paragraph. Answers will vary.

1. the importance of money

2. a holiday memory

3. an unexpected kindness

4. being an outsider

5. a bad habit

Freewriting

mywritinglab

Visit MyWriting Lab for additional practice freewriting.

Freewriting is nonstop writing on a topic for a set time. The point of freewriting is that your flow of words never ceases; your pen never stops moving. If you have nothing to say, repeat your last thought again and again until a new thought replaces it. Do not worry about spelling, about clarity, or about whether your thoughts are logically connected. Just write.

Example of Freewriting

Emily did the following freewriting when her instructor asked the class to write on the topic "Discuss one of your pet peeves and why it annoys you."

> Let's see. Right now I am peeved about having to write about a pet peeve. Ha! Seriously, I am an easygoing person and do not get too upset over anything. I don't like telephone salespeople. I don't like loud commercials. I don't like my ex-boyfriend. I don't like people who are late. I don't like it when a class or meeting is held up because some people are late. Yesterday, in Freshman Orientation, we had a quiz and when it was time for class to start, the instructor said, "We'll just wait a minute or two in case someone else comes in." Excuse ME, but I made it to class on time. Why should I wait for someone who is late? I can think of plenty of other examples. Is my ten minutes up yet? No. The minister at our church always starts services on time and it doesn't matter how many people come in late but when my cousin got married the ceremony was supposed to be at 7 P.M. and it did not start until 7:30. People just keep coming in, right up until about 7:25. I think spending a lot of money on a wedding is a waste—they should just buy furniture or something.

| EXERCISE 2 | **FREEWRITING** |

Freewrite on one of the following topics; then see if you have a focus for a possible paragraph. Answers will vary.

1. What is your pet peeve?
2. What is your favorite time of day?
3. Is honesty always the best policy?
4. What is your biggest complaint about college professors?
5. What can you tell about a person from the way he or she dresses?

Invisible Writing: A Computer Technique

Invisible writing is a freewriting technique especially for writing on a computer. Turn on your computer, and once you have a blank screen in front of you, type the words "Invisible Writing" at the top of the page. Then turn your monitor off or adjust the contrast until the words are no longer visible and your screen is completely dark.

Freewrite for five to ten minutes. It is especially important not to worry about spelling errors. With this method, you can hardly avoid them. At first, you may feel strange, even anxious, pouring your words into the dark computer screen. Soon, though, your fingers and your thoughts will start to fly.

EXERCISE 3   **INVISIBLE WRITING**

Prewrite by applying invisible writing to one of the following topics. Answers will vary.

1. taking chances
2. superstitions
3. television or radio commercials
4. driving habits
5. ending a friendship

Clustering

mywritinglab

Visit MyWriting Lab for additional practice with clustering.

Clustering is a technique designed to boost your creativity by stimulating both hemispheres of the brain. The left hemisphere, or "left brain," is used in logical tasks that move in 1-2-3 order. When you count to ten, write a sentence, or make an outline, you use your left brain. Your right brain, on the other hand, specializes in tasks involving visual images and intuition. Since clustering involves both listing (a left-brain task) and drawing (a right-brain task), it allows you to tap both your logical side and your creative side.

To cluster, begin with a circled word—your topic. From there, map out associations. Some people branch ideas from the central word like quills on a porcupine. Others group ideas when they cluster, with smaller clusters branching out from larger ones. When this type of cluster is finished, it resembles a diagram of a molecule in a biology textbook.

What your diagram looks like does not matter. In clustering, what matters is that you get your thoughts on paper using both images and words.

Look at the following examples of clustering.

Example of Porcupine Clustering

Brandon did his "porcupine" cluster on the topic "Your chosen career."

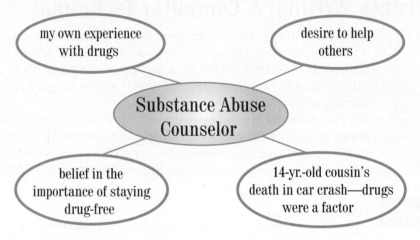

Example of Molecule Clustering

Here is Kara's "molecule" cluster on the topic "Internet shopping."

| EXERCISE 4 | CLUSTERING |

Draw a cluster diagram using one of the following topics. Answers will vary.

1. credit cards

2. your favorite sport

3. your best or worst date

4. advantages or disadvantages of public transportation

5. your eating habits

Outlining

mywritinglab

Visit MyWriting Lab for additional practice with outlining.

Outlining is often the last step in the prewriting process. Once you have used one of the other prewriting methods, making an outline will take you one step further in the writing process. Forget about the formal outline with its Roman numerals, ABCs, and 123s. A short paragraph calls for a short outline. Your outline may be just a few words jotted on a page, or it may include a topic sentence and a brief listing of support.

Example of Outlining

Below is Emily's outline of her paragraph describing her pet peeve.

Topic Sentence: I am an easygoing person, but it annoys me when a meeting, class, or other event does not begin on time because some people are late.

Freshman orientation class—quiz delayed because of people who were late.

Meeting with friends in restaurant—waited fifteen minutes to order until Kylie came.

Cousin's wedding—delayed a half hour because of late arrivals.

Summary sentence: Classes, meetings, and other gatherings should not be arranged for the convenience of latecomers, but for those who care enough to arrive on time.

| EXERCISE 5 | OUTLINING |

Take one of the topics on which you have done a practice prewriting and make an outline for a paragraph. Answers will vary.

✐ Journal Writing

Journals are "daily writings"—the word *journal* comes from *jour*, the French word for *day*. Journals are usually composed of informal writings on a variety of subjects. **Journal writing** allows you to experiment with the techniques you are learning in your writing class. In a journal, the only form of writing you should avoid is "diary mode." An "I-got-up-I-fed-the-dog-I-went-to-school" format makes for dull writing and even duller reading. Write about issues that matter to you. Tell your dreams. Describe your grandfather's tool shed. Work toward detailed writing that follows a logical pattern.

Whether or not you receive credit for it in class, make journal writing a habit. Practice is the only thing that is guaranteed to make you a better writer. Courses and texts are of limited value without time spent alone with a word processor or pen and paper. If you think, "It won't matter. I'll never be a good writer," ask yourself this: How good a driver would you be if the only driving you had done was in a driver education course? You *can* be a better writer. Journal writing will start you on your way.

Journal Topics

1. What are some reasons for keeping a journal or diary?
2. If you had one day of your life to live over, which one would it be?
3. If you were cleaning out your mental closet, what would you most want to throw away?
4. Who is your role model? Why?
5. Is it better to have an assertive, in-your-face personality or to be laid-back and slow to show anger?
6. Other than food, water, and sleep, what *must* you have every day? Why?
7. If every job or career paid the exact same salary, what kind of work would you choose?
8. Discuss one item that fits this description: "It plugs into the wall, and I couldn't live without it."
9. If people had fur, what changes would take place in society?
10. If you had to live without television, how would you spend your extra time?
11. If you could have one talent that you do not now possess, what would it be?
12. If you could bring one fictional character to life (for whatever reason—to be your friend, to benefit humanity, or to solve a problem), who would it be?
13. If you could travel to any place in the world, where would you go?

14. Describe one effective method you use to reduce stress.

15. Describe the one place that, for you, is "heaven on earth."

16. What can you tell about people from the way they carry themselves—that is, the way they stand, sit, or move?

17. Is it better to have a wide circle of casual friends or just a few close friends?

18. Describe your general style of dealing with problems. Do you meet problems head on, or do you hide your head in the sand and hope they will go away? Do you enlist the help of others, or do you try to solve your problems alone? Illustrate your journal entry with at least one example.

19. Which is more important, independence or security?

20. If you were granted a sneak peek one hundred years into the future, what change, development, or discovery would you most like to see? Why?

THE PROGRESSIVE WRITING ASSIGNMENT

How It Works

Begin by choosing one of the topics that follow; it will serve as the basis for your first paragraph. In this chapter, you will complete prewriting for the paragraph. Throughout the next four chapters, each Progressive Writing Assignment will take you a step further toward a paragraph. By the time you have finished the final assignment, you will have completed all the steps in the writing process and will have a complete paragraph.

Progressive Writing Assignment: Prewriting

In this chapter, your Progressive Writing Assignment is a prewriting assignment. Choose one of the following topics—one you would like to write a paragraph about—and follow the instructions.

Topic 1: Discuss the results of taking a specific piece of advice from a friend or family member.

TIPS FOR PREWRITING

Prewrite on the topic, using one or several of the methods outlined in this chapter. As you prewrite, consider the different types of advice you have been offered: bad advice, good advice, advice that got you in trouble, or advice that cost you money. Consider the different people who have offered you advice. Taking a broad approach allows you to consider many different possibilities.

What Now?

After you have completed your prewriting, you should have more material than you will be able to use. To prepare for the next step in the Progressive Writing Assignment, choose the piece of advice that you want to focus on in your paragraph.

Topic 2: Discuss your decision to attend college.

Tips for Prewriting

Prewrite on the topic, using one or several of the methods outlined in this chapter. As you prewrite, consider all the factors that surround your decision. What are they? Some people are motivated to attend college by the expectations of family or friends. Some are trying to put the past behind them, while others are trying to fulfill lifelong ambitions. Some people arrive certain of success; others fear failure. Consider everything surrounding your decision to attend college: your reasons, your expectations, the reaction of friends and family, and your own hopes and fears.

What Now?

After you have completed your prewriting, you should have more material than you will be able to use. To prepare for the next step in the Progressive Writing Assignment, decide which ideas you want to focus on.

Topic 3: Discuss your greatest fear.

Tips for Prewriting

Prewrite on the topic, using one or several of the methods outlined in this chapter. Consider that fears sometimes have a strong basis in reality: A person whose parents and grandparents died young may have a fear of not living long enough to see her children grow up. Just as often, though, fears seem irrational. A person with a steady job and a comfortable home may fear being homeless. Write down your fears, both rational and irrational, and try to determine what lies behind them. Consider also how you deal with your fears. Do you have a specific method for overcoming them, or do you just live with them?

What Now?

After you have completed your prewriting, you should have more material than you will be able to use. To prepare for the next step in the Progressive Writing Assignment, decide which ideas you want to focus on in your paragraph.

Topic 4: Discuss the types of stress experienced by college students.

Tips for Prewriting

Prewrite on the topic, using one or several of the methods outlined in this chapter. Everyone experiences stress from many sources, such as overwork, family problems, or even boredom. However, there are some kinds of stress that may be specifically associated with college. In this paragraph, you will write about some of the types of stress experienced by college students. Thinking about your own stress is a good starting point, but imagine the kinds of stress experienced by students who may not be like you: older students, working students, students who have children. What kinds of stress are common to all college students, and which are particular to certain groups?

WHAT NOW?

After you have completed your prewriting, you should have more material than you will be able to use. To prepare for the next step in the Progressive Writing Assignment, decide which types of stress you want to focus on in your paragraph.

For support in meeting this chapter's goal, log in to **www.mywritinglab.com** and select **Getting Started** and **Prewriting**.

CHAPTER 3

Writing Paragraphs:
Topic Sentences

Chapter Goal: Construct an effective topic sentence to give direction to your paragraph.

A Silly Riddle

How is a topic sentence like a compass?
a. It always points to magnetic north.
b. It's useful on a hiking expedition.
c. It shows exactly where you are headed.

The riddle above may be silly, but the comparison it makes is valid. A topic sentence *is* like a compass. It shows your reader exactly where your paragraph is headed, and it also helps to keep you on track as you write your paragraph. It gives **direction** to your paragraph.

Direction is one of the four characteristics of effective writing that you will read about in this text and learn to develop in your own writing. Before exploring the topic sentence further, look at the four characteristics of effective writing.

Characteristics of an Effective Paragraph

1. **Direction** means that the paragraph has a strong topic sentence that states the main idea and sets the course that the paragraph will follow.
2. **Unity** means that the paragraph makes one main point and sticks to that point.
3. **Coherence** means that the ideas in the paragraph are logically connected and easy to follow.
4. **Support** means that the paragraph contains a specific and detailed discussion of the idea stated in the topic sentence.

Focus on Topic Sentences: Setting Up the Paragraph

Avid fans know what to expect from James Bond movies: action-packed openers. Whether it's Sean Connery facing a SPECTRE agent, Pierce Brosnan diving off the Hoover Dam, or Daniel Craig maneuvering his Aston DB 5 through a spectacular chase scene, the openers grab the attention of moviegoers and make them want to see more. These opening scenes let audiences know that James Bond is an agent who can outmaneuver the toughest opponents and get out of the stickiest situations. The openers set up the entire movie.

Topic sentences do much the same thing. They are important because they help readers know what the paragraph will be about. And don't forget that, like the opener of a James Bond movie, a topic sentence must fit the overall picture.

Reflect on It

Look through the anthology section of this book, and find a topic sentence that interests you. On the basis of that sentence alone, what do you think the paragraph will be about? Read the whole paragraph only after you consider what it should say to see if you predicted something close to what was actually written.

Direction: Shaping the Topic Sentence of a Paragraph

mywritinglab

Visit MyWriting Lab for additional practice with the topic sentences.

A topic sentence provides direction by stating the main idea of a paragraph and answering the reader's unspoken question, "What is your point?"

Functions of a Topic Sentence

A topic sentence does two things. First of all, it states the *general topic* of the paragraph. Second, it makes a *specific point about the topic*.

Example Topic Sentences

                  topic   specific point about

✔ Carrying a homemade lunch instead of eating out has had unexpected

the topic
benefits.

                      topic   specific point about the topic

✔ Knowing how to research using a computer is an essential skill in college.

              specific point   topic

✔ There are many creative ways to hide thinning hair.

EXERCISE 1 **ANALYZING TOPIC SENTENCES**

In each of the following topic sentences, underline the topic and double-underline the specific point the writer is making about the topic.

1. Stromboli's Italian Grill is my favorite restaurant.

2. A successful letter of complaint has three essential elements.

3. My brother's fondness for loud music irritates the rest of the family.

4. The woman who lives next door is incurably nosy.

5. Poor organization can make studying difficult.

EXERCISE 2   **ANALYZING TOPIC SENTENCES**

In each of the following topic sentences, underline the topic and double-underline the specific point the writer is making about the topic.

1. Peer pressure can weaken even the strongest will.

2. My experience working at the Burger Basket convinced me to avoid fast-food places.

3. Trying to find information on the Internet can be frustrating.

4. Gas prices vary in different parts of town.

5. My vacation will give me a chance to do some work around the house.

EXERCISE 3   **COMPLETING TOPIC SENTENCES**

Complete the following topic sentences. Then underline the topic and double-underline the point about the topic. Answers will vary.

1. Taking an aerobics class _____

2. _____ is something no home should be without.

3. In the morning, _____ helps me prepare to face the day.

4. _____ is my favorite piece of furniture.

5. To avoid last-minute cramming for tests, _____

EXERCISE 4   **WRITING TOPIC SENTENCES**

Write five topic sentences. Underline the topic. Then double-underline your point about the topic. Answers will vary.

1. _____

   _____

2. _____

   _____

3. _____

   _____

4. _____
   _____

5. _____
   _____

Writing Topic Sentences That Fit

A topic sentence also provides direction by precisely outlining the territory the paragraph will cover. A topic sentence that is *too broad* outlines more territory than a paragraph can comfortably cover. A topic sentence that is *too narrow* draws the boundaries of the paragraph uncomfortably small, usually by focusing on some fact that would make a good supporting detail but that does not lend itself to development.

Example of a Topic Sentence That Is Too Broad

✗   Computers have changed modern society.

This topic sentence is too broad. It promises more than one paragraph can deliver. Think of all the ways computers have changed modern life: they have changed the way stores keep track of inventories, the way banks work, and the way groceries are checked out. They have created new jobs and made others obsolete. They have altered our ideas about which skills are essential and have raised new concerns about privacy and access to information. The topic "how computers have changed society" could easily be the subject of a book.

Example of a Topic Sentence That Is Too Narrow

✗   My computer has six USB ports.

This topic is too narrow. It tells the reader that the writer will discuss a specific computer, her own, and that the focus will be the computer's USB ports. Although the sentence might work as a supporting point in a paragraph, it is too narrow to be a topic sentence. A topic sentence that is too narrow is a dead-end statement, a fact that does not invite exploration. A good topic sentence opens a door to discussion.

Example of an Effective Topic Sentence

✔   A computer can link a person who is disabled or homebound to the outside world.

This topic sentence is neither too broad nor too narrow. Within this paragraph, the writer can discuss how a computer helps a disabled person to bank or shop online. She can tell how a computer links a homebound person to people and information sources around the world. The sentence opens a door to an area of discussion and exploration that is neither too narrow nor too broad to develop in one paragraph.

| EXERCISE 5 | ANALYZING TOPIC SENTENCES |

Each set of sentences below contains one topic sentence that is too broad, one that is too narrow, and one that would make a good topic sentence for a paragraph. In the blank to the left of each sentence, label it TB (too broad), TN (too narrow), or TS (topic sentence).

Set 1

TB **a.** The functions of a bank are many and varied.

TS **b.** Bank fees seem to target lower-income customers.

TN **c.** My checking account is with First National Bank.

Set 2

TN **a.** My brother Simon often stays awake until 2:00 or 3:00 A.M.

TS **b.** My brother Simon is a night owl.

TB **c.** My brother Simon has different levels of energy at different times of the day, week, month, and year.

Set 3

TS **a.** Ordering merchandise online has several advantages.

TN **b.** I received a promotional email from Land's End today.

TB **c.** American businesses thrive in the digital age by maintaining a strong presence online and in social media.

Set 4

TS **a.** Coping with my father's illness has been difficult for my family.

TB **b.** Life has its ups and downs.

TN **c.** Last year, my father had major surgery.

Set 5

TS **a.** The commercials for Mercedes project a classy image of the car.

TN **b.** CNN and MSNBC are news channels.

TB **c.** Television exerts a positive influence on American society.

| EXERCISE 6 | **ANALYZING TOPIC SENTENCES** |

Each set of sentences below contains one topic sentence that is too broad, one that is too narrow, and one that would make a good topic sentence for a paragraph. In the blank to the left of each sentence, label it TB (too broad), TN (too narrow), or TS (topic sentence).

Set 1

TN   a. My cat has a marking on her back that looks like the number three.

TS   b. Training a dog to sit on command is a simple process.

TB   c. Pets are wonderful.

Set 2

TB   a. Housing costs vary widely across the United States.

TN   b. A one-bedroom apartment in the Aspen Forest apartment complex costs $570 per month.

TS   c. A first-time homebuyer should consider several factors when searching for a home.

Set 3

TB   a. Gasoline stations have been a part of the American landscape for almost a century.

TN   b. In my grandfather's time, gasoline cost fifty cents per gallon.

TS   c. Gasoline stations of my grandfather's time offered services that are unheard of today.

Set 4

TS   a. Requiring fingerprints of citizens who obtain drivers' licenses is a bad idea.

TB   b. Many laws are unjust and should be repealed.

TN   c. In some states, a driver's license must bear the driver's fingerprint.

Set 5

TB   a. Fish are fascinating creatures.

TN   b. My sister's angelfish is named Gabriel.

TS   c. An aquarium is like a small entertainment center for the home.

Group Exercise 1 Writing a Topic Sentence: Confident? Go Solo!

Have you had enough test *taking?* Form a test-*making* team with two or three of your classmates and write an exercise similar to the one on page 30. Choose three to five of the following topics, and for each topic, write a topic sentence that is too broad, one that is too narrow, and one that would fit a paragraph. Then trade tests with another group and see how your group's performance—as test makers and as test takers—stacks up against theirs.

Topics

1. books
2. garbage
3. beverages
4. music
5. schools
6. furniture
7. nature
8. people
9. food
10. television

Where Should a Topic Sentence Go?

If you look carefully at the paragraphs in textbooks, essays, and news stories, you will see that a topic sentence may appear anywhere in a paragraph. However, the most common position for a topic sentence is at or near the beginning of a paragraph. Placing the topic sentence at the beginning of a paragraph lets your reader know exactly where the paragraph is going and gives the impression that you have thought about the organization of your paragraph. And you *will* have thought about it. The very act of constructing a topic sentence places your focus on the main idea of your paragraph and helps keep you on track in supporting that idea.

Topic Sentence First

Placing the topic sentence first is often your best choice. A topic sentence conveys your main idea and provides a strong, clear opening for your paragraph.

Example of a Paragraph with the Topic Sentence First

Since I began carrying a homemade lunch to my part-time job at the mall, I have discovered the benefits of brown-bagging. The most obvious benefit is that bringing a lunch from home saves money. At the mall's food court, the price of a sandwich and chips or a slice of pizza and a soft drink can easily exceed five dollars.

But for less than ten dollars, I can buy a loaf of bread and enough pimento cheese and peanut butter to make lunches for a week or more. Another benefit of brown-bagging—an unexpected one—is that I feel less rushed. Before I started bringing my lunch, my thirty-minute lunch break was consumed by a mad dash to the food court to stand in line, find a table, gulp down my food, and rush back to work. Now, I take a leisurely lunch in the employee break room, reading a magazine as I eat. Usually, I have an extra fifteen minutes to read and relax or take a stroll around the mall's upper level. I also benefit from the improved nutrition of my homemade lunches. Turkey on whole wheat bread or even a peanut butter and jelly sandwich from home is lower in fat and calories than a hamburger or slice of pizza from the food court. For me, brown-bagging means that a healthier wallet, a more relaxed lunch break, and improved nutrition are "in the bag."

Topic Sentence after an Introductory Sentence

Sometimes, you may wish to include background material before you state the main point of your paragraph. In these instances, condense the background material to one introductory sentence. After your introductory sentence, state the topic sentence.

Example of a Paragraph with a Topic Sentence after an Introductory Sentence

Baldness runs in my family, and at thirty-five, I have come to accept my hair loss. **But as my hairline receded over the years, I discovered several creative ways to hide thinning hair.** My first solution to baldness was to wear a hat. Baseball caps in summer and knit caps in winter were only the beginning. During an "arty" phase in my mid-twenties, I wore a beret, and in the back of a closet somewhere, I still have a dashing Indiana Jones–style hat. Another method I used to hide my thinning hair was the "comb-over"—combing hair over a bald spot. In the earliest stages of baldness, the method worked well for me. But as my hairline receded further, I stopped using the comb-over. I had seen too many men who looked ridiculous with just a few strands of foot-long hair covering a completely bald dome. The best method I have found to hide thinning hair is the one I use now. I have shaved my head completely. Now, no one can tell whether I am bald by nature or by choice. Shaving my head has helped me to get over my embarrassment at being bald. I have finally come to realize that bald is beautiful.

EXERCISE 7	FINDING TOPIC SENTENCES

One of the following paragraphs begins with an introductory sentence, while the other starts with the topic sentence. Underline the topic sentence in each paragraph.

Paragraph A

It has been said that fashion models are essentially walking, strutting, sashaying coat hangers to showcase designer fashions and that thin models show off clothing best. <u>But as models have gone from thin to emaciated, public outcry has risen against showcasing designer fashions on models who barely have any flesh on their prominent bones.</u> Some of the outcry followed the anorexia-related deaths of three models, including the French model Isabelle Caro, who was featured on several anti-anorexia billboards. Others who protest the presence of rail-thin models on the catwalk cite the influence on preteen and teenage girls, who may try to mimic an unrealistic and unhealthy body image. Health experts worry about the damage that compulsive dieting can wreak on still-developing bodies. The controversy has spilled into the fashion industry, which has responded with a greater awareness of the issue, with some designers, model agencies, and fashion shows refusing to use models whose body mass index (BMI) falls below a certain level and some working with underweight models to help them reach a healthy weight.

Paragraph B

<u>My brothers, Eric and Michael, are very different in their attitudes about money.</u> Eric and his wife Alexis believe in living for today. They have a new house on the north side of town, a new sport utility vehicle, and a two-year-old Volvo. Their clothes are always designer labels in the latest fashions, and their home is a showplace of fine furniture. But they seldom have time to enjoy these things because they both work two jobs to pay off the massive debt they have accumulated. It is as though their possessions own them. My brother Michael goes a bit too far in the opposite direction. He puts every spare penny away for the future. Though he has a good job, he drives a thirteen-year-old car that rattles as if only habit is holding it together. He argues constantly with his wife, who simply wants decent clothes for herself and their children. Worse yet, he insists on

buying nothing but practical gifts. I thought Kim would divorce him when he gave her a hand-held vacuum for her birthday so that she could vacuum the inside of her car at home instead of taking it to the car wash. My two brothers agree on politics, football, and religion, but they will never agree about money.

PROGRESSIVE WRITING ASSIGNMENT

Progressive Writing Assignment: Topic Sentence

If your instructor has assigned the Progressive Writing Assignment, you have already completed your prewriting for one of the topics below. In this chapter, you will complete your topic sentence.

Topics and Tips for Writing a Topic Sentence

The Topics

Topic 1: Discuss the results of taking a specific piece of advice from a friend or family member.

Topic 2: Discuss your decision to attend college.

Topic 3: Discuss your greatest fear.

Topic 4: Discuss the types of stress experienced by college students.

Tips for Writing a Topic Sentence

- Decide on the points you will cover in your paragraph and the order in which you will present them. Then write a tentative topic sentence.
- Make sure that the topic sentence presents a specific topic and makes a point about that topic.
- Check to make sure that your topic sentence is not too broad. For example, for Topic 4, "Discuss the types of stress experienced by college students," the following topic sentence would be too broad:

    ✗   Everybody experiences stress at one time or another.

The sentence is too broad because the paragraph is not about "everybody"; it is about college students. Two better topic sentences are shown below:

    ✔   College students are prone to certain kinds of stress.

✔ College students most often experience stress related to academic performance and lack of time.

- Check to make sure that your topic sentence is not too narrow. For example, for Topic 2, "Discuss your decision to attend college," the following topic sentence would be too narrow:

✗ I began college just two months ago.

The sentence is too narrow because it does not address the idea of a decision to attend college. Although the sentence might be appropriate as a supporting detail, it is too narrow to be a topic sentence. Two better topic sentences are shown below:

✔ Stuck in a dead-end job, I decided to attend college so that I could do something that will make a difference.
✔ Attending college will help me realize my lifelong dream of being a nurse.

mywritinglab   For support in meeting this chapter's goal, log in to www.mywritinglab.com and select **The Topic Sentence**.

CHAPTER 4

Writing Paragraphs: Support

> ✍ **Chapter Goal:** Construct sentences that support your topic sentence.

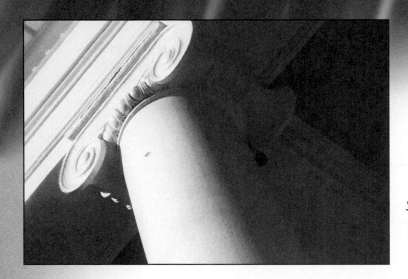

Support:
  Strong
  Solid
  Beautiful

Whether it is a column that holds up a roof or a sentence that helps to hold up a paragraph, support must be strong and solid. In fact, specific support is one of the keys to good writing. Before looking at paragraph support, review the following four principles of effective writing. The highlighted principle, support, is the focus of this chapter.

Characteristics of an Effective Paragraph

1. **Direction** means that the paragraph has a strong topic sentence that states the main idea and sets the course that the paragraph will follow.

2. **Unity** means that the paragraph makes one main point and sticks to that point.

3. **Coherence** means that the ideas in the paragraph are logically connected and easy to follow.

4. **Support** means that the paragraph contains a specific and detailed discussion of the idea stated in the topic sentence.

Focus on Support: Providing Convincing Detail

You may have heard about the court case involving McDonald's and Stella Liebeck: She won approximately $3 million (later reduced to just over half a million) because she was burned by scalding coffee after leaving a drive-through at McDonald's. Many who hear about this case are outraged. It seems to prove that Americans have become "lawsuit crazy."

But those who get angry may not know all the facts. Liebeck received third-degree burns on over 16 percent of her body, mainly in the genital area. McDonald's refused her initial request of $20,000 reimbursement of medical costs, saying that their coffee was not hot enough to cause such severe burns. However, during the trial, McDonald's admitted to heating their coffee to between 180 and 190 degrees Fahrenheit. At that temperature, McDonald's later admitted, the coffee would burn anyone it was spilled on. These are just a few of the items Liebeck's attorneys presented. (Source: http://www.centerjd.org/free/mythbusters-free/MB_mcdonalds.htm.)

The point here is that in court cases—as in academic papers and in all aspects of life—support is necessary to make something clear. If Liebeck's attorney had simply said, "Stella was burned, and here are her records," he would have lost the case. Strong supporting evidence helped win this case.

Reflect on It

Think about the last time you wanted something from someone—a parent, brother, sister, boss, or friend. Think of how you chose to present the problem and how you thought of all the reasons that would support your case. How important were your reasons to your presentation of your request? How much did your skill in presenting them affect the response to your request?

〰 Support: Using Specific Detail

A strong topic sentence, unity, and smooth transitions give a paragraph structure and style. Only **support** can give it life. Without specific details, a paragraph remains on a broad, general level. What is it like to read a paragraph without specific details? Imagine watching a movie, television show, or video that never shows a closeup but instead maintains a camera distance of ten feet from every character. You would probably feel detached and uninvolved. Readers feel the same way when a writer never gets close enough to the subject to describe it in detail.

The Difference Between Topic Sentences and Supporting Sentences

A topic sentence provides direction—the road map for a paragraph—but supporting sentences supply the scenery. While topic sentences are broad and general, large enough to encompass the entire paragraph, supporting sentences are specific, giving details and examples. The following exercise provides practice in distinguishing topic sentences from supporting details.

EXERCISE 1	DISTINGUISHING TOPIC SENTENCES FROM SUPPORTING DETAILS

Each numbered item contains three supporting details and one topic sentence. Write SD beside each of the three details and TS beside the topic sentence.

1. a. <u>SD</u> Finally, he began throwing a tennis ball for his dog, who barked loudly in appreciation.

   b. <u>SD</u> Then he put on a CD by a group called the Funk Brigade and turned the volume up.

   c. <u>SD</u> First, he turned on the television to provide background noise.

   d. <u>TS</u> It was too quiet in the room, so Marcus decided to make some noise.

2. a. <u>SD</u> In the second book, Harry meets Dobby, a house-elf who nearly kills Harry in an effort to help him.

   b. <u>TS</u> J. K. Rowling's popular *Harry Potter* books follow the adventures of a young wizard as he learns his craft.

   c. <u>SD</u> In the first book, Harry, who has always felt like the odd one out, finds out that he is a wizard and begins to discover his powers.

d. SD The third book introduces Harry to a mysterious character named Sirius Black and to the soul-sucking guardians of Azkaban Prison.

3. a. TS Being late is a harmful habit.

 b. SD People who are late to classes or meetings often miss important information.

 c. SD People who arrive late for appointments or meetings often anger those who have to wait.

 d. SD Although the impression may be inaccurate, people who are late are often perceived as rude or selfish.

4. a. SD Tires that are not properly inflated can pose a danger to both driver and passengers.

 b. SD Windshield wipers that are excessively worn can pose a danger in rainy weather.

 c. SD Bald tires, worn tires, and unevenly worn tread can cause a car to lose traction on the road.

 d. TS Failure to take care of small details of car maintenance can make driving dangerous.

5. a. SD The close companionship that arises between the adopted animal and its owner can benefit both animal and human.

 b. SD Shelter animals are euthanized if they are not adopted, so adopting a pet from the pound saves a life.

 c. TS Adopting a pet from the animal shelter can benefit both animal and owner.

 d. SD Pound puppies and kittens are usually spayed or neutered before adoption, saving the owner veterinary fees.

Recognizing Specific Detail

One of the most difficult tasks a writer faces is providing strong, specific supporting details. If a writer provides only vague, sketchy details, the picture presented to the reader will be fuzzy and out of focus. As details become sharper and more specific, the picture becomes clear. The following exercise will give you practice in recognizing sharp, clear detail.

| EXERCISE 2 | RECOGNIZING SPECIFIC DETAILS |

Each of the following topic sentences is supported by three details. Place a check (✔) beside the two details that are sharp and specific. Place an ✗ beside the detail that needs to be more specific. Then, in the space provided, rewrite the vague sentence to make the supporting detail more specific.

1. All day long, Nicole was haunted by the number 8.
   - ✔ a. At the driver's license bureau, she pulled the number 8 out of a machine marked "Take a number."
   - ✔ b. At lunchtime, the first potato chip she pulled out of her bag was shaped like the number 8.
   - ✗ c. On her way home, yet another incident occurred involving the number 8.

   _____
   _____

2. Rodrigo's search for an apartment was long and difficult.
   - ✗ a. He looked at several apartments that were not suitable in terms of his financial situation.
   - ✔ b. Many of the apartments he could afford were too far away from work and school.
   - ✔ c. Finally, he found a small, affordable attic apartment close to his work and within walking distance of the college.

   _____
   _____

3. For several reasons, majoring in the health sciences is a good idea.
   - ✔ a. An aging population ensures that health-care professionals will be in demand for decades to come.
   - ✔ b. A variety of fields from respiratory therapy to x-ray technology gives a student a wide range of choice.
   - ✗ c. A nursing shortage means that anyone with a nursing degree has it made.

   _____
   _____

4. The small, crowded office was messy.
   - ✔ a. In the corner, a trash can overflowed with paper and discarded soft-drink cans.
   - ✗ b. The desk was also in disarray.
   - ✔ c. Papers were spread in piles across the floor and around the desk, leaving little room for walking.

   _____
   _____

5. Elena worried that her memory was getting worse.

   _✗_   a. She forgot an important appointment last week.

   _✔_   b. She was constantly losing her glasses, her keys, and her wallet.

   _✔_   c. She could no longer remember the items she needed at the grocery store without making a list, and she often forgot to bring the list.

   _____

   _____

Using Specific Words

Sometimes, a simple change in word choice makes all the difference. You paint a clearer picture for your reader when you use specific words and phrases: *four hours of research in the library* instead of *a lot of work, Ella's Soul Food Café* instead of *a restaurant, glared* instead of *looked,* or *a map of Florida, a deck of cards, and two dollars in change* instead of *things.*

Making Nouns Specific

Consider the following sentence:

✔   Richard put *a heavy item* in his trunk, then drove away from the *building.*

Different readers will put different interpretations on this sentence. What did Richard put in his trunk? What kind of building did he leave? Specific detail would serve a twofold purpose: it would clearly convey the writer's meaning, and it would capture the reader's interest. Consider the following revisions.

✔   Richard put *a bulging briefcase* in his trunk, then drove away from *the law office.*

✔   Richard put *his ex-wife's body* in his trunk, then drove away from *the small white house where they had spent so many years together.*

✔   Richard put *a case of hymnals* in his trunk, then drove away from the *Harvest Religious Bookstore.*

Notice how the detail not only provides more specific information but also helps to characterize Richard. How does your impression of him change with each example?

| EXERCISE 3 | USING SPECIFIC WORDS |

Create a new impression of Richard by varying what he puts in the trunk and the location described in the sentence. Answers will vary.

1. Richard put _____ in his trunk, then drove away from the

   _____.

2. Richard put _____ in his trunk, then drove away from the

   _____.

3. Richard put _____ in his trunk, then drove away from the

   _____.

4. Richard put _____ in his trunk, then drove away from the

   _____.

5. Richard put _____ in his trunk, then drove away from the

   _____.

Making Vague Nouns Specific

Look at the following list. The nouns in the left-hand column provide little information, while those in the right-hand column are specific. Notice, too, that the more specific term is often not simply a noun, but a phrase.

Vague Term	Specific Term
✗ course	✔ Introduction to Social Problems
✗ clothing	✔ man's herringbone jacket, size 42
✗ student	✔ Gloria Hollinger, first-year nursing student
✗ car	✔ 1965 Ford Mustang
✗ sandwich	✔ turkey on five-grain bread with mayonnaise

| EXERCISE 4 | CHOOSING SPECIFIC TERMS |

From the three choices for each of the following sentences, circle the most specific choice to fill in the blank.

1. Carlos ate _____ at noon.
   a. a nutritious meal
   b. a tomato sandwich
   c. delicious food

2. When Larry took _____, he felt better.
   a. a pill
   (b.) two Excedrin tablets
   c. the advice of a respected physician

3. Ana said the _____ was breathtaking.
   a. spectacular view of the surrounding scenery
   b. work of some nineteenth-century poets
   (c.) ride on the Scream Machine

4. The vendor sold _____ from the back of a pickup truck.
   (a.) ripe peaches and black velvet art
   b. various wares in a wide range of colors
   c. electronic devices that may have been stolen

5. Melanie's mother said, "Would you help me _____?"
   a. complete a few simple household chores
   (b.) chop these onions
   c. do some errands

6. The little girl sat beside her mother in the veterinarian's waiting room, carefully holding _____.
   a. her animal companion
   (b.) a scrawny black kitten
   c. a cute, cuddly pet

7. On the refrigerator were _____.
   (a.) a child's drawing of a house, a grocery list, and a dentist's appointment card, held in place by colorful magnets
   b. photographs, papers, children's art, and reminders
   c. twelve magnets, along with the usual odds and ends that tend to accumulate under refrigerator magnets

8. Gerald's parents thought Kim was weird because _____.
   a. her appearance was unusual
   (b.) she had a pierced tongue and two-tone hair
   c. she did not look the way they thought a normal teenager should look

9. Because Harold did not believe in banks, he kept his money _____.
   a. in a place he thought was safe
   b. hidden away somewhere safe from thieves
   (c.) in a waterproof plastic pouch buried under a rock

10. Pat believed she was straightforward and open, but other people saw her as
    _____.

    (a.) rude and tactless
    b. something else
    c. a person with an attitude that was often perceived negatively by those
        who had to be around her

| EXERCISE 5 | CHOOSING SPECIFIC TERMS |

Three possible replacements follow each general term. One of the possible replacements is vague, while the other two are specific and thus would be acceptable substitutes. Circle the two specific terms in each of the following items.

1. tool
   (a.) hammer
   b. instrument
   (c.) spatula

2. test
   a. examination
   (b.) SAT
   (c.) math final

3. restaurant
   (a.) Vernon's Veggie Bar
   (b.) a hot dog stand on the corner
   c. an eatery

4. shoes
   (a.) sandals
   (b.) loafers
   c. footwear

5. noise
   a. sound
   (b.) earsplitting rock music
   (c.) click

6. pet
    a. animal companion
    b. Fluffy
    c. white hamster

7. home
    a. doublewide mobile home
    b. living space
    c. mansion

8. book
    a. telephone directory
    b. *War and Peace*
    c. published volume

9. ice cream
    a. delicious dessert
    b. pint of Rocky Road
    c. Ben & Jerry's Cherry Garcia

10. illness
    a. mumps
    b. disease
    c. food poisoning

Making Pronouns Specific

"I wanted to register today, but *they* wouldn't let me."

"*Everybody* says Ms. Torres is a tough teacher."

"The candidate says he will not increase taxes, but *nobody* believes him."

Sentences like these are common in conversation and usually go unchallenged. In writing, though, precision is necessary. Readers usually do not have access to the writers of the books, stories, and essays they read, and so they cannot ask questions like "Who are *they?*" or "What do you mean by *everybody?*" Look at the revised versions of the statements you just read:

I wanted to register today, but *the clerks in the Registrar's Office* wouldn't let me.

Two of the students in my sociology class say Ms. Torres is a tough teacher.

The candidate says he will not increase taxes, but *few voters* believe him.

Forcing yourself to be more specific may also force you to be more accurate. The "everybody" who tells you to enroll in a certain teacher's class may turn out to be two fellow students. And if you truly wanted to prove that "nobody" believes what a candidate says, you'd have to ask every voter—an impossible task.

| EXERCISE 6 | REPLACING VAGUE PRONOUNS |

Replace the italicized pronouns with more specific expressions. Answers will vary.

1. *It* was only getting worse, so Curtis decided to move out of his parents' house.

   The argument with his father

2. Sheila followed several leads from the help wanted ads and attended an interview arranged by her school's career counselor, hoping to find *something* before graduation.

   work as a preschool teacher

3. Dr. Madison did a brain scan on the patient but didn't find *anything*.

   a tumor

4. My trash container sat by the curb all day, but *they* didn't pick it up.

   the garbage collectors

5. The family walked into the dining room where the table was set for Thanksgiving. *Everything* looked delicious.

   The turkey, ham, and dressing

Making Verbs Specific

Verbs bring life and movement to writing. Vague, poorly chosen verbs add nothing to your writing or, worse yet, drag it down. Well-chosen verbs leap off the page, adding power and energy to your writing. Choosing effective verbs means rejecting the easy choice and looking for powerful verbs that express your meaning exactly.

A *thesaurus,* or dictionary of synonyms, helps you choose the best word for the situation. But shades of meaning vary, so don't just choose a synonym at random. If you are not sure of a word's exact meaning, check your dictionary.

Examples of Specific Verbs

✘ Exhausted after studying for the exam, I *went* to bed at midnight.

✔ Exhausted after studying for the exam, I *stumbled* to bed at midnight.

✘ At 3:00 P.M. on the last day of school, the doors *were opened* and students *came* from the building, yelling and shouting.

✔ At 3:00 P.M. on the last day of school, the doors *burst* open and students *streamed* from the building, yelling and shouting.

EXERCISE 7   USING SPECIFIC VERBS

Cross out the italicized verb in each sentence and replace it with a verb that more effectively conveys the sense of the sentence. Answers will vary.

1. Angrily, Beatrice *retrieved* the envelope from the table.
    snatched

2. Smoothly, the sailboat *moved* across the water.
    glided

3. When the cable snapped, the elevator *descended* fifteen stories.
    plummeted

4. Albright's glove *contacted* his opponent's jaw, sending the man reeling toward the edge of the ring.
    smashed

5. A small bird *was* on the highest branch of the cherry tree.
    perched

6. The garbage truck *moved* down the street, spewing noxious fumes.
    rumbled

7. The crowd *reacted* as fireworks appeared in the inky night sky.
    cheered

8. When asked if he wanted to speak before he was sentenced, the defendant *commented,* "Please believe me! I do not know who committed this horrible crime, but I swear that I am innocent."
    pleaded

9. Five thousand fans *filled* the small concert hall, screaming and shouting their approval.
   <u>packed</u>

10. The angry customer said that a loose shopping cart had *harmed* her new car.
    <u>dented</u>

EXERCISE 8 | **MAKING VERBS SPECIFIC**

Cross out the italicized verb in each sentence and replace it with a verb that more effectively conveys the sense of the sentence. Answers will vary.

1. The ball seemed to take flight, *going* over the outfield and into the stands.
   <u>sailing</u>

2. The squirrel grabbed the acorn and quickly *went* up the tree trunk.
   <u>scampered</u>

3. The roller coaster made a slow ascent, then *moved* toward the ground as its passengers screamed delightedly.
   <u>sped</u>

4. Suddenly, Tom *came* into the room, yelling, "Quick! Somebody call an ambulance!"
   <u>burst</u>

5. As Andrea flipped the light switch, dozens of cockroaches *moved* across the wall and into the cracks near the baseboard.
   <u>scurried</u>

6. Lightning *was seen*, and thunder rolled.
   <u>flashed</u>

7. The basketball *went* into the street just as a garbage truck rattled around the corner.
   <u>bounced</u>

8. As he stormed out of his boss's office, Phil *commented*, "And you know what you can do with your lousy job!"
   <u>shouted</u>

9. Annoyed at the interruption from a young fan, the athlete hastily *signed* his name on the program and abruptly turned away.
    <u>scrawled</u>

10. When the phone rang at 3:00 A.M., Channing sleepily *reached* for the receiver.
    <u>groped</u>

Making Sentences Specific

Sentences with specific language are sentences with power. As you write, strive for forceful verbs and vivid phrases. As you revise, look for opportunities to make vague language more specific. Look at the following examples to see how much stronger a sentence becomes when specific words replace vague words.

Examples of Specific Word Choice

Vague Word Choice

✗ Eager shoppers *entered the toy store* when the *popular toy* came in.

Specific Word Choice

✔ Eager shoppers *mobbed Toy World* when the *Avengers of Doom action figures* came in.

Vague Word Choice

✗ When my mother comes to visit, she brings *all kinds of stuff* with her.

Specific Word Choice

✔ When my mother comes to visit, she brings *four suitcases, a shopping bag filled with homemade goodies, and her miniature poodle, Pierre.*

Vague Word Choice

✗ When Martin looked in his refrigerator, he found *there was not much to eat.*

Specific Word Choice

✔ When Martin looked in his refrigerator, he found *only a half-empty jar of pickles and the two-week-old remains of a takeout dinner from Junior's Barbecue.*

Vague Word Choice

✗ Sylvester could not concentrate on the test. *The noises around him* grated on his nerves.

Specific Word Choice

✔ Sylvester could not concentrate on the test. *The popping of gum in the back of the room, a burst of laughter from outside the building, and even the breathing of the student beside him* grated on his nerves.

EXERCISE 9	MAKING SENTENCES SPECIFIC

Rewrite the sentences so that they contain more specific detail. Feel free to use more than one sentence if you wish. Answers will vary.

1. The newscaster reported that *a terrible thing* had happened in *a large city.*

   _____

2. The clock was shaped like *an animal* and painted *in bright colors.*

   _____

3. Lynn put a package from *a store* in the back seat because her trunk had *something* in it.

   _____

4. On their way to *their destination,* Asha and her husband stopped at *a little place by the roadside.*

   _____

5. *Bad weather* kept Mark from *doing what he had planned.*

   _____

6. When Percy saw *what had happened to his car,* he *reacted strongly.*

   _____

7. *A noise* startled the *animal.*

   _____

8. The mailbox held *several unimportant pieces of mail* and *one important piece of mail.*

   _____

9. On our street, *they* have organized a neighborhood watch because of *various crimes that have taken place.*

   _____

10. *In certain situations,* Jack gets *a bad feeling.*

    _____

EXERCISE 10	ANALYZING PARAGRAPHS FOR SUPPORT

One of the following paragraphs is well supported with specific details and examples, while the other is poorly supported with vague, general sentences. Read each paragraph and answer the questions at the end of the exercise.

Paragraph A

In my experience, college professors are the worst-dressed people in the world. If there were an award for "worst-dressed professor," my history professor, Dr. Bloom, would be a leading candidate. He must be among the ten most wanted by the fashion police. When I saw him walk into the classroom on the first day, I could not believe the clothes he was wearing. I thought that maybe he had just been in a hurry that morning, but on the second day of class, his clothing was just as bad. I cannot imagine where he finds that awful clothing. Then there is Professor Hunter, who teaches art. She wears the strangest clothes, even for an art teacher, who might be expected to have unusual taste. It is as if she were living in a different decade. It's a sure thing she hasn't looked at a fashion magazine lately. But I think my personal choice for the worst-dressed professor award is Mr. Nelson, my English teacher. Like clockwork, the same loud pants, jackets, and shirts appear in strict rotation, each for a different day of the week. When I go into his classroom, I make sure I sit in the back. I am not sure I could stand all those bright colors if I were sitting in the front row. I have great respect for my professors' knowledge, but most of them deserve an "F" in fashion.

Paragraph B

In my experience, college professors are the worst-dressed people in the world. If there were an award for "worst-dressed professor," my history professor, Dr. Bloom, would be a leading candidate. When I saw him walk into the classroom on the first day in a green checked shirt, red bow tie, and shapeless brown sweater vest, I thought perhaps he was just having a bad day. But each day in Dr. Bloom's class is a parade of mismatched rag-bag fashions: rumpled jackets, baggy pants, and shirts in checks, plaids, and polka dots. Professor Hunter, who teaches art, looks like a folk singer from the seventies with her straight hair and ankle-length dresses. She likes delicate rainbow colors and long strands of beads, an odd combination with her heavy white athletic shoes. But I think my personal choice for the worst-dressed professor award is Mr. Nelson, my English teacher, whose taste is not just bad, but annoyingly predictable. On Mondays, he wears a yellow and green checked polyester jacket with lime-green pants. On Tuesday, it's a polyester jacket in robin's-egg blue with a pair of mustard-colored pants. The polyester parade continues through Friday, when he wakes the class up with a pair of bright red pants worn with a pink shirt. I have great respect for my professors' knowledge, but most of them deserve an "F" in fashion.

Questions

Fill in the blanks of the questions below. Details in Item 2 will vary.

1. Paragraph ____A____ is less specific.

2. Paragraph ____B____ is more specific. Three specific details from the paragraph are shapeless brown sweater vest, delicate rainbow colors and long strands of beads, and mustard-colored pants.

TOPICS FOR WRITING

Small Scrawls: Imaginative Short Writings

What is a Small Scrawl? A "scrawl" is something written quickly. In this case, it is a page or so of quick writing that allows you to practice a writing skill, in this case, providing support. Have fun with it!

Small Scrawl 1: Soft Addictions

Author Judith Wright uses the term "soft addictions" to refer to actions that are not generally seen as harmful but, when carried to extremes, can get in the way of more productive activities. Soft addictions are not shameful; they are activities you would not mind confessing to your grandmother: watching television, surfing the Internet, shopping, drinking coffee, or playing video games. What activity or behavior are you addicted to? Write a paragraph describing your "soft addiction" or that of a friend. Be sure to include specific details about the behavior or activity.

Small Scrawl 2: Your Game Face

Are you a competitive person? Describe a situation that always makes you put on your "game face"—the expression that says, "Come on, just try to beat me at this!"

Small Scrawl 3: The Welcome Mat

Describe how you would make someone feel welcome in your home or your place of business.

PROGRESSIVE WRITING ASSIGNMENT

Progressive Writing Assignment: Providing Supporting Details and Examples

If your instructor has assigned the Progressive Writing Assignment, you have already completed your prewriting and your topic sentence. In this chapter, you will provide support for your paragraph.

Topics and Tips for Providing Supporting Details and Examples

THE TOPICS

Topic 1: Discuss the results of taking a specific piece of advice from a friend or family member.

Topic 2: Discuss your decision to attend college.

Topic 3: Discuss your greatest fear.

Topic 4: Discuss the types of stress experienced by college students.

Tips for Providing Supporting Details and Examples

- Make sure that your language is specific. Have you used words that create pictures by appealing to the reader's sense of sight, hearing, touch, taste, and smell? The following sentences illustrate how specific language might be used to support Topic 3, "Discuss your greatest fear."

   ✔ If I were homeless, I would have no shelter from the hot sun or the cold rain. On chilly nights, I would lie awake, listening to my stomach growl and feeling the damp chill creep into my bones.

- Check to see that you have supported your paragraph with specific examples. If you are writing on Topic 1, "Discuss the results of taking a specific piece of advice from a friend or family member," an example might be a *specific example* that describes what happened on a particular occasion.

   ✔ Thinking of my father's advice, I walked right into my boss's office and said, "Ms. Carmichael, the mix-up with the order yesterday was my fault." She looked at me and said, "Yes, I know that, but I really appreciate hearing it from you."

mywritinglab   For support in meeting this chapter's goal, log in to **www.mywritinglab.com** and select **Developing and Organizing a Paragraph**.

CHAPTER 5

Writing Paragraphs: Unity and Coherence

Chapter Goal: Recognize the characteristics of effective paragraphs (direction, unity, coherence, and support) and write paragraphs that embody these qualities.

Into the loom go many threads
That soon come out a whole,
Into your writing, many words,
Which you alone control.

Only you can weave those words
With skill and perseverance,
Creating paragraphs that have
Unity and coherence.

Characteristics of an Effective Paragraph

Review the following characteristics of an effective paragraph. You have already learned how to give your paragraph direction with an effective topic sentence and how to support that topic sentence with details and examples. This chapter looks at the two remaining characteristics of an effective paragraph, unity and coherence.

1. **Direction** means that the paragraph has a strong topic sentence that states the main idea and sets the course that the paragraph will follow.

2. **Unity** means that the paragraph makes one main point and sticks to that point.

3. **Coherence** means that the ideas in the paragraph are logically connected and easy to follow.

4. **Support** means that the paragraph contains specific and detailed discussion of the idea stated in the topic sentence.

Focus on Unity and Coherence: Pulling It All Together

The judges on American Idol often give the contestants seemingly conflicting advice: One week they may tell an aspiring Idol, "All we hear from you are ballads—give us an up-tempo song!" The next week, they may tell the same contestant, "This song is a poor choice for you. We want to hear songs that reflect who you are as an artist."

The Idol judges are asking for the qualities of unity and coherence, which apply to music as well as to writing. From the Rolling Stones to Rihanna, artists who have made it share one thing: an unmistakable style, a unifying thread within their body of work. And whether the song is sweet and tender or a little raunchy, Mick Jagger's throaty wail

or Rihanna's smooth, snappy style will unmistakably come through. Within an album, different tracks will relate to one another musically or thematically.

But music is not the only career in which unity and coherence are important. A business meeting or presentation will be unified—that is, it will have a single aim—and it will be coherent, moving smoothly from one part of the meeting or presentation to the next.

Unity and coherence are important to any career because they show how each part fits together (unity) and relates to each other part (coherence). In your writing, too, unity and coherence help you make your case to your reader.

Reflect on It

Think about the career you plan to pursue. How are unity and coherence crucial to that future job?

✐ Unity: Sticking to the Point

mywritinglab

Visit MyWriting
Lab for additional
practice revising
paragraphs for
unity.

Every topic sentence offers a promise of **unity** to the reader, a promise that you will discuss the point advanced in that sentence and no other. If your topic sentence is "My friend Ellen is the messiest person I have ever known," then you will discuss the specific ways in which she is messy. You will not mention the few times you have known her to be neat; you will not discuss the other qualities that make her so good to have as a friend. You will discuss only the piles of clothes stacked on every piece of furniture in her bedroom; the assortment of books, bills, and banana peels on her desk; and the mounds of fast-food wrappers in the back seat of her car. Your paragraph will have unity because it sticks to its topic and to the specific point you make about that topic.

EXERCISE 1   FINDING PROBLEMS IN UNITY

A list of possible supporting points follows each of the topic sentences in the exercise. In each group, circle the letter of the point that interferes with the unity of the paragraph.

1. Topic sentence: Some restaurant customers make trivial complaints in the hope of getting a free meal.
    a. Some customers gripe when service is a bit slow.
    b. Many complain if they have to make a trip to the emergency room because of food poisoning.
    c. Other customers grumble if the coffee is not piping hot or the iced tea is not cold enough.

2. Topic sentence: Fear of serious injury makes many parents hesitate to encourage their children to play football.
    a. Many parents fear that the child may break a bone in a football game.
    b. They fear their child might sustain head injuries during a game.
    c. Some parents fear their child will start to do poorly in academics.

3. Topic sentence: One way that I try to keep in shape is through a proper diet.
    a. I get plenty of exercise.
    b. I eat very few sweets or sugary treats.
    c. I stay away from too many fats.

4. Topic sentence: If I had to give up one modern convenience, I would get rid of my telephone.
    a. Getting rid of my phone would eliminate interruptions from salespeople.

b. My telephone is a vital link to emergency services.

c. Without a phone, I would waste less time chatting.

5. Topic sentence: My neighbor's yard is an eyesore.

a. In his front yard, he has an old Chevrolet up on blocks.

b. At the side of his house is a beautiful old oak tree.

c. Because he never mows his lawn, tall grass and weeds surround his house.

EXERCISE 2   **FINDING PROBLEMS IN UNITY**

A list of possible supporting points follows each of the topic sentences below. In each group, circle the letter of the point that interferes with the unity of the paragraph.

1. Topic sentence: Some crimes go unreported because crime victims believe they are not worth reporting.

   a. petty theft

   b. kidnapping

   c. graffiti

2. Topic sentence: Fear that they will do poorly in the classroom makes many adults hesitant to return to school.

   a. anxiety about taking tests

   b. fear of not understanding the ideas presented

   c. fear that their families will not accept their decision to return to school

3. Topic sentence: One way that I try to keep in shape is through exercise.

   a. lift weights

   b. eat nutritious foods

   c. attend aerobics classes

4. Topic sentence: Doing my writing on a computer has helped me improve my papers.

   a. modern computer lab

   b. ease of revising

   c. spelling check

5. Topic sentence: My neighbor's dog is an annoyance.

   a. "Heinz 57" mutt

   b. barks at night

   c. jumps fence and digs up my flowers

Reinforcing Unity: The Summary Sentence

One way to reinforce paragraph unity is to end the paragraph with a **summary sentence** that echoes the topic sentence. The summary sentence does not repeat the topic sentence; rather, it reinforces it. If the function of a topic sentence is to tell the reader where the paragraph is going, the function of a summary sentence is to tell where the paragraph has been, thus reinforcing the unity of the paragraph. A summary sentence also signals the end of the paragraph and provides a sense of closure.

Example of Unified Topic and Summary Sentences

Topic Sentence

✔ The most valuable lesson I have learned from my parents is to be independent.

Summary Sentence

✔ I will always be grateful that my parents taught me to rely on myself and not on others.

Example of Unified Topic and Summary Sentences

Topic Sentence

✔ A few minor changes could make our campus more welcoming to students with disabilities.

Summary Sentence

✔ These easy and inexpensive changes would ensure that all students feel safe and welcome on our campus.

EXERCISE 3 **ANALYZING PARAGRAPH UNITY**

In each of the following paragraphs, underline the topic and double-underline the specific point that is made about that topic. Then find and cross through the two sentences that interfere with the unity of the paragraph. If you have trouble, go back and look at the topic sentence to see the specific point that is made about the topic. Then read again to see which sentences do not support that specific point. Finally, underline the summary sentence of each paragraph.

Paragraph 1

¹I enjoy spring because it is a season when nature comes alive. ²Each tree sports a halo of tiny, delicate leaf buds of the palest green. ³Soon the leaves mature and unfurl, trumpeting

a brilliant green message to the world. [4]Flowers nudge their way through a new growth of grass, pushing up to find the sun. [5]Then they open into a rainbow of springtime colors. [6]Each evening, a symphony of sound serenades the listener from shallow ponds where frogs call solemn invitations to prospective mates. [7]Toward morning, as the frogs subside, birds begin their racket, their chatter reverberating from tree to tree. [8]~~In the ballparks, the crack of the bat and the umpire's cry of "Yer out!" echo again as baseball season opens.~~ [9]~~Lights blaze, the stands fill, and the aromas of hotdogs, popcorn, and beer blend on the evening breeze.~~ [10]It is spring, and nature awakens the world to new possibilities.

Numbers of the sentences that interfere with the unity of the paragraph: ___8___, ___9___

Paragraph 2

[1]The graduation ceremony at our college is dignified but dull. [2]In a large hall filled with well-dressed parents, relatives, and friends of the graduates, faculty and students file in, dressed in hot, heavy academic robes. [3]The ceremony follows a prescribed routine. [4]First, prospective graduates sing the alma mater, desperately searching their programs for the unfamiliar words. [5]The dean of the college, clad in a flowing robe, welcomes the assembled crowd with appropriate decorum. [6]The graduation speaker, usually a state legislator or a distinguished graduate, delivers a lengthy discourse as members of the audience yawn, read their programs, or pretend to listen. [7]~~Then, the anticipated moment arrives and the graduates begin to stir excitedly, waving at parents, who quickly ready cameras and video equipment.~~ [8]~~In spite of the dean's plea to hold the applause until all diplomas have been distributed, whoops and cheers ring out from the audience as eager graduates file across the stage.~~ [9]Finally, the majestic notes of "Pomp and Circumstance" rise in the air, and the graduates march out, heads held high with the dignity of their newly conferred degrees. [10]The ceremony, with its air of dull formality, is over for another year.

Numbers of the sentences that interfere with the unity of the paragraph: ___7___, ___8___

Coherence: Holding the Paragraph Together

mywritinglab

Visit MyWriting Lab for additional practice revising paragraphs for coherence.

If your writing does not have **coherence,** then the sentences in your paragraph are like a pile of loose bricks: There is little connection between them. Coherence is the mortar you use to make your paragraph a brick wall, with solid and strong connections between ideas. To achieve coherence, first make sure your ideas are logically related and well thought out. Then use **coherence tools** to cement the connections between those ideas in the most effective way possible. Two common and easy-to-use coherence tools are *transitional expressions* and *repetition*.

Transitional Expressions

As a writer, you must not only express an idea clearly, you must keep your reader oriented in time and space and aware of relationships between ideas. *Transitional expressions* help you juggle these multiple tasks without detracting from the ideas you express. Ideally, these words and phrases do their job in the background, as guideposts that show the path of your logic and the movement of your ideas through time and space. Following is a list of transitional words and expressions, organized by their function within the sentence.

Some Common Transitional Words and Expressions

Transitions of Time

after	during	later	now	suddenly	when
as	first	meanwhile	often	temporarily	while
before	immediately	next	previously	then	yet

Transitions of Space

above	beside	down	next to	toward
around	between	in	on	under
behind	by	near	over	

Transitions of Addition

also	finally	furthermore	in addition	next
another	first			

Transitions of Importance

as important	essential	major	primary
equally important	just as important	most important	significant

Transitions of Contrast

although	even though	in contrast	instead	on the other hand
but	however	in spite of	nevertheless	yet

Transitions of Cause and Effect

a consequence of	because	for	so	thus
as a result	consequently	since	therefore	

Transitions of Illustration or Example

for example	for instance	including	such as

EXERCISE 5   USING TRANSITIONAL EXPRESSIONS

In the following paragraph, provide the indicated type of transition in each blank. Answers will vary.

[1]Nothing had gone right lately, so _____ (time signal) the doorbell rang, Sam had a feeling it was not the Prize Patrol with a million-dollar check. [2]_____ (contrast signal), he did not expect quite as much trouble as he got. [3]Two police officers were standing _____ (space signal) his porch. [4]"Mr. Williams, we have information that your dog may have bitten a child who lives _____ (space signal) the street," said the tall officer. "It couldn't have been Killer," said Sam, [5]"_____ (cause-effect signal) he never goes outside except on a leash." [6]"Please bring the dog out _____ (time signal)," said the officer. "I'm afraid we'll have to take him to the pound." Sam knew that his dog had not bitten anyone, [7]_____ (contrast signal) he saw no alternative but to hand over his dog. Would he ever see Killer again? [8]_____ (time signal) he brought Killer out on a leash, the officers had their hands near their guns, as if fearful

of being attacked. [9]_____ (contrast signal), when they saw Killer, the officers began to laugh. "That's not the dog we're looking for," said the tall officer, bending to pet the tiny, trembling Chihuahua on the head. "We are looking for a large, fierce dog." [10]_____ (time signal), to Sam's relief, the two officers apologized for bothering him and left.

1. when
2. However
3. on
4. down
5. because
6. now
7. yet
8. When
9. However,
10. Then

EXERCISE 6 USING TRANSITIONAL EXPRESSIONS

In the following paragraph, provide the indicated type of transition in each blank. Answers will vary.

[1]_____ (time) the Fresh-Food Supermart was robbed, Shawna had the bad luck to be the only cashier on duty. The robber came in about 7:00 A.M., [2]_____ (time) the store opened. She noticed him right away [3]_____ (cause-effect) his ball cap was pulled low over his eyes and he wore a jacket [4]_____ (contrast) the morning was warm. He loitered for a while [5]_____ (space) the door; [6]_____ (time) he walked up to her register. She must have suspected him [7]_____ (cause-effect) she suddenly remembered Mr. Monroe, the store manager, saying: "If you are ever robbed, remember that your life is worth more than whatever is in that cash drawer. Stay cool and hand over the money." [8]_____ (time) the robber leaned [9]_____ (space) her and mumbled, "I have a gun. Put the money in a bag." Remembering Mr. Monroe's words, Shawna quickly withdrew the money from the register. [10]_____ (time) she reached for a bag, she was surprised at the words that automatically fell from her lips: "Paper or plastic?" Much [11]_____ (time) Mr. Monroe teased that not only had she remembered his instructions, she had [12]_____ (addition) remembered to offer her unwelcome "customer" a choice.

1. When
2. as
3. because
4. even though
5. near
6. then
7. because
8. Suddenly,
9. toward
10. As
11. later,
12. also

Using Transitions Effectively

Used skillfully, transitional expressions bring coherence to your writing, but moderation is the key. Using these words unnecessarily or artificially is worse than not using them at all.

Tips for Using Transitional Expressions and Examples

- Less is more. Skillfully weaving a few transitional expressions into a paragraph is better than forcing in as many as possible.

- For variety, place transitions somewhere other than the beginning of a sentence. Instead of "However, Arturo refused to place the pink plastic flamingo on his lawn," try "Arturo, however, refused to place the pink plastic flamingo on his lawn."

- Examples are sometimes more effective when they are not preceded by *for example* or *for instance*. If you feel uncomfortable putting an example in without announcement, try using *for example* in your rough draft and editing it out later.

EXERCISE 7   ANALYZING USE OF TRANSITIONS

Look at the two paragraphs that follow. Underline the transitional expressions in each. In which paragraph are transitional expressions used more skillfully? Can you pinpoint some of the reasons?

Paragraph 1

The third week of a student's first year in college is often a dangerous one. Like the "seven-year itch" that supposedly makes people give up on romantic relationships, the "three-week shock syndrome" sometimes signals the end of a student's academic career. After the excitement of the first week or two of classes begins to wear off, reality starts to set in. There is more than just the excitement of meeting new people and buying textbooks in a well-stocked bookstore. Those books, with their crisp pages and new smell, must be opened and read, marked and highlighted. The smiling professors who leaned on their lecterns and cracked jokes on the first day of class have turned into serious-faced people who talk faster than their students can write and whose lectures are sometimes boring. <u>Worst of all</u> is the work. Reading assignments, writing assignments, library assignments, and computer lab assignments pile up, waiting to be completed. Who has time to remember it all, much less do it all? Students who make it past the third week of classes usually find that they can adjust, that they can keep up. <u>But</u> some, faced with the shock that college means work, never stay long enough to find out whether they can succeed or not.

Paragraph 2

    <u>First of all,</u> the third week of a student's first year in college is <u>often</u> a dangerous one. <u>For example,</u> the "seven-year itch" supposedly makes people give up on romantic relationships, and the "three-week shock syndrome" <u>often</u> signals the end of a student's academic career. <u>In addition,</u> the excitement of the first week or two of classes begins to wear off, and reality starts to set in. <u>More important,</u> there is more than just the excitement of meeting new people and buying textbooks in a well-stocked bookstore. <u>In contrast,</u> those books, with their crisp pages and new smell, must be opened and read, marked and highlighted. <u>Furthermore,</u> the smiling professors who leaned on their lecterns and cracked jokes on the first day of class have turned into serious-faced people who talk faster than their students can write and whose lectures are sometimes boring. <u>Worst of all</u> is the work. <u>To enumerate,</u> there are reading assignments, writing assignments, library assignments, and computer lab assignments. <u>Further,</u> who has time to remember it all, much less do it all? <u>Nevertheless,</u> students who make it past the third week of classes usually find that they can adjust, that they can keep up. <u>In conclusion,</u> some, faced with the shock that college means work, never stay long enough to find out whether they can succeed or not.

    The paragraph in which transitions are used more successfully is paragraph <u>1</u>.

Some reasons: <u>In paragraph 1, transitions are used naturally between ideas.</u> <u>They often come in the middle of a sentence rather than being automatically</u> <u>plugged in at the beginning.</u>

Look at the two paragraphs that follow. Underline the transitional expressions in each. In which paragraph are transitional expressions used more skillfully? Can you pinpoint some of the reasons?

Paragraph 1

<u>One</u> characteristic of successful students is that they know how to study. They know, <u>for instance,</u> that the time to begin studying is not the night before the test <u>but</u> much earlier. <u>The first time</u> they read a section of the textbook, successful students begin their study. They highlight or underline important sections and jot down key terms. <u>When</u> taking notes in class, they use a similar technique, jotting down the most important ideas and <u>later</u> transcribing their notes into a format that will be easy to study. Unsuccessful students, <u>on the other hand,</u> often postpone highlighting the text and organizing their notes until the night before the test, when time is short. Successful study, <u>then,</u> partly depends on beginning well before the date of the test.

Paragraph 2

<u>First,</u> successful students know how to study. <u>First of all,</u> they know that the time to begin studying is not the night before the test but much earlier. <u>For example,</u> successful students usually begin their study the first time they read a section of the textbook. <u>In addition,</u> they highlight or underline important sections and jot down key terms. <u>Next, when</u> taking notes in class, they jot down the most important ideas. <u>Furthermore,</u> they transcribe their notes into a format that will be easy to study from later. <u>However,</u> unsuccessful students postpone highlighting the text and organizing their notes until the night before the test. <u>Therefore,</u> successful study partly depends on beginning well before the date of the test.

The paragraph in which transitions are used more successfully is paragraph <u>1</u>.

Some reasons: <u>In paragraph 1, transitions are used naturally between ideas.</u> <u>They often come in the middle of a sentence rather than being automatically</u> <u>plugged in at the beginning.</u>

Repetition

Repetition of Key Words and Phrases

Often, repetition is seen as a negative quality in writing. However, *repetition of key words and phrases* is a method of tying your ideas together and achieving coherence. While no one would advise endless hammering of unimportant words or ideas, repetition of key words and ideas helps to bring your point home strongly.

| EXERCISE 9 | EXAMINING REPETITION OF IMPORTANT TERMS |

The following paragraph is about business telephone manners. Underline the repetitions of the key words *business, telephone* (or *phone*), and *manners.*

At a time when voice mail, answering machines, and computerized <u>telephone</u> answering systems have all but replaced the <u>business telephone</u> call, good <u>telephone manners</u> remain essential. Because the caller on the other end of the <u>phone</u> cannot read lips or minds, it is important for anyone who answers a <u>business telephone</u> to speak clearly, giving his name and the name of the department or company. If it is necessary to ask the caller to hold, it is never good <u>manners</u> to say "Hold, please" and leave the person wondering when, if ever, the <u>phone</u> will be picked up again. Good <u>telephone manners</u> require an explanation, such as "Ms. Smith, our manager, will be happy to help you with that. Would you mind holding for a minute while I get her?" Above all, <u>business telephone manners</u> require giving the caller the idea that her <u>business</u> is appreciated and that the <u>phone</u> call has been a pleasure, not a chore. For example, if the caller says, "Thank you," then the proper reply is not "Yeah, right, no problem." A reply such as "Thank you, Ms. Crabtree. We appreciate your <u>business</u>," demonstrates good <u>telephone manners</u> and excellent <u>business</u> sense. In an impersonal age, adding a personal touch to <u>business telephone</u> calls is not just good <u>manners</u>. It's good <u>business</u>.

Repetition Through Pronouns

Pronouns aid coherence by allowing you to refer to someone or something without tedious repetition. Following is a partial list of pronouns often used to substitute for nouns. (For more information about using pronouns, see Chapters 18 and 19.)

Common Pronouns

Subject pronouns:	I, we, you, he, she, it, they, who
Object pronouns:	me, us, you, him, her, it, them, whom
Possessive pronouns:	my, mine, our, ours, your, yours, his, her, hers, its, their, theirs, whose
Indefinite pronouns:	one, anyone, everyone, nobody, some, somebody

In the following sentences, it's easy to see how much more smoothly the words seem to flow when pronouns link sentences and ideas together.

Example Paragraph Without Pronouns

✗   *The dog* woke up, stretched out *the dog's* legs, and yawned hugely. Then, as if realizing that *the dog* was supposed to be guarding *the dog's* yard, *the dog* shambled over to the gate and gave a halfhearted bark.

Example Paragraph with Pronouns That Aid Coherence

✔   *The dog* woke up, stretched out *his* legs, and yawned hugely. Then, as if realizing that *he* was supposed to be guarding *his* yard, *he* shambled over to the gate and gave a halfhearted bark.

PROGRESSIVE WRITING ASSIGNMENT

Progressive Writing Assignment: Unity and Coherence

If your instructor has assigned the Progressive Writing Assignment, you have already completed your prewriting, a topic sentence, and supporting details. In this chapter, you will make sure your paragraph has unity and coherence.

Topics and Tips

The Topics

Topic 1: Discuss the results of taking a specific piece of advice from a friend or family member.

Topic 2: Discuss your decision to attend college.

Topic 3: Discuss your greatest fear.

Topic 4: Discuss the types of stress experienced by college students.

Tips for Unity and Coherence

STAYING ON TRACK: TIPS FOR UNITY

- Check each paragraph to make sure that every sentence supports the topic sentence.
- Include a summary sentence at the end of the paragraph to reinforce the topic sentence.
  - ✔ Whatever else they may learn on campus, most college students also learn to live with stress.
  - ✔ Becoming a nurse will be the fulfillment of a lifelong dream and the beginning of a long and rewarding career.

TRANSITIONS: TIPS FOR COHERENCE

- Read your paragraph aloud to make sure it flows logically.
- Check to make sure that transitions between supporting ideas are smooth and that transitional expressions are used where needed.
  - ✔ Academic stress *also* affects most college students.
  - ✔ *However,* I have found ways of coping with my fear of public speaking.

mywritinglab   For support in meeting this chapter's goal, log in to **www.mywritinglab.com** and select **Developing and Organizing a Paragraph** and **The Topic Sentence**.

CHAPTER 6

Revising, Proofreading, and Formatting

> ✍ **Chapter Goal:** Develop an understanding of the importance of revision and analyze, revise, proofread, and format a paragraph or essay.

A ragged shrub can be revised
To form a topiary
In almost any shape you want—
Dog, tiger, or canary.

To get your words whipped
into shape,
You'll also need revision
To make sure that your writing
Is just what you envision.

To many writers, revising, proofreading, and formatting are afterthoughts, hastily completed just before the paper is turned in. But these final steps in the writing process help you present your ideas in the best possible way. Revising helps you capture your ideas more clearly and accurately, and proofreading and formatting help give them the polish they need before they are ready for an audience.

Focus on Revision: Getting It Right the Fourth Time

One of the greatest composers of all time, Johann Sebastian Bach, was also one of the messiest composers of all time. He constantly revised his music, writing all over his sheet music until he created something he thought was suitable for performance. But most people who hear Bach's music don't ever consider his revisions. After all, we are hearing it in perfect condition. Why should we consider the multiple changes Bach made to his music when we hear it in its final form?

The truth is that composers revise their music just as writers revise their texts. As writers, we go through many drafts and make multiple changes, just as Bach did with his music. Whether you are writing music or an essay, think through and revise multiple times to make it sound its best.

Reflect on It

Think about something that you do that requires revision, double-checking, or attention to format. Do you ever "revise" your clothing before going out? What else do you do that has to be "just so"?

 Revising

mywritinglab

Visit MyWritingLab for additional practice revising your work.

If you have ever watched your golden ideas clatter onto the page like a load of rough gravel, you understand the need for revision. **Revising** helps you do justice to your ideas, to capture some of their original sparkle.

There are also more practical reasons for revision, reasons that have their roots in the difference between writing and conversation. Conversation is constantly under revision. When your listener says, "What do you mean?" and you explain, you are revising. When your listener disagrees and you reinforce your argument or concede a point, you are revising. In a conversation, revision is a response to the listener. But writing does not offer the same opportunity for response. Your reader cannot ask questions. So you have to *anticipate* a reader's objections and meet them before they arise. That means that you need to spot possible misunderstandings and clarify them before the reader sees the finished work. Revising is a process of stepping back and looking at your work through the eyes of a reader.

The word *revise* combines the Latin root meaning *to see* with the prefix meaning *again.* "Seeing again" is the essence of good revision. The difficult part is distancing yourself far enough from the work to see it with new eyes. When the work is fresh from your pen or computer, you often see what you *meant* to say rather than what is actually on the page.

To see your work again, you need to create a space, a mental distance, between yourself and the work. Time is your best ally. Lay the writing aside for at least a twenty-four-hour period. When you return to it, words that aren't precise, sentences that aren't clear, and explanations that don't explain enough are easier to spot.

If you do not have twenty-four hours to lay the work aside, it may help to have someone else look at it. Ask your reader to focus on content and to ask questions about any point that does not seem clear. The written word carries no facial expression, no gesture, and no tone of voice, so it is more open to misinterpretation than is face-to-face communication. Discussing work with a reader can help close the gap between what you *think* you said and what your reader actually sees.

In addition to letting a work "cool" before revising and enlisting the help of a reader, you can also check your paragraph point by point to make sure that it fulfills the purpose you had in mind. There is nothing mysterious about this procedure. It works like the diagnostic test a mechanic might perform to evaluate a car, checking all the major systems to make sure they are working as they should. The following revision checklist will help you to go through a paragraph, part by part, to make sure that each part is doing the job you intend it to do.

Checklist for Revision

The Topic Sentence

✔ Does the paragraph have a topic sentence that clearly states the main idea of the entire paragraph?

✔ Is the topic sentence the first or second sentence in the paragraph?

The Supporting Sentences

✔ Does each sentence of the paragraph support the topic sentence?

✔ Do your examples and explanations provide specific detail to support the topic sentence?

✔ Is each point you raise adequately explained and supported?

The Ending

✔ Is the last sentence satisfying and final sounding?

✔ Does the last sentence serve as a summary or closing sentence for the entire paragraph?

Checking Coherence

✔ Is the order of ideas clear and logical?

✔ Are transitional words used effectively?

EXERCISE 1	ANALYZING TWO VERSIONS OF A PARAGRAPH

Read the two versions of the paragraph "Some Purposes of Urban Legends." Using the preceding Checklist for Revision as your guide, decide which version is the revision and which is the rough draft.

Version 1

Some Purposes of Urban Legends

[1]Some urban legends, such as the story of a man caught speeding by a high-tech surveillance system, are meant to amuse. [2]The man was mailed a photo of his car's license plate, a radar reading of his speed, and a ticket for $120. [3]He mailed back a photo of a check. [4]The police responded with a photo of a pair of handcuffs. [5]The motorist quickly relented and sent a check. [6]Urban legends are meant to sound a warning. [7]Urban legends that tell of escaped murderers haunting lovers' lanes, of babies left alone for "just a moment" with tragic consequences, or of predators stalking women down lonely roads fit this category. [8]I myself cannot imagine a parent being careless with his or her child. [9]There is so much that can happen to a defenseless baby in seconds. [10]These legends remind us, as we go about our lives, to be careful. [11]A final type of urban legend, the "David and Goliath" story, shows how an average person can fight big business or government and win. [12]One example is the story of a woman who asked a waitress in a department store's tearoom for the store's chocolate chip cookie recipe. [13]She was told she would be charged "two-fifty," and she agreed to what she thought was a $2.50 charge on her credit card. [14]Later, she received a charge card bill for $250. [15]This legend, which still haunts the Internet, reminds its readers that even ordinary people have some measure of

power. [16]Urban legends, although mostly untrue, serve a purpose as they tell of funny incidents, tragedy, or an ordinary person's revenge.

Version 2

Some Purposes of Urban Legends

[1]Urban legends, the modern equivalent of ancient folktales, serve a variety of purposes. [2]Some urban legends, such as the story of a man caught speeding by a high-tech surveillance system, are meant to amuse. [3]The man was mailed a photo of his car's license plate, a radar reading of his speed, and a ticket for $120. [4]He mailed back a photo of a check. [5]When the police responded with a photo of a pair of handcuffs, the motorist quickly relented and sent a check. [6]Another type of urban legend is meant to sound a warning. [7]In one story of warning, a couple goes to a lovers' lane in spite of a news broadcast telling of an escaped murderer called "Hook Hand." [8]When they hear a noise outside the car, they become frightened and start to leave. [9]The car seems to be stuck, but finally they pull away and drive home. [10]As they get out of the car in the young woman's driveway, they notice something caught on the bumper: a hook hand. [11]A final type of urban legend, the "David and Goliath" story, shows how an average person can fight big business or government and win. [12]An example is the story of a woman who asked a waitress in a department store's tearoom for the store's chocolate chip cookie recipe. [13]She was told she would be charged "two-fifty" and she agreed to what she thought was a $2.50 charge on her credit card. [14]Later, she received a charge card bill for $250. [15]When the department store refused to remove the charge, the woman's revenge was swift. [16]She posted the recipe on the Internet for the world to enjoy, along with a letter of explanation. [17]This legend, which still haunts the Internet, reminds its readers that even ordinary people have some measure of power. [18]Urban legends, although mostly untrue, serve a purpose as they tell of funny incidents, tragedy, or an ordinary person's revenge.

The revised version of the paragraph is version __2__

EXERCISE 2   ANALYZING AN UNREVISED PARAGRAPH

Go back to the unrevised version of "Some Purposes of Urban Legends" and fill in the blanks in the following questions.

1.   A topic sentence should appear before sentence __1__ in the unrevised version.

2. A transitional word or expression is needed as the writer moves to a new point in sentence __6__.

3. Two sentences that do not support the topic sentence are sentence __8__ and sentence __9__.

4. More support is needed to fully make the writer's point after sentence __14__.

Proofreading

mywritinglab

Visit MyWriting Lab for additional practice proofreading your work.

Think about the last time you saw a misspelled word in a newspaper. The minute you saw it, your thoughts moved away from the story itself and focused on the error. Similarly, errors in your writing take a reader's focus away from your ideas and put emphasis on grammar, spelling, or punctuation. Naturally, you want the ideas to stand in the foreground while grammar, spelling, and punctuation remain in the background. Proofreading, then, is an essential last step in your writing. Though proofreading is usually a chore, it is a necessary chore.

After you have completed the final revision of your work, proofread it at least twice, once from the top down and once from the bottom up. If you have a special problem area, such as comma splices or subject-verb disagreement, you should do at least one extra proofreading focusing on finding such errors.

Proofreading is the job that never seems complete. No matter how thorough you are, some little error may still escape your notice. Then, just as you are turning in your beautifully handwritten or typed manuscript, the error pops out at you as if it were written in neon. Therefore, the more thorough your approach to proofreading, the better.

The Top-Down Technique

On the first proofreading, scan from the top of the page down. Check to make sure the connections between ideas are smooth and solid and that sentences and paragraphs flow smoothly into one another. Check for parallel structure, clear pronoun reference, and appropriate transitional expressions. After correcting any problems you find in the top-down proofreading, move to the second type of proofreading, the bottom-up proofreading.

The Bottom-Up Technique

The bottom-up proofreading technique is more labor-intensive and more focused than top-down proofreading. When you read from the bottom up, you are no longer reading your essay as a single piece of writing but as disconnected sentences that do *not* flow into one another. Because your focus is on a single sentence, you can look at it closely, as if it is a sentence in a grammar exercise. Read it carefully, correct any errors you find, and then move up to the next sentence.

The Targeting Technique

If you have a "favorite" error—one that seems to plague you more than any other—try an additional proofreading to target that error. Following are some common errors and shortcuts to finding those errors. As you become more experienced, you will find yourself devising your own strategies to target your problem areas.

Subject-verb agreement. Check each subject-verb sequence. Look for present-tense verb forms and make sure they agree with their subjects.

Comma splices and run-ons. Target long sentences; they are more likely to be run-ons. Target commas and see if there is a sentence on each side of the comma; if so, you have a comma splice.

Other comma errors. Target each comma and ask yourself why you put it there. If you aren't sure why it is there, maybe it doesn't belong. Check for the correct usage in this text or another reliable source.

Pronoun agreement. Look for the plural pronouns *they* and *their*, and make sure that they have a plural, not a singular, antecedent.

Sentence fragments. Using the bottom-up technique, read each sentence to see if it could stand on its own.

Proofreading the Computer-Generated Paragraph

Spelling and grammar checkers can be helpful in proofreading, but they are no substitute for personal knowledge and judgment. A spelling or grammar checker can find possible errors and suggest possible solutions. However, it is up to you to decide what, if anything, is wrong and how to fix it.

Even when you use spelling and grammar checkers, you should do at least two separate proofreadings. The following sentence, in which all words are spelled correctly, illustrates the need:

✔ Weather or knot ewe use a spelling checker, you knead too proofread.

Whether to proofread onscreen or print out a hard copy to proofread is a personal choice. Some writers find it easier to scroll up and down on the computer screen, viewing the paragraph in small segments. Others swear that they cannot see their errors until they hold the printed copy in their hands. Find out what works best for you and proceed accordingly.

Group Exercise 1   Proofreading a Paragraph
Confident? Go solo!

Each of the twenty sentences in the following paragraph contains an error. Form a small proofreading team with two or three of your classmates. Pooling your knowledge, see how many errors you can identify and correct.

An Urban Legend

[1]Urban legends are stories that are often told but is seldom true. [2]One urban legend involves a young college woman traveling home for the Thanksgiving holiday's. [3]As she leaves, the dorm's custodian warned her to take precautions against the Road Killer, who is known to prey on women driving alone. [4]On the road, she stops before dark to get gas, however; she can't get the pump to work. [5]She drives off, planing to stop somewhere else. [6]But as she drive's, she begins to feel more and more apprehensive. [7]It is now fully dark, so she decide to stop at a full-service station. [8]So that she won't have to get out of the car again. [9]It seems like hrs. before she finds a station with a sign that says, "We pump." [10]She hands the attendant her credit card, she notices he is looking at her and at her car with a strange expression. [11]As he walks toward his booth to check her credit, she feels majorly creeped out. [12]The attendant comes back and said a representative of the credit card company wants to talk to her on the phone. [13]She fears a trick but, the attendant is insistent. [14]One gets out of the car. [15]And walks toward the attendant's booth. [16]He follows closely, goes in behind her slams the door, and locks it. [17]Just as she is about to scream, he says, "I've called the police, and they're on there way. There is a man crouched in the back seat of your car." [18]Urban legends like this one are all most never true. [19]However people find them interesting. [20]Because they represent events that could happen.

Corrections

1.	are	11.	frightened
2.	holidays	12.	says
3.	warns	13.	trick, but
4.	gas; however,	14.	She
5.	planning	15.	car and walks
6.	drives	16.	her, slams
7.	decides	17.	their
8.	station so that	18.	almost
9.	hours	19.	However, people
10.	card, and she	20.	interesting because

✍ Formatting

You have heard it all your life: First impressions count. The document you hand to your instructor, the résumé you submit to a prospective employer, or the letter you send to the editor of a newspaper has the ability to present a positive first impression or a negative one. When an instructor sees a carefully formatted paper with no smudges, crossovers, or dog-eared edges, the instructor expects that paper to be a good one, written as carefully as it was prepared. On the other hand, a hastily scrawled document smudged with eraser marks or heavily laden with white-out suggests that the writer did not take the time to create a good impression—or to write a good paper.

Manuscript format is so important that entire books have been written about it. An instructor who asks you to use MLA style, APA style, or Chicago style is referring to styles outlined in books published by the Modern Language Association, the American Psychological Association, and the University of Chicago.

If you are given instructions for formatting a document, follow those instructions carefully. If you have no specific instructions, use the guidelines in the following section. They will help you to format a document effectively, whether that document is written in class or out of class, by hand or on a word processor.

Handwritten Documents

Paragraphs and Essays

For handwritten paragraphs and essays, use lined white 8½ × 11-inch paper and blue or black ink. Write on one side of the paper only, and leave wide margins.

In the upper right-hand corner of the page, write your name and the date. If you wish, include your instructor's name and the name of the class for which you are preparing the assignment. Center your title, if any, on the first line of the paper, but do not underline the title or put it in quotation marks. Indent each paragraph about three-quarters of an inch. In a handwritten document, do not skip lines unless your instructor specifically requests it. If you make an error, draw a single line through the error and rewrite your correction above the crossed-out error. Put a single paper clip, not a staple, in the upper left corner to join the pages.

Essay Tests

When you take an essay test, you may be required to use a "blue book" or to write on the test itself. If you are allowed to use your own paper, use lined paper and write on one side only.

Answers to questions on essay tests should be written in blue or black ink. Since time is too limited for a rough draft, take a moment to organize your thoughts, and then answer the question. Indent each paragraph about three-quarters of an inch. State your main idea first; then add specific supporting details and examples.

If you misspell a word or make a mistake, cross through it with a single line. Be sure to write clearly and legibly, and if your handwriting is difficult to read, try printing instead.

Computer-Generated Documents

Setting up the Word-Processing Software

Choose a font and a font size that are easily readable, such as Times New Roman in a 12-point size. Do not use a bold or italic font.

Margins should be one inch all around. One-inch margins are the default on most word processors, so you probably will not have to set margins. Set the word processor to double-space the text. Leave the right edge ragged rather than justifying it. (To justify means to line up in a straight edge, like a newspaper column. Most word processors have settings that allow you to justify, but these settings are not commonly used for academic work.)

Formatting the Document

Your instructor may ask you to follow a particular style when formatting your papers. If your instructor does not, place your name and the date in the upper right corner of the page. Other information, such as the name of your instructor or the class for which you are preparing the assignment, is optional. Center the title and indent each paragraph as shown in the sample that follows. A title page is not necessary unless your instructor asks for one.

> Derek Smith
>
> April 1, 2011
>
> Format Reform
>
> I am ashamed to say that I used to be a format abuser. I used strange fonts such as Adolescence and Space Toaster. I tried to make my papers look longer by using two-inch margins and 14-point font. At my lowest point, I turned in a report with the text in 15-point Star Trek font printed on lime-green paper. A caring instructor saw that I had a problem and helped me to turn my formatting around. Now I know how to format a document perfectly.
>
> The first step in formatting a document is setting up the word processor. Margins should be set at one inch all around—left, right, top, and bottom. Choose easy-to-read fonts, such as Times New

Printing and Presenting Your Document

When the document has been revised and proofread, print it on good-quality, 8½ × 11-inch white paper. To hold the pages together, place a single paper clip in the upper left corner. Do not staple your document or put it in a report cover.

PROGRESSIVE WRITING ASSIGNMENT

Progressive Writing Assignment: Revising, Proofreading, and Formatting

If your instructor has given you the Progressive Writing Assignment, you are almost finished. All that remains is to revise the paragraph, proofread it carefully, and put it in the proper format.

Topics and Tips

THE TOPICS

Topic 1: Discuss the results of taking a specific piece of advice from a friend or family member.

Topic 2: Discuss your decision to attend college.

Topic 3: Discuss your greatest fear.

Topic 4: Discuss the types of stress experienced by college students.

TIPS FOR REVISING, PROOFREADING, AND FORMATTING

- Set aside your writing for 24 hours, or ask someone else to look at your paragraph and tell you if any point is not clear or if any idea needs further explanation.
- Evaluate your paragraph using the "Checklist for Revision" in this chapter.
- Use your word processor's spelling and grammar checkers, but don't forget to proofread the document at least three times yourself.
- Check the formatting of your paragraph against your instructor's instructions or against the guidelines in this chapter. Improper formatting can be distracting to a reader, but proper formatting allows your paragraph to shine.

mywritinglab   For support in meeting this chapter's goal, log in to **www.mywritinglab.com** and select **The Paragraph**.

CHAPTER 7

Showing and Telling: Description, Narration, and Example

> **Chapter Goal:** Analyze and write descriptive, narrative, and example paragraphs and essays.

Five senses countdown:
Walking down a city street, what are
5 things you might see?
4 things you might hear?
3 things you might smell?
2 things you might touch or feel?
1 thing you might taste?

Description, narration, and example are useful when you need to provide specific details. With *description*, you can show your reader what you see, hear, smell, touch, or taste. With *narration*, you can tell a reader a story that makes a point. With *example*, you can provide specific illustrations. Your writing comes alive when you describe, tell a story, or give a specific example.

Focus on Description, Narration, and Example

You've seen them: the ads on TV that try to entice you to go visit one of the United States. You see images of couples walking along a beach or children playing in an open field or a man hiking up a mountain and taking in the amazing view. The voiceover says, "Visit California" or "Come meet us in Texas."

Advertisers know that the way into consumers' minds, hearts, and pocketbooks is through effective description, narration, and example. An ad for a state as a vacation destination may show viewers vivid landscapes (description) as the activities tell a story of an enjoyable vacation (narration and example). These three modes of writing are important when you want to show your readers something instead of just telling them.

Reflect on It

Find a commercial on TV or in a magazine that does absolutely nothing to sell the product other than using description, narration, and example. Is the ad effective? Why or why not?

Description, Narration, and Example in Action

In this chapter, you will have the opportunity to examine and use the techniques of description, narration, and example. To help you become skilled in using these techniques, the text analyzes and explains each one separately. In reality, they are rarely used that way. Instead, authors combine techniques, using the ones that best suit their purpose for writing.

Before looking at description, narration, and example separately, look at how a professional writer uses all three techniques together. The following essay, from Knight-Ridder/Tribune Information Services, is a story about the Vietnam Veterans Memorial in Washington, D.C. This story, written by an anonymous newspaper reporter, is an example of *journalistic writing*. Journalistic writing is less formal than academic writing, and the shorter paragraphs are suited to the narrow columns in newspapers and magazines.

The essay embodies all three of the writing techniques featured in this chapter. The article is framed as a **narrative**, or story, that follows a park ranger around the memorial as he picks up items left at the wall. As the story continues, the writer gives specific **examples** of items left at the wall, along with **description** that helps the reader visualize the items and the people they commemorate.

Narration, description, and example are three of the most basic and useful writing techniques. By using them, you can show and tell your reader exactly what you mean.

Against the Wall

Knight-Ridder/Tribune Information Services

They come every day, years, even decades after their loved ones were lost.

They leave the kinds of things that people have been leaving ever since the Wall was built—poems, letters, medals, black lace panties, teddy bears, cans of sardines, six-packs of Bud, toilet paper, wedding rings.

Years pass. People get older. But the emotions evoked by the Vietnam Veterans Memorial Wall never seem to change.

At night, park ranger Pete Prentner walks along the Wall with his flashlight, picking up the tangible pieces of lives broken by grief. In the 15 years since the wall was dedicated, nearly 54,000 items have been left here.

"No one ever expected this to happen," he said. "It's so personal. It caught everyone by surprise."

It now takes almost an hour a night to collect everything left at the Wall and even longer on holidays like Memorial Day.

Through the years, people have left dollar bills, rosaries, locks of hair, an empty bottle of Chandon champagne and two goblets, a golf trophy with this note, "It's a beautiful day. We'd be playing golf. I'd be beating you by two strokes, sucker."

Many remembrances are for people unknown, but loved anyway. There's the gold-framed sonogram images for Sgt. Eddie E. Chervony, with a letter that says "Happy Father's Day, Dad! Here are the first two images of your first grandchild. . . . Dad, this child will know you, just how I have grown to know and love you even though the last time I saw you I was only four months old. Your daughter, Jeanette."

The National Park Service collects, catalogs and stores the items in a gigantic, climate-controlled warehouse in suburban Maryland.

A few things are exhibited at the Smithsonian Institution and four other museums. Next month, the story of the mementos left at the Wall will be told on a Web site. The collectors plan to take some items to schools around the country to teach another generation about the war most know little about.

This collection is different from all others, which typically reflect a curator's conscious selections. In this case, the public is the curator.

"It is the public saying this is important," said Duery Felton, Jr., the park service curator and himself a Vietnam vet. "Only the donor and maybe the recipient understand the meaning of the items."

Many artifacts are left anonymously, such as blue diaper pins, a pacifier, Mickey Mouse ears. Others are directly personal, such as this letter to Sgt. Andres Massa: "My sister, Carmen, misses you very much and so do I. P. S. I'm looking out for her. Coco."

Even though Washington is a town full of imposing monuments, no other has provoked such an emotional torrent of tokens and trinkets as the Wall, which draws some three million visitors a year.

The first artifact actually arrived when the Wall's foundation was being poured. A man wanted to leave a Purple Heart medal awarded posthumously to his brother in the concrete.

For the first two years, the items were gathered nightly by maintenance people and stored in cardboard boxes in sheds. When the flood didn't stop, they realized they had quite a phenomenon on their hands. Each item collected gets a bar code, is placed in a plastic Zip-Loc bag, and is carted to the warehouse, known as the Museum Resource Center. There, items are handled by technicians in white cotton gloves.

Some items have shocked the rangers, such as cremated ashes dumped on the concrete. "The first time, we didn't know what to do," Prentner recalled. "We called the police. We wondered: Is this like disposing of a body? Luckily, it rained that night, and that's probably what the guy wanted."

There was the flesh-toned double-leg prosthesis, complete with running shoes and black socks, that once belonged to Stephen E. Belville. He was wounded in a foxhole in 1968 and died April 15, 1994.

There was the cardboard covered with cigars and this message for Francis Eugene Sanders: "For 28 Christmas mornings, I've thought of you and our last cigar together. Now for your birthday, it's time for you to catch up to me." It was from his buddy, Sgt. J. Kornsey.

The item that haunted all who saw it: A wrinkled photo of a young North Vietnamese soldier and a little girl with braided pigtails. The accompanying letter said:

"Dear Sir, For twenty-two years, I have carried your picture in my wallet. I was only eighteen years old that day we faced one another on that trail in Chu Lai, Vietnam. Why you didn't take my life I'll never know. You stared at me for so long, armed with your AK-47, and yet you did not fire. Forgive me for taking your life, I was reacting the way I was trained, to kill V. C. . . . So many times over the years

I have stared at your picture and your daughter, I suspect. Each time my heart and guts would burn with the pain of guilt."

At times, it is hard for the rangers and the museum workers to even look at the mementos. "You learn to read, but not read," said Felton, the curator.

In the darkness, with tourists still milling around the wall, Prentner stumbled upon a letter addressed to Fred: "I always looked up to you without you even really knowing it. Man, you looked so good in your uniform, jump wings, spit-shined boots. . . . Love, Frank."

The 35-year-old ranger, who served four years in the Army himself, cannot help being moved.

"I try to distance myself," he said. "Some of these guys disappeared more than 25 years ago, but it is obviously still so emotional. Each one had a name. Each one had a family and friends. You never know all the people and what they could have been."

THINKING ABOUT THE ESSAY

1. Examples provide specific instances that help a reader understand a more general point. Choose two examples of items left at the Vietnam Veterans Memorial from the essay. What do those items and the notes left with them, if any, tell you about the soldier who died, the person who left the item, and their relationship?

2. Narration helps essay writers make a point by telling a story. While there are certainly stories in the items left against the memorial wall, the author chose to frame the article as a walk through the memorial with a park ranger. How do the ranger's remarks at the end of the story help to reinforce what readers learn about the emotional impact of the items?

3. Description helps readers understand an essay in the same way that they understand the world: through sight, hearing, taste, touch, and smell. Which of the senses is used most prominently to describe the items in this essay?

Laying the Groundwork for Descriptive Writing

Writers on Effective Description

Don't tell me the moon is shining; show me the glint of light on broken glass.

   —Anton Chekhov

Detail makes the difference between boring and terrific writing. It's the difference between a pencil sketch and a lush oil painting. As a writer, words are your paint. Use all the colors.

   —Rhys Alexander

Look at the photograph of the diner; then use your imagination to visualize the interior. How is it furnished and decorated? How are the people dressed? What types of food are served? Write a paragraph describing the interior of the diner. Your challenge in this assignment is to make everything you describe seem so real that the reader can almost see it, hear it, touch it, taste it, and smell it.

Description

mywritinglab

Visit MyWriting Lab for additional practice with description.

Effective descriptive writing paints a picture for the reader. Just as an artist uses canvas, brushes, and paints, the successful painter of word pictures also employs tools of the trade to create an effective picture. Your tools as a writer of descriptive paragraphs and essays include sense impressions, spatial order, and use of a dominant impression.

Sense Impressions

Every scrap of information you collect about the world around you comes through your five senses: sight, hearing, smell, taste, and touch. It is logical, then, that descriptions using **sense impressions** present a real and vivid picture to your reader.

Sight

Visual impressions are strong and lasting. People are not fooled by a clerk's "Thank you" if his facial expression says, "I hate my job." In fact, psychological studies confirm that people are likely to rely more on facial expressions and gestures than on spoken words. If it really is true that "seeing is believing," then creating a visual picture for the reader is particularly important in descriptive writing.

Hearing

Our sense of hearing also gives us information about the world around us. We are warned by the blast of a horn, energized by the beat of rock music, or soothed by the thunder of the ocean. Imagery that appeals to a reader's sense of hearing is an essential dimension of descriptive writing.

Smell

The sense of smell has a powerful connection to memory. The smell of freshly popped popcorn may summon the claustrophobic feel of a dark, crowded movie theater. A whiff of furniture polish can bring back memories of an elderly aunt's stately dining room. Using imagery related to smell helps to complete the picture you are creating for your reader.

Taste

Taste imagery will probably play only a small role in your writing, unless you are writing about food. However, used sparingly, references to taste can add a touch of spice to your descriptive writing.

Touch

The sense of touch is a backdrop for all experience. As you sit reading this, you may feel beneath you the hard surface of a wooden chair or the softness of sofa cushions. You may be aware of the chill of air conditioning or the warmth of sunlight, the scratch of a wool sweater or the cottony caress of an old pair of jeans. Imagery that brings out textures and temperatures adds the stamp of reality to the picture you are drawing for your reader.

| EXERCISE 1 | RECOGNIZING WORDS OF THE SENSES |

In the following paragraph, underline words and phrases that convey sense impressions.

Water Aerobics

Although I am not athletic, I enjoy my water aerobics class. I feel comfortable around the other women in my class because, like me, they are not athletes. They are not <u>picture-perfect models with smoothly muscled arms and concave stomachs</u>, but <u>real women with pudgy stomachs, wide hips, or skinny, toothpick calves</u>. Around them, I feel less self-conscious about the extra twenty pounds I am carrying. I also enjoy the music that accompanies our exercise. The music system is just a small portable CD player, but if it is turned up loudly enough, the energizing <u>beat of disco music echoes throughout the pool area</u>. It is impossible to hear "Shake Your Groove Thing" without wanting to dance. Once the music starts, we move from the <u>hot concrete</u> at the side of the pool into the shock of <u>the cool blue water</u>. The exercise itself may be my favorite part of the experience. The water <u>buoys me up</u> so that the laws of gravity no longer fully apply. <u>Each bounce sends me a foot into the air</u>, and I land <u>lightly and easily</u>. When the class is over, the crisp <u>smell of chlorine</u> stays with me, reminding me of the <u>laughter of classmates, the blare of music, and the temporary freedom from gravity</u> that I experience in my water aerobics class.

| EXERCISE 2 | WRITING SENSORY DESCRIPTIONS |

Write a phrase that describes each of the following words in sensory terms. Then note whether you describe the word through sight, hearing, smell, taste, or touch. The first one is done for you. Answers will vary.

1. cup

   a smooth, heavy ceramic cup (touch)
   _____

2. chair

   _____

3. grass

   _____

4. hat

   _____

5. moonlight

    _____

6. air freshener

    _____

7. french fries

    _____

8. tire

    _____

9. cloud

    _____

10. dirt

    _____

Spatial Order

Spatial order shows the layout of anything that takes up space. Use spatial order to present physical objects in a way that makes sense: bottom to top, left to right, background to foreground, outside to inside—in short, in any organized fashion. Below is a partial list of words commonly used when referring to space.

above	beyond	near	right
ahead	by	next to	south
around	down	north	toward
behind	east	on	under
beside	in	over	underfoot
between	left	overhead	west

EXERCISE 3   **RECOGNIZING EFFECTIVE USE OF SPATIAL ORDER**

Look at the following short paragraphs. In which paragraph is spatial order used in a more organized and coherent way?

Paragraph 1

    The top drawer of my desk was a mess. The tape I was looking for was all the way in the back. A deck of playing cards secured with a rubber band sat beside a flashlight that had no batteries. The first thing I saw when I opened the drawer was a jumble of papers. Near the front of the drawer were a crumpled yellow sheet with an email address written on it, several grocery store and gas receipts, and an envelope that had once contained a bank statement. Pencils without points, paper clips, and assorted change were scattered in the tray at the front of the drawer. It was difficult to explain why some of the items near the back of the drawer had been saved at all: a catnip mouse without a tail, an empty tape dispenser, and an unfolded gum wrapper on which someone had written "23cd" seemed to have no use. I took the roll of tape, then closed the drawer, resolving to clean it out the moment I had time.

Paragraph 2

The top drawer of my desk was a mess. The first thing I saw when I opened the drawer was a jumble of papers. Near the front of the drawer were a crumpled yellow sheet with an email address written on it, several grocery store and gas receipts, and an envelope that had once contained a bank statement. Pencils without points, paper clips, and assorted change were scattered in the tray at the front of the drawer. A deck of playing cards secured with a rubber band sat beside a flashlight that had no batteries. It was difficult to explain why some of the items near the back of the drawer had been saved at all: a catnip mouse without a tail, an empty tape dispenser, and an unfolded gum wrapper on which someone had written "23cd" seemed to have no use. The tape I was looking for was all the way in the back. I took the roll of tape, then closed the drawer, resolving to clean it out the moment I had time.

The paragraph that uses spatial order more effectively is paragraph __2__.

Establishing a Dominant Impression

Description is more than a tangle of unrelated details. In descriptive writing, all the details should join to convey a single **dominant impression**. Imagine that your job is to describe a house that you pass every day. If your description is to stick in your reader's memory, it must be more than simply a jumble of shutters, bricks, and roofing tiles. A dominant impression not only makes your description more memorable, but it also adds to the unity of the description. What is your overall impression of that house? Is it cheerful? Eerie? Prim? Dignified? The word that you choose to describe the house conveys your dominant impression. As you describe the house, each detail should contribute to the dominant impression.

If you are describing a house that is eerie, include details designed to send chills up the reader's spine: the loose, creaking shutters and the blankly staring windows. If cheerful dandelions bloom in the yard, let them bloom unseen. Details that do not reinforce the dominant impression do not belong in your description.

EXERCISE 4   **SUPPORTING THE DOMINANT IMPRESSION**

In each list below, circle the letter of the detail that would *not* support the dominant impression of the topic sentence.

1. The bank building looks *dignified*.
    a. Black marble covers the front of the building.
    b. The tinted glass doors look heavy and substantial.
    c. Graffiti is spray-painted on the sidewalk that leads up to the door.
    d. Gold letters spell out the bank's name.

2. The bathroom is *messy*.
    a. Toothpaste is spattered on the sink and mirror.
    b. Damp towels have been thrown on the floor.
    c. Children's tub toys are scattered on the sink and in the tub.
    d. Clean towels are folded and stored on a shelf.

3. My brother is *studious*.
    a. He finishes his homework as soon as he comes home from school.
    b. He likes to play video games.
    c. He researches subjects like astronomy and geology on the Internet.
    d. He hates to see school let out for the summer.

4. The basement is *a fire hazard*.
    a. Newspapers dating back to 1972 are stacked beside the furnace.
    b. Boxes of firecrackers sit near an open can of charcoal starter.
    c. A black widow spider has made her nest on a box of broken glass and rusty nails.
    d. A rusty chainsaw with a frayed cord is plugged into the wall.

5. The man seemed *prosperous*.
    a. He drove a new Mercedes.
    b. He lived in a large, expensive brick house on the north side of town.
    c. His battered wallet held two dollars and a picture of his family.
    d. His designer suit was tailored to perfection.

Wordsmith's Corner: Sample Descriptive Paragraphs

Below are two examples of descriptive writing. Read each paragraph and answer the questions that follow.

Descriptive Paragraph 1

In this paragraph, the writer draws a portrait of a homeless man.

Interstate Sam

<u>Interstate Sam is a figure of weary dignity.</u> His tired face is an ebony mask, ancient and unreadable. His shoulders bend as if under a heavy load. Sometimes he stands slumped onto his shopping cart as if he has fallen asleep. In winter, a battered green coat shrouds the many layers of clothing that sag from his thin frame like tattered robes. In rain, his cape is a yellow plastic banner, positioned so that the word SALE stretches from shoulder to shoulder across his stooped back. He leans on his rusty cart, shifting the weight from his overburdened feet, but he carries no sign reading "Stranded" or "Will Work for Food." He asks for nothing, and people say he accepts nothing that is offered. He scrounges through dumpsters for food or, less likely, buys it with the thick sheaf of bills he is rumored to carry. Interstate Sam lives his life in the street, yet holds the world at arm's length with his stoic solitude.

Questions

Answers may vary.

1. Underline the topic sentence of the paragraph. Does it state the dominant impression?

   Yes.
   _____

2. What is the dominant impression in this paragraph? List three details that reinforce it.

   The dominant impression is that Interstate Sam is a figure of weary dignity.
   _____

   "tired face is an ebony mask, ancient and unreadable"
   _____

   "shoulders bend as if under a heavy load"
   _____

   "layers of clothing that sag from his thin frame like tattered robes"
   _____

3. Is the sensory imagery in the paragraph mainly sight, hearing, smell, taste, or touch? List three details expressed in sensory terms.

   The imagery is mainly sight imagery.
   _____

"a battered green coat shrouds the many layers of clothing"

"his cape is a yellow plastic banner"

"the word SALE stretches from shoulder to shoulder across his stooped back"

Descriptive Paragraph 2

Luis writes about a subway station as seen through a child's eyes.

The Subway Station

When I was a child, the subway station seemed like a strange and frightening place. Going down the steep steps into the dark subway, with its smell of dirt, shoes, and sweat, I felt like I was descending into a sinister underground world. In the station, standing with my father on a cement floor that was lumpy with ingrained chewing gum, I looked around at the people. They leaned against pillars, read newspapers, or sat on benches, appearing ordinary enough. But I had been warned against strangers, and here they were, loitering in close proximity. The woman in the striped dress could be a kidnapper, or the thin man's briefcase might hold a gun. I watched the strangers warily, occasionally getting an annoyed glare in return. Then my attention would turn to the steep drop at the edge of the platform. There was always one daredevil standing right at the edge, peering into the dark tunnel as if to make the train arrive faster. I hung well back. If I approached the edge, some unseen force might propel me over the steep drop and onto the third rail. Even if I survived the fall, contact with the third rail would mean instant electrocution. As I watched the person at the edge of the platform, wondering when he would fall, my ears caught the distant rumble of an approaching train. As the strangers folded their papers and rose from their benches, I covered my ears in dread. The rumble became a huge, echoing roar, and the roar became a piercing screech of brakes as the subway came to a stop. On board the train, my fears subsided as clacking, noisy wheels carried us through the dark tunnel and toward the light.

Questions

Answers may vary.

1. Underline the topic sentence of the paragraph. Does it state the dominant impression?

   Yes.

2. What is the dominant impression in this paragraph? List three details that reinforce it.

The dominant impression of the subway is that it is strange and frightening.

"The woman in the striped dress could be a kidnapper, or the thin man's briefcase might hold a gun."

"Some unseen force might propel me over the steep drop and onto the third rail."

"The rumble became a huge, echoing roar, and the roar became a piercing screech of brakes."

3. Give examples from the paragraph of imagery expressed in terms of smell, touch, and hearing.

Smell: "smell of dirt, shoes, and sweat"

Touch: "a cement floor that was lumpy with ingrained chewing gum"

Hearing: "a piercing screech of brakes"

TOPICS FOR PRACTICING DESCRIPTIVE WRITING

Small Scrawls: Imaginative Short Writings

What is a Small Scrawl? A "scrawl" is something written quickly. In this case, it is a page or so of quick writing that allows you to practice a particular type of writing—in this case, descriptive writing. Have fun with it!

Small Scrawl 1: A Walk Outside

Take a walk outside on your college campus. This should not be a rapid, head-down walk like you may take when you are rushing to class, but a slow, appreciative stroll. Look around you and observe with all of your senses. What do you see, hear, smell, taste, or touch? After taking your walk, come back and write a page describing what you have experienced.

Small Scrawl 2: Fish Tale

You are a fish, living in the depths of a cool blue lake. Your days are peaceful, and food is plentiful. You spend most of your time half hidden among the rocks and weeds, but sometimes you swim quickly, darting through the cool water. At other times, you are so filled with the joy of life that you leap high out of the water, your iridescent scales shining in the sun. Today, as you venture from among the weeds, you see a quick flash near the surface of the lake. Maybe it's food. Describe what happens, focusing on your five senses.

Small Scrawl 3: An Interesting Person

In one page, describe one of the people above as completely as possible.

Descriptive Assignment 1: A Place

Paragraph or essay

In a paragraph or essay, describe a place. It can be a store, an office, a nightclub, a park, a church sanctuary, or any place of your choosing. In your topic sentence or thesis statement, state the dominant impression in one word, choosing a word from the following list or thinking up your own word. Make sure all details of your description reinforce that dominant impression. *Hint:* Your topic sentence will follow this pattern:

The ___(place)___ was/is ___(dominant impression)___.

bleak	crowded	filthy	noisy
chaotic	depressing	gloomy	orderly
cheerful	dull	impersonal	serene
colorful	eerie	lonely	shabby
cozy	elegant	messy	spotless

Descriptive Assignment 2: A Person

Paragraph or Essay

Write a paragraph or essay describing a person. You may describe someone you know well, such as a friend or relative, or someone you see often but don't really know, such as a library worker or a fellow student. Be sure that you state a dominant impression in your topic sentence. A few possibilities are listed below. Make sure that all the details in your paragraph support the dominant impression. Focus on details that can be expressed through sight, hearing, smell, taste, and touch.

arrogant	easygoing	graceful	neat
dignified	elegant	gruff	unhappy
disorganized	forbidding	messy	upbeat

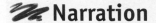 Narration

mywritinglab
Visit MyWriting
Lab for additional
practice with
narration.
Narration is the art of storytelling. A good story pulls your readers in, captures their imaginations, and keeps them wondering what will happen next. What is the difference between a narrative that succeeds and one that fails? To make your narrative a success, try some of the following techniques.

Laying the Groundwork for Narrative Writing

Look at the photograph of the woman with her finger held in front of her lips. What is she thinking or saying? To whom is she gesturing?

Write a narrative that leads up to the moment shown in the picture. Use dialogue to show what the people are saying and description to show the people who are speaking and their reactions during the conversation. Here's a special challenge: Make sure that in your narrative, the conversation is short—five minutes or so—but that it shows, through dialogue, what happened before the conversation took place and what might happen afterward.

Steps to Writing a Successful Narrative

Select Detail Carefully

A good narrative is not burdened by endless details. Provide details that move the story forward, but leave out anything that might slow its progress. In a successful narrative, every detail is significant. Suppose you are telling about the time you locked yourself out of your house and had to convince a passing police officer that you were not a burglar. Details about what you ate for breakfast, the decor of your house, or how you spent the hours or days leading up to the event do not matter. Focus instead on the incident itself.

Use Chronological Order

Most stories are best told in the order in which the events in it happen, with background details near the beginning of the narrative.

Keep the Timespan Short

In a short paragraph- or essay-length narrative, you can't tell your whole life's story. Your narrative packs more punch if you tell a story with a short timespan— preferably less than an hour and certainly less than twenty-four hours.

Center on Conflict

Most successful narratives center around conflict. It may be inner conflict, conflict with another person, or conflict with an outside force—a tornado, an economic recession, or something else beyond the individual's control. When the conflict ends, the story ends, too.

Use Dialogue

Use dialogue for dramatic moments when you want to show your reader exactly what was said and done or when you want readers to draw their own conclusions about the events that took place. For the strongest effect, use dialogue sparingly.

Know Your Purpose

The purpose of the story is its reason for existence, the reason that you find it worth telling. If no change takes place, if no lesson is learned, if nothing happens, your reader will ask impatiently, "What is the *point?*" Before you tell a story, know your reasons for telling it.

Building CONNECTIONS

Descriptive writing skills can also be incorporated into narrative writing. Your narrative becomes even stronger when you present it in terms of sight, sound, touch, taste, and smell.

EXERCISE 5   CHOOSING RELEVANT DETAILS

Imagine that you are writing a narrative about being stranded on a lonely high-way. You have brainstormed to gather every available detail about the incident without trying to judge the importance of each detail. Now it is time to choose the details you will include in your paragraph. Place a check (✔) beside those details that you would include in the finished paragraph and an ✗ beside those that you would leave out. If there are details you are unsure about, mark them with an "**M**" for "maybe." Then compare your answers with those of your classmates and discuss the items on which you do not agree. Answers may vary.

Topic Sentence: A few months ago, I had a frightening experience on a lonely highway.

✔ **a.** It was dark, and few other cars were on the road.

✗ **b.** The temperature outside was a comfortable 72 degrees.

M **c.** The radio was turned up loud, and I was singing with it.

✔ **d.** I heard a loud pop, and my car became hard to steer.

✔ **e.** I realized my tire was going flat and pulled to the shoulder of the road.

✔ **f.** I found my cell phone in my purse.

✗ **g.** I found a pack of spearmint gum in my purse.

✗ **h.** I really prefer cinnamon gum.

✔ **i.** The cell phone was out of range.

✔ **j.** I saw a single headlight in the distance.

✗ **k.** I remembered a story on last night's news about the economy.

✔ **l.** I remembered a story on last night's news about the "Motorcycle Murderer" who preys on stranded motorists.

✔ **m.** My heart pounded as a motorcycle pulled up and stopped.

✔ **n.** When the driver took off his helmet, I realized that it was my neighbor, Jack.

✔ **o.** He helped me change the tire, and I drove safely home.

Wordsmith's Corner: Sample Narrative Paragraphs

In the following paragraphs, look at the way two writers approach narrative writing. Then answer the questions that follow each narrative.

Narrative Paragraph 1

Melanie, the writer of this narrative paragraph, tells how a crab supper became less than appetizing.

A Painful Meal

A few years ago, I was invited to a "catch your own" crab supper at my uncle's rented beach house. <u>It was not the pleasant experience I expected.</u> It started enjoyably enough as we lowered baited traps from the dock and pulled them up, sometimes with two or three crabs in each of them. Then we went back to the beach house, and Uncle Ed began preparations, using tongs to place the twitching crabs in a large pot and then adding vinegar and water. "Wait a minute," I said. "You aren't going to boil them alive, are you?" Uncle Ed looked at me in surprise but patiently explained, "That's the way they're cooked. They can't feel anything—crabs are just one step above insects." I watched as he turned on the heat. As the water became warmer, I could hear the crabs scrabbling against the sides of the metal pot. Uncle Ed looked at me and laughed at my horrified expression. "It's just a reflex," he said. But as the water became warmer, the noise from the pot grew more desperate. Finally, there was silence. Uncle Ed took the crabs from the pot and dumped them on newspapers spread on the kitchen table. Uncle Ed looked at me and said, "Mel, you're not still worried about these crabs, are you?" My mother was giving me a warning glance, so I said, "No, it's fine." I felt my stomach do a flip as my uncle put three large crabs in front of me. The crabs' white flesh was tender, but for me, it might as well have been Styrofoam. Since that day, I have not eaten crab. No one can tell me they don't suffer.

Questions

1. Underline the topic sentence of the paragraph.

2. About how much time does the narrative cover?

   The narrative covers a few hours.

3. What is the main point of the narrative, the writer's reason for writing it?

The writer wants to tell about the experience that convinced her that crabs suffer a cruel

death when they are cooked.

Narrative Paragraph 2

In this paragraph, André writes about the night that changed his life.

My Last Night at the Kwik-Stop #7

Just a few months ago, as I worked the night shift at the Kwik-Stop #7, my entire life changed direction. It was about 11:00 P.M., and the store was deserted. A man came in, a baseball cap pulled low over his eyes and his jacket collar turned up to cover his face. In a flash, he was standing in front of me, pointing the metallic nose of a revolver at my head. "Give me all the money in that register. Don't pull any tricks or I'll kill you," he said. I could hear his voice trembling, and I realized he was scared. All I could think of was that a scared robber was more likely to pull the trigger. Time seemed to slow down. I could hear the robber yelling at me to hurry, but the words barely registered. Beneath the counter, I saw the red "panic button" that would silently summon the police if only I would press it. I could not. I opened the drawer and placed each stack of bills on the counter, twenties, tens, fives, and ones. The robber scooped them off the counter, jabbed the gun at me, and said, "Don't call the police for at least an hour." I don't know how many minutes passed before I grabbed the keys with trembling hands, locked the door, walked back behind the counter and pushed the red button. The next day, when I took stock of the life I had almost lost, I realized I had lived twenty-three years and had done absolutely nothing I could be proud of. That day, I quit my job at the Kwik-Stop and filled out a college application. I had always said I would go to college someday, but I never thought someone would have to hold a gun to my head to make me do it.

Questions

1. Underline the topic sentence of the paragraph.

2. About how much time does the narrative cover?

The narrative covers about 24 hours, although the main portion covers just a few

minutes.

3. What is the main point of the narrative, the writer's reason for writing it?

The writer wants to tell about the life-threatening experience that made him

realize that he couldn't wait for "someday" to come to carry out his plans for the future.

TOPICS FOR PRACTICING NARRATIVE WRITING

Small Scrawls: Imaginative Short Writings

What is a Small Scrawl? A "scrawl" is something written quickly. In this case, it is a page or so of quick writing that allows you to practice a particular type of writing—in this case, narrative writing. Have fun with it!

Small Scrawl 1: Wake-Up Call

You wake with the sun in your eyes, wondering why your bed seems to be rocking underneath you. Then you realize that you are not in your bed, but in a small boat on a vast ocean. In the distance, you see what looks like a small island.
Tell the story.

Small Scrawl 2: An Unusual Adventure

As you hike through the woods on a familiar trail, you see a small cave entrance that has somehow escaped your notice on past occasions. Because you are a curious person with a high-powered flashlight in your backpack, you decide to enter the cave. Write about your adventure in a one-page narrative. Have fun!

Small Scrawl 3: A Day in the Life

Write a Small Scrawl about one of the people pictured above, imagining the day or the hour during which the photo was snapped. Write a narrative telling what is happening.

Narrative Assignment 1: Treat or Mistreat?

Paragraph

Write about a time when someone treated you in one of the following ways. Make sure your one-paragraph story has a purpose by focusing on the way the incident made you feel. Were you sad? Surprised? Angry?

Someone misjudged you.

Someone gave you praise or credit you did not deserve.

Someone encouraged you.

Someone ridiculed you.

Someone treated you with unexpected kindness.

Someone treated you unfairly.

Narrative Assignment 2: Transformation

Paragraph

Write a narrative paragraph describing a life-changing event that took place in less than an hour.

Narrative Assignment 3: A Significant Goodbye

Paragraph or Essay

Write a narrative paragraph or essay about a significant ending in your life. Some possibilities include your last day of high school, a time when you said goodbye to a person who was important in your life, or your last day on a job. Alternatively, you might focus on a symbolic ending when you realized that the end of something was at hand: the end of your childhood, the end of a relationship, or the end of a grudge or other feeling that you had held for some time. Make sure that the incident you choose is one that will fit into a paragraph or essay. It would be hard, for instance, to write a narrative that fully discussed your first marriage or first job—unless it lasted only an hour or two.

Examples

mywritinglab

Visit MyWriting Lab for additional practice with examples.

Examples are one of the best ways to get a point across because they provide a concrete illustration of your point. If you say your father is sentimental, your reader gets the general idea. If you say he gets teary-eyed over Hallmark commercials, you give specific support to the general idea. Examples are specific illustrations, exact instances. They may range in length from a single word to a single sentence to an entire paragraph.

Laying the Groundwork for Writing Using Examples

Look at the photograph of the appliance energy guide. Buying energy-efficient appliances is one example of ways to save energy. Make a list of other specific examples of ways you can conserve energy at home. Then, write a paragraph on how to save energy, supporting it with some of the examples you have generated.

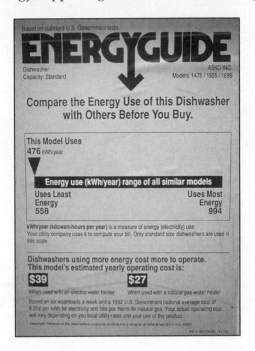

The Short Example

A **short example** may be a word or a phrase, but it must be a specific, concrete example. It cannot simply be a synonym. The word *canine*, for instance, is a synonym for *dog*, not an example of a dog. An example illustrating the word *dog* might be *Dalmatian, Chihuahua, Raffles, my two-year-old terrier*, or *that mangy mutt across the street.*

| EXERCISE 6 | ADDING YOUR OWN EXAMPLES |

For each of the words or phrases below, an example is given. Add your own example in a word or phrase. Answers will vary.

1. song
   a. "Take Me Out to the Ball Game"
   b. _____

2. sport
    a. soccer
    b. _____

3. a proverb or familiar saying
    a. "A stitch in time saves nine."
    b.

4. an uncomfortable sensation
    a. walking barefoot across hot sand
    b. _____

5. an uncomfortable social situation
    a. Going on a date for the first time since your breakup and running into your ex's parents.
    b. _____

The Sentence-Length Example

Sometimes you need more than just a word or phrase to illustrate an idea. In such cases, try using a **sentence-length example**. Again, the example needs to be a specific, detailed illustration of the general idea you are discussing. It should not simply be a vague restatement. Look at the following examples to see the difference between a vague restatement and a specific example.

Examples

✗ *Idea + vague restatement:* The new disk jockey on the morning show is really obnoxious. He has an unpleasant attitude that makes listening to his show a bad experience.

✔ *Idea + specific example:* The new disk jockey on the morning show is really obnoxious. He tries to humiliate listeners who call in, and his jokes border on the offensive.

✗ *Idea + vague restatement:* The new grocery store has added whimsical touches to some of its departments. It's enjoyable to shop in a store that is entertaining.

✔ *Idea + specific example:* The new grocery store has added whimsical touches to some of its departments. In the produce department, "thunder" rolls and "lightning" flashes above the vegetable bins before the automatic sprinkler turns on. On the dairy aisle, recordings of mooing cows and clucking hens amuse passing shoppers.

| EXERCISE 7 | ELIMINATING VAGUE EXAMPLES |

Circle the letter of the sentence that is not a specific example.

1. The car was dirty.
   - (a.) The entire vehicle had a filthy appearance.
   - b. Brown streaks of mud covered the bumpers and doors.
   - c. The windows were specked with the tiny, squashed bodies of dead insects.

2. The man seemed angry.
   - a. He spoke loudly and used vulgar language.
   - (b.) He seemed to be in a state of fury.
   - c. As he left, he slammed the door behind him.

3. I have spent money carelessly this weekend.
   - a. At the mall, I bought two CDs that I could not afford.
   - (b.) Money seemed to run through my fingers like water.
   - c. I spent twenty dollars on dinner at the Steak-Out, an expenditure I had not planned.

4. Alfred spent an hour cleaning his apartment.
   - a. He picked up magazines, clothes, and papers that cluttered his bedroom.
   - b. He vacuumed the carpet and mopped the kitchen floor.
   - (c.) He took the time to get the place looking good.

5. The plant had obviously been neglected.
   - (a.) Someone had ignored the poor philodendron.
   - b. Its leaves were dusty and limp.
   - c. The soil in its pot was dry.

| EXERCISE 8 | PROVIDING SPECIFIC EXAMPLES |

For each of the following general ideas, provide a specific example in a sentence or two. Answers will vary.

1. The garage was a mess.

   _____

   _____

2. After two cups of coffee, I started to come awake.

     _____

     _____

3. In the hallway, Leon complained about his professor.

     _____

     _____

4. The evidence indicated that the accused man was guilty of burglary.

     _____

     _____

5. The mailbox contained nothing but junk mail.

     _____

     _____

The Extended Example

Sometimes you may wish to develop an idea with an **extended paragraph-length** example. In this case, your topic sentence states the general idea and the rest of the paragraph provides a detailed example. This sort of paragraph usually ends with a summary sentence that connects the specific example back to the general idea, as in the following short paragraph.

Example

topic sentence

Not long ago, I found myself caught in an uncomfortable social situation. I was out on my first date since the breakup of my three-year marriage. As my date and I entered the restaurant where we were going to eat, I saw my ex-wife's parents. I half hoped that they would not speak to me, but they called out, "Andy! Hello!" I had to introduce them to my date, and, to make matters worse, they insisted on filling me in about how well my ex-wife was doing without me.

summary sentence

I tried to handle the situation gracefully, but I felt uncomfortable, and I am sure my date did, too.

extended example

EXERCISE 9	WRITING AN EXTENDED EXAMPLE

Write an extended example (four sentences or more) to support one of the following topic sentences. Then write a summary sentence to end the paragraph. Answers will vary.

1. Not long ago, I found myself caught in an uncomfortable social situation.

2. I can remember how nervous I was on my first day at college.

3. Some of my classmates can be annoying.

4. Some professors can be a real pain.

5. I remember one of the proudest moments of my life.

Wordsmith's Corner: Paragraphs Developed by Example

In the paragraphs below, the writers develop their topics by using examples. Read each paragraph and answer the questions that follow.

Example Paragraph 1

In this paragraph, Justin gives examples of the excuses his friend Leo constantly makes.

No More Excuses

My friend Leo makes up lame excuses whenever there is something he doesn't want to do. Just two weeks ago, he was at my house when he decided he did not want to go in to work. He called his boss and said he had to get a new set of tires put on his truck. Then he sat down and watched TV with me. Not only had he lied, but his excuse was not a very convincing one. Another time, he canceled a date with his girlfriend at the last minute, telling her he had to get a new battery for his truck. She was angry and refused to go out with him again until he apologized. Last weekend, Leo offered the lamest excuse yet. He had promised he would help me move my furniture from my parents' house to my new apartment. He was supposed to bring his truck over about eight o'clock Saturday morning. I waited, then called and left a message on his machine. About 11:30 he called and said he was sorry, but he had been getting a new set of tires put on his truck. I guess he had forgotten he used the same excuse when he called his boss from my house. I think I need a new set of friends—I am beginning to tire of Leo's excuses.

Questions

1. Underline the topic sentence of the paragraph.
2. List three examples given in the paragraph.

   Answers may vary.

   Leo called his boss and said he had to get new tires.

   Leo told his girlfriend he had to get a new battery.

   Leo told the writer he had to get a new set of tires, forgetting that his friend had heard

   that excuse before.

3. Double-underline the paragraph's summary sentence.

Example Paragraph 2

Olivia's paragraph describes the ways her college's wellness center benefits students.

Athletics for Everyone

Many students at the college I attend complain about paying an athletic fee along with tuition. However, I don't complain because I know that the athletic fee supports a wellness program that benefits all students. The athletic fee funds a health club equipped with weight machines, treadmills, stationary bikes, and free weights. The fee also helps pay the salary of a director who runs the club and teaches classes like stretch and tone, step aerobics, and water aerobics. Fees at private health clubs run hundreds of dollars per year, but the college's athletic fee is only thirty dollars per term. Another benefit of the wellness program is its medical services. A nurse-practitioner offers advice on diet and nutrition, dispenses remedies for colds and allergies, and schedules private consultations on health-related matters. The athletic fee also subsidizes tetanus immunizations and flu shots. For commuter students, many of whom are not covered by health insurance, the service is essential. At some colleges, only athletic teams benefit from student athletic fees, but at our college, the athletic program benefits everyone.

Questions

1. Underline the topic sentence of the paragraph.
2. List three examples given in the paragraph.

   Answers may vary.

The athletic fee funds a health club equipped with weight machines, treadmills, stationary

bikes, and free weights.

The fee also helps pay the salary of a director.

A nurse-practitioner offers advice on diet and nutrition, dispenses remedies for

colds and allergies, and schedules private consultations on health-related matters.

3. Double-underline the paragraph's summary sentence.

TOPICS FOR PRACTICING WRITING WITH EXAMPLES

Small Scrawls: Imaginative Short Writings

What is a Small Scrawl? A "scrawl" is something written quickly. In this case, it is a page or so of quick writing that allows you to practice a particular type of writing—in this case, writing supported by example. Have fun with it!

Small Scrawl 1: Television

Are there types of television shows you hate to watch? Love to watch? Write a Small Scrawl about your television preferences, giving plenty of specific examples and briefly describing each show that you mention.

Small Scrawl 2: Other People

In Jean-Paul Sartre's play *No Exit*, a character says, "Hell is other people." Even Sartre rejected the idea that *all* other people were hell or that every relationship was doomed. But most people will admit that the expression is true sometimes, or true of certain people. Write a Small Scrawl giving an example (or more than one example) that supports the statement "Hell is other people."

When you write something that supports a particular quotation, it's best to state the quotation and properly attribute it at the beginning of your piece of writing. Here are a couple of ways you might open such a piece:

> Jean-Paul Sartre wrote, "Hell is other people." Although this is not ordinarily my philosophy, I had an experience the other day that made me believe it might be true.

> A character in Jean-Paul Sartre's play *No Exit,* says, "Hell is other people." I wonder if Sartre knew my (mother-in-law, boss, brother, ex . . .).

Small Scrawl 3: A Familiar Face

Every day, you see familiar faces. They may include the faces of the barista in the coffee shop where you go for your morning jolt of caffeine, the delivery man who comes every day to the office where you work after classes, or the librarian who smiles at you as you enter the library to grab some quiet study time.

Write a Small Scrawl giving examples of the people you see every day. Describe these people and the effect they have on your day. Have fun!

Example Assignment 1: Quotations and Illustrations

Paragraph

Choose one of the following quotations and write a paragraph agreeing or disagreeing with it. Your support should take the form of specific examples that help to prove or disprove the quotation. Your topic sentence will look something like this: "I agree/disagree with Juvenal's statement 'Luxury is more deadly than any foe.'"

Quotations

Luxury is more deadly than any foe.
—Juvenal

The impossible is often the untried.
—James Goodwin

It is impossible for a man to be cheated by anyone but himself.
—Ralph Waldo Emerson

Success is never final.
—Winston Churchill

How glorious it is—and also how painful—to be an exception.
—Alfred de Musset

In poverty and other misfortunes of life, true friends are a sure refuge.
—Aristotle

There is nothing so easy but that it becomes difficult when you do it reluctantly.
—Terence

Example Assignment 2: Saving and Spending

Paragraph

Are you a person who likes to save money or a person who likes to spend it? In one paragraph, support your answer with specific examples.

Example Assignment 3: People

Paragraph or Essay

Choose one topic from the following list and write a paragraph or essay that illustrates the topic with examples.

a loyal friend	an inefficient person
a jealous person	a productive person
a good or bad boss	an optimist
a good or bad teacher	a pessimist
a giving person	a self-sufficient person
a thrifty person	a bad influence

TOPICS FOR COMBINING METHODS OF DEVELOPMENT

Description, narration, and example are methods of showing or telling a reader exactly what you mean. Combining the methods adds even more power to your writing. The assignments that follow ask you to combine two or more of the methods of development in this chapter.

Building CONNECTIONS

Methods of development are tools of a writer's trade. Like a carpenter's hammer, saw, and sander, they each do a specific job. Which one should you use? It depends on the job you have to do. Some pieces of writing will require just one method, but most will require you use more than one of your tools of the trade.

Mixed Methods Assignment 1: Brief Encounter

Narration and Description

Narrate a brief encounter that you have had with someone. That person may have been a stranger, a relative, a coworker, or a friend. The meeting you describe may have been your first meeting with that person or your last, a friendly encounter or an unfriendly one, but it should have been significant in some way. As you narrate the encounter, weave in a description of the other person—his appearance, her voice. Try to narrate and describe the encounter so vividly that your reader feels as though he was there with you.

Mixed Methods Assignment 2: The Joy of Life

Description and Example

Runners sometimes experience a rush of endorphins, which has been described as a "runner's high." An old song by John Denver describes the feeling of being in the mountains as a "Colorado Rocky Mountain high." Both terms describe a special and rare feeling of self-awareness and joy that some might call a "high" and others might simply call "the joy of life." What places or activities bring you joy? Describe those places or activities and give specific examples.

Mixed Methods Assignment 3: Childhood Unhappiness

Narration and Description

Write a paragraph narrating an event that upset you when you were a child but that does not seem so serious now. It could be an argument with a childhood friend, trouble with a teacher at school, or a lost game or competition. Make sure that you narrate an event that took place in a very short span of time—fifteen minutes or less is suggested. As you narrate the event, make sure to weave in relevant details so that your reader sees the fall leaves or the dust that you kick up as you walk across the playground; hears the musical sounds of the ice cream truck or the angry tone in your teacher's voice; or feels the cold rain that soaked you to the skin.

REAL-WORLD ASSIGNMENTS

The Real-World Assignments that follow allow you to mix methods in writing assignments that mirror the types of writing you might do outside the classroom.

Real-World Assignment 1: Signs and Symptoms

Description and Example

You are a school health coordinator in a medium-sized school district. You wish to educate parents to look for signs that indicate a child has an eating disorder, is using drugs, or is being bullied. Write a letter to parents giving descriptions of physical symptoms and examples of behavior that may indicate a child has one or more of these problems.

Real-World Assignment 2: Name Game

Narration and Description

You are the tourism director of one of the towns listed below. Your job is to make up a story about how the town got its unusual name, since the actual story is not known. The story should be interesting and entertaining to tourists. (*Note:* Because these are all real towns or cities, there may well be actual stories connected to their names.)

Aimwell, Alabama

Surprise, Arizona

You Bet, California

Santa Claus, Georgia

French Lick, Indiana

Sandwich, Massachusetts

Hot Coffee, Mississippi

Offer, Montana

Worms, Nebraska

Love Ladies, New Jersey

Toast, North Carolina

Idiotville, Oregon

Sweet Lips, Tennessee

Imalone, Wisconsin

Real-World Assignment 3: Civic Duty

Description and Example

You are a member of a citizens' coalition to improve the roads in your city. In order to be heard before the city council, your group needs to submit a brief description of the problem you wish to address. Write a paragraph describing the poor road conditions that exist in your town and giving specific examples of those problems. If one of the problems is potholes, for instance, you might mention that and then describe in more detail the large pothole on Third Street that is almost impossible to avoid without hitting a pedestrian or veering into an oncoming lane of traffic.

Real-World Assignment 4: Children's Hour

Narration and Description

You are a teacher at a preschool. It is the practice at this preschool to keep a log on each child. This log includes brief notations on what the child eats, whether he naps, and what special projects he works on. In the case of a problem, such as illness or misbehavior, a more extensive note is written, indicating in objective, unemotional language what the child did and what disciplinary actions were taken (at this school, time-outs and loss of privileges are the only disciplinary actions used). On this particular day, a child has had a behavioral problem, and you are writing a paragraph about it in the log so that the parents can be informed.

mywritinglab For support in meeting this chapter's goal, log in to **www.mywritinglab.com**, and select **Paragraph Development: Narrating**, **Paragraph Development: Describing**, and **Paragraph Development: Illustrating**.

CHAPTER 8

Limiting and Ordering: Definition, Classification, and Process

> 🖋 **Chapter Goal:** Analyze and write definition, classification, and process paragraphs and essays.

Mary had a little lamb,
She kept it in a pen.
Whenever it got out,
She'd put it back again.

Then Mary took another pen
And wrote her whole life's story.
Her well-told tale propelled her
From infamy to glory.

The techniques in this chapter
May never bring you fame,
But writing well will always be
Good reason for acclaim.

🖋 Definition, Classification, and Process

As a writer, you may find that your ideas are sometimes hard to pin down—they prefer to roam free. Writing an essay can be a bit like herding sheep into a pen—finding ideas that go together, separating them from their natural environment, and confining them within the fences of an essay. The techniques of definition, classification, and process help fence in your ideas—to limit and order information and to answer the questions *What is it? How many different types exist?* and *How does it work?*

Focus on Limiting and Ordering: Making Your Case

The trial pictured here is one of the most famous trials in history. Popularly known as the Scopes Monkey Trial, it is the trial of John Scopes, a teacher from Tennessee who  *was tried for teaching evolution. When presenting their case, the prosecutors at the Scopes trial used definition, classification, and process. First, they defined the crime to the jurors as a violation of the Butler Act, which prohibited teachers from teaching about evolution. Next, they classified the charge as unlawful and not protected by freedom of speech. Finally, they outlined the process that led to the charge, from Scopes teaching a chapter about evolution to students testifying to a grand jury that they had learned about evolution.*

Reflect on It

Every profession in some way limits and orders. Think about your future career and the various ways you will be asked to explain something, define something, or show how something small fits into a larger picture (or vice versa). In what ways will these methods be crucial to that career?

Definition, Classification, and Process in Action

In this chapter, you will have the opportunity to examine and use the techniques of definition, classification, and process. In this text, each technique is explained separately. However, writers seldom use them in isolation. Just as an aspiring tap dancer would learn and practice the ball change, the shuffle-flap, and the hop-step separately before employing them together to do the Shim Sham Shimmy, so is it useful for writers to learn and practice techniques of writing separately before using them together in a composition.

Before looking at definition, classification, and process separately, look at how one writer uses all three techniques together. The following essay, by Constance Faye Mudore, appeared in *Career World.*

The essay embodies all three of the writing techniques featured in this chapter. The essay begins with a **definition** of difficult people. Next, the author

classifies difficult people into different types. After each type of difficult person, the author shows the reader a **process** for coping with that type of person.

Working with Difficult People

Constance Faye Mudore

Friction on the job is a fact of life. With the right know-how, it doesn't have to get the better of you.

Travis waited tables on weekends at a popular restaurant. He had worked there for more than a year and he liked the job. But his feelings toward work changed after Helene, an assistant manager, was hired. This was because Helene often exploded at Travis in front of customers.

He complained to the manager, who only made excuses for Helene. Travis wondered how much longer he could work with such a difficult person.

Difficult people are the folks who frustrate and dampen the spirits of the people who work for them. While we can all be difficult at times, difficult people are seen as problems by most of the people around them most of the time. Worst of all, they tend to be reluctant to change their ways.

The good news is that there are ways to cope with difficult people. But make no mistake. Coping has nothing to do with changing someone else. The only person's behavior you can change is your own. It also has nothing to do with winning or losing battles with others. Coping requires that you learn ways to help you and the difficult person function together at work as effectively as possible.

What follows is a guide to dealing with three difficult personality types you're likely to meet on the job: Helen Hostile, Walter Whiner, and Corey Clam.

R$_X$ for Hostiles

Helen Hostile gets her way at work by bullying others. Hostiles usually have strong opinions about how others "should" behave. When they sense a lack of confidence in others, they attack. When their targets run from them, they become even more aggressive.

Dr. Robert Bramson, a business management consultant and author of *Coping with Difficult People in Business and in Life,* says, "The first rule of coping with anyone aggressive is that you stand up to that person." But, Bramson emphasizes, you must stand up to them without fighting.

Why? Hostiles are good at fighting. If you become aggressive toward them, they'll probably become even more aggressive toward you. You are likely to lose.

And even if you do win a particular battle, by becoming aggressive yourself, you damage your own reputation at work.

How do you stand up for yourself without fighting? Bramson suggests that you give hostiles time to run down. Then, get their attention and state your opinions firmly.

Travis says, "I figured I had nothing to lose since I was ready to quit anyway. So the next time she blew up at me—which was the next time I worked with her—I let her vent a little. I was nervous, but I looked her in the eye and said, 'Helene, you have the right to discuss my work. But you don't have the right to humiliate me.'"

She looked at me like she'd never seen me before and walked away. I've worked with her since then. She still explodes, but not at me.

The Silent Treatment

Corey Clam volunteers little information, typically answering questions with one word, if he responds at all. A clam's most comfortable response to new information or potential conflict is to shut down.

Take Laura. She needed Corey's approval to begin a plan to train employees more effectively. She scheduled a meeting with him and enthusiastically laid out her ideas. At the conclusion, she expected him to comment. He said nothing. Confused, she asked, "Do you need more information?" He said no and indicated that he had another appointment.

Laura felt like she had had the wind knocked out of her. She didn't know how to interpret his silence. But if her plan was to proceed, she had to draw him out.

How do you get clams to tell you what they think? Ask open-ended questions. These are questions that can't be answered with one word. Instead of asking, "Do you need more information?" Laura should have asked, "What's your reaction to what I'm proposing?"

It's also important to give clams time to answer. This might mean you have to get comfortable with long silences. At such times, Bramson suggests "friendly, silent staring," preferably focusing your eyes on the clam's chin. (Direct eye contact can be threatening to clams.) Friendly staring communicates that you're expecting the clam to start speaking at any moment.

If the clam still doesn't talk, comment on what's happening by saying, "I'm noticing that you're not commenting. What does that mean?" If none of this works, let the clam know that you will make another appointment to discuss the issue.

Laura went back to see her boss and got him to open up. She says, "Corey liked my plan. When I left his office after our first meeting, I was sure that his silence meant he hated it. I'm glad I checked out that assumption."

Warning: Whiners at Work

Walter Whiner is another difficult person on the work scene. Whiners complain about problems on the job, but don't do anything to improve things. They tend to believe that it is someone else's responsibility to "fix it."

The employees at the bank where Walter works avoid him when he starts complaining about the bank being mismanaged. Missy, who works there after school, says, "I groan inside when Walter comes over to talk to me. I know I'm in for a long monologue of gripes. Sometimes, he even blames me. To top it off, he never tries any of the things I suggest."

How to cope? Listen to what whiners have to say, Bramson says, but put a time limit on it. This allows them to let off steam, but doesn't lock you into having to listen indefinitely. Let them know that you heard what they said by restating their complaints. Don't agree or apologize for any of the things they might be dumping on you as "your fault." And try to get them to problem solve.

Here's what Missy did. "The next time Walter came over, I listened to what he said for several minutes. He was complaining about the office manager because she gets to work late every day."

"I let him know that I could tell he was frustrated with the manager. But I also let him know that the manager was always available when I needed help. I asked him to think about whether there was anything he could do about the situation and to get back to me. Then I told him I had some work to finish before I left for the day. He went back into his cubicle. Walter still complains a lot, but I don't feel so helpless in dealing with him."

Waiting Doesn't Work

Wishing that a difficult person were different is a waste of time. It's only by developing our own interpersonal and problem-solving skills that we can cope with them. Viewed positively, difficult people are some of the best teachers we will ever have.

THINKING ABOUT THE ESSAY

1. A dictionary will not list a definition of a "difficult person." Where do you think Mudore got her definition?
2. Classification of ideas deals with types or kinds. In the essay, Mudore outlines various types of difficult people. What are these types? What do they have in common?
3. When writers describe a process, they often give examples to illustrate the process, as Mudore does in this essay. Name one of Mudore's specific examples of a way to deal with difficult people.

✍ Definition

mywritinglab
Visit MyWriting Lab for additional practice with definition paragraphs.
Most people think of a definition as a "dictionary definition"—a brief explanation of the meaning of a word and little else. But your **definition** paragraph goes beyond a bare-bones statement of a word's meaning because you give your reader your own personal definition of a term.

In a personal definition, the way you define a term reflects your own feelings about it. Two dictionaries might have very similar definitions for the word *love*. Two people probably will not. A new parent might define love as a feeling that is tender but protective, while someone who has recently been disappointed in romance might define it as the quickest route to a broken heart.

Laying the Groundwork for Writing a Definition

Look at the photo of the firefighter rescuing a child. Write a paragraph defining the word *courage*. Do not worry about the dictionary definition of the word; instead, use your personal experience and observation to provide one or more examples that define the word.

Setting Up Your Definition Paragraph

The key element in a definition paragraph is the topic sentence, which presents your personal definition of the term you are defining. Look at the following examples, all defining the word *vacation*. Notice that some of the topic sentences employ personal terms like "for me" or "I can define." Although phrases such as these are not always a part of a personal definition, they often help mark the definition as the writer's personal definition rather than a dictionary definition.

Examples of Topic Sentences for Personal Definition Paragraphs

✔ To me, a vacation is a brief escape from my everyday responsibilities.
✔ A vacation is the fastest way to waste a large amount of money in a short time.

✔ For most people, vacations are a time of rest, but for me, they are a time of stress.

✔ When I think of the boring family vacations I was forced to go on as a teenager, I can only define a vacation as a living nightmare.

EXERCISE 1   RECOGNIZING PERSONAL DEFINITIONS

For each term below, circle the definition that is a personal definition rather than a dictionary-type definition.

1. music
   a. Music is a rhythmic sound made by various instruments or with the human voice. In all cultures, it is a way of collectively expressing emotion.
   (b.) Music, for me, is a way of expressing or even changing my moods. I choose quiet music for quiet moods and peppy music when I am feeling energetic. If I am in a bad mood, music with a strong beat picks me up immediately.

2. test
   (a.) A test may be a teacher's way of measuring knowledge, but for me, it is an hour of anxiety. No matter how well I know the material, anxiety grips me as the test papers are passed out and does not let go until I have turned in my paper and left the room.
   b. A test is a way for a teacher to assess how well students know the material that has been taught. Tests come in a variety of formats. *Subjective tests* are oral or written tests that allow students to respond to a question in their own words. *Objective tests* may feature question formats such as multiple choice, true-false, or matching that require a student to choose a single correct answer.

3. computer
   (a.) A computer is a machine as addictive and alluring as any slot machine Las Vegas can offer. One can play games on it for hours or pursue any subject on the Internet. Through chat rooms and email, the user can contact people all over the globe. A computer provides access to a web of pure fun.
   b. A computer is a machine with many applications for work and play. Using word processing software, financial software, and databases, a person may run a small business from a home computer. Computer games and the Internet add recreational value, and educational software and online libraries provide tools for research.

4. car

    a. A car is a means of personal transportation. It comes in many different sizes, styles, and price ranges, and may be rented, leased, or bought outright. Many see a car as preferable to public transportation, and in many areas where mass transportation is unavailable, a car is a necessity.

    (b.) For many, a car is just a means of transportation, but for me, my 1969 Volkswagen Beetle is a source of pride. The hours of work I put into lovingly restoring every detail pay off when heads turn as I drive down the road.

Wordsmith's Corner: Sample Definition Paragraphs

Read the two definition paragraphs that follow to see how two writers define two ordinary terms. Then answer the questions that follow each paragraph.

Definition Paragraph 1

In this paragraph, Shakira describes how her family experience affected the way she defines money.

Money

Some people see money as evil, while others see it as something to spend on life's pleasures. <u>My definition of money can be summed up in one word: security.</u> My definition stems from my childhood experience. When I was growing up, my family was comfortable and my parents had good jobs, but I was always told that money was not important. It was family, love, and home that mattered. Then when I was fourteen, my father lost his job when his company downsized. My mother was carrying the financial load for the family, and my parents' marriage became more strained. Finally, my parents sat us down and told us we could no longer afford to keep the house we had lived in all my life. We moved to a cramped apartment. We were crowded together, and it was much harder for my sister and me to avoid hearing the fights my parents had almost daily. When my father finally found a job two hundred miles away, he moved, but we stayed here. My parents called it a "trial separation," but it ended in divorce. I felt cheated, and I felt that everything my parents had told me about money was a lie. They had said money was not important, but without it, the things that were important were soon gone. <u>Now, I see that money is important.</u> <u>It can never replace family, home, and love, but it can help to make them more secure.</u>

Questions

1. Underline the topic sentence of the paragraph. Does it state a personal definition?

   Yes.

2. Does the paragraph contain an introductory sentence?

   Yes. The first sentence is an introductory sentence.

3. Double-underline the two sentences that summarize the paragraph.

Definition Paragraph 2

Michael writes a definition that reveals his humorous view of his customers' shortcomings.

What Is a Customer?

<u>Since I started working part time at a grocery store, I have learned that a customer is more than someone who buys something.</u> To me, a customer is a person whose memory fails entirely once he or she starts to push a shopping cart. One of the first things customers forget is how to count. There is no other way to explain how so many people get in the express line, which is clearly marked "Fifteen items or less," with twenty, twenty-five, or even a cartload of items. Customers also forget why they came to the store in the first place. Just as I finish ringing up an order, a customer will say, "Oops! I forgot to pick up a big jar of pickles for my wife! I hope you don't mind waiting while I go get it." Five minutes later, the customer is back with the jar of pickles, a bottle of catsup, and three rolls of paper towels. Strange as it seems, customers also seem to forget that they have to pay for their groceries. Instead of writing a check or looking for a debit card while I am ringing up the groceries, my customer waits until I announce the total. Then, in surprise, she says, "Oh! Now what did I do with my checkbook?" After five minutes of digging through her purse, she borrows my pen because she has forgotten hers. <u>But I have to be tolerant of customers because they pay my salary—and that's something I can't afford to forget.</u>

Questions

1. Underline the topic sentence of the paragraph. Does it state a personal definition?

   Yes.

2. What examples support the writer's definition?

   Customers who come to the express lane with more than fifteen items.

   Customers who forget items until they are in the checkout lane.

   Customers who forget to pull out a checkbook until the total is announced.

3. This paragraph contains an introductory sentence and a summary sentence. Double-underline those sentences.

TOPICS FOR PRACTICING DEFINITION

Small Scrawls: Imaginative Short Writings

What is a Small Scrawl? A "scrawl" is something written quickly. In this case, it is a page or so of quick writing that allows you to practice a particular type of writing—in this case, definition. Have fun with it!

Small Scrawl 1: Trouble with a Capital T

Think of a person or animal about whom you might say, "I knew he was trouble the moment I saw him." Define "trouble" in any way you wish. The individual may be a mischief-maker, one who wishes to harm you in some way, or one whose charms you cannot resist. Write a Small Scrawl about this individual in which you define the kind of trouble that the person or animal was for you.

Small Scrawl 2: Spaced Out Definition

You are walking along minding your own business when a friendly extra-terrestrial approaches you, wishing to learn about your planet. The alien is especially curious about the object in your hand, what it is for and how you use it. In a Small Scrawl, define the object for the alien creature, keeping in mind that he has no knowledge of Earth customs or ideas. It is up to you to decide what you might be holding in your hand, but it should be an object familiar to most Earthlings.

Small Scrawl 3: Dueling Definitions

Write a Small Scrawl defining the word "cookout" from the two points of view described below.

> *Human's point of view.* You live on a small farm, and every Fourth of July, you kill six fat chickens and roast them on an outdoor barbecue. You and your family and friends enjoy the feast, which has become a tradition. Write a definition of a cookout.

> *Chicken's point of view.* You are a chicken, living on the small farm mentioned in Topic 1. As you peck around the chicken yard, you wonder where Uncle Albert is. You haven't seen him for a while. There seem to be some others missing, too. Suddenly, through the chicken wire, you see an outdoor barbecue. On it are six shapes, and one of them looks a lot like Uncle Albert. Write a definition of a cookout.

Definition Assignment 1: Defining Ordinary Terms

Paragraph

Write a paragraph giving your personal definition of one of the following ordinary terms.

> jeans
>
> a computer
>
> dog
>
> music
>
> a particular food or beverage

Definition Assignment 2: Personal Definitions

Paragraph

Write a paragraph defining one of the types of people on the following list. Use a specific person (or persons) as an example if you wish, but be sure to give a precise personal definition before you give the example. See the sample topic sentences below for further help.

    ✗   My neighbor, Madeleine, is incredibly nosy.

The topic sentence above does not provide a definition.

    ✔   Some people might define a neighbor as a helpful friend, but to me, a neighbor is a person who always has her nose in other people's business.

This topic sentence works because it presents a definition. After the topic sentence has been stated, Madeleine the neighbor can be used as a supporting example.

Choose a term to define from the following list:

mother	son	daughter	teacher
father	minister	coach	neighbor
spouse	friend	boss	sister/brother

Definition Assignment 3: Defining an Activity

Paragraph

Write a paragraph defining one of the following activities, or substitute an activity of your own.

fishing	dancing	aerobics	shopping	running
reading	eating	jogging	driving	swimming
studying	working	cooking	gardening	sleeping

Classification

mywritinglab

Visit MyWriting Lab for additional practice with classification paragraphs.

Whether you know it or not, **classification** comes naturally to you. From the time you are born, you explore, discovering that some things are pleasurable and others are painful, that some things are edible and others are not. Those are your first lessons in classification.

By the time you reach adulthood, you divide people, articles of clothing, words, teachers, and ways of behaving into different types or categories so automatically that you are barely aware of it. When you answer a classmate's question, "What kind of teacher is Dr. Burton?" or reply to a friend who asks what kind of day you have had, you are classifying.

When you write a classification paper, you must analyze this familiar process of classification to apply it to your writing.

Laying the Groundwork for Classification

Look at the photograph showing a variety of foods. Think about the foods you eat. How would you classify them? In other words, what are the different categories of food that you eat? Group the foods into three or four major categories and write a paragraph discussing each category. For each category, write a sentence or two of example or discussion. When you are finished, it should be clear to your reader how the three categories differ from one another.

Establishing a Basis for Classification

In the following list of kinds of shoppers, which item does not belong?

    a. the spendthrift

    b. the bargain hunter

    c. the male shopper

If you chose c, "the male shopper," you are right. You have recognized, consciously or subconsciously, that the first two have the same basis for classification: attitude toward money. The third item has a different basis for classification: gender.

When you write a classification paper, it is important that your classification have a single basis or underlying principle.

EXERCISE 2   **CLASSIFYING ITEMS IN A LIST**

Part 1: Cross out the item that does not belong in each of the following lists. Then determine the basis for classification of the other items and write it in the blank to the right of the list. The first one is done for you.

1. sweaters   Basis for classification: neckline style
   a. crew neck
   b. ~~wool~~
   c. V-neck
   d. turtleneck

2. dogs   Basis for classification: breed
   a. Dalmatian
   b. cocker spaniel
   c. ~~toy~~
   d. Chihuahua

3. stars   Basis for classification: stars in constellations
   a. Sirius
   b. Castor
   c. Polaris
   d. ~~Denzel Washington~~

Part 2: To each list, add one item that fits the existing basis for classification and one item that does not fit.

Answers will vary. Typical answers are given.

4. drugs
   a. aspirin
   b. cough syrup
   c. antacid
   d. laxative _____ (a drug that belongs on this list)
   e. crack cocaine _____ (a drug that belongs on another list)

5. games
   a. basketball
   b. softball
   c. tennis
   d. football _____ (a game that belongs on this list)
   e. Monopoly _____ (a game that belongs on another list)

6. car
   a. Toyota
   b. Renault
   c. Honda
   d. Mitsubishi _____ (a car that belongs on this list)
   e. Ford _____ (a car that belongs on another list)

7. clothing
   a. evening wear
   b. swimwear
   c. sportswear
   d. casual wear _____ (a type of clothing that belongs on this list)
   e. bikini _____ (a type of clothing that belongs on another list)

8. shoes
   a. Reebok
   b. New Balance
   c. Adidas
   d. Nike _____ (a shoe that belongs on this list)
   e. athletic _____ (a shoe that belongs on another list)

EXERCISE 3 FINDING THE POINT THAT DOES NOT FIT

The following paragraph contains one point that has a basis for classification that is different from that of the other three. Read the paragraph and answer the questions that follow.

Types of Workers

At school and at work, I have noticed that people have different kinds of work habits. Some people are collaborators who like to work in groups. They find that doing a project with someone else makes the job more pleasant and the load lighter. Collaborators never work alone unless they are forced to. A second category I have noticed is the advice seeker. An advice seeker does the bulk of her work alone, but frequently looks to others for advice. When this worker has reached a crucial point in her project, she may show it to a classmate or coworker just to get another opinion. Getting the advice of others makes this worker feel secure about her project as it takes shape. Another type of worker I have noticed is the slacker. A slacker tries to avoid work whenever possible. If he seems to be busy at the computer, he is probably playing solitaire, and if he is writing busily, he's probably making his grocery list. Slackers will do anything except the work they are paid to do. The final type of worker is the loner. This type of worker prefers working alone. He has confidence in his ability and is likely to feel that collaboration is a waste of time. Loners work with others only when they are forced to. Collaborators, advice seekers, slackers, and loners have different work styles, but each knows the work habits that help him or her to get the job done.

Questions

Answers will vary.

1. Which point does not have the same basis for classification as the others?

   The slacker is classified on a different basis of classification—how much effort he

   puts into his work.

2. What is the basis for classification of the other three points?

   The other three types of workers—collaborators, advice seekers, and loners—are

   classified by the extent to which they prefer to work with others.

Wordsmith's Corner: Sample Classification Paragraphs

Read the two following classification paragraphs. Then answer the questions that follow.

Classification Paragraph 1

Danielle's paragraph classifies the kinds of stress she experiences when she goes on vacation.

Kinds of Vacation Stress

<u>No matter how much fun I have on vacation, I always experience several kinds of stress.</u> Physical stress is always part of the picture. If I take my children to a theme park, the endless walking and standing in line take their toll. In the mountains or at the lake, insect bites, poison ivy, and sunburn are often our traveling companions. In addition to physical stress, the forced togetherness of a vacation often causes emotional stress. After being cooped up in a car together all day, my children start bickering. I lose patience and begin to think how nice it would be just to have a quiet half hour by myself. Finally, there is financial stress. Renting a hotel room is just the beginning. We have to eat all of our meals in restaurants, and even fast food is more expensive than eating a meal at home. Tickets to attractions are expensive, and souvenirs make the hole in my wallet a little deeper. After a week, I am ready to trade the stresses of vacation for the everyday stresses of home and work.

Questions

1. Underline the topic sentence of the paragraph.
2. How many classifications of vacation stress are mentioned in the paragraph?

   The three classifications mentioned are physical stress, emotional stress, and financial

   stress.

3. In this paragraph, vacation stress is classified on the basis of
   a. who causes it.
   b. how it affects the person.
   c. how long it lasts.
   d. who experiences it.

Classification Paragraph 2

Cassie writes about kinds of road trips she has taken.

Road-Tripping

It has been said that it is not the destination that is important but the journey. <u>When I go on a road trip, the kind of journey I take depends entirely on the people I travel with.</u>

My grandmother has taken my sister and me on several trips, usually to historic sites. She is never in a hurry and is always eager to stop at flea markets, restaurants, and shopping centers along the way. Sometimes, the trip itself is much more fun than whatever we do once we arrive at our destination. With my grandmother, a road trip is a leisurely ramble. When I travel with friends, we are more focused on getting to our destination. We pack a cooler with snacks and drinks, and we rarely take side trips. But the journey seems short because we laugh all the way. When I travel with friends, my trip is an amusing adventure. On a trip with my father, however, the name of the game is "Beat the Clock." His only purpose is to make good time to wherever his destination may be. Getting us there alive is secondary, though an accident would be regrettable because it would keep him from making good time. Needless to say, bathroom breaks or stops for food are strongly discouraged, so no one dares drink the bottled water that sits on the floorboard of the car throughout the entire journey. We arrive at our destination hungry, thirsty, tired, and in desperate need of a visit to the bathroom. Trips with my father are highway marathons. Road trips come in different types, but somehow, I manage to enjoy them all.

Questions

1. Underline the topic sentence of the paragraph.
2. What are the classifications of road trips in the paragraph?

   The classifications are leisurely ramble, amusing adventure, and highway marathon.

3. In this paragraph, road trips are classified on the basis of
   a. money spent.
   b. degree of hurry.
   c. destination.
   d. distance traveled.

TOPICS FOR PRACTICING CLASSIFICATION

Small Scrawls: Imaginative Short Writings

What is a Small Scrawl? A "scrawl" is something written quickly. In this case, it is a page or so of quick writing that allows you to practice a particular type of writing—in this case, classification. Have fun with it!

Small Scrawl 1: Summer Fun

Whether you work or attend school in summer or whether you take the whole glorious summer off, summertime is fun time. In a Small Scrawl, classify the kinds of fun you have in the summertime and give examples of each. You might classify the kinds of fun on the basis of the types of activity: summer sports, summer reading, and summer movies, for example. Or you might classify on the basis of the company you keep; fun with family, fun with friends, and solitary fun, for instance.

Small Scrawl 2: Kinds of Foods You Enjoy

In a small scrawl, classify and describe the kinds of food you most enjoy. You may classify them on the basis of taste (salty, sweet, sour), on the basis of ethnicity (Indian, Chinese, Italian), or on any other basis you desire to use.

Small Scrawl 3: Classifying Your Moods

Even people who seem cheerful most of the time have low moods occasionally. How about you? Think about your moods, from high to low, and classify them according to type in a Small Scrawl.

Classification Assignment 1: Personal Style

Paragraph

Every day you see people eating, walking, taking tests, and having conversations. Think about some of the ordinary (and not so ordinary) behaviors you see on a regular basis. Then, in a paragraph, classify people according to the way they perform a specific task or action. Use one of the suggestions below or come up with an idea of your own.

Classify people by the way they:

eat	greet people	sit
drink	drive	study
chew gum	talk	dance
walk	sing	enter a classroom

Classification Assignment 2: Kinds of Kind People

Paragraph

Even kindness comes in more than one type. Some people will do a favor only if they receive something in return. Others are kind only when they receive recognition or praise for it. Others do kind acts in secret, when no one else will see. Write a paragraph classifying kinds of kind people. If you prefer, write your paragraph on kinds of mean people.

Classification Assignment 3: Fill in the Blank

Paragraph or Essay

Write a classification paragraph or essay on "Kinds of _____." Fill in the blank with one of the words that follow.

social media	happiness	sadness	procrastination
tests	bosses	teachers	music
TV shows	games	sports fans	clothing

 Process

mywritinglab

Visit MyWriting Lab for additional practice with process paragraphs.

When you write a **process** paragraph, you describe how to do something or how it works. Process writing surrounds you. Recipes, instruction manuals, and any of the many self-help books that promise to tell you how to become fit, lose weight, save money, or lead a more satisfying life are examples of how-to process writing. A chapter in an American government text describing how a bill becomes a law, the page in your biology text on the life cycle of the fruit fly, and the fine print on the back of your credit card statement explaining how interest is applied are examples of "how it works" process writing.

Laying the Groundwork for Process Writing

What process is this woman engaged in? Have you ever taught an animal to do a trick or taught a person a skill?

Teaching is a process all its own. Think of a time when you have taught something to a person or to a pet. List the steps involved in the process. Are the steps interchangeable, or do they need to be done in a particular order?

Now, write a paragraph describing the process you followed when you taught someone to do something. Clearly describe each step so that anyone wanting to do this process could follow your steps and perform the process himself.

Organizing the Process Paper

Some processes are **fixed processes**—that is, ones in which the order of the steps cannot vary. If you tell someone how to change the oil in a car, for instance, you can't place the step "add new oil" before the step "drain old oil." If you explain how a bill becomes a law, you can't place "goes to president for signing or veto" before "approved by both houses of Congress." If you are describing a fixed process, list the steps in chronological order.

Other processes are **loose processes**. They have no fixed, predetermined order. Loose processes include such activities as handling money wisely or becoming physically fit. In describing these processes, it is up to you to choose the most logical order.

Imagine that you are writing a paper on handling money wisely. You decide that the steps involved include paying down debt, developing a spending plan, and saving for the future. Developing a spending plan seems logical as a first point, but you can't decide whether to place "saving" or "paying down debt" next in the order. You may say, "It's hard to save until debts are paid. Therefore, paying debt before saving is logical." Or you may reason like this: "Most people stay in debt for most of their lives. If it's not a credit card, it's a car loan or a mortgage. To save, pay yourself first, no matter what." Either order is logical. What is important is that you have thought about it and chosen the order that best suits your own philosophy.

One important point to remember when organizing the how-to process paper is that many processes require tools or certain conditions. Usually, then, step one of your process will direct the reader to gather the necessary tools and make preparations. Whether you're telling how to make a cake or how to defuse a bomb, your reader won't appreciate being led to a crucial point and then being instructed to use a tool that isn't handy. Ideally, a how-to paper is written so clearly and logically that the reader could carry out the process on the first read-through.

Wordsmith's Corner: Sample Process Paragraphs

In the next two paragraphs, look at the ways two other writers handle a process paragraph. Then answer the questions that follow each paragraph.

Process Paragraph 1

In this process paragraph, Ravi tells how to make a car an asset instead of an embarrassment.

How to Keep Your Car from Ruining Your Social Life

If that cute guy or gal from your algebra class just happened to walk out to the parking lot with you after class, would you be embarrassed by the appearance of your car? With a bit of attention and a bit of work, you can have a car that is an asset to your social life, not an obstacle. It all starts inside your car, with the basic understanding that a car is not a trash can or a file cabinet. Banana peels and fast-food containers should not be tossed in the back seat, and old test papers and handouts should not be filed in the trunk. Instead, trash and other items should be removed each day. If you never leave anything in your car, it will never start to look messy. Once the inside is neat, it's time to make sure the outside is taken care of. It is as simple as this: Wash your car every week or, at the very least, every other week. It does not matter whether you wash it yourself with a hose and sponge or whether you take it to a car wash. What matters is that if you and the person from algebra class go out together in your car, you will see the blue sky or the golden moon through your windshield, not two months' worth of dead bugs. There are enough obstacles to a successful social life—don't let your car be one of them.

Questions

Answers may vary.

1. Underline the paragraph's topic sentence.
2. Is the process described in this paragraph a fixed process or a loose process?

   A loose process—the steps do not have to be in any particular order.

3. Double-underline the paragraph's summary sentence.

Process Paragraph 2

Sarah's process paragraph tells how she and her roommates eat well on a budget.

How to Eat Well on a Budget

As poverty-stricken students sharing an apartment, my roommates and I find eating well a challenge. We have very little money, and, as students carrying full-time class loads, we have almost no time. But we have come up with some ways to eat plentifully and somewhat nutritiously even on our small budget. Our first way of saving money and time is simple: noodles, noodles, noodles. They are cheap, are low in fat, and are a basis for many easy-to-make meals. Spaghetti, chili mac, and macaroni and cheese are often on our menu. Baked ramen noodles are lower in fat than fried noodles and make a quick meal any time. When we tire of noodles, we turn to what we call our twenty-four-hour breakfast. Breakfast foods are cheap, tasty, and can be eaten at any meal. Scrambled eggs are quick to make, and a few pieces of toast complete the meal. Pancakes are filling, cheap, and satisfying. But the easiest breakfast of all is cereal. Any time of day, it's easy to pour a bowl of Cheerios or corn flakes, slice a banana over it, and pour on milk. Cereal and milk are always on our menu. Finally, on those days when we don't feel like cooking but want plenty to eat, we order the two-for-one special from the pizzeria down the road. It's the most affordable take-out food we can find, and sometimes we even have pizza left over. Refrigerated overnight, it makes a great cold breakfast in the morning. <u>Our unconventional meals may break a few nutritional rules, but they are quick and easy and never break our budget.</u>

Questions

1. Underline the paragraph's topic sentence.
2. Is the process described in this paragraph a fixed process or a loose process?

   A loose process—the steps do not have to be in any particular order.

3. Double-underline the paragraph's summary sentence.

TOPICS FOR PRACTICING PROCESS WRITING

Small Scrawls: Imaginative Short Writings

What is a Small Scrawl? A "scrawl" is something written quickly. In this case, it is a page or so of quick writing that allows you to practice a particular type of writing—in this case, writing about a process. Have fun with it!

Small Scrawl 1: Getting out of Trouble

Have you ever talked your way out of a traffic ticket or some similar form of trouble? Write a Small Scrawl in which you tell your reader how to get out of the ticket that the officer is writing in the photo on the previous page.

Small Scrawl 2: How to Have a Bad Morning

Have you had mornings that just don't go right? The alarm does not go off. It's a bad hair day. You spill coffee on your interview outfit. Just in case there is someone in the world who has never had one of those mornings, you are going to write instructions for how to have a bad morning. Write a Small Scrawl telling your reader how to have a bad morning. Feel free to draw on your own (perhaps ample) experience.

Small Scrawl 3: The Small Stuff

Write a Small Scrawl telling your reader how to do a simple, everyday process. Describe it so well and so completely that a reader could do it successfully based on your directions alone. Include at the beginning of the paper any tools that the reader will need. A few suggestions follow.

tying shoelaces	putting on and buttoning a shirt
brushing your teeth	starting a car
making toast	putting on makeup
making coffee	shaving

Process Assignment 1: Advice Guru

Paragraph

You are an advice columnist, and you need to answer one more letter to complete tomorrow's column. Choose one of the following letters and write a process paragraph telling the letter writer how to solve his or her problem.

Dear Advice Guru,

I am twenty-three years old and plan to be married next month. My fiancé and I have planned a wonderful trip to the Bahamas as our honeymoon. The only problem is that my husband-to-be has announced that he wants to take his mother with us. I love my fiancé and I like his mother, but I do not want her on our honeymoon. How can I resolve the situation without hurting anyone's feelings?

Signed,
Three's a Crowd

Dear Advice Guru,

I have a problem with my upstairs neighbors in the apartment building where I live. Every day, all day, they play loud, obnoxious music. Even when they are gone, they leave the stereo blaring. At night, they watch television in bed with the volume up loud. They fall asleep and leave it on all night. I am hesitant to approach them because I am afraid of making the situation worse. What should I do?

Signed,
Quiet Please

Process Assignment 2: Getting Physical (or Mental)

Paragraph

Choose a physical or mental process and write a paragraph describing how it's done. Write about a process of your own choosing, or pick one from the following lists.

Mental Processes	**Physical Processes**
deciding between two job offers	working out with weights
studying	mowing a lawn
appreciating a sunset	washing a car
overcoming procrastination	packing belongings for a move

Process Assignment 3: You're the Expert

Paragraph or Essay

Write a paragraph or essay telling your reader how to do something that you do well. It might be a physical skill such as pitching a baseball, being a goalie on a hockey team, or doing an aerobic exercise routine. It might be a social skill such as the ability to make people feel comfortable or to successfully mediate an argument. Or it might be a practical skill or a craft, like getting the most for your money at the grocery store or making a stained-glass window. Whatever it is, you're the expert, so write with confidence.

TOPICS FOR COMBINING METHODS OF DEVELOPMENT

Definition, classification, and process are methods of showing the limits of a topic—the borders that define it—and of ordering it into steps, stages, or types. The following assignments ask you to combine one or more methods of development as you complete the assignment.

Mixed Methods Assignment 1: Courage

Definition and Classification

In this paragraph, your job is to define the term *courage* and to divide it into types. Your definition must be broad enough to cover all the types of courage that you explore in your paragraph. Then, list and define each type of courage. For example, you might discuss *moral courage,* the ability to stand up for what is right, or *physical courage,* the willingness to put oneself in danger for a cause. Because classification often incorporates examples, you may wish to provide examples that help the reader get a clear picture of each type of courage.

Mixed Methods Assignment 2: Problems and Solutions

Definition and Process

Define a particular problem that exists in your home, workplace, or school. It may be a problem that affects you, or it may simply be a problem you have observed. Once you have defined the problem, your job is to suggest a process for solving it.

Mixed Methods Assignment 3: Classmates

Definition and Classification

As you observe the students in your classes, you probably classify some as serious students, others as perpetual latecomers, and still others as class clowns. Write a paragraph defining and classifying the types of students in your classes. To make your paragraph more unified, discuss either the students you enjoy having in class with you or the students you dislike having in your classes.

REAL-WORLD ASSIGNMENTS

The Real-World Assignments below allow you to mix the methods in your class writing assignments that mirror the types of writing you might do outside the classroom.

Real-World Assignment 1: Job Description

Definition and Example

You have been asked to write a definition of your career (or intended career). Write a paragraph listing your primary duties and giving examples of the procedures that you perform (or will perform) in the course of your duties.

Real-World Assignment 2: Party Planner

Classification and Example

You are a professional party and event planner. You plan weddings, all types of parties, and business events such as conferences. You have hired an advertising firm to publicize your company's services. The advertising firm has asked you to prepare a short statement classifying the types of services you offer and giving concrete examples of exactly what you do for your clients with each type of service.

Real-World Assignment 3: Themed Resort

Process and Description

You are the human resources manager for a new themed resort hotel. Employees are expected to dress and act according to the theme and stay in character while on duty. For example, if you name the hotel Blackbeard's Pirate Hideaway, the staff might wear modified pirate costumes and greet guests with, "Ahoy, mateys! Welcome to Blackbeard's Pirate Hideaway!" If the hotel is Hawaiian-themed, different costumes and greetings might be in order.

Write a memo to the head of one of the hotel's divisions (Housekeeping, Front Desk, Bell Captain, or Food Services) introducing them to the costumes and procedures that their employees should follow in the course of their duties to promote the hotel's theme.

The details are up to you. Feel free to adopt one of the themes from the following list or to make up your own.

Island
Sports (skiing, tennis, snorkeling, etc.)
Disco
Safari
Casino
Western

Real-World Assignment 4: Safety Assessment

Classification and Process

You are an environmental safety specialist, and your team is performing a surprise safety assessment of a restaurant at the owner's request. You find the following problems, listed in no particular order:

Employees in food prep area not wearing hairnets or hats

Grease on the kitchen floor

Bleach stored on shelf along with food

Insecticide spray sitting out on food prep counter

Empty fire extinguishers in kitchen

Waitstaff smoking in kitchen

Flooring coming up near door

Your job is to write a report for the restaurant owner, classifying the problems into health and hygiene matters, hazardous materials, and accident hazards and recommending actions to take.

mywritinglab   For support in meeting this chapter's goal, log in to **www.mywritinglab.com** and select **Paragraph Development: Definition**, **Paragraph Development: Division/Classification**, and **Paragraph Development: Process**.

CHAPTER 9

Examining Logical Connections: Comparison-Contrast, Cause-Effect, and Argument

Chapter Goal: Analyze and write comparison-contrast, cause-effect, and argument paragraphs and essays.

The chasm of confusion is
Spanned by a slender bridge,
A logical connection
That runs from ridge to ridge.

But logic can unravel,
And arguments can fail;
It's only careful writing
That helps the span prevail.

Focus on Connections: Getting the Joke

Look at the cartoon above. What is it suggesting about the two genders? How is this comparison stereotypical? Do you agree that it is typically an accurate commentary about both men and women?

We often hear jokes about the differences between men and women, some of them harmless and funny, others hurtful or biased. Often, the jokes play on our expectations, using stereotypes or preconceived notions. However, when you argue a point, make a comparison, or show cause and effect, you will need to go beyond preconceived notions. You may even want to surprise your reader by arguing against something that "everybody knows." Logical connections between ideas will help you show your reader that what "everybody knows" is not necessarily so.

Reflect on It

Find another cartoon that is funny because it plays on preconceived notions. What is the underlying idea that makes the cartoon funny in the first place? How accurate is it?

When you compare alternatives, when you look for causes and effects, or when you argue for a particular course of action, you are using logic to explore connections between ideas. If your logic is thin or your connections weak, your reader will notice, and the bridge of communication between you and your reader will weaken. The methods in this chapter call for rational thought and careful planning. The skills that go along with these methods of development—pinpointing differences and similarities, discovering reasons, predicting results, and arguing an issue logically—are essential. These higher-order tools of thought can help you in the college classroom and beyond.

Comparison-Contrast, Cause-Effect, and Argument in Action

In this chapter, you will have the opportunity to examine and use the techniques of comparison-contrast, cause-effect, and argument and a closely related technique, persuasion. The text explains the techniques separately so that you can become thoroughly familiar with them and learn to use them successfully. Later, you will mix techniques to suit your purpose for writing.

Before looking at comparison-contrast, cause-effect, and argument separately, look at how a professional writer uses all three techniques together. The following essay is by Leonard Pitts, a columnist for the *Miami Herald*.

The essay embodies all three of the writing techniques featured in this chapter. The first technique that the writer incorporates is cause-effect. Mainly, the essay shows the way that permitting one small offense opens the door for others. The essay also contrasts Pitts' reactions toward profanity in a comic book with that of an outraged letter writer. Finally, the author argues that unconcerned attitudes like his own contribute to making problems worse, whether those problems are broken windows or offensive words in comic books.

Broken Windows

Leonard Pitts

I guess it was only a matter of time before Sue Richards said "ass." I mean, everybody else has. Why not her?

It's right there in black and white, Page 2, "Fantastic Four No. 38: the Invisible Woman," an offhand reference to "knocking Dr. Doom on his ass."

It was too much for a fellow named Marcus Lusk. He wrote Marvel Comics a letter, which the company published last week.

"What in the world were you thinking?" he demanded. "This is wrong. Just flat-out wrong."

Truth to tell, I can think of several ways to punch holes in Lusk's indignation. I could point out, for instance, that it's unlikely the majority of readers exposed to the offending word were young children. As Jim Welker of Tropic Comics in North Miami Beach points out, comics fans tend to range in age from 17 to 25 years. I could observe, too, that it's only "ass"—hardly the big kahuna in the hierarchy of naughty terms. Finally, I could note that you can hardly watch a TV sitcom or drama these days without some character spouting the same word.

Yet for all of that, Lusk's complaint resonates with me, though my discomfort stems from a different place.

What bothers me is that I'm not bothered. Or, at least, I wasn't. I read right over the passage in question and it registered only as a lamentable sign of the times. Then I read Lusk's letter, I see that he is indignant, and I begin to wonder why I was not.

Media used to set stuff with bad language or suggestive pictures aside, consigning it to hours and locations where young people were unlikely to encounter it. Now it's everywhere. To the point that a comic book heroine talks about knocking the bad guy on his ass.

Another barrier is breached, another small crudity seeps into a forbidden place.

I wouldn't even mind the intrusion if there was some point to it. Thirty years ago, for instance, this same company bucked the Comics Code Authority—the industry's censoring group—to publish a controversial tale about drug addiction. That was brave.

This is . . . lazy.

And if you're thinking, "So what? Comic book character says a bad word. That isn't such a big thing,". . .well, you're right. That's the point.

I'm reminded of the "broken windows" theory of crime prevention. It says that if one window is shattered in a factory and allowed to go unrepaired, people will perceive that no one cares, that this is a lawless place. And it won't be long before all the windows are shattered and the street becomes one where prudent people do not walk.

I wonder if something similar isn't true of the tendency of crude material to seep into inappropriate places, if hesitancy to raise a ruckus over small breaches isn't analogous to leaving the window shattered.

"We are doing our best to balance the demands of a new generation with the expectations of our more traditional readers," went the company's response to Marcus Lusk.

In other words, the lines of propriety are shifting, blurring away to irrelevance. And you wonder where or whether they'll ever take shape again.

THINKING ABOUT THE ESSAY

1. How does Pitts's attitude toward the reference to "knocking Dr. Doom on his ass" compare or contrast with that of Marcus Lusk, who wrote the letter to Marvel Comics?

2. This essay contains more than one argument: Lusk's argument that offensive words do not belong in comic books, Pitts's counterargument that it's really not that big a deal . . . or a very shocking word. Finally, Pitts fashions a third

argument that hinges on his own argument that the word is no big deal. What is that argument, and how is it supported?

3. Cause-effect writing can be mainly about causes, mainly about effects, or a detailed discussion of both. In this essay, there are multiple causes and multiple effects. Discuss the effect of leaving a broken window unrepaired. How does that relate to Pitts's argument about offensive words in comic books?

Comparison-Contrast

mywritinglab
Visit MyWriting Lab for additional practice with comparison-contrast paragraphs.
One of the most effective ways of describing something that is unfamiliar to your reader is by comparing or contrasting it with something familiar. When you make a **comparison**, you show how two things are similar. If a friend asks you about a class you are taking, you may describe it by comparing it to a class that the two of you have taken together. When you **contrast** two things, you show how they are different. If you are asked on a political science exam to discuss the legislative and judicial branches of government, you may contrast the ways each branch shapes the country's laws. In an English class, you might use both comparison and contrast to show how two writers develop similar themes in different ways. Used alone or together, comparison and contrast are useful tools for any writer.

Laying the Groundwork for Comparison and Contrast

Look at the photographs of the two nurses. One is clearly old-fashioned, while the other is very modern.

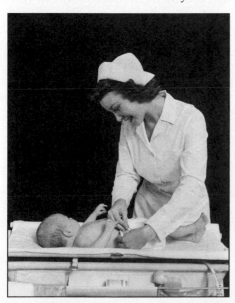
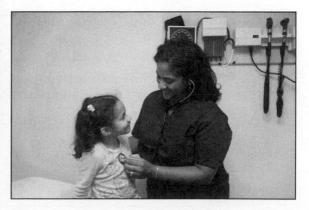

Think about yourself. Do you consider yourself traditional or modern? Now, think about a family member who is just the opposite. Write a paragraph contrasting yourself with a family member who is more old-fashioned or more modern than you.

Setting up a Comparison-Contrast Paragraph

The first step in setting up a comparison-contrast paragraph is to choose points of comparison or contrast and to decide whether to compare or contrast. One way to decide is through prewriting. Prewriting can help you determine whether your primary focus is on comparison or on contrast. Below is a sample brainstorming that sets the focus for a paragraph.

Brainstorming—Two Brothers

Eric

- ✔ quiet
  even-tempered, patient,
  does not care about what he wears
- ✔ good student
- ✔ curious about ideas,
  likes music,
  good sense of humor

Rashad

- ✔ outgoing,
  easygoing,
  dresses well
- ✔ average student
- ✔ curious about people,
  likes music,
  funny and always joking

Though there are points of comparison, there are even more points of contrast. The writer decides to focus on three contrasting points.

The next step in planning the comparison-contrast paragraph is to decide whether to use a point-by-point pattern or a block pattern to discuss the points. In a **point-by-point** pattern, each point of comparison or contrast is considered separately. Following is a point-by-point paragraph outline.

Personality
Eric: Quiet
Rashad: Outgoing

Academic Performance
Eric: Good student
Rashad: Average student

Interests

Eric: Curious about ideas

Rashad: Curious about people

Another way of presenting a comparison or contrast is in a **block** pattern. In this pattern, information about one subject is presented in one big block, followed by information about the other subject in a second big block. A block paragraph outline is shown below.

Eric: Quiet—a listener rather than a talker

                  A good student—demands perfection

                  Interested in ideas

Rashad: Outgoing—keeps people entertained

                  Average student

                  Interested in people

EXERCISE 1 **RECOGNIZING COMPARISON-CONTRAST PATTERNS**

Following are two paragraphs written from the outlines shown earlier. Read each paragraph and decide which follows the point-by-point pattern and which follows the block pattern.

Paragraph A

My two brothers, Eric and Rashad, are from the same family, but they are different in many ways. Eric, my older brother, is the quiet one. He is a listener rather than a talker, and it takes a while to get to know him and see the friendly, funny person he is inside. He has always been a good and careful student. If he turns in a paper, it has been proofread several times, and he always checks math problems twice. He demands perfection of himself and isn't really happy unless he makes A's. Eric has always been interested in ideas, immersing himself in books and in the Internet and joining scholastic clubs such as the Science Club. Rashad, on the other hand, is an outgoing person who makes friends easily. Maybe it is because he is the youngest child in our family and had to compete for attention, but he is a natural entertainer who keeps everyone laughing. As a student, he is just average. He procrastinates in studying, doing assignments, and preparing for tests. If he makes a C on an exam, he is satisfied. He is not so much intellectually curious as he is curious about people. He is always interested in what people are doing, and he wants to understand their behavior and know what motivates them. He would make a good counselor, coach, or psychologist. I have two wonderful brothers, but they are very different in their personalities, academic performance, and interests.

Paragraph B

My two brothers, Eric and Rashad, are from the same family, but they are different in many ways. Eric, my older brother, is the quiet one. He is a listener rather than a talker, so it takes a while to get to know him and see the friendly, funny person he is inside. Rashad, on the other hand, is an outgoing person who makes friends easily. Maybe it is because he is the youngest child in our family and had to compete for attention, but he is a natural entertainer who keeps everyone laughing. The two are also different in their approach to academics. Eric has always been a good and careful student. If he turns in a paper, it has been proofread several times, and he always checks math problems twice. He isn't really happy unless he makes A's. Rashad is more casual about studying. As a student, he is just average. He procrastinates in studying, doing assignments, and preparing for tests. If he makes a C on an exam, it does not bother him for too long. My brothers' interests are also different. Eric is idea-focused, immersing himself in books and in the Internet and joining scholastic clubs such as the Science Club. Rashad, however, is not so much intellectually curious as he is curious about people. He is always interested in what people are doing, and he wants to understand their behavior and know what motivates them. He would make a good counselor, coach, or psychologist. I have two wonderful brothers, but they are very different in their personalities, academic performance, and interests.

Questions

1. The paragraph organized in point-by-point format is paragraph _____B_____

2. The paragraph organized in block format is paragraph _____A_____

3. Look at the two paragraphs. In which paragraph do you find more transitions? Why?

    Paragraph B contains more transitions because the writer moves back and forth from Eric to Rashad instead of making one switch in the middle of the paragraph.

Transitional Expressions

In setting up your comparison-contrast paragraph, you may find the following transitional expressions helpful. The transitions of contrast alert your reader to a change of direction, while transitions of comparison help to point out similarities.

Transitional Expressions Used to Compare and Contrast

Transitions of Contrast

| although | even though | in contrast | instead | on the other hand |
| but | however | in spite of | nevertheless | yet |

Transitions of Comparison

in the same way   like   similarly

Wordsmith's Corner: Sample Comparison-Contrast Paragraphs

Below, see how two writers handle topics using comparison-contrast. Read each paragraph and answer the questions that follow.

Comparison-Contrast Paragraph 1

Jesse's paragraph contrasts two different times of the week at the same car wash.

At the Car Wash

Once a week, on Friday night or Saturday morning, I take my car to the self-serve car wash. But the car wash on a Friday evening is quite different from the car wash on a Saturday

morning. On Friday nights, as the sun goes down and the fluo-
rescent lights come on, the car wash comes alive with sound.
As I pull into the wash bay, I hear the thumping rhythms of
rap and rock, and from somewhere, a smooth ballad. The people at the car wash are mostly in their teens or early twenties.
Parked beside the vacuum with all four doors open wide, they
clean their cars as their music competes with the sound coming from the other cars parked nearby. Laughter, flirting, and
enthusiastic greetings among friends are as much a part of the
scene as soap and water. The Friday night crowd is young, fun,
and noisy. On Saturday mornings, the car wash attracts mostly
families and older people. Children dart through the spray of
the hose while their mothers scold. Older couples tackle the
job together, while dads let their kids help with vacuuming the
seats or polishing the tires. The only sounds are the spray of
water on metal, the roar of the vacuum, and the shrieks and
laughter of children. <u>The bays and the vacuums remain the
same, but the atmosphere of the car wash changes completely
from Friday night to Saturday morning.</u>

Questions

1. Underline the paragraph's topic sentence.
2. Is the paragraph comparison or contrast? What is being compared or contrasted?

   The paragraph contrasts a car wash on Friday nights with the same car wash on

   Saturday morning.

3. Is the paragraph written in point-by-point or block format?

   The paragraph is written in block format.

4. Double-underline the paragraph's summary sentence.

Comparison-Contrast Paragraph 2

Karen discusses how she functions in the morning and in the evening.

Morning and Evening

Most people function better at certain times of the day, but
I take it to extremes. <u>In the morning, I am a barely functioning
human being, but when evening comes, I have energy to spare.</u>
Every morning, I stumble out of bed in a semiconscious state,
only waking up after the second cup of coffee. My family knows

that conversation with me before 10:00 A.M. is impossible. My end of the conversation consists of a few grunts, and whatever anyone else says does not stay in my sleep-fogged brain for more than a few seconds. I know better than to take an 8:00 A.M. class. Even if I could drag myself out of bed to get to class on time, I would never remember a word the professor said. By midafternoon, however, my engines start humming. When everyone else is in a midafternoon slump, I am out jogging around the lake or doing research for my term paper in the library. If I go out with friends, my energy increases as the night wears on, while my friends wilt like tired flowers as midnight approaches. If I am at home, I watch my family drift away to bed, one by one, in spite of my attempts to keep them awake with conversation and jokes. It's not easy to be a night owl when I am surrounded by larks.

Questions

1. Underline the paragraph's topic sentence.

2. Is the paragraph comparison or contrast? What is being compared or contrasted?

   The paragraph contrasts the writer's energy level in the morning and in

   the evening.

3. Is the paragraph written in point-by-point or block format?

   The paragraph is written in block format.

Building CONNECTIONS

When you make comparisons or draw contrasts, *examples* are often useful in making the similarities or differences clear to your reader.

TOPICS FOR PRACTICING COMPARISON-CONTRAST WRITING

Small Scrawls: Imaginative Short Writings

What is a Small Scrawl? A "scrawl" is something written quickly. In this case, it is a page or so of quick writing that allows you to practice a particular type of writing—in this case, comparison-contrast. Have fun with it!

Small Scrawl 1: Apples and Oranges

It's the classic contrast. When two things are very different, people say, "They're like apples and oranges." In this Small Scrawl, you are invited to compare and/or contrast apples and oranges.

Small Scrawl 2: High School and College

What are the main differences you have noticed between high school and college?

Small Scrawl 3: Sunrise, Sunset

Write a Small Scrawl contrasting two different times of day. Decide how you will approach this assignment. Will you talk about things external to you, such as people rushing to classes in the mornings with their coffee versus people sitting under trees and studying in the afternoons? Or will you discuss internal feelings or personal activities, or will you combine both? This Small Scrawl is ideal for combining both description and comparison-contrast.

Comparison-Contrast Assignment 1: Family Traits

Paragraph

In a paragraph, discuss some of the ways in which two members of your family are alike.

Comparison-Contrast Assignment 2: What Would You Change?

Paragraph

What area of your life would you like to change, and how would you make it different from the way it is now? Make sure that your paragraph shows both sides: how it is now and how you would like it to be. Some possible areas of change are:

a family relationship

relationship with a friend or significant other

finances

living conditions

job

transportation

Comparison-Contrast Assignment 3: Thumbs Up, Thumbs Down

Paragraph or Essay

Think of the best and the worst in any of the following categories. Then write a comparison-contrast paragraph or essay contrasting the two.

the best/worst job you have held

the best/worst date you have been on

the best/worst place to go on a date

the best/worst place you have lived

the best/worst vacation

the best/worst TV show or movie

Cause and Effect

mywritinglab

Visit MyWriting Lab for additional practice with cause and effect paragraphs.

When you look for the **causes** of an event, you are looking for the reasons it happened. In other words, you are looking for answers to *why* questions. Why did your last romantic relationship end badly? Why is your uncle Fred's car still humming along at 150,000 miles? Why are so many schools plagued by violence?

When you look for the **effects** of an action, you are looking for its results. You are answering the question *What would happen if?* What would happen if every community had a neighborhood watch? What would happen if you decided to devote just one hour a day to an important long-term goal? What is the effect of regular maintenance on an automobile?

When you explore both cause and effect, you look at both the reason and the result. You may explore actual cause and effect, as in "Uncle Fred performs all scheduled maintenance on his car and changes the oil every 5,000 miles; as a result, his car is still going strong at 150,000 miles." You may also explore hypothetical cause and effect, as in "Many members of my generation are bored and cynical because everything—material possessions, good grades, and even the respect of others—has come to them too easily."

Laying the Groundwork for Cause-Effect Writing

Look at the two friends in the photograph below. Then, think about your own friendships. Friendships often seem to arise naturally, but there must be reasons that a friendship forms—the causes of a friendship. List as many things as you can think of that might make people likely to become friends. The list is started for you below.

1. Working in the same place or attending the same school.
2. Knowing the same people.
3. _____
4. _____
5. _____
6. _____
7. _____
8. _____
9. _____
10. _____

Once you have made the list, look it over and decide which items are most important. Then write a paragraph about the reasons people might be likely to become friends. After each reason, include a sentence or two of discussion.

Identifying Causes and Effects

A cause is a *reason*. If you are asking a "why" question, the answer is probably a cause. Why do toilets flush in a counterclockwise spiral above the equator and in a clockwise spiral below it? Why did I do so poorly on my history test? Why did the chicken cross the road? From the scientific to the silly, these "why" questions can be answered by finding reasons or causes.

An effect is a *result*. If you ask "What will happen if . . ." or "What were the results of . . ." then your answer is an effect. What would the results be if the speed limit were lowered by ten miles per hour? What would happen if I set aside an hour a day to exercise? What would happen if I threw these new red socks into the washer with my white underwear? When you answer these and other "what if" questions, your answer is an effect.

EXERCISE 2   **CAUSES OR EFFECTS?**

For each topic listed, indicate whether a paragraph on the topic would involve a discussion of causes (reasons) or effects (results).

causes   **1.** Why do so many people enjoy watching wrestling?

effects   **2.** What would the results be if attending college became mandatory?

causes   **3.** Why are so many Americans overweight?

causes   **4.** Describe your reasons for choosing the career you are preparing for.

effects   **5.** What would happen if every television station in the United States stopped broadcasting for a one-month period?

effects   **6.** How do you react to music?

causes   **7.** What good habit have you taken up lately? Why?

causes   **8.** Why do so many people watch talk shows?

effects   **9.** What can result from the habitual overuse of alcohol?

causes   **10.** Are you superstitious? Why or why not?

Wordsmith's Corner: Sample Cause-Effect Paragraphs

Following are two paragraphs dealing with causes and effects. Read each piece and answer the questions that follow.

Cause-Effect Paragraph 1

In this paragraph, Maria discusses obnoxious behavior at ball games.

Obnoxious Fans

The last time I went to a professional baseball game, a fan sitting near me shouted insults at the players until his voice became hoarse. <u>Instead of enjoying the action on the field, I spent nine innings wondering why a fan would behave so obnoxiously at a game.</u> One possible reason is that the fan is letting out pent-up aggression from some other, unrelated situation. Maybe his boss yells at him and insults him, and he can't yell back for fear of losing his job. So he takes out all his aggression for the price of a ticket to the ball game. Another possibility is that he is a coward who only strikes out at targets that won't strike back. Publicly humiliating people, shouting at them, or insulting their mothers is usually dangerous. However, ball players are relatively safe targets because their job is to focus on the game, and usually, they ignore abuse. Confrontational behavior might also be part of the fan's personality. Maybe he picks fights with everyone and sees no reason to behave differently just because he is at a ball game. While suppressed aggression, cowardice, or a confrontational personality could be the problem, there is one other possibility. Maybe the fan is just a jerk.

Questions

1. Underline the topic sentence of the paragraph.

2. Does the paragraph mainly discuss causes or effects? <u>mainly causes</u>

3. Identify the effect(s) and the cause(s) in this paragraph.

    Answers may vary. Effect: Fan shouts insults at baseball players.

    Possible causes: The fan has pent-up aggression from another situation.

    The fan is a coward who only strikes at targets that will not strike back.

    The fan is simply an aggressive person who picks fights with everyone.

    The fan is a jerk.

Cause-Effect Paragraph 2

Anthony uses cause and effect to write about his credit card blues.

Credit Card Blues

Shortly after I enrolled in college, I received a credit card offer in the mail. <u>My decision to accept had several negative effects.</u> For one thing, having a credit card gave me the illusion of unlimited buying power. I would go into a store, see something I wanted, and pull out my shiny new credit card. Magically, that little piece of plastic gave me the power to buy, even if I had no money in the bank. When the first bill came, I was shocked to see that I had charged almost $300 on my card, almost as much as I cleared in a month on my part-time job. A second effect of having a credit card was the illusion that I could easily pay off my debt. On a $300 balance, the credit card company wanted only a $10 minimum payment. I paid the minimum, not realizing that it would take me well over two years to pay off my card at that rate. I continued charging, rationalizing that the $2,000 limit on my card would act as an automatic barrier and keep me from spending too much. But when I reached that amount, the credit card company raised my limit to $3,000. I felt proud, thinking I must really be a creditworthy person. I was more like a fish, attracted by a flashy plastic lure and caught on a line of credit. Finally, when my credit card balance reached $5,000, I called a halt to credit and cut up my card. But the card is still exercising its negative effects. I am now working extra hours at my part-time job to pay off my balance, and the amount I can spend day to day is reduced. Now, when envelopes come in the mail saying "preapproved" or "low interest," I tear them up without even opening them.

Questions

1. Underline the topic sentence of the paragraph.

2. Is the paragraph mainly about causes or effects?
    The paragraph is mainly about effects.

3. Identify the cause(s) and effect(s) discussed in the paragraph.
    Answers may vary. Cause: The writer accepted a credit card offer.

    Effects: He felt that he could spend without restriction.

    Cause: The minimum payment was very low.

    Effects: He felt that his debt was under control and could easily be

    paid off. He continued charging.

    Cause: The credit card company raised his limit.

    Effect: He felt like a creditworthy person who must be handling debt well.

    Cause: His balance reached $5,000.

    Effect: He cut up his card.

TOPICS FOR PRACTICING CAUSE AND EFFECT WRITING

Small Scrawls: Imaginative Short Writings

What is a Small Scrawl? A "scrawl" is something written quickly. In this case, it is a page or so of quick writing that allows you to practice a particular type of writing—in this case, writing about causes and effects. Have fun with it!

Small Scrawl 1: Waiting in Line

Think of a time when you were in a hurry and had to stand in line. What are the effects of having to wait in line, on you or on other people? Discuss in a Small Scrawl.

Small Scrawl 2: People and Pets

Around 63 percent of all households in the United States include at least one pet. What are some of the reasons people choose to share their lives with animals?

Small Scrawl 3: It's a Gas

Write a Small Scrawl discussing the effects of high gas prices.

Cause-Effect Assignment 1: Just Causes

Paragraph

Discuss only the causes of one of the following in a paragraph.

poor grades
divorce
financial problems
shoplifting
stress or burnout

Cause-Effect Assignment 2: Writing about Effects

Paragraph

Discuss the effects of one of the following in a paragraph.

exercise
violence in television programs, movies, and music
technology on everyday life
loss of a close friend or relative

Cause-Effect Assignment 3: A Painful Decision

Paragraph or Essay

Write a paragraph or essay discussing the reasons for a painful decision in your life. A decision to divorce, to have an abortion or to give up a child for adoption, to break off a friendship, or to quit a job are some possibilities.

🖋 Argument and Persuasion

mywritinglab

Visit MyWriting Lab for additional practice with argument.

Argument and **persuasion** are related techniques of writing in which you take a side on an issue and defend your position. Much of the writing you do on the college level will require you to provide evidence to defend a position and will thus require argument or persuasion. **Argument** involves taking and defending a position on an issue, whereas **persuasion** imposes the added burden of trying to win others over to your side.

Argument and persuasion answer questions such as the ones that follow:

- Is it ethical to keep animals in zoos?
- Should physician-assisted suicide be legalized for terminally ill people?
- Should television advertisements aimed at children be banned?

Aristotle's Influence on Argument and Persuasion

Much of what we believe today about effective persuasion and argument comes to us from the ancient Greek philosopher Aristotle. Aristotle identified three elements of an argument: ethos, pathos, and logos. Look at these ideas one by one to see what an ancient Greek philosopher has to say about your writing in the twenty-first century.

Ethos (*eeth-ahse* or *eeth-ohse*), according to Aristotle, involves the reputation and image of the writer. *Ethos* is the root of the English words *ethics* and *ethical*. What does this have to do with writing in the modern world? Everything. Readers want to know that your reputation and the reputation of any sources you use as references are ones of honesty and reliability. That is why it is important to write honestly and not twist your words or anyone else's to suit your purpose. That's why it's important, when you research a topic, to choose sources carefully rather than just grabbing the first few sources that come up in an Internet search. The stronger the reputation of your sources, the stronger your paper will be.

Ethos also has to do with the image you project as a writer, the way you present yourself. Writers project a poor image when they don't proofread or when they use poor grammar and careless spelling. Their image suffers when they try to cover up lack of knowledge and understanding with long words or when they do not put sufficient thought into their writing. Your reader's acceptance of you as a credible writer will be all the stronger if you put thought into your writing and if you construct a paper that does not distract the reader with poor grammar and careless errors.

Pathos (*payth-ahse* or *payth-ohse*), in Aristotle's framework, has to do with persuading your reader with appeals to emotion and feeling. The Greek word *pathos* is at the root of the English words *sympathy* and *empathy*, both of which deal with a feeling of connection between people. Here are three ways to connect with your reader more easily.

Know your reader. When you write an essay, it's good to know who your intended audience is. How much are they likely to know about your subject? What is their position likely to be? For example, if you are writing about using a designated driver, your primary audience is probably people who drive to destinations where alcohol is served. However, anyone who shares the same roads or who has loved ones who drive will be a secondary, and supportive, audience. Knowing your audience makes it easier to persuade your audience.

Remember that tone is important. Have you ever heard someone say, "It wasn't so much what he said; it was the way he said it"? People take offense if they feel they are being talked down to or lectured to. Your goal is to make your tone conversational, peer-to-peer, as though you are talking to someone you know and like.

Engage your reader with anecdotes and examples. Stories and examples can liven your writing and draw your reader in. Here is where you provide specific examples, real or hypothetical, to back up and drive home your argument.

Logos (*low-gahse* or *low-gohse*), or logic, according to Aristotle, is the final element in argument or persuasion. The Greek word *logos* is at the root of English words such as *logic* and *logical*. Logic is extremely important in making an argument or persuading an audience. No matter how strong the other elements of your writing are, they will count for nothing if your argument does not make sense.

Signs of Flawed Logic in Argument

Here are some danger signs that may signal flawed logic:

Painting with too broad a brush. If you say "Older people are *usually* bad drivers because their reflexes have slowed and their reaction time is poor," you are generalizing, or painting an entire group of people with a single brush-stroke. On the one hand, words like *usually, never,* and *always* increase your responsibility to make sure that what you are saying is absolutely accurate. On the other hand, words like *often, can,* and *may* allow you to make a point without using too broad a brush. Saying "Older drivers *may* lose their ability to react quickly as they age" is much more realistic.

Staying on the surface. If you find yourself repeating generalizations instead of analyzing, providing strong support, and giving examples, your argument is a surface argument. Look at the two paragraphs that follow to see the difference between a paragraph that remains on the surface and one that goes into more depth.

Paragraph A

Television advertisements aimed at children should be banned. Children lack the maturity to distinguish between fiction and fact, and if an advertisement tells them that a particular fast-food restaurant is "the fun place," they will pressure their parents to go there. It's easy to say that the parents can just say "no," but add to that advertisement the commercials of every other restaurant, toy manufacturer, cereal maker, and candy manufacturer that is trying to influence the child, and the parents have a hundred such battles to fight. In addition, young children form their values early, and though parents may try to help their children resist the message to consume, consume, consume, they do not have millions of dollars to pour into the delivery of their message. Children form brand allegiance easily, and corporations are not going to easily give up their fight for the youngest consumers. It will take pressure from voters and perhaps an outright ban to keep advertisers from targeting children.

Paragraph B

Television advertisements aimed at children should be banned. Children can't distinguish between fiction and fact, and if an advertisement tells them that a certain thing is true, they will believe whatever the advertisement or commercial says. If children believe the commercials that they see on TV, then they will constantly be pestering their parents to buy the products that they viewed while watching commercials, and parents will have to refuse their children time and time again. Children also form their values early, and what kinds of values will commercials teach them? Though most parents wish to help their children resist the consumerist message of advertisers, they are not as well equipped to drive home their message as are the well-funded multinational corporations. Children are easily led, and corporations are happy to have very young consumers. Corporations will not give up these young consumers without a fight. Voters and lawmakers must put these corporations under pressure and, if necessary, ban commercials aimed at young children.

Making exaggerated claims. Have you seen ads that make claims like these?

"Have the body of your dreams in just ten minutes a day!"

"Make $100,000 a year from home in your spare time!"

"Attract the person of your dreams with our phenomenal pheromone spray!"

"Call our psychics now to find out what the future holds for you. They already know you are going to call!"

Advertisements like these probably make you skeptical, even if they tempt you just a bit. And you are right to be skeptical, because the claims of those ads are clearly exaggerated. In an argument essay, you are expected to take a position and support it, but that does not mean you want to exaggerate. Think through your topic thoroughly, and be aware of the complexity of the problem you are discussing.

Look at the two sample paragraphs that follow. Though they are on the same topic, the similarity ends there. One takes an exaggerated approach that is likely to turn a reader off, while the other is more moderate and thus more believable. Which is which?

Sample Paragraph 1

The Internet can be a dangerous place for those who are not careful. You need to password-protect personal and financial information and to use "strong" passwords that contain numbers and both upper- and lowercase letters. Any email that asks for personal information and especially for account numbers and passwords is not legitimate, even if it seems to be from your bank or credit union. It is a "phishing" scheme, fishing for information, which of course you will not provide. In addition to safeguarding financial information, it is important to safeguard the children in the family. Monitor the sites they visit, make sure they surf the Internet in a family area where adults can watch, and be sure that the children know the dangers of revealing personal information or of physically meeting anyone they have met on the Internet. Many adults use Internet dating sites. If you choose to try Internet dating, be sure that you use a reputable site and that, if you decide to meet in person, you meet in a public place for at least the first few times. Reveal personal information with caution, and if you sense that something is "not right" about the person you have met, trust your instincts and back off. The Internet is a valuable tool for business and personal use, but it requires caution.

Sample Paragraph 2

The Internet is a dangerous place. Wherever you go on the Internet, someone is waiting to steal your personal information and your identity, perhaps ruining you financially. When you log on to your bank's Internet site to pay your bills electronically, how do you know that someone is not stealing your information even as you go about this everyday task? If you have children, beware! Children's sites are filled with predators whose only purpose is to find out where you live and steal your child from you. Some even lure children to meet them, children who may never be seen or heard from again. As for you, are you interested in joining an Internet dating site to find love or companionship? What you are more likely to find is a serial killer who wants to kill you slowly and painfully, or, if you are lucky, someone who merely wants to scam you out of your hard-earned money and disappear. The Internet is the playground of perverts, pedophiles, and pretenders, and you would be wise to stay away.

Laying the Groundwork for Writing Argument and Persuasion

Look at the photograph on the next page of the man riding a bus. Public transportation is one alternative to one's own car. Make a list of the advantages and disadvantages of public transportation. Consider personal convenience, cost, effects on the environment, and effects on traffic congestion. Then consider this question: Should individuals use public transportation in preference to driving a private vehicle? Write a paragraph supporting the use of public transportation or the use of a private vehicle, using the reasons you have listed.

Taking Sides

It has been said that there are two sides to every argument. Your paragraph, however, should favor just *one* side. In an argument paragraph, it is important to make your position clear, and that means starting with a strong topic sentence. Look at the following examples.

Examples of Unclear and Clear Topic Sentences

✗ Music education is often the first program to feel the axe when a budget crisis hits the public schools. (This topic sentence does not state a position.)

✗ Music education is considered essential by many, but others see it as a non-essential frill. (This topic sentence states two positions.)

✓ Music education is an essential part of a child's education. (This topic sentence states a clear position.)

✓ Although some see music education as nonessential, I believe it should be a part of every child's education. (This topic sentence mentions the opposing viewpoint but makes it clear where the writer stands.)

EXERCISE 3	RECOGNIZING TOPIC SENTENCES THAT TAKE A SIDE

Look at the following pairs of topic sentences. Place a check beside the sentence that takes a side on the issue being discussed.

1. _____ A museum is a place that houses artifacts and collections and educates and entertains the public.

   ✔ The proposed science museum would be an asset to our city.

2. ✔ The death penalty, while unquestionably harsh, is justified in some instances.

   _____ The death penalty is an issue that generates much argument, both for and against.

3. _____ Ever since I can remember, my family has always driven Toyotas.

   ✔ The Toyota Corolla is the best car in its price range.

4. _____ Many people favor electing Ed Macklehouse as our next mayor, but then again, some people say he is a crook.

   ✔ Ed Macklehouse should be our next mayor.

5. _____ Many people enjoy playing state lotteries that fund education and other state programs.

   ✔ State lotteries are nothing more than a tax on people who don't understand math.

Will You Change Anyone's Mind?

A good argument is aimed at changing people's views. On some topics, a convincing argument may change someone's mind. On other topics, though, you will find it next to impossible to sway an opinion that may have been molded by a lifetime of experience. Particularly on such hot-button issues as abortion, assisted suicide, or the death penalty, the best you can realistically hope for is to open a window to your viewpoint. In this case, success means coaxing your reader to look through that window long enough to say, "I see what you mean, and I understand your point of view."

Building CONNECTIONS

Arguing a point often involves *contrast* and *cause-effect*. Making an argument sometimes involves contrasting one side with another. An argument favoring a particular course of action (for example, making handgun ownership illegal) often involves examining both the positive and negative effects of that action.

Wordsmith's Corner: Sample Argument and Persuasion Paragraphs

Following are two examples of writing arguing a point. Read each piece and answer the questions that follow.

Argument Paragraph 1

Carmen argues for the usefulness of creatures that give some people the shivers.

Let Them Be

For many people, the immediate reaction to a spider, snake, or lizard is to yell, "Kill it!" <u>But in most cases, the best thing to do is simply let it be.</u> Spiders may look creepy, but they eat harmful insects. A wolf spider, for example, does not trap its prey, but actively hunts down ticks, cockroaches, and other insects. So when I see a wolf spider in my garage, I let it alone. Though it is ugly and its size is formidable, I know that it is beneficial. Occasionally, I see a snake in my yard or garden, but I do not run for a hoe to kill it. I know that snakes eat insects and small rodents that feed on plants. So if I have beautiful flowers or delicious tomatoes and squash, it is partly thanks to the snakes that keep pests from devouring my garden. Some creepy creatures are valuable just for their entertainment value. A resort hotel my family visited once was home to many geckoes, small darting lizards that lived in the bushes and in the spaces between the boards on the outside of the hotel. Instead of trying to eliminate them, the hotel made mascots of them. The gift shop and restaurant sold gecko keychains, gecko postcards, and small stuffed geckoes to take home as souvenirs. <u><u>Spiders, snakes, and lizards may not be warm and cuddly, but they are mostly harmless and often helpful creatures that deserve a better fate than most people would allow them.</u></u>

Questions

1. Underline the paragraph's topic sentence.
2. List the arguments that the writer makes in favor of spiders, snakes, and lizards.

   Spiders eat harmful insects. Snakes eat insects and small rodents that feed on plants.

   Geckoes are entertaining.

3. Double-underline the paragraph's summary sentence.

Argument Paragraph 2

In this paragraph, the writer argues that curfews are a form of age discrimination.

City Curfews: Legalized Age Discrimination

The issue of whether a teenager had a curfew used to be between the teen and his or her parents, but lately, some cities have begun imposing curfews on teenagers. <u>The reasons for the curfews sound convincing on the surface, but a closer look shows that curfews are a form of legalized age discrimination.</u> Lawmakers say that teenagers are responsible for more crimes than other age groups, and teens who are out late are more likely to commit crimes. True, a teenager who is out late might be committing a crime, but he also might be returning home from work, coming back from a study session, or simply having fun. Even convicted felons, once their time is served, are allowed to walk the streets freely. Keeping teenagers off the streets because of crimes they might commit is nothing more than discrimination. The same applies to the argument that curfews cut down on drinking and driving. A teen who drinks is violating the law, and if he gets behind the wheel, he is doubly guilty. But why should teens who are not drinking and driving be penalized for the actions of those who do? A better idea is to focus on those who do wrong and leave the innocent alone. A final argument often made in favor of curfews is that they keep teens safe. But concern for safety is sometimes a convenient excuse for discrimination. For instance, women were denied jobs as police officers and firefighters for decades on the grounds that those jobs were "too dangerous." But danger, whether on the job or in the streets, is an equal-opportunity threat. If the streets are unsafe, then they are unsafe for all age groups, not just for teenagers. <u>Cities should leave the power to set curfews where it belongs—in the hands of parents.</u>

Questions

1. Underline the paragraph's topic sentence.
2. What arguments does the writer use in saying that teen curfews are discriminatory?

   It is discriminatory to keep teens off the streets because of crimes they might

   commit. Teens who don't drink and drive should not be penalized for the actions of

   those who do. If streets are unsafe, they are unsafe for everyone, not just teens.

3. Double-underline the paragraph's summary sentence.

TOPICS FOR PRACTICING ARGUMENT AND PERSUASION

Small Scrawls: Imaginative Short Writings

What is a Small Scrawl? A "scrawl" is something written quickly. In this case, it is a page or so of quick writing that allows you to practice a particular type of writing—in this case, argument or persuasion. Have fun with it!

Small Scrawl 1: Sell It!

You apply for a sales job, and the manager tells you, "If you can sell flowers from this display to the next customer who walks through the door, you have the job." Here comes your first customer. In a Small Scrawl, sell those flowers!

Small Scrawl 2: Money and Happiness

An old saying tells us that money can't buy happiness. Actress Bo Derek once said that anyone who believed money did not buy happiness just didn't know where to shop. What do you think? Explain in a Small Scrawl.

Small Scrawl 3: Policy Matters

Write a Small Scrawl arguing why one of your school's policies is unwise. Some students object to policies limiting the number of absences, while others fret at library policies that allow a book to be checked out for only two weeks. Still others object to exams that all students must pass before graduating. Brainstorming with other students will help you to get your thoughts focused on your school's policies.

Argument Assignment 1: Child Care

Paragraph

Does attending day care while their parents work harm children or help them? Write your argument in one paragraph.

Argument Assignment 2: Banned

Paragraph

Write a paragraph supporting the following fill-in-the-blank topic sentence:

"If I ran the world, _____ would be banned."

Note: On this topic, you might get a better paragraph from a small, concrete topic than from a large, abstract one. For example, "television" or "open-toed sandals" might be more manageable topics than "hatred" or "racism."

Argument Assignment 3: Testing, 1, 2, 3 . . .

Paragraph

The following topics deal with testing in one form or another. Choose one of the topics and write a paragraph supporting one side of the issue.

1. Is the practice of employers testing job applicants for illegal drugs a good idea?
2. Should colleges require students to take a test demonstrating competence in reading and writing before issuing a diploma?
3. Should every newborn be tested for AIDS?
4. Should teachers be periodically tested in their subject area to make sure their knowledge is current?

TOPICS FOR COMBINING METHODS OF DEVELOPMENT

Comparison-contrast, cause-effect, and argument are methods of looking at logical connections between ideas. How are they alike? How do they differ? How does one affect another, and what logical arguments can be made for or against an idea? The following assignments ask you to combine one or more methods of development as you complete the assignment.

Mixed Methods Assignment 1: Community Service

Argument and Cause-Effect

Some colleges are incorporating a community service component into the graduation requirements of the college or into the requirements of specific programs. As you argue for or against such a requirement in your own college, base your argument on the effects of mandatory community service on students or on the community at large.

Mixed Methods Assignment 2: Same or Different?

Comparison-Contrast and Cause-Effect

Write a paragraph that discusses the ways in which you and a close friend or family member are alike or different. As you discuss each similarity or difference, describe the effect that it has on your relationship. Focus on either similarities or differences.

Mixed Methods Assignment 3: Givers and Takers

Argument, Comparison-Contrast, and/or Cause-Effect

Although most people fall somewhere between the two extremes, clearly some people are givers and others are takers. Givers work for the betterment of their community, give to their families, and always seem to be doing something for others. Takers rely on the help of others. It may even sometimes seem as though they are using other people to accomplish their own goals. If one has to make a choice, is it better to be a giver or a taker?

In this paragraph, you will answer the question with an argument—that is, your topic sentence will state that it is better to be a giver or better to be a taker. Although the paragraph is essentially an argument, structure it to include either comparison-contrast or cause-effect. If you include comparison-contrast, do so by showing the contrasts between being a giver and being a taker. If you include cause-effect, focus on one of the two alternatives (It is better to be a giver . . .) and show the effects of choosing that particular alternative.

REAL-WORLD ASSIGNMENTS

The Real-World Assignments below allow you to mix methods in writing assignments that mirror the types of writing you might do outside the classroom.

Real-World Assignment 1: Vet on a Roll

Argument and Description

You are an advertising copywriter. You have been hired to promote a service that is completely new in your area. A local veterinarian, Dr. Karen Goodhart, has outfitted a large truck as a mobile veterinary facility. In this facility, she can perform lab tests and even some surgeries. Her practice will consist entirely of home visitation of pets. It is your job to decide which advantages and features of Dr. Goodhart's practice should be stressed. Write a sixty-second radio spot to advertise Dr. Goodhart's mobile veterinary practice to the public.

Real-World Assignment 2: Snack Attack

Comparison-Contrast and Argument

You are a second-term college student. During your first term, you attended classes in two different buildings on campus. In these buildings, vending machines dispensed soft drinks, water, and snacks, which you were allowed to bring into class. This term, a new building has opened, and in this building, the rules have changed. The friendly vending machines are gone, and no food or drink (not even bottled water) is permitted on the classroom floors. Write a letter to the editor of the student newspaper in which you compare and contrast the situation in the older buildings and the newer building and argue for a loosening of the rules in the new building.

Real-World Assignment 3: Parking Dilemma

Cause-Effect and Argument

You are a resident in a historic town that depends heavily on tourism. The town's historic preservation board has turned down the idea of an aboveground parking garage near the historic district, and a new proposal has been made to build a more costly underground facility at taxpayers' expense. You can take the part of a merchant who favors building the garage, a member of the historic preservation board who does not want traffic congestion near the historic district, or a taxpayer favoring or opposing the garage. Write a paragraph stating your position and explaining the positive or negative effects that a parking garage will have.

Real-World Assignment 4: Computer Purchase

Comparison-Contrast and Argument

You are the technology resources manager for a large company. The company is planning to purchase state-of-the-art desktop computers for all employees. Because technology is your area of expertise, you have been asked to recommend two computers, comparing and contrasting the two in terms of price, memory, and other features, and to recommend the one you think is best for the company. For this project, you will need to do some online research to find two comparable computers.

mywritinglab   For support in meeting this chapter's goal, log in to **www.mywritinglab.com** and select **Paragraph Development: Comparing and Contrasting**, **Paragraph Development: Cause and Effect**, and **Paragraph Development: Argument**.

CHAPTER **10**

Writing an Essay

> ✎ **Chapter Goal:** Write a clear, organized essay that includes an engaging introduction, supportive body paragraphs, and an effective conclusion.

·ADMIT ONE·

T
I
C This ticket entitles those who have
K mastered the essay to move freely
E within the academic world, to express
T themselves in a way that professors will
respect, and to modify the essay format
to fit any type of academic writing.

·ADMIT ONE·

You are about to meet a form of writing that offers a ticket to just about anywhere in the academic world. When you master the fundamentals of the essay,
you master a form of writing that can be used to express an opinion, analyze a
poem, or compare two methods of government. Shrunk down a bit, it can be used
to answer a question on an essay test or an employment application. Expanded
a bit, it can be used to write a research paper, a term paper, or even a master's
thesis. Even this textbook is, in many ways, an expansion of the essay format.

Focus on the Essay: Beginning to End

The Dark Knight, *which featured Heath Ledger as the Joker and Aaron Eckhart as Two-Face, is considered perhaps the best Batman movie to date.*

The movie opens as the Joker robs a bank and continues with the villain robbing mob bosses of their money. Then the movie develops into the classic Batman versus Joker struggle that defines many Batman stories. Though the basic plot is a familiar one, the movie is wildly entertaining. Why? The answer is that while the movie's structure may have been typical, the set-up, action, and ending were unexpected, well scripted, and well acted. These elements made the movie fun to watch.

Writing an essay is much like creating a movie: You need a beginning scene for the set-up (the introduction), action in the middle (the body), and a fantastic ending that leaves the audience wanting more (the conclusion). Essays may follow certain patterns, but each one will be different depending on what you as the writer want to say and how you want to say it.

Reflect on It

Take a movie you've recently seen, and explain the "introduction," the "body," and the "conclusion." How does this particular movie follow the organization of an academic essay?

Parts of an Essay

mywritinglab

Visit MyWriting Lab for additional practice recognizing the essay.

Once you learn to write an essay, you can modify the essay form and length to suit your purpose for writing. Here's how an essay looks: First comes an introduction that catches the reader's attention, provides background, introduces the subject, and states the **thesis**, or the main idea of the essay.

Then come the **body paragraphs**. Each one discusses one aspect of your thesis. The topic sentence of each paragraph tells which thesis point the paragraph will develop.

The essay ends with a **conclusion** that sums up the points you have made and lets your reader know that you have ended the essay.

A diagram of a five-paragraph essay follows. Study it to get a mental map of the essay; then use it for planning and checking your own essays.

Structure of an Essay

Introduction

- The first sentence attracts the reader's attention.
- The introduction provides background and introduces the subject.
- The last sentence states the thesis (main idea) and may list the points of development.

First Body Paragraph

- The topic sentence states the first thesis point that you will develop.
- Support sentences give specific examples, information, and explanation of the topic sentence.
- A summary sentence (optional) sums up the entire paragraph.

Second Body Paragraph

- The topic sentence states the next thesis point that you will develop.
- Support sentences give specific examples, information, and explanation of the topic sentence.
- A summary sentence (optional) sums up the entire paragraph.

Third Body Paragraph

- The topic sentence states the third thesis point that you will develop.
- Support sentences give specific examples, information, and explanation of the topic sentence.
- A summary sentence (optional) sums up the entire paragraph.

Conclusion

- The first sentence of the conclusion is a broad, thesis-level statement. It may restate the thesis.
- The last sentence of the conclusion is satisfying and final-sounding.

Sample Essay

Like Father, Like Son

attention-getting opening

"Like father, like son," my aunt always said. Then her eyes would slide over to my mother in a secretive way, and I knew even as a child that it was not a compliment. Now that I have a child of my own, it is important to me to prove my aunt's words

thesis statement

wrong. As a parent, I plan to be different from my own father in all of the ways that count.

topic sentence 1

The first difference that my aunt—and my child—will see in me is that I will lead a more sober life than my father did. During all my growing-up years, my father abused alcohol and drugs.

support

Since he and my mother were not together, I never saw the worst of it. But even on our rare visitation days, he could not take me to a ball game or a mall without stopping by a convenience store for a six-pack. Maybe because of that example—or maybe because I was young and stupid—I followed in my father's footsteps for a while. But now that I am older and have a son, my wild days are over. I realize the importance of setting a good example and of

summary sentence

being a role model to him. Drugs and alcohol will never be a part of the image of me that my son Brandon carries through life.

topic sentence 2

Another difference will be in my financial support of my child. My father drifted from job to job and had periods of unemploy-

support

ment, so his financial support was undependable. To make ends meet, my mother had to work two jobs, one in the mornings on a hotel janitorial staff and the other waiting tables on a part-time basis. Even then, times were often tough. Financial support is part of being a father. It is the reason that I work, and the reason

summary sentence

I am enrolled in school. Brandon's mother will never have to work an extra job because I am not meeting my obligations.

topic sentence 3

Unlike my father, I am going to be there for my child. My

support

father's visits were as unpredictable as his support checks. He was not there when I was six and had my tonsils taken out, and he was not there for my high school graduation. I will be there for Brandon. Brandon's mother and I have chosen to live separately, but both of us agree that I should have an active role in his life. When he was a baby, I held him and fed him and changed his diapers. Now, I am the one who takes him to T-ball practice and

summary sentence

attends all his games. He can count on me to be there during the important moments in his life.

(continued)

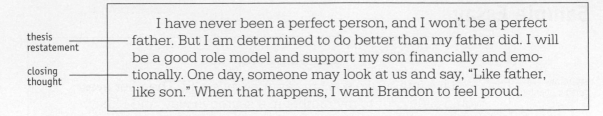

thesis restatement ——

closing thought ——

I have never been a perfect person, and I won't be a perfect father. But I am determined to do better than my father did. I will be a good role model and support my son financially and emotionally. One day, someone may look at us and say, "Like father, like son." When that happens, I want Brandon to feel proud.

Meeting the Challenge of Essay Writing

How do you get from an idea or assignment to a polished, fully developed essay? It is sometimes difficult to make the transition from paragraph-length compositions to essays. The length and the format of your assignments have changed. But the basic principles you have been following have not changed. The writing process is still the same: You still prewrite, plan, draft, revise, and proofread.

Similarly, the characteristics of an effective paragraph also apply to the essay. **Direction, unity, coherence,** and **support** are part of the makeup of effective paragraphs *and* essays. Review those characteristics below, and see how these qualities of effective writing apply to the essay.

Characteristics of an Effective Essay

1. **Direction** means that the essay has a strong thesis sentence that states the main idea and sets the course that the essay will follow.
2. **Unity** means that the essay makes one main point and sticks to that point. Each body paragraph may discuss a different thesis point, but the essay never strays from the idea expressed in the thesis.
3. **Coherence** means that the essay is logically connected and easy to follow.
4. **Support** means that the essay contains specific and detailed discussion of the idea stated in the topic sentence.

Writing the Essay

mywritinglab

Visit MyWriting Lab for additional practice writing an essay.

Because the essay is so much longer than the paragraphs you have been writing, it may appear to be not so much a writing exercise as a major construction project. Like any major project, the construction of an essay is accomplished word by word, sentence by sentence, paragraph by paragraph. The next few sections of the chapter deal with the major parts of the essay and with how those parts fit together to form a coherent whole.

Providing Direction: Writing the Thesis Statement

mywritinglab

Visit MyWriting Lab for additional practice with the-sis statements.

Your **thesis statement** is the most important sentence in your essay. It states the main idea of your essay, often states or implies your attitude or opinion about the subject, and gives your essay **direction**. In an essay, the thesis statement is the controlling force behind every sentence and every word. It is a promise to your reader that you will discuss the idea mentioned in the thesis statement and no other.

Types of Thesis Statements

When constructing your thesis statement, you have a choice. You may write a **thesis with points** that lists the points the essay will cover or a **thesis without points** that does not list the points of development.

The Thesis with Points

A thesis with points presents the main idea and the points of development, listed in the order in which you will discuss them in the essay. The thesis with points has a long tradition in college writing. Listing your thesis points provides a road map that lets the reader see where the essay is headed.

Examples of a Thesis with Points

       point 1   point 2

1. Playing with my children, shopping with my mother and sister, and

           point 3

   spending time with my husband are my weekend pleasures.

         point 1

2. Older students may attend college to prepare for a new career, to

     point 2   point 3

   advance in their present career, or to satisfy a hunger for learning.

     point 1   point 2   point 3

3. Action, an exciting plot, and strong characters are essential ingredients for

   any movie.

EXERCISE 1 | **COMPLETING THESIS STATEMENTS**

Complete the following thesis statements. Answers will vary.

1. Our camping trip was a disaster. We were pelted by rain, bitten by <u>mosquitoes</u>, and <u>chased</u> by <u>a bear</u>.

2. Writing an essay requires good ideas, <u>strong organization</u>, and <u>the patience to revise and proofread</u>.

3. <u>Intelligence</u>, <u>generosity</u>, and <u>a sense of humor</u> are my mother's best qualities.

4. These days, the best candidate for the job is usually the one <u>who knows comput-</u><u>ers</u>, <u>possesses strong language skills</u>, and <u>thinks independently</u>.

5. Some of the things people fear about getting old are <u>loneliness</u>, <u>poverty</u>, and <u>poor health</u>.

The Thesis without Points Listed

A thesis without points listed presents the central idea of the essay without enumerating the points of development. Without the "road map" that listing your points provides, it is even more important that your essay flow logically and smoothly. Therefore, topic sentences require careful planning so that they are clearly connected to the thesis. When you plan a thesis without listed points, plan each topic sentence, too, to ensure that you stay on track. Not listing thesis points does not mean that you do not plan them, it simply means that you do not list them.

Examples of Thesis Statements without Points Listed

Thesis: My weekend pleasures revolve around my family.

Topic sentence 1: On Friday evenings, my husband and I often enjoy a movie.

Topic sentence 2: On Saturdays, I take the children shopping or swimming.

Topic sentence 3: Every Sunday, we visit my parents or my husband's parents.

Thesis: Starting an exercise program has made me a healthier person.

Topic sentence 1: For one thing, exercise has improved my aerobic capacity.

Topic sentence 2: I also feel stronger since I began exercising.

Topic sentence 3: Thanks to my exercise program, I have also dropped a few unwanted pounds.

Thesis: Losing my parents at the age of eighteen was the hardest thing I have ever gone through.

Topic sentence 1: The accident was so sudden and my parents were gone so quickly that I was numb for weeks.

Topic sentence 2: My parents' death left me with a tremendous amount of responsibility.

Topic sentence 3: It is still difficult seeing the milestones ahead that my parents will never share with me.

EXERCISE 2	WRITING THESIS STATEMENTS

For each of the following topics, write a thesis statement without points.
Answers will vary.

1. What was the best (or worst) day of your life?

    _____

2. Should drivers and their passengers be required to wear seat belts?

    _____

3. Is there ever any justification for cheating?

    _____

4. If you could spend a week visiting any place in the world, where would you go?

    _____

5. What popular activity do you consider overrated? Why?

    _____

Getting Started: Introducing the Essay

mywritinglab

Visit MyWriting
Lab for additional
practice with
introductions.

It is said that you will never have a second chance to make a first impression. Because first impressions are so important, it pays to put extra effort into your introduction. However, an introduction is more than just a way to make a good impression. It does several jobs that no other part of the essay could do quite so effectively.

Purposes of an Introduction

1. *An introduction draws your reader into the essay.* The first sentence of your introduction should be irresistible. It won't always turn out that way, but aim high anyway.
2. *An introduction presents the general topic of your essay.* When you ease into the thesis by bringing up your general topic first, your reader has time to turn her thoughts away from whatever is on her mind—the price of gas or what to eat for lunch—and to get in the mood to listen to what you have to say.
3. *An introduction provides necessary background.* Background information is not always necessary. But if it is, the introduction is a good place for it. Background information tucked into the introduction gives the necessary details to set up the rest of the essay.

4. *The introduction presents your essay's thesis.* The most important job of an introductory paragraph is to present your essay's thesis. Every sentence in the introduction should follow a path of logic that leads directly to your thesis, which will be the last sentence of your introduction. Once you have stated the thesis, stop. Your body paragraphs will flow naturally from a thesis that comes at the end of the introduction.

Writing the Introductory Paragraph

Introductions that draw a reader in don't just happen; they are carefully crafted. Three common types of introduction follow. Try them all, using the examples as models.

The Broad-to-Narrow Introduction

The *broad-to-narrow introduction* is a classic style of introduction. Sometimes called the *inverted triangle introduction,* it funnels your reader from a statement of your topic to the narrowest point in the introduction: your thesis.

Example of a Broad-to-Narrow Introduction

Driving is a great American pastime. Roads and highways swarm with drivers going back and forth from work, school, shopping, or recreation. And with so many drivers on the road, there are bound to be a few who should never have been trusted with that little plastic card called a license. The worst drivers on the road are those who tailgate, those who weave in and out of traffic, and those who drive drunk.

The Narrow-to-Broad Introduction

Instead of beginning with a statement of your general topic, the *narrow-to-broad introduction* begins at a point that is smaller than your thesis—often just a detail—and expands toward that thesis. With this method, you can create an unusual and intriguing opening.

Example of a Narrow-to-Broad Introduction

I see the tires first, grimed with the dirt of a long journey. Then I catch a glimpse of a face in the window of the long, boxy vehicle. The RV passes, giving me a last look at the bikes hooked to the back and "The Wanderer" painted above the rear window. I just don't get it. Why would anyone want an RV? An RV is a poor choice for vacationing because of its cost, size, and the chores that come along with it.

The Contrast Introduction

Gold placed on black velvet in a jeweler's window takes on extra luster against the contrasting background. In a *contrast introduction*, your ideas can shine through the drama of contrast. Starting with a contrasting idea is an easy and effective technique to use. Make sure that your introduction contains a change-of-direction signal such as *but* or *however* so that the two contrasting elements are clearly set apart.

Example of a Contrast Introduction

Modern life often means that people work long hours to buy possessions that they don't have time to enjoy. Sometimes, it means that children have too many toys and not enough of their parents' time. But many people have decided to leave the rat race. Instead of striving for more, these families live on less in exchange for working fewer hours or sometimes quitting their jobs entirely and working for themselves. A simpler lifestyle can reduce stress, teach self-reliance, and encourage family unity.

The Body Paragraphs: Unity

mywritinglab

Visit MyWriting Lab for additional practice revising essays for unity.

Once you begin writing the body of your essay, you are in familiar territory once again. You already know how to write a topic sentence and support a paragraph. In writing the three body paragraphs of a five-paragraph essay, you are simply doing that familiar task three times. In an essay, however, each of the three body paragraphs is directly related to the thesis statement. Specifically, each body paragraph discusses one aspect of the thesis statement. This arrangement gives an essay **unity**. Look at the thesis from an earlier sample essay:

Thesis: As a parent, I plan to be different from my own father in all of the ways that count.

From reading the thesis, it is clear that the writer plans to discuss *ways his parenting style will be different from his father's.* Each body paragraph, then, will discuss one way in which the writer will be different from his own father.

Now look at the topic sentences from the sample essay and notice how each relates directly to the thesis (*being different from his father*) and also discusses a distinct and separate point of that thesis:

Topic sentence 1: The first difference that my aunt—and my child—will see in me is that I will lead a more sober life than my father did.

Topic sentence 2: Another difference will be in my financial support of my child.

Topic sentence 3: Unlike my father, I am going to be there for my child.

A thesis statement gives your essay direction. The topic sentences must follow that direction, or the unity of the essay will be compromised.

EXERCISE 3   ELIMINATING FAULTY TOPIC SENTENCES

Each of the following thesis statements is followed by three topic sentences. Circle the letter of the topic sentence that does *not* support the thesis statement.

1. Football is my favorite sport.
   a. When I was in high school, I was on the football team three out of four years.
   b. During football season, I am glued to my television set to watch the games.
   c. Attendance at professional football games has risen in recent years, demonstrating the sport's popularity.

2. Like dogs themselves, there are several kinds of dog owners.
   a. Like the wolves they are descended from, dogs are pack animals and need to be part of a social structure.
   b. Some dog owners simply want a companion around the house or apartment.
   c. Another type of dog owner wants the protection that a dog can provide.

3. The city's new indoor skating park will have several positive effects.
   a. Skaters and skateboarders will have a place to call their own.
   b. Pedestrians will no longer be endangered by fast-moving skaters on downtown streets.
   c. Skating can be dangerous, so skaters and skateboarders should always wear safety equipment.

4. Our college should consider scheduling classes around a "Wonderful Wednesday" or a "Fabulous Friday," a day during the week when no classes meet.
   a. A weekly day off would give students time to go to the library and work on class projects.
   b. The idea has been rejected by the school's administration because students might not use the day productively.
   c. The day would also give professors a chance to catch up on grading and have conferences with students.

5. Looking at the movies of the 1950s and the movies of today, it is easy to see how their differences reflect social changes over the years.
   a. Romantic comedies of the 1950s almost always ended in marriage, but today's movies reflect a different social trend.
   b. Special effects in 1950s movies were unsophisticated, but today's advanced techniques produce impressive effects.
   c. Minorities and women were often stereotyped in the 1950s movies, but today's films have fewer stereotyped characters.

The Body Paragraphs: Support

Once you have written the thesis and the topic sentences, you have an outline composed of the main idea and the major subpoints of the essay. All that remains is to flesh out the body paragraphs with strong, vivid, detailed **support**, just as you would in any paragraph. Review the principles of support by completing the exercise below.

| EXERCISE 4 | RECOGNIZING SPECIFIC SUPPORT |

The introduction on recreational vehicles (RVs) is extended here with three sets of body paragraphs. In the blank to the left of each paragraph, mark *S* if the paragraph contains specific support and *V* if the paragraph contains vague support.

Body Paragraph 1a

_____*V*____ First of all, an RV is extremely expensive. As anyone who has ever visited an RV dealer or an RV show can testify, the initial outlay for a new RV is considerable. In addition, there are numerous other expenses associated with RV ownership. Some of those expenses relate to traveling, while others relate to maintenance. For the cost involved in owning and maintaining an RV, a person might be able to enjoy a luxury vacation at the finest hotel.

Body Paragraph 1b

_____*S*____ First of all, an RV is extremely expensive. A new RV can cost $100,000 or more, as much as some houses. Add to that the cost of gas, maintenance, hookup at RV parks, storage, and repairs, and an RV becomes even more expensive. If a person put $100,000 in the bank at 5 percent interest instead of buying an RV, he would get $5,000 in interest each year, enough to take a vacation or two every year and still keep his $100,000.

Body Paragraph 2a

_____*S*____ Second, an RV is just too large. Its size makes it difficult to maneuver and gives it a greater stopping distance, thus requiring greater driving skill. It can't be parked just anywhere, nor can its driver just whip into a drive-through for a hamburger when the travelers get hungry. Its size also makes storage a problem during the months when it is not being used. My neighbors' RV is too large to fit into their garage, so they had to build a separate storage barn in their backyard just to keep their RV out of the weather. That's fine for people who have the money and the space to build a storage facility, but people who live in condominiums or who have small lots have to make other arrangements. An RV's size makes it more of a liability than an asset.

Body Paragraph 2b

_____V_____ Second, an RV is just too large. The size of an RV is enormous, dwarfing every car on the road. Size has several disadvantages. Many of the maneuvers that drivers of smaller vehicles take for granted cannot be performed by an RV because of its size. Further, there is the consideration of RV storage, which must take size into account. An RV's size makes it more of a liability than an asset.

Body Paragraph 3a

_____S_____ Finally, an RV is just too much work. People who travel in RVs have to clean, cook, make beds, and empty toilets. If they run out of food, they have to shop. If I have to take all that work on vacation with me, I might as well stay at home. When I go on vacation, I want to eat in restaurants and have my food brought to me perfectly prepared. I do not want to stand over a hot stove and know that I have to wash dishes after I eat. In the morning, I want to leave my bed unmade and my towels in the tub, walk on the beach, and come back to my room to find everything in perfect order. In an RV, I would have to do all the work myself.

Body Paragraph 3b

_____V_____ Finally, an RV is just too much work. People who travel in RVs have to do all the work normally associated with maintaining a house. In many cases, there are other associated tasks that relate to travel. Why would a person take all of those household chores on vacation? It seems to me that the purpose of a vacation is to leave everyday chores behind. In a hotel these tasks are accomplished by the hotel staff, so that the traveler has little to do. That seems like the ideal situation for any traveler. That way, when the traveler returns home, he is rested and refreshed, not worn out from trying to accomplish all the tasks associated with traveling in an RV.

The Body Paragraphs: Coherence

An essay requires not only coherence *within* paragraphs, but coherence *between* paragraphs. That is, movement from one paragraph to the next should seem graceful, natural, and seamless.

Coherence within paragraphs is provided by transitional words, use of pronouns, and use of repetition. (To review these principles, glance back at the section on coherence in Chapter 5.) Look below for tips for making graceful transitions between paragraphs.

Tips for Smooth Transitions

1. In the first body paragraph, you do not necessarily need a transitional word. If you want to use one to indicate that this paragraph is making the first of several points, the choices are easy: *first of all, one reason* (*factor, cause,* or similar term), or *first.*

2. The second body paragraph gives you more choices. You can use a phrase like *a second reason* or a word such as *next, another,* or *also.* For variety, try slipping the word or phrase in the middle of your topic sentence instead of using it at the beginning: "Job security is *another* reason I have chosen a career in the medical field."

3. The third body paragraph gives you all of the transitional options of the second body paragraph and a few others as well. Since the third body paragraph is your last, you can use expressions such as *finally* or *the last reason.* If you are using emphatic order (order of importance), you might want to try *most important, the major factor, best,* or *worst.*

4. Transitions of time and place are preferable in narrative or descriptive essays and can be used in any essay organized around time or place. Transitions of time might include phrases such as *after I had finished my classes for the day, the next morning,* or *a few weeks later.* Transitions of place might include phrases such as *just down the hall, across the room,* or *on the other side of town.* (A more complete listing is provided in Chapter 5.)

5. Avoid anything that would confuse your reader or make it seem as though you are just mechanically plugging in transitions instead of trying to write an artful essay. A reader would be confused, for instance, if you used a phrase such as *in conclusion* to begin your last body paragraph. The last body paragraph contains your last major point, but it is not your conclusion. (In fact, *in conclusion* is not even a recommended opening for conclusions.)

Any transitional sequence that uses counting throughout—*first, second, third; my first reason, my second reason, my third reason*—gives your reader the impression that you are using transitions mechanically and unthinkingly rather than choosing them for best effect. If you use numbers, combine them with other transitional expressions for best effect: *the first reason, another factor,* and *the final cause.*

A Graceful Exit: The Conclusion

mywritinglab

Visit MyWriting Lab for additional practice with conclusions.

The etiquette of concluding an essay, like that of ending a telephone conversation, is simple: Keep the goodbye short, and don't introduce any new information that keeps the other person hanging on too long.

After the specific and detailed support of the body paragraphs, the first sentence or two of your conclusion takes the reader back to a broad, thesis-level view of the topic. Often, this takes the form of a thesis restatement.

Then comes the closing statement, harder to write but vital because it is the last impression your reader takes away from the essay. The key requirement of a closing statement is that it should *sound* like a closing statement. It should sound as final as the slam of a door.

Sample Conclusion 1: A Summary Conclusion

The summary conclusion sums up the main points and ends with a sentence that provides a ring of finality.

Example of a Summary Conclusion

Recreational vehicles are too costly, too big, and too labor intensive. When I go on vacation, I'll drive my own car, stay at a reasonably priced motel, and let someone else do all the work.

Sample Conclusion 2: A Recommendation

A recommendation conclusion suggests a solution to a problem raised in the essay. A logical way to end an essay that discusses a problem is to offer a solution or suggest that one is on the horizon.

Example of a Recommendation Conclusion

In spite of a few problems, our school library is a valuable resource for all students. Extending weekend and evening hours, keeping the computer room open whenever the library is open, and setting aside a special group study area for students who need to converse will go a long way toward easing the frustrations many students experience when they visit the library.

Sample Conclusion 3: A Prediction

A look toward the future is another good way of ending an essay. The example below ends an essay discussing the advantages of online music stores with a summary and a prediction.

Example of a Prediction Conclusion

Online music stores have a wide selection of merchandise, offer convenience, and allow customers to listen before they buy. With all of the advantages on online music stores, it won't be long until the conventional music shop ceases to exist.

Wordsmith's Corner: Sample Essays

Below are two essays. One explores "inner space"—the writer's search for who she is—while the other discusses exploration of outer space. Read each essay and answer the questions that follow.

Essay 1

In the essay, Autumn discusses her lifelong search for her heritage.

A Mixed-up Kid

I opened the wedding invitation and read, "As we form a new union, we draw on the strength of our heritage and the unity of our family. Celebrate with us." A wave of longing and downright envy swept over me. I do not envy Kim her marriage. I envy her strong sense of who she is and where she comes from. It is a feeling I have never known. All my life, I have been searching for who I am.

When I look at the two people who adopted me twenty years ago, I feel lucky, secure, and loved, but I see nothing of where I came from. My mom's red hair and freckles tell of her Irish heritage, but say nothing of mine. She sets our Thanksgiving table with her great-grandmother's crystal and linen and tells me to look forward, not back. She just doesn't understand. My dad, who has Scottish and Cherokee ancestry, understands a bit more. When I was younger, he would stretch his arm out, comparing his fawn-colored skin to mine. "That's a pretty close match," he'd say. "You might have a little Cherokee in you somewhere." Hearing him say that always made me feel connected and secure.

When I look in the mirror, I see no clear clues to my heritage. I see light caramel skin, coarse, wavy hair, and brown eyes. My face is wide, with a small, flat nose and delicate lips. I am short—just 5'2"—with a sturdy build. When I was in the sixth grade, a new girl at school asked me what race I was. I told her that my parents had told me my background was mixed, but I was adopted and not sure what the mixture was. "I'm a mixed-up kid, too," she said. I thought that was the perfect way of expressing how I felt—a mixed-up kid.

When I look to society to find out who I am, I get no answers. My adoption records are sealed, and my mom and dad know nothing about my birth parents. Was I given up by a teenage mother who loved me but couldn't keep me? Was I thrown into a dumpster by an uncaring parent or left on a doorstep by a desperate one? I may never know. Because I know so little about my background, I have tried to seek a mirror in many different social groups, and I have friends of all races. Yet there is still a part of me that feels like an outsider in any group because I am not sure where I come from.

For the most part, I am a happy person who feels fortunate in her family and friends. Mostly, I follow my mother's advice to look forward and not back. But when I look around, hoping to see a reflection of who I am, all I see is a mixed-up kid.

Questions

1. Underline the thesis statement. Is it a thesis with points listed or without points listed?

The thesis statement has no points listed.

2. Underline the topic sentence of each body paragraph.

Essay 2

Harley, the writer of this essay, discusses the value of the U.S. space program.

The Final Frontier

On the day that I was born, Neil Armstrong, the first person on the moon, took "one small step for man, one giant leap for mankind." I guess that is why I have always taken an interest in our space program. The space program, unlike many government programs, has something to give to every American.

The space program links every American to the mysteries that lie beyond Earth's atmosphere. Human beings have always looked to the heavens with a sense of wonder. Only in the last century have we actually been able to explore our moon and other planets. The Mars *Pathfinder* mission in 1997 gave us a closer look at the red planet with a mobile rover that took soil samples and pictures from all angles, even showing us a Martian sunset. The *Voyager* traveled outward among the planets, taking photographs of red Mars, ringed Saturn, and blue Neptune. In photographing the planet Jupiter and its moons, *Voyager* discovered ice on one of the moons, and where there is water or ice, there is the possibility of some form of life. What could be more exciting than the discovery of life beyond Earth's boundaries?

Another important contribution of the space program is that it gives us heroes in a time when heroes are few. Alan Shepard, the first American in space, had the courage to go "where no one had gone before" as Americans sat mesmerized in front of black-and-white TV sets. Neil Armstrong, the first to set foot on the moon, was my hero for many years. Sally Ride, the first woman in space, inspired people all over the United States to cheer her on with the words "Ride, Sally Ride!" And who can forget Christa McAuliffe, the first teacher in space, who died tragically in the explosion of the space shuttle *Challenger?* John Glenn, a veteran space traveler, was the first senior citizen to test the effects of space travel on an aging body. All of these people are heroes because they are pioneers, among the first to travel where our descendants may one day live.

The most important contribution of the space program is the hope it gives for the future. All around us, the earth's resources are being depleted. If we don't replenish the forests, repair the ozone layer, and repopulate endangered species, life on Earth will be in danger. The growth of the human population also raises the possibility that one day, Earth may no longer have room for everyone. The vast, cold reaches of space may hold a solution to these problems. Human beings have lived for months on the *Mir* space station, and that is just the beginning. Self-sustaining space colonies could eventually provide room for a spreading human population. People may one day find a way to populate the planets in the solar system or even to reach other solar systems through interstellar travel. In the future, space may hold the key to human survival.

Space travel has fascinated me since I was old enough to know that on my birthday, the first human set foot on the moon. I believe that the space program returns value for every penny that is spent on it. It links us to the ancient mysteries of the universe, it provides us with heroes, and it brings hope for a brighter future for every human being.

Questions

1. Underline the thesis statement. Is it a thesis with points listed or without points listed?

   The thesis statement has no points listed.

2. Underline the topic sentence of each paragraph.

Topics for Writing Essays

Constructing Your Essay

No matter which topic you choose, the method of constructing your essay is the same. Follow the steps below as you write your essay.

Step 1: Prewrite using one of the methods in Chapter 2. Prewriting is even more important in longer compositions, which usually require more thought. Try **freewriting** for ten minutes about the image that you have of yourself and that various other people or groups have of you. Or try a cluster diagram, with each branch of the cluster showing a different view of the person you are. Next, review your prewriting and choose the three viewpoints you want to include in your essay. Make sure that they are separate and distinct viewpoints. If all three viewpoints show you as the exact same person, your three body paragraphs will be nearly identical in content.

Step 2: Plan, making a brief outline of the essay you plan to write. Here's where you'll decide on the order in which to present your paragraphs and get some idea of the supporting examples you want to use. After you've done a scratch outline, write out your thesis statement and your three topic sentences. You may want to change the wording later, but completing a thesis statement and topic sentences prepares you for the next step.

Step 3: Draft your essay as completely as you can. If you have trouble with the introduction, start with your thesis and proceed from there. You can always come back and write your introduction later. Complete each paragraph as if it were a freestanding paragraph, much like the ones you have been writing in class, and include plenty of specific support for each topic sentence. When you have completed your draft, including the introduction and conclusion, lay it aside for a while before proceeding to the next step.

Step 4: Revise your essay. First, do a visual check. Does your essay look balanced, with the three body paragraphs approximately equal in length? Are the body paragraphs framed by an introduction and conclusion that are shorter than the body paragraphs?

Next, check your word count. If you are writing on a computer, your word processor can check the count for you. If you have handwritten your essay, pick three lines at random. Count the number of words in each line, add them together, and then divide by three. The result is your average number of words per line. Count the number of lines, then multiply by the average number of words per line. The result is your approximate word count. If your word count is between 400 and 550, you are in the ballpark. If the count is over 600, check to make sure that everything you are saying supports your thesis and that you are not repeating yourself. If your word count is under 400, you probably need to add more support.

Finally, check the specific parts of your essay, using the Checklist for Revision at the end of this chapter.

Once you have completed the Checklist for Revision, you might want to show your essay to a classmate. Ask your classmate to focus on content and clarity. Does he or she understand everything you say? Are examples plentiful and specific?

Once you have looked at your essay, completed the revision checklist, and perhaps gotten a second opinion, rework the essay.

Step 5: Proofread after you have revised your essay and are satisfied that it is the essay you want to turn in. Correct any errors in grammar or spelling.

Essay Assignment 1: Among Your Belongings

Imagine that someone wanted to get to know you, but being the busy person you are, you were unavailable. Instead, you give the person the key to your place and let them look through your things. What things might they find that reveal who you are? The things you choose to write about should say something about who you are, what you like to do, and what you value. This assignment gives you a framework in which to discuss the things you value most. An introduction, three topic sentences, and a conclusion have been written for you. Your job is to fill in the content of the paragraphs, to flesh them out and give them strong support. Choose things, not people or animals, to discuss, though it is certainly fair to choose something that reminds you of a special person or animal in your life. As you complete the essay, feel free to change anything about the introduction, conclusion, or topic sentences that does not fit your essay.

Among My Belongings

If I gave a stranger the key to my home and permission to look through my things, that person would get to know me even if she had never met me before. The things that I value are not necessarily worth a lot of money, but they have meaning for me. Among the electronic devices, T-shirts, and keepsakes, an observer would find three things that reveal various aspects of my personality and my values. These things are _____, _____, and _____.

_____ is the first item of interest that might tell a stranger something about me _____
_____
_____.

As the observer looked a little further, she would see my _____
_____
_____.

The final item that would tell someone who I am is my _____
_____
_____.

Though I am clearly more than the sum of my possessions, the things that I own can tell someone a lot about who I am. My interests and my values would be apparent to anyone who saw my _____, my _____, and my _____.

Essay Assignment 2: Reflections of You

In Sample Essay 1, "A Mixed-up Kid," the writer speaks of searching for her reflection in her adoptive parents, in her own mirror, and in society. Write an essay discussing who you are in your own eyes and in the eyes of two other groups or individuals. Possibilities include your parents, friends, teachers, children, or members of various groups you belong to. Or you might move in a widening circle, first discussing how you see yourself, how your close friends see you, and how casual acquaintances see you. Another possibility, particularly if your view of yourself has changed radically over the years, is an essay explaining how you saw yourself in the past, how you see yourself now, and how you hope to see yourself in the future.

Essay Assignment 3: What Interests You?

In Sample Essay 2, "The Final Frontier," the writer discusses a lifelong interest in the space program. What interests you, either as an onlooker or as a participant? Are you a movie buff, a music lover, or a follower of a particular sport? Do you read every book and watch every TV special about a particular historical period? Are you into collecting teacups, playing the alto sax, riding motorcycles, attending garage sales, or singing in a choir or chorus?

Whatever your interest, write about it, following the steps of the writing process as outlined in Constructing Your Essay. To get started, think of the following questions:

How long have you been pursuing your interest?

Who got you started?

What is it that inspires and fascinates you about it?

Are there people associated with it that you admire?

What activities do you participate in that involve your interest?

Essay Assignment 4: Mountains or Beach?

If you were hired by a company that had facilities in both mountain and beach locations, which would you choose? Think of the scenery, the terrain, and the activities available in both places. Once you have chosen, write an essay discussing three reasons for your preference.

Essay Assignment 5: Description of a Place

Think of a place where you go often. Perhaps it is a library, a coffee shop, a quiet bench on your campus, or a favorite place to shop. Whatever place you choose, it should be a relatively small place, not a town, an entire campus, or a giant theme park. It should be small enough for you to describe it completely.

Now that you have thought of this place, think about the sights, sounds, smells, and textures of the place. Jot down your impressions. Decide on the particular features of the place that you would like to describe, and then decide on the order in which to describe them. Feel free to include not just the place itself, but also the people you ordinarily see there. Try to make your reader feel as though he or she is there with you.

Essay Assignment 6:

What kinds of students do you most enjoy or dislike having in class with you? Give specific examples.

Checklist for Revision

The Introduction

✔ Does the introduction draw the reader in?
✔ Does the introduction provide background information, if needed?

The Thesis

✔ Is the thesis the last sentence of the introduction?
✔ If the thesis does not include points of development, does it state the main idea broadly enough to include all the points you raise in your body paragraphs?
✔ If the thesis lists points, does it list three separate and distinct points?

Topic Sentences

✔ Does each topic sentence raise one separate and distinct thesis point?
✔ If the thesis lists points, are body paragraphs arranged in the same order as thesis points?

The Body

✔ Does each body paragraph provide specific detail and examples for each thesis point?
✔ Have you provided enough specific support for each thesis point?
✔ Does each sentence of each body paragraph support the topic sentence?

The Conclusion

✔ Is the first sentence of the conclusion a broad, thesis-level statement?
✔ Is the conclusion short, with no new information introduced?
✔ Is the last sentence satisfying and final-sounding?

Checking Coherence

✔ Have you used transitional words effectively within paragraphs?
✔ Have you used transitional words effectively between paragraphs?

mywritinglab   For support in meeting this chapter's goal, log in to **www.mywritinglab.com** and select **Recognizing the Essay, Essay Organization**, and **Thesis Statement**.

CHAPTER 11

Writing Summary Reports

> ✍ **Chapter Goal:** Summarize and paraphrase the work of others appropriately and write effective summary reports.

It usually takes a long time to find a shorter way.
—Author Unknown

W hile the saying above is probably intended as a warning against taking shortcuts, it could just as easily apply to writing a summary. Summarizing is a painstaking process, involving fully understanding the material to be summarized, determining the most important ideas, and condensing them in your own words. A summary may be a shorter way of saying something, but writing one can be a time-consuming process.

Focus on Summary: Choosing Relevant Detail

Police officers have to write reports on crimes, accidents, and arrests. It's their job to write these reports as condensed yet accurate portrayals of the events that occurred.

To do this, they must choose relevant facts to include in their reports—for instance, that a driver had alcohol on his breath and failed a roadside sobriety test. They also must omit unnecessary detail that doesn't help readers understand what happened—for example, that the driver wore a blue shirt. Since police reports are legal documents and may be used in court, police officers have to be very careful in their summary of events and their choice of details. A blue shirt that is extraneous to one report may become important if the officer is trying to provide a description of a perpetrator who fled the scene of a crime. Officers must therefore be selective in their accounts, depending on the situation and the purpose of the report.

Whatever profession you choose to go into, you will need to summarize information to tell a boss, client, or coworker. Because you will not want to waste anyone's time, including your own, it is to your advantage to learn how to summarize effectively and concisely.

Reflect on It

Consider all the different professions that interest you. In what ways do you see the art of summary helping you further your career in those professions?

Writing a Summary Report

mywritinglab
Visit MyWriting Lab for addi-tional practice summarizing

A **summary report** condenses and presents information, often from a single source. When you write a summary, your goal is to concisely present information from an essay, article, or book so that your reader understands the main points. In a summary, present the author's ideas objectively, without including your opinion of them. At the end of your report, if the assignment calls for it, write a brief evaluation of the essay, article, or book.

Five Steps in Writing an Article Summary

The following section shows you the steps in summarizing an article.

Step 1: Choose a Topic and Find Sources of Information

Your instructor may assign a topic or area of investigation, or you may be asked to choose your own topic. Choose a topic that interests you and on which information is readily available.

Articles on your topic may be found in periodicals, databases, or on Internet sites. An overview of each type of information source is provided below.

Periodicals

Periodicals are publications such as newspapers, magazines, and scholarly journals that are published on a regular basis—daily, monthly, or quarterly, for example. Newspapers and magazines are written for the general public, while journals are written for scholars in a particular field.

Subscription and CD-ROM Databases

Periodical articles are also available through subscription databases or CD-ROM databases. Most college libraries subscribe to databases such as ABI/INFORM, Academic Search Premier, ERIC, and Research Library. These databases may contain full-text articles from journals, newspapers, or magazines, or they may contain article abstracts. **Full-text articles** are complete articles, exactly as originally published. **Article abstracts** are summaries intended to help you decide if a particular article is appropriate for your purposes. If it is, you will need to find the original article in the periodical in which it originally appeared.

What Does the Suffix of an Internet Site Mean?

An Internet site's suffix can tell you a bit about the person or group behind the site. Here's a key to decoding Internet suffixes.

.org: A nonprofit organization

.edu: A college or university

.gov: A U.S. government site

.com: A business or private individual

Internet Sources

Some websites may contain articles previously published in print media; others may contain articles written for and published on the Internet. Internet sources vary widely in quality; it is up to you to evaluate the credibility of each site you visit.

Advice for Online Researchers

Go Online

Research used to mean poring through stacks of books and periodicals. Today, it usually means sitting in front of a computer screen. Even print sources must be located through online catalogs, indexes to periodicals, and databases. These resources may still seem alien to you at first, even if you are comfortable using a computer. If you need help, do not hesitate to ask for it.

Find a Friend

Find someone in class who will agree to be your research partner. You don't need an expert; nor do you need someone who is working on the same topic. All you need is someone who is willing to go through the process with you. The two of you can work side by side and handle the rough spots together.

Ask a Librarian

Librarians are experts in finding information, and they are there to help. Explain your project and the kind of information you are looking for, and a librarian will point you in the right direction.

Print the Information

When you find useful articles online, print them out so that you will not have to go looking for them should you need them again. Documentation of online sources requires that you note the database you are using and the date you accessed the information.

Be Patient

Be patient with yourself and with the process of finding information—it always takes longer than you think it will.

Step 2: Evaluate Sources of Information

Once you have found articles on your chosen topic, evaluate them to make sure they are suitable for your summary. Use the following evaluation criteria to find suitable articles.

- *Length.* If an article summary covers all the major points in the article, it will probably be 25 to 50 percent of the length of the article. Therefore, if you are assigned a five-hundred-word summary, choose an article of between one thousand and two thousand words. These figures are only an approximation. The idea is not to choose an article so short that a few sentences can summarize it or one so long that you cannot summarize the entire article.

- *Readability.* In any article that you choose, expect to find unfamiliar terminology and concepts that are new to you. After all, the purpose of research is to learn something new. However, some articles are written for experts in the field and may be hard for a layperson to understand. If you read the article three times and still feel as though you are trying to comprehend ancient Egyptian hieroglyphics, choose another article.

- *Publication Date.* A publication date helps you evaluate the timeliness of the source. In fields where change is rapid, such as medicine or computer technology, finding the most up-to-date-sources is essential.

- *Author.* Is the author an authority in the field? If not—if the author is a journalist, for example—does the author consult and quote credible, authoritative sources? These questions help you evaluate the authority and credibility of your source.

Step 3: Read Your Article Thoroughly

Before taking any notes, read your article through once or twice. Then, highlighter in hand, look for the following information.

- *Main idea and major ideas.* Read through the article, highlighting the main idea and the major ideas. Remember, the main idea is often found at the beginning of an article and repeated at the end. Major ideas are often stated at the beginning of a paragraph or after a headline, and they are often supported by examples. Don't worry if this step takes more than one reading.

- *Examples and supporting details.* Once you have found the main and major ideas, go back and highlight the supporting details and examples that most directly support those ideas. A summary contains a minimum of the detail that fleshes out the main idea, so be selective and choose only necessary and important details.

- *Information for the Works Cited list.* The final step in taking notes from your source is to write down the information you will need for your Works Cited list. In a summary of a single article, you have only one work to cite, but it is important to cite it correctly. A list of information needed for your Works Cited list follows.

For all sources:

- Author
- Title of article
- Title of the magazine, journal, or newspaper in which the article was published
- Date of publication
- Volume and issue number of periodical, if available
- Page numbers

For online sources, note the following additional information:

- Date of access
- The URL (Universal Resource Locator, or complete Web address) of an article from a website; or other identifying information such as site name or Digital Object Identifier (DOI)
- The name of the database for articles accessed from subscription databases through a college (or other) library, and the name of that library

Step 4: Draft Your Paper

Drafting a summary report is similar to drafting an essay. Your draft should contain the following elements:

- *Introduction.* The introduction includes the author's name, the title of the article, and the central idea of the article.

Sample Introduction to a Summary

Interviews are crucial for both employer and prospective employee. The employer needs to find the best person for the job; the prospective employee wants a fulfilling job and perhaps even a career. In his article, "The Interview: Rights and Wrongs," David Butcher describes techniques that can be employed by both interviewer and job-seeker to make the interview process easier and more productive.

- *Body paragraphs.* The body paragraphs outline the most important points in the article. The topic sentence of each body paragraph should state the idea that the paragraph will develop and incorporate a reference to the author.

Sample Topic Sentence

Smith believes that the Internet can be especially beneficial for senior citizens.

The inclusion of the author's name in each topic sentence makes it perfectly clear to the reader that you are still discussing the ideas of another person rather than your own ideas.

The body paragraph itself will paraphrase the author's ideas; that is, you will state the ideas in your own words. Quoting the author is also permissible, but use quotations sparingly. Most of the summary should be in your own words.

- *Conclusion.* The conclusion sums up the author's ideas and presents your evaluation of or reaction to the article. Placing your evaluation in the conclusion is a way of clearly separating your reaction to the article from the summary, but if your evaluation is lengthy, you may place it in a final body paragraph before beginning the conclusion.

Step 5: Format, Proofread, and Cite Your Source

The final draft of your paper will include proper formatting and a Works Cited page. Use the documentation style recommended by your instructor, or follow the brief guide to MLA and APA style that appears later in this chapter. Your instructor may also ask you to provide a copy of the article you are summarizing.

Paraphrasing: An Essential Skill

One of the most difficult tasks of writing a summary is to put an author's ideas in your own words. When you **paraphrase**, you capture an idea using your own sentence structure and your own words. Here are some pointers to help you when you paraphrase:

- It's always permissible to repeat key terms. If the author uses the term "geriatric medicine," there's no need to rephrase it as "medical care of the elderly."
- Unusual phrasings should be reworded. If the author refers to a spider web as "a spider's gossamer trap," a paraphrase should simply call it a spider web.
- The sentence structure of a paraphrase should vary from that of the original material.

Making the Switch to Academic Writing

As you move from personal writing to academic writing, you need a new set of strategies. Here are five helpful strategies for academic writing:

A Learning Approach

While personal writing allows you to write about the things you know best, academic writing requires a willingness to read, understand, and evaluate the ideas of others.

Objectivity

Personal writing is *subjective*—that is, it allows you to express your own feelings and opinions. Academic writing, on the other hand, is *objective*. It requires you to put aside your own opinions and to look without bias at the ideas of another person—even if you disagree with those ideas.

Knowledge of Key Terms

When you read and write about academic subjects, understanding key terms is essential. Make an effort to learn the meanings of unfamiliar terms. This essential step will help your comprehension of the article you are reading and will help you to use the terms knowledgeably in your writing.

Use of Third Person

When you write from personal experience, you often use the *first person* (*I*, *me*, or *my*). In academic writing, *third person* is preferred, even when you are expressing your own opinion. Thus, you would write, "Several of Emily Dickinson's poems reflect an obsession with death," not "I think that Emily Dickinson's poetry reflects an obsession with death."

Careful Acknowledgment of Others' Work

If you are quoting or using the ideas of other writers, it is important to acknowledge your sources both informally within the text of your paper and formally through parenthetical references and a Works Cited page. Failure to acknowledge sources is called **plagiarism** and is considered cheating.

EXERCISE 1   RECOGNIZING EFFECTIVE PARAPHRASES

For the numbered items below, circle the letter of the better paraphrase.

1. Original material:
    From retail buying to bargain hunting, the Internet has revolutionized shopping. Shoppers used to be limited to the retail stores in their area; now, online stores across the country or even across the world are open to them if they have

an Internet connection and a credit card. Shoppers can find items that are not available locally and can compare prices to get the best deal. Bargain hunters no longer have to get up early and spend a Saturday morning scouring area yard sales. Now they can sign on to eBay or similar auction sites to find second-hand items in a variety of places, from Alaska to Nebraska and beyond. Both buyers and sellers have benefited from the availability of online shopping.

(a.) Because of the Internet, shoppers are no longer limited to stores within driving distance. Online shopping has made a wider range of goods available to both retail shoppers and bargain hunters. Online stores and auction sites have benefited both buyers and sellers.

b. The Internet has revolutionized shopping from retail buying to bargain hunting. Shoppers are not limited to items that can be bought locally. From Alaska to Nebraska, online shoppers can get better deals from eBay and other auction sites as well as from online retail stores the world over.

2. Original material:
    The cat's eye is different from the human eye in several respects. The first and most obvious difference is the shape of the pupil as it contracts. The pupil in the human eye is round, and when exposed to light, it contracts, retaining its circular shape. The round pupil of the cat's eye, on the other hand, contracts from each side to form an ellipse. Unlike a human eye, a cat's eye shines in the dark. The cat's eye contains a reflective layer of cells that picks up and reflects available light, enhancing the vision of these nocturnal animals. A final feature that distinguishes the cat's eye from the human eye is the nictitating membrane, an inner eyelid that serves to clean and protect the cat's eye.

    a. The cat's eye is different from the human eye in the shape of the pupil as it contracts. The pupil in the human eye retains its circular shape when it contracts, but the round pupil of the cat's eye contracts from each side to form an ellipse. Unlike the human eye, the cat's eye shines in the dark. Finally, the cat's eye has a nictitating membrane, an inner eyelid that cleans and protects the cat's eye.

    (b.) Though they perform the same function, the cat's eye and the human eye are different in some ways. While the pupil of the human eye remains round as it contracts, a cat's pupil becomes elliptical. The cats' eye also reflects in the dark, something the human eye cannot do. In addition, the cat's eye possesses a protective inner eyelid called the nictitating membrane.

EXERCISE 2   PARAPHRASING SHORT PASSAGES

Paraphrase the following short passages.

Passage 1

Aggressive driving is characterized by the tendency to view driving as a competition rather than as a means of getting from one place to another. While most drivers are content to move along with the flow of traffic, aggressive drivers weave from lane to lane, seeking any advantage that will place them ahead of others. Aggressive drivers are also more likely to tailgate and honk the horn in an effort to intimidate other drivers or simply to move them along faster. When confronted with heavy traffic, aggressive drivers often engage in dangerous behavior such as passing on the right, using utility or turn lanes as driving lanes, and ignoring traffic signals. Paradoxically, aggressive drivers often pride themselves on their skill. They see other, more cautious drivers as the problem, not themselves.

Answers will vary.

_____

_____

_____

_____

_____

_____

_____

Passage 2

The National Academies' Institute of Medicine now recommends an hour per day of total physical activity such as walking, stair-climbing, or swimming. Many Americans fall far short of reaching this goal. Some are still trying to catch up to the previous guidelines of thirty minutes of activity five days per week. A century ago, Americans would have found it easier to exercise for an hour per day. Without cars, people walked more, and without modern labor-saving devices, life required more physical exertion. Today, however, many Americans sit at a desk all day and come home to sit in front of a TV or a computer. Even those who make an effort to exercise often find that they lack the time.

Answers will vary.

_____

_____

_____

_____

_____

_____

EXERCISE 3   SUMMARIZING A PASSAGE

In a paragraph, summarize the following longer passage. Use your paraphrasing skills to condense the ideas in the original material.

Developing Focus

One of the most valuable skills a student can develop is focus. Focus is the ability to concentrate on one thing for an extended period of time, shutting out everything else. The person who is focused has no trouble with homework; her mind is on the task until it is finished. The focused person has no trouble concentrating during a test. She does not even notice the voice of the lecturer in an adjacent classroom, the tapping pencil of the student two rows over, or her instructor's squeaky chair.

People differ widely in their ability to concentrate. Some seem capable of laserlike focus on any job until it is completed. Others are easily distracted, jumping up from homework to do a hundred small but suddenly urgent tasks as the homework gets pushed further into the background. Like any other skill, the ability to focus can be learned and reinforced through practice. To improve your ability to concentrate, start by establishing a set time and place to study. If possible, study at the same time and in the same place every day. Establishing a routine gives study the importance it deserves and helps make studying a habit. Then, to keep yourself on task, set a small timer as you begin studying. Start by setting the timer to go off after fifteen minutes. Until the timer goes off, give studying your full attention. If your mind wanders—and it will—pull it back to the task. Then reward yourself with something small: five minutes of solitaire on your computer or a trip to the refrigerator for a glass of iced tea. Time your reward, too—about five minutes should be sufficient. Then set the timer for another fifteen minutes.

As concentration becomes a habit, that habit will spill over into the classroom, too. You will be better able to focus on your instructor's words or on the test you are taking. If extraneous noises during tests still distract you, invest in a pair of earplugs to shut out noise as you take your test.

The ability to concentrate is a necessary skill. Fortunately, it is a skill that can be improved with effort.

Answers will vary.

_____

_____

_____

_____

_____

_____

_____

_____

_____

_____

_____

Using Documentation Styles

When you write a college paper, you will likely be asked to use one of two documentation styles: APA (American Psychological Association) style or MLA (Modern Language Association) style. In general, MLA style is used in fields such as English language and literature, media studies, and cultural studies. APA style is used in fields such as psychology, sociology, business, economics, nursing, and criminal justice. There are other documentation styles, such as Chicago style, which is used in fields such as art and art history, music, theology, and women's studies, and CSE (Council of Science Editors) style, which is used in the sciences, but MLA and APA styles are the focus of this chapter.

Why Use a Documentation Style?

Documentation styles help you document, or cite, sources that you use in your research. One reason to cite your sources properly is to avoid accidental plagiarism. But the use of documentation styles goes beyond the need to avoid plagiarism. Documentation styles have their own methods of formatting, titling, and spacing.

The driving force behind documentation styles is the need for consistency. Imagine if spelling were as inconsistent today as it was in Shakespeare's day, when even Shakespeare's name had several variants, including "Shakspear" and "Shaxberd." It would be easy to become sidetracked wondering about different spellings of a word or name and to lose sight of the content entirely. By requiring a particular format for your papers, your professors help ensure that style remains a background issue and content moves to the foreground.

In addition, when your instructors require you to use a particular style or format, they are preparing you for a time when you might be a writer yourself and be required to use the style that is required in your field. At the very least, your instructors are preparing you for a time when you will be required to adapt your writing to a particular style or format on the job. Every workplace has a format for writing memos, letters, and reports. Again, consistency keeps the focus on the content of those documents. In addition, just as academic writing has certain conventions that must be followed, workplaces, too, have particular writing styles. A police report would never say, "The low-down slimeball tried to get away from me, so I grabbed the sucker, and got him in a headlock." Instead, an officer would choose factual, unemotional words, such as "The subject attempted to escape and was restrained."

In addition to requiring a particular format, each documentation style requires a list of sources. The list of sources is an important part of your research paper. Ideas are the currency of the academic community, and a list of references in a standardized style makes it easier to share those ideas. You list sources so that other researchers in your field could go back to the original source, read it, and form their own conclusions.

Brief Guide to APA (American Psychological Association) Style

The following section outlines a few basic principles of APA style. For complete information on APA style, consult the *Publication Manual of the American Psychological Association*, available in most college libraries and bookstores.

Formatting Your Paper

- Use 8½-by-11 inch paper.
- Preferred fonts are 12-point Times Roman and 12-point Courier.
- Double-space the text, including the references page.

- Use one-inch margins all around.
- Indent paragraphs one-half inch.

Preparing the Title Page

The title page will include a page header in the upper left corner, a page number in the upper right corner, and the title, author, and affiliation are centered and double-spaced in the upper half of the page, as illustrated below. The page header should be an abbreviated (one- or two-word) version of the title.

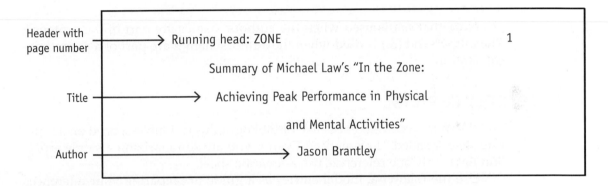

Referencing Sources within Your Paper

Within your summary, references to your source are **parenthetical references**, not footnotes. APA style calls for brief references enclosed in parentheses and placed immediately after the referenced idea or at the end of the sentence that contains the idea.

The following examples show the APA style of reference.

Examples of Parenthetical References

Single Author

✔ According to Steven Pinker (2002), the idea that parents are at fault if children turn out badly is an outgrowth of the "tabula rasa" or "blank slate" theory. This theory holds that cultural influence, not genetics, determines personality and character.

✔ The idea that parents are at fault if children turn out badly is an outgrowth of the "tabula rasa" or "blank slate" theory. This theory holds that cultural influence, not genetics, determines personality and character (Pinker, 2002).

Note that when the author's name is used as part of the sentence rather than in a separate citation, the date follows in parentheses.

Two Authors

✔ Skybo and Buck (2007) reported that children mentioned physical symptoms of stress, such as headache or stomachache, more often than emotional symptoms such as fear or anxiety. The authors say this occurs because children tend to report stress only when it manifests as a physical symptom.

✔ Children mentioned physical symptoms of stress, such as headache or stomachache, more often than emotional symptoms such as fear or anxiety because children tend to report stress only when it manifests as a physical symptom (Skybo & Buck, 2007).

Note that *and* is used when the authors' names are part of the sentence. The ampersand (&) is used when the authors' names are part of a parenthetical citation.

The References List

In APA style, your references list, or bibliography, is double-spaced on a separate sheet headed "References." Even if you are summarizing a single article and have only one reference, use a separate sheet.

Use the following model entries as a guide to preparing your references list. When there are two examples, the first is from an online source, the second from a print source.

Journal Article

No Author Listed

Anxiety disorders in primary care patients. (2007, March 6). *Annals of Internal Medicine, 146*(5), 317–325. Retrieved from www.annals.org

John and Abigail Adams: The original power couple. (2008, April). *American History, 43*(1), 38–41.

One Author

Gearhart, G. (2006, October). Controlling contraband. *Corrections Today, 68*(6), 24–29. Retrieved from www.aca.org /publications/ctmagazine

Bergerson, A. (2007, January). Exploring the impact of social class on adjustment to college: Anna's story. *International Journal of Qualitative Studies in Education, 20*(1), 99–119.

Multiple Authors (up to Seven)

Budnitz, D., Shehab, N., Kegler, S., & Richards, C. (2007, December 4). Medication use leading to emergency department visits for adverse drug events in older adults. *Annals of Internal Medicine, 147*(11), 755–W229. Retrieved from www.annals.org

Skybo, T., & Buck, J. (2007, September). Stress and coping responses to proficiency testing in school-age children. *Pediatric Nursing, 33*(5), 410–418.

In APA style, when an article has two to seven authors, all authors are listed.

Eight or More Authors

Schlooz, W., Hulstijn, W., Broek, P., van der Pijll, A., Gabreëls, F., . . . van der Gaag, R. (2006, December). Fragmented visuospatial processing in children with pervasive developmental disorder. *Journal of Autism & Developmental Disorders, 36*(8), 1025–1037. doi:10.1007/s10803-006-0140-z

In APA style, include a DOI (digital object identifier) whenever one is available. If you include a DOI, you do not need a URL for Web sources.

Tzimos, A., Samokhvalov, V., Kramer, M., Ford, L., Gassmann-Mayer, C., . . . Lim, P. (2008, January). Safety and tolerability of oral paliperidone extended-release tablets in elderly patients with schizophrenia: A double-blind, placebo-controlled study with six-month open-label extension. *American Journal of Geriatric Psychiatry, 16*(1), 31–43.

When an article has more than seven authors, the first six are listed, followed by an ellipsis (. . .) and then the final author's name.

Magazine Article

Zimmer, E. (2007, February). Taming the gypsy in her soul. *Dance Magazine, 81*(2), 62–66. Retrieved from www.dancemagazine.com

Socha, M., & Zargani, L. (2005, April 8). Viktor & Rolf turns retailing on its head. *WWD: Women's Wear Daily, 189*(74), 16.

Newspaper Article

Scott, A. (2007, November 12). Contagious cancers: Scientists are only beginning to discover the hidden role of some viruses and bacteria. *Boston Globe*. Retrieved from www.boston.com

Sabin, R. (2008, January 28). Constant struggle to conquer bacteria: Beating bad bugs: Economics and evolution frustrate effort to eliminate a growing threat. *San Francisco Chronicle*, p. A.1.

Article on a Website

Potts, T. L., & Reichenstein, W. (2008). What grads need to know about finances. *Forbes*. Retrieved from: http://www.forbes.com

Brief Guide to MLA (Modern Language Association) Style

The following section outlines a few basic principles of MLA style. For complete information on MLA style, consult the *MLA Handbook for Writers of Research Papers*, available in most college libraries and bookstores.

Formatting Your Paper

- Double-space the text, including the Works Cited page.
- Use one-inch margins.
- Indent paragraphs one-half inch.
- Do not include a title page. Instead, place your name, your instructor's name, your course name, and the date at the top of the first page, each on a separate line, each line flush with the left margin. Center the title above the first paragraph. This material, like the rest of your paper, should be double-spaced.

Referencing Sources within Your Paper

Within your paper, MLA style requires **parenthetical references**, not footnotes. For a paragraph in which you mention the author's name, the only parenthetical reference necessary is the page number placed at the end of the paragraph. If you use a direct quotation, place the page number after the quotation.

Example

✔ According to Steven Pinker, the idea that parents are at fault if children turn out badly is an outgrowth of the "tabula rasa" or "blank slate" theory. This theory holds that cultural influence, not genetics, determines personality and character (16).

✔ The idea that parents are at fault if children turn out badly is an outgrowth of the "tabula rasa" or "blank slate" theory. This theory holds that cultural influence, not genetics, determines personality and character (Pinker 16).

The Works Cited List

Use the following model entries as a guide to preparing your Works Cited list. The first example in each section is from an online source, the second from a print source. MLA style requires that sources be labeled according to medium: "Print," "Web," "Interview," or "Film," for example. Online sources also include the database and the date of access.

Journal Article

Berman, Ron. "Hemingway's Michigan Landscapes." *Hemingway Review* 27.1 (2007): 39–54. *Advanced Placement Source.* Web. 29 Jan. 2011.

Zapf, S. A., and R. B. Rough. "The Development of an Instrument to Match Individuals with Disabilities and Service Animals." *Disability & Rehabilitation* 24.1–3 (10 Jan. 2002): 47–58. Print.

Magazine Article

"Four Things We Don't Want to Smell." *Skiing* Dec. 2007: 114–115. *Academic Search Complete.* Web. 29 Jan. 2011.
Pinker, Steven. "The Blank Slate." *Discover* Oct. 2002: 34–40. Print.

Newspaper Article

Hummer, Steven. "Surviving the Sweet Science." *ACJ.com.* Atlanta Journal-Constitution, 13 Oct. 2002. Web. 13 Jan. 2011.

Axtman, Kris. "The Newest Prison Contraband: Cellphones."
Christian Science Monitor 11 June 2004: 1. Print.

Article on a Website

Dunleavy, M. P. "Twenty Ways to Save on a Shoestring." *MSN/ Money.* MSN, 29 Dec. 2001. Web. 16 Oct. 2011.

Note that the date of publication is followed by the date of access.

A Model Summary Report

For her summary report, Sandra chose an article dealing with college graduates and the job market. The article, along with Sandra's highlighting and annotations, appears below, followed by the final draft of her summary report.

Graduated? Seven Job Tips for College Graduates

Susanne Goldstein

The job data might seem rosier, but finding a job is harder than ever—especially for the nearly 2 million college students who will have graduated this year. Newly minted college graduates are up against experienced mid-career professionals who are also out there searching. Use these seven career tips to change your job search into a job offer.

main idea

#7 Claim your career as your own

Here's a secret: Careers don't just happen, they are made. If you want to have the job and career that you want and need, it will take an enormous amount of work on your part. Many graduating seniors mistakenly believe that it is the responsibility of their career service officers to get them a job. Not true. Until you are ready to take charge of, and own, your career, you won't have one.

major point: own your career

Owning your career takes discipline and true commitment. Sending 20 standard cover letters and résumés to Monster.com and hoping for a response isn't enough. To land the job you want, you need to make it your full-time job. Yes, this is hard—you have finals and papers to write, and friends to party with—but if you don't work hard, you won't get a job. Guaranteed.

Make a commitment to yourself and to your job search by claiming your career as your own. By pledging to do this, you will stop being a victim of the job market and will begin to take control over your future. This may sound hokey, but this symbolic act will help you accelerate your job search. Raise your hand and make the pledge.

#6 Know who you are and what you have to offer

Take a moment and think about what kind of car you drive. Or if you don't drive a car, what you'd like to drive if you had one? What adjectives or characteristics do you associate with your car? Safe? Well-engineered? Versatile? Eco-friendly? Car companies spend gazillions of dollars crafting the brands of the cars they sell. Looking for safety? Buy a Volvo. Superior engineering? Audi. Versatile? How about a Ford minivan? Want to save the planet? You better drive a Toyota Prius.

When we decide to purchase a car, we consciously or subconsciously have certain attributes in mind that will make the car "feel like me." That is exactly why car companies pour money into brand development, brand marketing, and advertising.

You are no different. As you go out and try to "sell" yourself to future employers, it's essential that you know exactly who you are and what you want to be. *major point: brand yourself* By being clear about what you can offer to hiring managers, you will be able to get people to buy into the brand that is you.

Discovering your own brand is an essential component of differentiating yourself from other hungry job seekers. Think about what makes you different, what skills you have to offer, what you're passionate about, and what you can bring to an employer that will make them want to pick you. If you were a car, what would be your best selling points? If you don't know what they are, ask a counselor, a parent, or friend to help you uncover what makes you a great product for employers to buy.

#5 Say goodbye to "um," "ah," and LOL

major point: communication It doesn't matter how smart or qualified you are, if you can't write, speak, and act like a professional, no one will hire you to be a professional. If you've never learned to communicate in a serious and capable manner, it's going to be very difficult to get hiring managers to take you seriously as a candidate. Here are some critical tips for communicating like a pro:

Practice conducting conversations in an articulate and confident way. Cut the words "um," "like," "you know," and "ah" out of your vocabulary. Do your homework. Prepare and research a company, organization, or person before you speak or write to them. In written correspondence, it is never okay to use text-isms (ENUF, LOL, GR8) or other 140-character shortcuts. Double-check your written work. Typos and misplaced words reflect poorly on you. Follow up from all communications with written notes that show your appreciation, summarize the conversation, and suggest a next course of action. Be personable. People buy people. If they like you, they are more likely to want to help, and maybe even hire you.

#4 Reverse engineer the job market

Most job searchers today spend hours sifting through job listings trying to cook up ways to fit themselves into an existing job opening. This rarely works and is akin to finding a needle in a haystack.

What if you were to turn this model on its head? Instead of looking for specific job openings at various companies, use job listing sites to reverse engineer the job market and find specific companies where you want to work.

The goal is to identify the types of places where you believe you'd be a good fit. Most people coming out of college think more about skills they possess rather than the "fields" or "industries" they want to work in. Use sites like Monster.com, CareerBuilder.com, and Idealist.org, which provide robust company profiles, as a place where you can research the kinds of organizations that appeal to you. Learn what products or services they provide.

Think about who you are, and seek out places that are doing the things you want to be doing. Do NOT look to see if there are any current job openings. That's not your objective right now. Your goal is to find out what companies you should be approaching as part of your job search—and the best companies for you are those where you feel like you'd be a great fit.

major point: find companies that fit you

#3 Find "in" people—and build lasting relationships

If you find a company you really like, look at its website—specifically its staff, management, and board pages to see who works there.

Why? Because getting a job today is based as much on who you know, as it is on what skills and experience you have. Luckily, in a technologically networked world, getting access to people is easier than ever. Whereas in the past, knowing "in" people was confined to the privileged few who had enough influence to make connections, in today's world, offline and online connections can be made by just about anyone, just about any time.

You need to embrace this reality to be successful at career development. With LinkedIn, Facebook, and other social networks, your circle of contacts is no longer limited to who you know; it's now expanded to who those people know as well.

major point: use the computer to find connections

Take a look at the team pages on a company's website. See if you can find someone in your networked-network that can make an introduction, or help you get an introduction. This is how you get "inside" an industry or a company and start building lasting relationships with people who are not only already doing the kind of work you want to be doing, but are recommending and hiring as well. Knowing these people is the absolute best way to get a job.

Sometime you'll face a situation where you just don't have a way "in." In this case, gather your strength and make a cold call. Remember that to get what you want in life, you might need to step out of your comfort zone. Try new things and be a little daring.

#2 Network by 5s

Once you meet an "in" person, it's time to start networking. Networking is a vitally important part of 21st century career success, and is something you should embrace, not something "fake" or "manipulative." "Networking by 5s" is a technique that will enable you to build a network of supporters in lightning speed.

Here's how it works:

major point; network by 5's

Ask your "in" person to give you the names of five people who might be willing to share five minutes of their time to tell you about what they do for a living. Set up these "information sessions" with the intention of getting to know this person, and that is all.

Whether in person or on the phone, become an interested listener, and learn everything you can about what this person does, and how they got to be doing their job. Know that this meeting is not about you. Ignore your need for a job and focus on letting the person in front of you tell their story.

The funny thing is that by being a good listener and letting people talk about themselves, they'll end up thinking that you're wonderful. By showing genuine interest in them without asking for anything in return, you are giving them the affirmation that all humans need.

Because of this, they will take an interest in you, and when they do tell them a little about yourself and what you're interested in doing. Share your résumé with them, and before the meeting concludes, ask them for the name of five of their colleagues who might be willing to talk to you for five minutes.

This technique, of meeting five people for five minutes at a time, is the absolutely best way to fast track your job search. With each successful meeting you have, with each new group of five names, you increase your career network exponentially by a factor of five. Within weeks, you can know tens of people who are doing the kind of work you want to be doing. When an opening for a job interview materializes, your new connections will be ready to recommend you!

#1 Be the solution to your interviewer's problems

Interviewing is hard and scary. It always feels like there's too much on the line and you're nervous about getting the job that you can't focus in the moment. With the right kind of preparation, you can make your interview anxiety melt away. How? By becoming a great teller of stories.

Do you freeze up when someone asks you to talk about yourself? Or asks you to share a past work challenge? The reason answering these questions is hard is because you don't have a framework for your answers.

Aristotle gave us this framework when he first described the concept of storytelling in three acts. Good storytelling, he taught, has a beginning (the setup), a middle (the action) and an end (the resolution), and can be used to take listeners on a rewarding journey.

major point: be the solution to your interviewer's problem.

You can utilize this simple framework to become masterful at telling your own story, the story of your greatest challenge, and the best story of all—how you can be the solution to your interviewer's problems.

In today's work environment, hiring managers are overstretched and barely have time to hire the people needed to help them solve the challenges in front of them. Their immediate goal is to make the best, most appropriate hire and know that their problems are going to get solved.

1/2 inch

1 inch

Lopez 1

Double-spaced
throughout

Sandra Lopez

Business 1101

Dr. Wilder

7 February 2012

Title, centered ——————Article Summary: "Graduated? Seven Job Tips for College Graduates"

The class of 2011, with roughly two million college graduates, faces
fierce competition in the job market. Susanne Goldstein's article "Graduated? Seven Job Tips for College Graduates" offers seven ways to stand
out in a crowd of applicants.

Goldstein's article is structured like David Letterman's "Top Ten,"
in countdown form. The number seven tip is "Claim your career as your
own." This is not a mystical mental process, but the act of embracing the
hard work of sending résumés and setting out on the job search.

Tip number six is "Know who you are and what you have to offer."
This may seem simple, but Goldstein suggests that job seekers "brand"
themselves much in the same way an automaker might brand a particular
car, highlighting its most outstanding features. In a similar fashion, college graduates should know and market their own product: themselves.

The fifth tip concerns clear, effective communication. The article
advises graduates to drop "um," "like," and "you know" from their speech
before going on job interviews. After the interview, graduates should also
follow up with written, carefully proofread notes that do not contain tex-
tisms such as LOL and GR8.

Tip number four, "Reverse engineer the job market," suggests that
instead of trying to convince an employer that she is a "good fit," the
job seeker should use career websites to find companies that would be
a good fit for her. The best place to start the job search, the author

believes, is with companies that are in tune with the job seeker's own values and interests.

Tip number three involves finding the "in" people. The author confirms what we have often heard: Finding a job involves knowing the right people. Through social networking and career sites like Facebook and LinkedIn, the savvy job seeker might be able to connect with all the right people.

Tip two in the countdown is the most complex, a technique called "networking by fives." The job seeker asks one of his "in" connections for the names of five people who might be willing to give him five minutes of their time to talk about their work. This is not a job interview, but a further building of the network of people that the job seeker knows in the field or company in which he wants to be employed.

The final and number one tip in the countdown is "Be the solution to your interviewer's problems." How does the job seeker do this? By following Aristotle's advice and becoming a teller of stories. Stories give a framework in which to answer questions and in which to make a point. It's a way to speak of personal challenges and a way to be the solution to an interviewer's immediate problem of finding the right person to hire.

Susanne Goldstein's article provides much food for thought, and gives the reader new ways to think about meeting the challenges of finding a job. That is not to say that her advice gives any easy solutions. The art of storytelling may take years to master, and even eliminating the "ums" and "ahs" from speech is difficult, especially during a tense job interview. But every piece of advice is worth taking to heart and at least making a start on. These tips will work not only for a job interview but also for advancement throughout one's career.

First line is
flush with left
margin; any
subsequent
lines are
indented one-
half inch.

Lopez 3

Works Cited

Goldstein, Susanne. "Graduated? Seven Tips for College Graduates."

    CSMonitor.com. Christian Science Monitor, 13 May 2011. Web.

    25 May 2011.

SUMMARY REPORT ASSIGNMENTS

Summary Report Assignment 1: Summarizing an Article about Your Career or Major

Write a summary of an article that deals with some aspect of your chosen career or major. The article may be one about job opportunities in your field, or it may focus on a particular\ issue central to your field. Follow the step-by-step process outlined in this chapter to find your article, evaluate it, read it to find the main ideas, and write your summary.

Summary Report Assignment 2: Summarizing an Article That Solves a Problem

Write a summary of an article that helps you solve a problem in your life. Whether you are trying to find ways to save more money, impress an interviewer, organize your time, choose an automobile, or eat more nutritiously, dozens of articles await you in the library or on the Internet. Because articles of this type vary widely in length, be sure to choose an article substantial enough to lend itself to summarizing. Follow the step-by-step process outlined in this chapter to find your article, evaluate it, read it to find the main ideas, and write your summary.

Summary Report Assignment 3: Summarizing an Article That Explores a Social Issue

Write a summary of an article that explores a current social problem. You will find articles on homelessness, drug abuse, domestic violence, school violence, and many more issues of current concern in the library or on the Internet. Articles may vary in length, so be sure to choose an article substantial enough to lend itself to summarizing. Follow the step-by-step process outlined in this chapter to find your article, evaluate it, read it to find the main ideas, and write your summary.

mywritinglab   For support in meeting this chapter's goal, log in to
www.mywritinglab.com and select **Summary Writing**.

CHAPTER 12

Verbs and Subjects

🎵 **Chapter Goal:** Recognize subjects, verbs (including action, linking, and irregular verbs), and prepositional phrases and use them appropriately.

I couldn't do anything.
My verb didn't show up.

Without a verb, a subject would not get very far. A sentence is written about a subject, but the **verb** carries the action and relates that action to the other words in the sentence. Some verbs, called **linking verbs**, function as connectors for related words.

A **subject** is what the sentence is about. It is usually a noun or a pronoun. It is probably not the only noun or pronoun in the sentence, but it is the only one that enjoys such a direct grammatical connection to its verb. If you ask, "Who or what _____?" putting the verb in the blank, the answer to your question is always the subject of the sentence.

🎵 Action and Linking Verbs

Verbs work in two ways within a sentence. They show the action, physical or mental, of the subject of the sentence, or they link the subject with other words in the sentence.

Action Verbs

Action verbs show physical or mental action performed by a subject. Look at the action verbs below, highlighted in italic type.

Examples with Action Verbs

✔ Beth *sat* at her desk. (physical action)

✔ She *noticed* that her clock *had stopped.* (mental action, physical action)

✔ She *wondered* how long she *had been studying.* (mental action)

PRACTICE 1   RECOGNIZING ACTION VERBS

Underline the action verb in each sentence.

1. Buzz <u>leaped</u> for the volleyball.
2. Pilar quickly <u>ate</u> her tuna salad sandwich.
3. A crop duster <u>droned</u> overhead.
4. The dog <u>barked</u> loudly at the stranger's approach.
5. Melvina <u>returned</u> two books to the library's drop box.

Linking Verbs

A **linking verb** links its subject with a word that describes or renames it. The most common linking verb in English is the verb *to be,* in all its various forms: *is, are, was, were, has been, will be,* and so on. Look at the following examples to see how the verb *to be* functions as a linking verb.

Examples with *to be* Used as a Linking Verb

✔ The glass *is* empty.

The verb *is* links the subject, *glass,* with an adjective describing it.

✔ Li *has been* student body president for the past year.

The verb *has been* links the subject, *Li,* with a noun, *president,* that renames him. In other words, he could be referred to as either "Li" or "the student body president." (*Student* and *body* are adjectives.)

Other common linking verbs include the verbs *to seem, to appear, to grow,* and *to become.* Verbs of the senses, such as *to smell, to taste, to look, to sound,* and *to feel,* can be action or linking verbs, depending on how they are used.

Examples with Verbs of the Senses

L   The book *seems* interesting. (The verb links *book* with an adjective that describes it.)

L   The burned potatoes *looked* terrible. (*Looked* is a linking verb. The potatoes are performing no action.)

A   Terralyn *looked* at the schedule of classes. (The verb shows Terralyn's physical action.)

L   The sliced turkey *smelled* bad. (The verb links *turkey* with an adjective that describes it.)

A   The dog *smelled* his owner's pockets, hoping for a treat. (The verb shows the dog's physical action.)

The Linking Verb Test

To tell if a verb is a linking verb, see if you can substitute *is* or *was* in its place. If the substitution works, the verb is probably a linking verb.

Examples of the Linking Verb Test

?   The drone of the engine *grew* louder as the plane approached the airport.

L   The drone of the engine ~~*grew*~~ *was* louder as the plane approached the airport.

The substitution makes sense; therefore, *grew* is used here as a linking verb.

?   The friendship between Della and Miriam *grew* quickly because they shared many interests.

A   The friendship between Della and Miriam ~~*grew*~~ *was* quickly because they shared many interests.

The substitution does not makes sense; therefore, *grew* is used as an action verb.

?   After drinking four cups of coffee, Martin *felt* jittery.

L   After drinking four cups of coffee, Martin ~~*felt*~~ *was* jittery. (linking verb)

?   Casey *felt* someone tap her shoulder and turned to see who it was.

A   Casey ~~*felt*~~ *was* someone tap her shoulder and turned to see who it was. (action verb)

PRACTICE 2   RECOGNIZING ACTION AND LINKING VERBS

Underline the verb in each sentence. In the blank to the left, write *A* if the verb is an action verb and *L* if it is a linking verb.

L   **1.**   The picture on the wall <u>is</u> crooked.

A   **2.**   Lu Ana <u>smelled</u> the week-old milk.

L   **3.**   This crossword puzzle <u>looks</u> difficult.

A   **4.**   The squirrel <u>scampered</u> up the trunk of the tree.

A   **5.**   Kim <u>prepared</u> her report carefully.

A   **6.**   The company's representative <u>asked</u> for Zelda's account number.

L   **7.**   The scrambled eggs <u>tasted</u> good.

A   **8.**   Anna <u>tasted</u> the eggs cautiously.

A   **9.**   Two young men <u>lounged</u> against a car in the parking lot of the fast-food place.

L   **10.**   The mail carrier <u>seemed</u> cheerful.

Recognizing Verbs and Subjects

Finding the Verb

mywritinglab

Visit MyWriting Lab for additional practice recognizing verbs and subjects.

Finding the subject and verb of a sentence is easier if you look for the verb first. Following are some guidelines to help you spot the verb in a sentence.

1. A verb may show action.
   ✔ Laney <u>laughed</u> aloud at the cartoon.
   ✔ Kirsten <u>wondered</u> what was so funny.

2. A verb may link the subject to the rest of the sentence.
   ✔ The inspection sticker in the elevator <u>was</u> four years old.
   ✔ The broken glass on the floor <u>looked</u> dangerous.

3. A verb may consist of more than one word. Some verbs include a main verb and one or more *helping verbs.*
   ✔ Zeke <u>has been working</u> in the campus bookstore for three months.

✔ Melanie <u>had</u> not <u>planned</u> to attend a commuter college.
✔ Gavin <u>might have been expecting</u> me to return his call.

4. Some verbs are compound verbs.
   ✔ Nick <u>pulled</u> a muscle in his shoulder and <u>went</u> to see the doctor.
   ✔ The loan officer <u>calculated</u> the payments and <u>handed</u> the customer a loan agreement.
   ✔ Angelo <u>ate</u> octopus once but <u>did</u> not <u>know</u> what it was.

5. An infinitive (*to* + verb) cannot act as a verb in a sentence.
   ✗ Kendall has begun <u>to accept</u> too many credit card offers.

   The phrase *to accept* is an infinitive and cannot be the main verb of the sentence. The verb in this sentence is *has begun*.

   ✗ The advertiser's claims about the new skin cream sounded too good <u>to be</u> true.

   The phrase *to be* is an infinitive, not the verb of the sentence. The verb in this sentence is *sounded*.

6. A verb form ending in -*ing* cannot act as a verb in a sentence unless a helping verb precedes it.
   ✗ The smell of baking bread drifted into the street, <u>inviting</u> passersby into the bakery.

   Inviting cannot be the verb because a helping verb does not precede it. The verb in this sentence is *drifted*.

   ✗ The basset hound's <u>drooping</u> jowls gave him a mournful appearance.

   Drooping cannot be the verb because a helping verb does not precede it. The verb in this sentence is *gave*.

   ✔ Elaine's mother <u>was waving</u> from the porch.

   The verb in this sentence is *was waving* (helping verb + main verb).

   ✔ Jeff said he <u>had</u> not <u>been sleeping</u> well for the last few months.

   The verb in this sentence is *had been sleeping* (helping verb + main verb).

PRACTICE 3   RECOGNIZING VERBS

Underline the verbs in each sentence.

1. Vernon <u>shared</u> his hamburger with a stray dog.
2. Melanie <u>noticed</u> a footprint on the kitchen wall.
3. The woman's hair <u>was</u> long enough to brush the pockets of her jeans.
4. April <u>did</u> not <u>move</u> except to turn a page of her book now and then.

5. The employee <u>guided</u> a long line of grocery carts, pushing them through the parking lot toward the store.

6. The governor <u>announced</u> a new program to help preschool children.

7. The photograph on the calendar <u>showed</u> a polar bear relaxing on an ice floe.

8. Sleepily, Tony <u>poured</u> a cup of coffee and <u>popped</u> a frozen waffle into the toaster.

9. According to my grandmother, people <u>behave</u> more irrationally during a full moon.

10. A rumor about the company's closing <u>had been circulating</u> for some time.

Finding the Subject

A subject answers the question *"Who or what* _____?" To find the subject of a verb, ask the question "Who or what _____?" The verb fills in the blank.

  Note: Be sure the words *who* or *what* are stated *before* the verb, or you will find the object rather than the subject.

✔ Inside Maurice's briefcase, his cell phone <u>rang</u>.

Who or what rang? The cell phone rang. *Cell phone* is the subject of the verb *rang*.

✔ The hot coffee <u>burned</u> Adrienne's tongue.

Who or what burned? The hot coffee burned. *Coffee* is the simple subject of the verb *burned*. (The words *the* and *hot* are modifiers and are part of the complete subject.)

✔ Katelyn and Marie <u>wanted</u> to ride the Ferris wheel.

Who or what wanted? Katelyn and Marie wanted. *Katelyn and Marie* is the compound subject of the verb *wanted*.

✔ Carefully, Tom <u>measured</u> the olive oil and <u>folded</u> it into the pizza dough.

Who or what measured? Tom measured. Who or what folded? Tom folded. *Tom* is the subject of the compound verb *measured and folded*.

✔ Carefully, Tom <u>measured</u> the olive oil while Ruthie <u>kneaded</u> the pizza dough.

Who or what measured? Tom measured. *Tom* is the subject of the verb *measured. Who* or what *kneaded?* Ruthie kneaded. *Ruthie* is the subject of the verb *kneaded*.

PRACTICE 4   RECOGNIZING VERBS AND SUBJECTS

Double-underline the verb in each sentence. Then find the subject by asking "Who or what _____?" Underline the subject once.

1. Marvin squeezed behind the wheel of the small sports car.
2. A candy jar sat on top of the filing cabinet.
3. The photograph showed a much thinner Bert.
4. The computer emitted a strange clunking noise.
5. Gwyn opened the door and called the dog.

Recognizing Prepositional Phrases

A subject will not be part of a prepositional phrase. In many sentences, prepositional phrases intervene between subject and verb.

✔ The top *of the refrigerator* was covered with dust.

When we pick out the subject of the verb by asking "What is covered with dust?" it is tempting to say, "The refrigerator is covered." But *refrigerator* cannot be the subject of the verb in this sentence. Grammatically, it already has a job: It is the object of the preposition. The subject of this sentence is *top*.

To avoid mistakes in picking out the subject of the sentence, cross out prepositional phrases before picking out the subject and the verb.

Below are a few tips for recognizing prepositional phrases:

• **Prepositional phrases always begin with a preposition.** Prepositions are often short words such as *of, to, by, for,* or *from.* They are often words of location such as *behind, beside, beneath, beyond,* or *below.* Below is a list of common prepositions.

Frequently Used Prepositions

about	before	during	next to	under
above	behind	except	of	underneath
across	beneath	for	off	until
after	beside	from	on	up
along	between	in	outside	upon
along with	beyond	into	over	with
around	by	like	to	within
at	down	near	toward	without

- **Prepositional phrases always end with a noun or pronoun.** The object of a preposition, always a noun or pronoun, comes at the end of a prepositional phrase: of the *ceiling*, beside the *restaurant*, with *us*, to *Rita and Dean*, within *four months*.

FAMOUS PREPOSITIONAL PHRASES

The following prepositional phrases have been used as titles for songs, television shows, movies, and books. How many do you recognize? Can you think of others?

Above Suspicion	In Living Color
Against the Wind	Of Mice and Men
Around the World in Eighty Days	On Golden Pond
At Long Last Love	On the Waterfront
At the Hop	Over the Rainbow
Behind Closed Doors	Under the Boardwalk
Behind Enemy Lines	Under the Yum Yum Tree
Beneath the Planet of the Apes	Up a Lazy River
Beyond the Sea	Up on the Roof
In Cold Blood	Up the Down Staircase

Real-World Writing: Is it okay to end a sentence with a preposition?

How else would you say, "Will you pick me up?" or "I feel left out"?

Sometimes, what seems to be an objection to a preposition at the end of a sentence is really an objection to an awkward or redundant construction. "Where are you at?" will bring a scowl to any English teacher's face—not because it ends in a preposition, but because it is redundant: *where* and *at* are both doing the same job—indicating location.

But by all means, say "I have nothing to put this in" or "The dog wants to go out." Except in the most formal writing, ending sentences with prepositions is something almost everyone can live with.

- **Prepositional phrases often have a three-word structure.** Often, prepositional phrases have a three-word structure: preposition, article (*a, an,* or *the*), noun. Thus phrases like *of an airplane, under the bleachers,* and *with a frown* become easy to recognize. But prepositional phrases can also be stretched with modifiers and compound objects: Everyone made fun *of Sam's extra-distance, glow-in-the-dark, Super-Flight golf balls and his tasseled, monogrammed golf club covers.* More often, though, the three-word pattern prevails.

PRACTICE 5   ELIMINATING PREPOSITIONAL PHRASES

Cross out prepositional phrases in the each sentence. Underline subjects once and verbs twice.

1. The smell ~~of cough drops~~ and the sound ~~of sneezing~~ filled the waiting room ~~of the doctor's office~~.
2. Siren blaring, the fire truck pulled ~~into the street~~.
3. The cracked and uneven cement walk ~~in front of the science building~~ posed a danger ~~to students and faculty~~ walking ~~to class~~.
4. The sugary taste ~~of the cereal~~ and the bright colors ~~on the box~~ were appealing ~~to children~~.
5. The smell ~~of fried chicken~~ wafted ~~from the kitchen~~, tantalizing Fran.

Regular and Irregular Verbs

mywritinglab
Visit MyWriting Lab for additional practice with regular and irregular verbs.

Regular verbs follow a predictable pattern in the formation of their **principal parts**. Every verb has four principal parts: the present-tense form, the past-tense form, the past participle (used with helping verbs), and the present participle (the *-ing* verb form used with helping verbs). Regular verbs add *-ed* to form their past tense and past participles. Some examples of regular verbs follow.

Regular Verb Forms

Present	Past	Past Participle	Present Participle
walk	walked	(have) walked	(are) walking
change	changed	(have) changed	(are) changing
add	added	(have) added	(are) adding
pull	pulled	(have) pulled	(are) pulling

Irregular verbs, on the other hand, follow no predictable pattern in their past and past participle forms. Sometimes a vowel changes: *sing* in the present tense becomes *sang* in the past tense and *sung* in the past participle. Sometimes an

-n or *-en* will be added to form the past participle: *take* becomes *taken, fall* becomes *fallen.* Some verbs, such as *set,* do not change at all. Others change completely: *buy* in the present tense becomes *bought* in the past and past participle forms.

Below are some common irregular verbs and their principal parts. If you are unsure about a verb form, check this list or consult a dictionary for the correct form.

Principal Parts of Common Irregular Verbs

Present	Past	Past Participle	Present Participle
become	became	(have) become	(are) becoming
begin	began	(have) begun	(are) beginning
blow	blew	(have) blown	(are) blowing
break	broke	(have) broken	(are) breaking
bring	brought	(have) brought	(are) bringing
burst	burst	(have) burst	(are) bursting
buy	bought	(have) bought	(are) buying
catch	caught	(have) caught	(are) catching
choose	chose	(have) chosen	(are) choosing
come	came	(have) come	(are) coming
cut	cut	(have) cut	(are) cutting
do	did	(have) done	(are) doing
draw	drew	(have) drawn	(are) drawing
drink	drank	(have) drunk	(are) drinking
drive	drove	(have) driven	(are) driving
eat	ate	(have) eaten	(are) eating
fall	fell	(have) fallen	(are) falling
feel	felt	(have) felt	(are) feeling
fight	fought	(have) fought	(are) fighting
find	found	(have) found	(are) finding
fly	flew	(have) flown	(are) flying
freeze	froze	(have) frozen	(are) freezing
get	got	(have) gotten (or got)	(are) getting
give	gave	(have) given	(are) giving
go	went	(have) gone	(are) going
grow	grew	(have) grown	(are) growing
have	had	(have) had	(are) having
hear	heard	(have) heard	(are) hearing

Present	Past	Past Participle	Present Participle
hide	hid	(have) hidden	(are) hiding
hold	held	(have) held	(are) holding
hurt	hurt	(have) hurt	(are) hurting
keep	kept	(have) kept	(are) keeping
know	knew	(have) known	(are) knowing
lay (put)	laid	(have) laid	(are) laying
lead	led	(have) led	(are) leading
leave	left	(have) left	(are) leaving
lend	lent	(have) lent	(are) lending
lie (recline)	lay	(have) lain	(are) lying
lose	lost	(have) lost	(are) losing
put	put	(have) put	(are) putting
ride	rode	(have) ridden	(are) riding
rise	rose	(have) risen	(are) rising
run	ran	(have) run	(are) running
see	saw	(have) seen	(are) seeing
set (place)	set	(have) set	(are) setting
sing	sang	(have) sung	(are) singing
sit (be seated)	sat	(have) sat	(are) sitting
speak	spoke	(have) spoken	(are) speaking
swim	swam	(have) swum	(are) swimming
take	took	(have) taken	(are) taking
tear	tore	(have) torn	(are) tearing
throw	threw	(have) thrown	(are) throwing
write	wrote	(have) written	(are) writing
be, am, are, is	was, were	(have) been	(are) being

PRACTICE 6   USING IRREGULAR VERBS

Fill in the blank with the correct form of the verb shown to the left of each question. For help, consult the list of irregular verbs above.

(become)   1.   Tamiki has __become__ an avid baseball fan.

(break)   2.   Before putting the eggs in his grocery cart, Ed opened the carton to make sure none were __broken__ .

(drink)   **3.**   Someone has ___drunk___ all the orange juice.

(eat)   **4.**   Did you ___eat___ breakfast this morning?

(go)   **5.**   The secretary said Mr. Cavanaugh had ___gone___ for the day.

(lead)   **6.**   The kindergarten teacher ___led___ the children down the hall in single file.

(lend)   **7.**   A classmate ___lent___ me a pen, but I forgot to return it.

(run)   **8.**   The cashier ___ran___ to catch the customer who had forgotten his keys.

(see)   **9.**   When David's parents ___saw___ his grade report, they told him they were proud.

(swim)   **10.**   When Jennifer had ___swum___ fifteen laps, she stopped to rest.

Puzzling Pairs

Some irregular verbs are easily confused with other words. The following section will help you make the right choice between *lend* and *loan, lay* and *lie,* and *sit* and *set.*

Lend and Loan

Lend is a verb meaning "to allow someone to borrow," as in "*Lend* me ten dollars until payday," or "She *lent* her book to another student." *Loan* is a noun meaning "something borrowed," as in "He went to the bank for a mortgage *loan.*"

> ### Real-World Writing: Lend? Loan? Who Cares?
>
> People who care about English also care about the distinction between *lend* and *loan.* Though the use of *loan* as a verb is widespread, it is not considered acceptable by careful writers and speakers of English.
>
> Therefore, it's best to avoid such constructions as "Loan me a dollar for the vending machine," or "He loaned me his car."

Examples Using Lend and Loan

✗   I hoped my neighbor would *loan* me his lawnmower.

✔   I hoped my neighbor would *lend* me his lawnmower.

✗   Shakespeare wrote, "Friends, Romans, countrymen, *loan* me your ears."

✔   Shakespeare wrote, "Friends, Romans, countrymen, *lend* me your ears."

✔   Without a good credit record, it's hard to get a *loan.*

PRACTICE 7   Using *Lend* and *Loan*

Underline the correct word in each sentence.

1. Calvin wanted a car, but knew he could not afford payments on a (lend, <u>loan</u>).
2. We can get the job finished quickly if Andrew (<u>lends</u>, loans) a hand.
3. Before Josh went to camp, his mother warned him not to (<u>lend</u>, loan) his toothbrush or comb.
4. "Before you can get a (lend, <u>loan</u>) from a bank," said Portia, "you have to prove you don't need the money."
5. Would you mind (<u>lending</u>, loaning) me a dollar?

Lay and *Lie*

Lay and *lie* are often confused, partly because their forms overlap. The present-tense form of *lay* and the past-tense form of *lie* are both the same: *lay*. Look at the following chart to see the different forms of each verb.

Present	Past	Past Participle	Present Participle
lay (put)	laid	(have) laid	(are) laying
lie (recline)	lay	(have) lain	(are) lying

*   The verb *lay* means "to put or place." It always takes an object: that is, there will always be an answer to the question "Lay what?"

Examples Using *Lay*

Whenever I need help, Manuel <u>lays</u> his <u>work</u> aside to assist me.

Carol <u>laid</u> her <u>purse</u> on the table and went to answer the phone.

Spiros <u>has laid</u> the <u>brick</u> for his patio.

The company <u>is laying</u> the <u>groundwork</u> for further expansion.

*   The verb *lie* means "to recline." It does not take an object.

Examples Using *Lie*

When Morgan had the flu, she <u>lay</u> in bed for almost two days.

verb
The town <u>lay</u> in a little valley surrounded by hills.

verb
Grady's back was aching because he <u>had lain</u> too long in one position.

verb
The dog <u>has been lying</u> on the sofa again; his fur is all over the cushions.

PRACTICE 8   USING *LAY* AND *LIE*

Underline the correct verb forms in the paragraph below.

When Jack came home from work, he found his wife [1](laying, <u>lying</u>) unconscious on the kitchen floor. He [2](<u>laid</u>, lay) his briefcase on the table and quickly dialed 911, wondering how long she had been [3](laying, <u>lying</u>) there. He listened numbly as the operator said, "Don't move her; just let her [4](lay, <u>lie</u>) there until the ambulance arrives. [5](<u>Lay</u>, lie) the phone down and check her breathing, but don't hang up." When the ambulance arrived, the paramedics [6](lay, <u>laid</u>) Arlene on a stretcher and put her in the ambulance. At the hospital, Jack paced the small waiting room, [7](laying, <u>lying</u>) in wait for the doctor and news of Arlene. Dr. Rodriguez finally emerged from the treatment room and told Jack that his wife had a mild concussion. "We'd like to observe her and make sure she [8](lays, <u>lies</u>) quietly for a day or two," the doctor said. Later, Jack brought his overnight bag and [9](lay, <u>laid</u>) it on the spare bed in Arlene's hospital room. "Stay with her if you like," said the nurse, "but it's not necessary. She will be fine." "I'll stay," said Jack. "I have [10](laid, <u>lain</u>) beside that woman every night for thirty-two years, and I see no reason to stop now."

Sit and *Set*

- The verb *sit* means "to take a seat" or "to be located." It does not take an object.

Examples Using *Sit*

verb
The class members <u>sit</u> in a circle to discuss what they have read.

verb
The dog <u>sat</u> on the porch, waiting for her owner to return.

verb   verb
We <u>had</u> just <u>sat</u> down to dinner when the telephone rang.

- *Set* means to "put" or "place." The verb *set* always takes an object; that is, you will always find an answer to the question, "Set what?"

Examples Using *Set*

            verb   object
Please set the pizza on the kitchen counter.

            verb   object
The company has set minimum sales goals for its staff.

            verb   verb object
The instructor has not set a due date for the research paper.

PRACTICE 9   USING *SIT* AND *SET*

Underline the correct verb form in each sentence.

1. "I can't (sit, set) any longer in this uncomfortable chair," said Leo.
2. Carrie and Josh are engaged but have not (sat, set) a date for their wedding.
3. Two old men were (sitting, setting) at a small table playing checkers.
4. Michael says that he was never able to meet his goals until he (sat, set) them down in writing.
5. "I used to have a crock pot," said Camille, "but I never used it. It just (set, sat) on a shelf."

Review Exercises

Complete the Review Exercises to see how well you have learned the skills addressed in this chapter. As you work through the exercises, go back through the chapter to review any of the rules you do not understand completely.

REVIEW EXERCISE 1

Cross out prepositional phrases in each sentence. Then underline the subject once and the verb twice.

1. In many theaters, advertisements for local businesses are shown before the movie.
2. More rain is forecast throughout next week.
3. Because of an unusually high number of accidents at the intersection of Kay Street and Brennan Avenue, the city installed a traffic light.
4. The bulletin board was covered with memos, reminders, and photographs.

5. The math quiz had not been announced ~~in advance~~.

6. ~~Across the top of Nan's computer monitor~~ sat a row ~~of small stuffed animals~~.

7. The noise ~~of a lawnmower~~ could be heard ~~in the distance~~.

8. Warren accidentally spilled coffee ~~on his computer keyboard~~.

9. ~~By five o'clock~~, the office was deserted.

10. Junk mail and a few bills were stuffed ~~into Kevin's mailbox~~.

REVIEW EXERCISE 2

Cross out prepositional phrases in each sentence. Then underline the subject once and the verb twice.

1. Glancing ~~at her salad~~, Erin saw a bug ~~on one of her tomatoes~~.

2. The sales associate sighed ~~at the sight of the coffee cup on top of the rack of clothes in the store~~.

3. Mitchell had received bad news ~~on the night before his exam~~.

4. Every instructor ~~at the college~~ holds office hours.

5. A large percentage ~~of the population~~ is lactose intolerant.

6. ~~In just a few years~~, the development ~~of the Internet~~ has revolutionized many industries.

7. ~~At the airport~~, Rodrigo bought a book and a magazine ~~for the flight~~.

8. ~~At the Mexican restaurant~~, Kelly dribbled salsa ~~onto her blouse~~.

9. The cake is frosted ~~in pink with blue lettering~~.

10. ~~At the gas station with the lowest prices~~, the line wrapped ~~around the block~~.

REVIEW EXERCISE 3

Choose the correct form of *lend* or *loan*, *lay* or *lie*, and *sit* or *set*.

1. The sign in the veterinarian's office said, "(Sit!, Set!) Stay! The doctor will be with you in a moment."

2. Despite the risk of sunburn or skin cancer, many people spend their vacations (laying, lying) in the sun.

3. Fernando (lent, loaned) a set of socket wrenches to his brother.

4. Linda has promised to (lend, loan) a hand when I try to repair the washer.

5. Discarded cans, fast-food wrappers, and cigarette butts (<u>lay</u>, laid) alongside the road.

6. "I need to be doing something," said Jacquelyn. "I can't just (lay, <u>lie</u>) around the house."

7. His mother's calm in the face of the thunderstorm (lay, <u>laid</u>) Timmy's fears to rest.

8. "I have great news!" Kelly told her mother. "Are you (<u>sitting</u>, setting) down?"

9. "Would you (loan, <u>lend</u>) me a dollar until tomorrow?" Craig asked.

10. "My roommate leaves her stuff (laying, <u>lying</u>) all over the place," said Ebony.

REVIEW EXERCISE 4

Fill in the blank with the correct form of the verb shown to the left of each question. For help, consult the list of irregular verbs in this chapter.

(lie)   1. Several motorists stopped to help gather the boxes that _____lay_____ scattered around the overturned truck.

(burst)   2. After the meal, James leaned back in his chair and said, "I feel like I am about to __burst__."

(fly)   3. "Have you ever __flown__ before?" the flight attendant asked.

(put)   4. Alison asked her daughter if she had _____put_____ away her toys.

(hurt)   5. "I think I _____hurt_____ my ankle, coach," said Ben.

(begin)   6. The student apologized for entering after class had __begun__.

(leave)   7. "Has Mr. Simmons already _____left_____?" asked Mandy.

(buy)   8. Kali _bought_ four boxes of Girl Scout cookies this year.

(fight)   9. For as long as they could remember, the couple had __fought__ over money.

(throw)   10. The student said he had __thrown__ away the rough draft of his paper.

REVIEW EXERCISE 5

Fill in the blank with the correct form of the verb shown to the left of each question. For help, consult the list of irregular verbs in this chapter.

(bring)   1. The councilwoman said that the year had __brought__ many changes to the town of Newton.

(rise)	2.	The morning was so cloudy and dark that it seemed as if the sun had not <u>risen</u>.

(ride)   3. Amiko said that she had never <u>ridden</u> a subway.

(see)   4. Paco did not come with us because he had already <u>seen</u> the movie.

(drink) 5. Who <u>drank</u> all the orange juice?

(lie)   6. For warmth, the cat <u>lay</u> on top of the television.

(break) 7. Harold was fired because he had <u>broken</u> the company's rules.

(go)   8. "I would never have <u>gone</u> to the party if I had known Amanda would be there," said Tom.

(forget) 9. Sherrod has <u>forgotten</u> his computer password again.

(drive) 10. Carol and Monty were bleary-eyed on their first day of vacation because they had <u>driven</u> all night.

mywritinglab   For support in meeting this chapter's goal, log in to www.mywritinglab.com, and select **Subjects and Verbs** and **Regular and Irregular Verbs**.

CHAPTER 13

Subject–Verb Agreement

🎵 **Chapter Goal:** Identify and correct problems with subject-verb agreement.

Eh, those two can never agree.

Fortunately, the rules for agreement between subjects and verbs are much simpler than the rules for human relationships. All of the rules for subject-verb agreement presented in this chapter have the same idea behind them: **A singular subject requires a singular verb, and a plural subject requires a plural verb.**

🎵 The Basic Pattern

Most subject-verb agreement problems occur in the present tense. Look at the conjugation of the present-tense verb *speak*. You can see exactly where trouble is likely to occur if you ask the question "Where does the verb change its form?"

	Singular	**Plural**
First person	I speak	we speak
Second person	you speak	you speak
Third person	he, she, it *speaks*	they speak

As you see, the verb changes its form in the third person with the addition of an *s* to the singular form. As a result, the third-person verb has two forms, a singular form and a plural form. The third-person singular verb ends in *-s*; the third-person plural verb does not. Most problems with subject-verb agreement in the present tense occur in the third person.

PRACTICE 1   CONJUGATING A VERB

All regular verbs follow the pattern above. Using the previous sample as a model, fill in the forms of the verb *look* in the spaces below.

	Singular	**Plural**
First person	I <u>look</u>	we <u>look</u>
Second person	you <u>look</u>	you <u>look</u>
Third person	he, she, it <u>looks</u>	they <u>look</u>

Did you remember to add the *-s* in the third-person singular form? Notice that the pattern of third-person verbs is exactly the opposite of the pattern seen in nouns. When you look at the noun *dog*, you know that it is singular and that the plural form is *dogs*. But verbs in the third person, present tense, work in exactly the opposite way. The third-person singular form of the verb, not the plural form, ends in *-s*. When you see the verb *walks*, you know it is singular because it ends in *-s*.

Examples Using Third-Person Singular Verbs

A third-person singular subject and verb usually follow this pattern:

> The *dog walks*. (The singular noun does not end in *-s*; the singular verb does end in *-s*.)

A third-person plural subject and verb usually follow this pattern:

> The *dogs walk*. (The plural noun ends in *-s*; the plural verb does not end in *-s*.)

Memory Jogger

If you have trouble with third-person verbs, remember the following verse.

The Singular S

When verbs are in the present tense,
You never need to guess.
The singular third-person verb
Always ends in *s*.

PRACTICE 2   CONJUGATING VERBS

On your own sheet of paper, fill in the first-, second-, and third-person forms of the regular verbs *install, shop, play, insist,* and *enjoy.* Remember to add the *-s* to the third-person singular form.

	Singular	**Plural**
First person	I _____	we _____
Second person	you _____	you _____
Third person	he, she, it _____	they _____

Verbs Ending in *-es*

Now look at the regular verb *impress* in the present tense. Here, when the verb already ends in *-s,* the third-person singular form also changes, adding *-es.*

	Singular	**Plural**
First person	I impress	we impress
Second person	you impress	you impress
Third person	he, she, it impress*es*	they impress

Using Third Person

Third person is sometimes confusing. One reason is that it is the only person where the verb form changes. The biggest reason, however, is that third person includes much more than just the pronouns *he, she, it,* and *they.* Third-person singular also includes any noun or pronoun that can be replaced by *he, she,* or *it. Janis, Mr. Brown, otter, desk, toddler, someone, convenience store clerk, one,* and *George Washington* are all in the third-person singular form. Thus each requires a present-tense verb ending in *-s* or *-es*.

Any noun or pronoun that can be replaced by *they* is in the third-person plural form. *The Smiths, both, gas and groceries, poodles, sport utility vehicles,* and *many* are words that could be replaced by *they.* Thus all are in the third-person plural form and require a present-tense plural verb, the form that does not add *-s* or *-es*.

The Verb *to be*

Now look at the most common irregular verb, the verb *to be.*

	Singular	**Plural**
First person	I am	we are
Second person	you are	you are
Third person	he, she, it is	they are

Notice that the pattern still holds: the third-person singular form of the verb always ends in *-s* or *-es.*

A Fundamental Rule

Knowing the pattern that present-tense verbs follow should make it a bit easier to apply the fundamental rule of subject-verb agreement:

A singular subject requires a singular verb, and a plural subject requires a plural verb.

Examples

     S   V
<u>Angela</u> <u>phones</u> home every day to check on her dog Hector. (singular subject, singular verb)

     S   V
<u>Halloween</u> <u>is</u> celebrated across the United States. (singular subject, singular verb)

        S   V
Many <u>students</u> <u>have</u> some difficulty adjusting to college life. (plural subject, plural verb)

       S   V
<u>Strawberries</u> <u>give</u> Clifford hives. (plural subject, plural verb)

PRACTICE 3   MAKING SUBJECTS AND VERBS AGREE

Underline the correct verb form in each sentence.

1. Like most people, Norma (<u>resists</u>, resist) trying new things.
2. Michael (impress, <u>impresses</u>) everyone with his determination and hard work.
3. The candy jar (<u>holds</u>, hold) only paper clips and spare change since Cecile decided to eat more nutritiously.
4. Two cups of coffee (is, <u>are</u>) barely enough to keep Roberto alert during his eight o'clock class.
5. Wolves (lives, <u>live</u>) in closely knit social groups, just as humans do.

Problems in Subject-Verb Agreement

Prepositional Phrase between the Subject and the Verb

mywritinglab

Visit MyWriting Lab for additional practice with subject-verb agreement.

When a prepositional phrase comes between the subject and the verb, it is easy to make mistakes in subject-verb agreement. Crossing out prepositional phrases will help you avoid errors and will help you remember this important rule:

The subject of a verb is never found in a prepositional phrase.

Example with a Prepositional Phrase between the Subject and the Verb

Consider the following problem in subject-verb agreement:

The members of the chorus (rehearses, rehearse) in the auditorium every Tuesday.

Which verb is correct? If you try to find the subject without crossing out prepositional phrases, you might ask the question "Who or what rehearses or rehearse?" It seems logical to say, "The *chorus* rehearses, so *chorus* is the subject of the sentence and *rehearses* is the verb." However, *chorus* cannot be the subject of the sentence because it already has a job: it is the object of a preposition. Remember, *the subject of a sentence is never found in a prepositional phrase.*

Incorrect Solution

✗ The members of the <u>chorus</u> <u>rehearses</u> in the auditorium every Tuesday.

Correct Solution: Cross Out the Prepositional Phrases to Find the Subject

✔ The <u>members</u> ~~of the chorus~~ <u>rehearse</u> ~~in the auditorium~~ every Tuesday.

Example with a Prepositional Phrase between the Subject and the Verb

✔ The <u>bumper stickers</u> on Nat's car <u>reveal</u> his changing political attitudes over the years.

The verb agrees with its subject, *stickers,* not with the object of the preposition.

PRACTICE 4   MAKING SUBJECTS AND VERBS AGREE

In each of the following sentences, cross out the prepositional phrases to find the subject of the sentence. Then underline the subject and double-underline the correct verb.

1. Several <u>signs</u> ~~in front of the store~~ (warns, <u><u>warn</u></u>) that cars parked ~~in the fire lane~~ will be towed.

2. The <u>popularity</u> ~~of some brands of athletic shoes~~ (<u><u>makes</u></u>, make) some people willing to pay high prices.

3. The driving <u>beat</u> ~~of the music in the fitness center~~ (<u><u>helps</u></u>, help) people exercise longer.

4. <u>Writing</u> ~~in her journal~~ every day (<u><u>is</u></u>, are) difficult ~~for Susan~~.

5. The free <u>samples</u> ~~of food~~ ~~in the supermarket~~ ~~on Saturday~~ (attracts, <u><u>attract</u></u>) many shoppers.

Indefinite Pronouns as Subjects

Problems in subject-verb agreement are also likely to occur when the subject is an **indefinite pronoun,** a pronoun that does not refer to a specific person or thing. The following indefinite pronouns are always singular and require singular verbs.

each	everybody	anyone	anything
either	somebody	everyone	everything
neither	nobody	someone	something
anybody	one	no one	nothing

Memory Jogger

Remember the singular indefinite pronouns more easily by grouping them:

    Each, either, neither

    All the bodies (anybody, everybody, nobody, somebody)

    All the ones (anyone, everyone, one, no one, someone)

    All the things (anything, everything, nothing, something)

Examples of Indefinite Pronouns as Subjects

                                 subject verb
Janna answered the telephone, but <u>no one</u> <u>was</u> on the other end.

The subject, *no one*, is singular, as is the verb, *was*.

subject   verb
<u>Each</u> of the cupcakes <u>has been decorated</u> with a jack-o'-lantern face.

The singular verb, *has been decorated*, agrees with the singular subject, *each*. The plural object of the preposition, *cupcakes*, does not affect the verb.

PRACTICE 5   **MAKING VERBS AGREE WITH INDEFINITE PRONOUNS**

In each sentence, cross out prepositional phrases and underline the verb that agrees with the indefinite pronoun subject.

1. Neither ~~of the cars~~ (<u>has,</u> have) all the features that Carl wants.

2. Everybody ~~in the apartment complex~~ (<u>believes,</u> believe) the manager is doing a poor job of groundskeeping.

3. Someone ~~in one of Helen's classes~~ (<u>is,</u> are) organizing a study group.

4. Everything ~~in the store~~ (<u>has,</u> have) been reduced ~~to half price~~.

5. Each ~~of the barbers~~ (<u>pays,</u> pay) rent ~~to the shop owner~~.

Subject Following the Verb

In most English sentences, the subject comes before the verb. However, the subject follows the verb in these situations:

1. When the sentence begins with *here* or *there*

2. When the sentence begins with a prepositional phrase that is immediately followed by a verb

3. When the sentence is a question

Examples of Subjects Following Verbs

       verb   subject

✔ There <u>are</u> several <u>oranges</u> ~~in the bowl~~.

The plural subject, *oranges,* requires the plural verb, *are.* The word *there* is not the subject of the sentence.

                   verb   subject

✔ In front of the fireplace <u>sit</u> two comfortable <u>chairs</u>.

The prepositional phrases *in front* and *of the fireplace* are immediately followed by a verb. Since the subject is never found in a prepositional phrase, it must be somewhere *after* the verb. The plural verb, *sit,* agrees with the plural subject, *chairs.*

        verb   subject

✔ What <u>was</u> the <u>price</u> of the small soft drink?

The singular subject, *price,* follows the singular verb, *was.*

        verb   subject

✔ What <u>were</u> those strange <u>noises</u> that I heard outside?

The plural subject, *noises,* follows the plural verb, *were.*

PRACTICE 6   MAKING VERBS AGREE WITH SUBJECTS THAT COME AFTER VERBS

Cross out prepositional phrases in each sentence. Then underline the subject and double-underline the correct verb.

1. Nestled ~~in the crawl space~~ ~~under the house~~ (was, <u>were</u>) a mother cat and four scrawny little <u>kittens</u>.

2. Why (<u>does</u>, do) <u>Rodney</u> <u>have</u> two cars when he can drive only one ~~at a time~~?

3. There (<u>is</u>, are) a <u>package</u> ~~outside Jamie's front door~~.

4. (<u>Does</u>, Do) <u>anyone</u> know where to get a parking permit?

5. There (wasn't, <u>weren't</u>) any seats available ~~for Friday night's concert~~.

Compound Subjects

Compound subjects may also cause confusion in subject-verb agreement. The rules for subject-verb agreement with compound subjects are outlined in the sections that follow.

Compound Subjects Joined by *and*

Because *and* always joins at least two elements, compound subjects joined by *and* require a plural verb. Remember this rule:

Compound subjects joined by *and* require a plural verb.

Examples of Compound Subjects Joined by *and*

       compound subject   verb
✔ A <u>pizza</u> *and* a rented <u>movie</u> <u>are</u> Kim and Anthony's way of relaxing on Friday nights.

       compound subject   verb
✔ <u>Winning</u> modestly *and* <u>losing</u> gracefully <u>are</u> two ways of demonstrating good sportsmanship.

       compound subject
✔ A prickly <u>cactus</u>, a <u>pot</u> of geraniums, *and* a <u>doormat</u> that says "Go

       verb
Away" <u>sit</u> on my neighbor's front porch.

       compound subject   verb
✔ Discarded beer <u>cans</u> *and* cigarette <u>butts</u> <u>dot</u> the convenience store's parking lot.

PRACTICE 7 MAKING VERBS AGREE WITH SUBJECTS JOINED BY *AND*

Cross out prepositional phrases. Then double-underline the verb that agrees with each compound subject.

1. A trip ~~to the mall~~ ~~with three children~~ and a visit ~~to a fast-food restaurant~~ (was, <u>were</u>) not Harriet's idea ~~of relaxation~~.

2. A tight waistband and the numbers ~~on his scale~~ (tells, <u>tell</u>) Arthur that it's time to start a diet.

3. ~~At the movie theater~~, a giant soft drink, a large bag ~~of popcorn~~, and a candy bar (costs, <u>cost</u>) more than the price ~~of admission~~.

4. Finishing ~~on time~~ and remembering all the material (is, <u>are</u>) just two ~~of the pressures of taking tests~~.

5. A timer shaped like a hen and a glass jar filled ~~with spare change~~ (sits, <u>sit</u>) ~~on top~~ ~~of the microwave~~ ~~in Natalie's kitchen~~.

Compound Subjects Joined by *or*, *either/or*, or *neither/nor*

When subjects are joined by *or, either/or,* or *neither/nor*, it is not always possible to use logic to determine whether the verb should be singular or plural. Therefore, one rule applies to all compound subjects joined by *or, either/or,* or *neither/nor*:

When a compound subject is joined by *or*, *either/or*, **or** *neither/nor*, **the verb agrees with the part of the subject that is closer to it.**

Consider the following sentence:

Seth or his brother (is, are) opening the shop on Saturday morning.

How many will open the shop? The answer is "just one": either Seth *or* his brother. Therefore, using the singular verb is logical. The singular verb *is* also agrees with *brother,* the part of the subject that is closer to the verb.

✔ <u>Seth</u> *or* his <u>brother</u> <u>is</u> opening the shop on Saturday morning.

Now, let's change the sentence a bit.

Seth's brothers or his assistants (is, are) opening the shop on Saturday.

How many will open the shop? In this sentence, *more than one:* either Seth's brothers or his assistants. It makes sense, then, to use a plural verb. The plural verb *are* also agrees with *assistants,* the part of the subject closer to the verb.

✔ Seth's <u>brothers</u> *or* his <u>assistants</u> <u>are</u> opening the shop on Saturday.

The next two sentences do not respond to logical examination.

Seth or his assistants (is, are) opening the shop on Saturday.
Seth's assistants or his brother (is, are) opening the shop on Saturday.

How many will open the shop? There is no way to tell. Simply follow the rule and make the verb agree with the part of the subject that is closer to it.

✔ Seth or his <u>assistants</u> <u>are</u> opening the shop on Saturday.

✔ Seth's <u>assistants</u> *or* his <u>brother</u> <u>is</u> opening the shop on Saturday.

Examples with Compound Subjects

✔ A five-dollar donation *or* two nonperishable food <u>items</u> <u>are</u> required for admission to the concert.
✔ Two nonperishable food items *or* a five-dollar <u>donation</u> <u>is</u> required for admission to the concert.
✔ *Either* two nonperishable food items *or* a five-dollar <u>donation</u> <u>is</u> required for admission to the concert.
✔ *Neither* the alarm clock *nor* her two <u>cats</u> <u>were</u> successful in getting Kendra out of bed.

MAKING VERBS AGREE WITH SUBJECTS JOINED BY *OR*, *EITHER/OR*, OR *NEITHER/NOR*

Cross out prepositional phrases. Then double-underline the verb that agrees with each compound subject. Some subjects are joined by *and*, while others are joined by *or*, *either/or*, or *neither/nor*.

1. Soup or a microwaveable pizza (<u>was</u>, were) all that Elton had ~~on hand for lunch~~.

2. Either a sweatshirt or a warm sweater (<u>feels</u>, feel) good ~~on a cool day~~.

3. Strawberries or a sliced banana (<u>tastes</u>, taste) good ~~over cereal~~.

4. Neither Deon nor his two brothers (talks, <u>talk</u>) ~~about anything except sports~~.

5. Taking drugs or drinking alcohol to escape problems often (<u>leads</u>, lead) ~~to even bigger problems~~.

Review Exercises

Complete the Review Exercises to find out how well you have learned the skills addressed in this chapter. As you work through the exercises, go back through the chapter to review any of the rules you do not understand completely.

REVIEW EXERCISE 1

Underline the correct verb in each sentence.

1. The room (<u>was</u>, were) too warm, and Larry found it difficult to stay awake.
2. Only one of the members of the jury (believe, <u>believes</u>) the defendant committed the crime.
3. When Emily or her brothers (needs, <u>need</u>) money, their father tells them to get it the old fashioned way—to earn it.
4. Each of the cashiers (<u>has</u>, have) a good reason for being late.
5. Long hours and her supervisor's habit of calling her in on weekends (is, <u>are</u>) forcing Shayna to consider quitting her job.
6. Running and weight lifting (keeps, <u>keep</u>) Brandon in shape and feeling good.
7. There (was, <u>were</u>) too many distractions in the room during the test, and Andy had a hard time concentrating.
8. Inside Marcie's lunch bag (is, <u>are</u>) a diet soft drink, an apple, and a gooey snack cake.
9. Why (does, <u>do</u>) Cathy and Dennis bother to come to class when they never do any of the assigned work?
10. The Mason jars sitting on the table (is, <u>are</u>) filled with homemade jam.

REVIEW EXERCISE 2

Write C in the blank to the left of the sentence if the italicized verb agrees with its subject. If the verb is incorrect, write the correct form in the blank. Two of the sentences are correct.

<u>makes</u> **1.** The large crowd in the doctor's waiting room *make* me think I will be here awhile.

<u>C</u> **2.** The noise from the washers, the dryers, and the television *makes* it hard to hold a conversation in the laundromat.

<u>is</u> **3.** "One of the mechanics *are* going to call me when my car is ready," said Ann.

<u>has</u> **4.** Everybody in the path of the hurricane *have* been warned to prepare for evacuation.

<u>were</u> **5.** A jacket, a hat, and a pair of gloves *was* lying on the kitchen floor.

<u>has</u> **6.** "Either the telephone bill or the cable bill *have* to wait till next week," said Burton.

<u>C</u> **7.** The bright sunshine and the music on her car radio *were* not enough to lift Natasha's gloomy mood.

<u>are</u> **8.** There *is* the keys that Nathan was looking for a few minutes ago.

<u>has</u> **9.** Why *have* the professor changed the due date of the assignment?

<u>gives</u> **10.** Andrea says everyone *give* her strange looks whenever she wears her purple outfit.

REVIEW EXERCISE 3

Cross out the two incorrect verb forms in each item. Then write the correct forms on the lines provided.

1. When she goes on vacation, Becky doesn't spend her entire vacation on a beach; instead, she ~~sunbathe~~ for a few hours. Her friends ~~soaks~~ up the sun all day.

   Sentence 1: <u>sunbathes</u>   Sentence 2: <u>soak</u>

2. Li's full-time job and her heavy class schedule ~~makes~~ it almost impossible for her to find enough time to study. "Either full-time work or full-time school ~~are~~ okay," she says, "but not both."

   Sentence 1: <u>make</u>   Sentence 2: <u>is</u>

3. Vanessa's coworkers ~~treats~~ themselves to an ice cream every day during their

lunch break. Vanessa goes with them, but never ~~buy~~ a cone because she is watching both her waistline and her budget.

Sentence 1: <u>treat</u>   Sentence 2: <u>buys</u>

4. As he ~~approach~~ graduation, Brad ~~think~~ more about his future career.

Sentence 1: <u>approaches</u> Sentence 2: <u>thinks</u>

5. Tricia had a terrible day. First, she found out her car's repairs ~~was~~ beyond her budget. Then, after waiting over an hour for a bus, she ~~were~~ shocked to discover the entire route had been eliminated.

Sentence 1: <u>were</u>   Sentence 2: <u>was</u>

REVIEW EXERCISE 4

In each numbered item, cross out the two verbs that do not agree with their subjects. Then write the correct verbs on the lines provided.

1. Sonya has never met the people in the apartment next door to her, but she has already decided she ~~don't~~ like them. Their music, pounding from the other side of the wall at all hours, ~~annoy~~ her.

Sentence 1: <u>doesn't</u>   Sentence 2: <u>annoys</u>

2. Inside the huge grocery superstore ~~is~~ a bank, a dry-cleaning shop, a fast-food restaurant, and a hair salon. "A person ~~need~~ hiking boots to get around in that huge store," Josh complained.

Sentence 1: <u>are</u>   Sentence 2: <u>needs</u>

3. In the fall, the leaves on the oak tree in our front yard ~~bursts~~ into a beautiful blaze of red. They are not so beautiful when they fall off the tree and my brother and I ~~has~~ to rake them up.

Sentence 1: <u>burst</u>   Sentence 2: <u>have</u>

4. There ~~are~~ no faculty member or staff person on duty in the grammar lab on Saturday. However, Sunday through Friday, computer tutorials and help with grammar ~~is~~ available for students of the college.

Sentence 1: <u>is</u>   Sentence 2: <u>are</u>

5. The twins' mother is angry because their membership in several of the school's clubs and activities ~~require~~ them to sell merchandise to raise funds. "It is bad enough that I end up buying most of it," she says, "but even worse, each new item that I buy ~~seem~~ tackier and more expensive than the last."

Sentence 1: <u>requires</u>   Sentence 2: <u>seems</u>

REVIEW EXERCISE 5

Underline the ten subject-verb agreement errors in the following paragraph. Then write the correct verbs on the lines provided.

[1]In my rural neighborhood, at the end of a long gravel driveway, <u>sit</u> a house that is a mystery to everyone. [2]It was built over a year ago, but neither I nor my neighbors <u>has</u> ever seen it. [3]A chain, heavy and made of metal, <u>run</u> between two thick posts at the end of the driveway. [4]Hanging from the chain and nailed to the posts <u>is</u> several signs: "Keep Out," "No Trespassing," "Private Property." [5]Though it is customary in our area to welcome new neighbors with a visit and a basket of fruit, nobody in the neighborhood <u>have</u> dared to go past those unfriendly signs. [6]Instead, everyone <u>speculate</u>. [7]Maybe the woods that hug the property conceal a drug manufacturing plant, or perhaps the residents <u>is</u> growing marijuana. [8]Or they could be members of a militia group, stockpiling guns and preparing for war with anyone who <u>venture</u> beyond that chain at the end of the driveway. [9]There <u>is</u> many possibilities, but one thing is certain. [10]Our new neighbors <u>prefers</u> to keep to themselves.

1. sits
2. have
3. runs
4. are
5. has

6. speculates
7. are
8. ventures
9. are
10. prefer

mywritinglab   For support in meeting this chapter's goal, log in to **www.mywritinglab.com** and select **Subject-Verb Agreement**.

CHAPTER **14**

Verb Shifts

✍ Chapter Goal: Avoid and correct unnecessary verb shifts; use passive voice correctly.

A Shifty Excuse

"Professor, I brought my term paper with me, but when I opened my notebook, it's gone. I can't print out another copy because the file was erased by me."

The excuse above is shifty—but not just because it is unconvincing. It contains two common types of **verb shifts**. The first sentence contains an unnecessary shift from the past tense to the present tense, and the second contains an unnecessary shift from active voice to passive voice.

In this chapter, you will learn to avoid and correct unnecessary shifts from the past tense to the present tense and to make necessary shifts into the past perfect tense. You will also learn to recognize active voice and passive voice and to correct unnecessary shifts between the two.

〰️ Shifts in Tense

Verb tenses give the English language its sense of time, its sense of *when* events occur. The timeline below shows six verb tenses, and the chart that follows the timeline briefly explains how each tense is used.

Verb Tense Timeline

	past I walked	present I walk	future I will walk

past ◁←- - - * - - - - - - - * - - - - - * - - - * - - - - - - - - - - - * - - - * - - - →▷ **future**

	I had walked past perfect	I have walked present perfect	I will have walked future perfect

Verb Tense Chart

◁◁◁	Furthest in the past; happened before another past action	past perfect *had* + *-ed* verb form	I *had walked* up the stairs, and I was out of breath.
◁◁	In the past; happened before now.	past *-ed* verb form	I *walked* all the way around the nature trail.
◁ •	In the past but extending to the present	present perfect *have* or *has* + *-ed* verb form	I *have walked* every day for the last month. He *has walked* a mile already.
•	Happens regularly or often, or is happening now	present base verb form or base verb + *-s*	I *walk* at least five miles a week. She *walks* quickly.
▷	Happens in the future but before another future event	future perfect *will have* + *-ed* verb form	By the time you join me on the track, I *will have walked* at least two miles.
▷▷	Happens at some time in the future	future *will* + base verb	I *will walk* with you tomorrow if we both have time.

Avoiding Unnecessary Tense Shifts

With so many ways to designate time, writers of English are bound to slip up occasionally. The most common error in verb tense is an unnecessary shift from past tense to present tense. Writers can easily become so caught up in the past event they are describing that it becomes, at least temporarily, a part of "the now." Unnecessary shifts from present to past, although not quite as common, should also be avoided.

Examples of Necessary and Unnecessary Shifts

Necessary Shift:

    past   present

✔ James <u>was</u> sick yesterday, but he <u>is feeling</u> better today.

Unnecessary Shift from Past to Present:

           past   present

✗ Cameron <u>was driving</u> on Route 42 when all of a sudden a bus <u>pulls</u> out in front of her.

Unnecessary Shift Corrected:

           past   past

✔ Cameron <u>was driving</u> on Route 42 when all of a sudden a bus <u>pulled</u> out in front of her.

Unnecessary Shift from Past to Present:

          past   present   present

✗ When we <u>arrived</u> at the theater, we <u>notice</u> that the line <u>stretches</u> all the way around the building.

Unnecessary Shift Corrected:

          past   past   past

✔ When we <u>arrived</u> at the theater, we <u>noticed</u> that the line <u>stretched</u> all the way around the building.

Unnecessary Shift from Present to Past:

    present   past

✗ Jerry <u>comes</u> home every day and <u>turned on</u> the television set to watch the news.

Unnecessary Shift Corrected:

    present   present

✔ Jerry <u>comes</u> home every day and <u>turns on</u> the television set to watch the news.

PRACTICE 1   MAINTAINING CONSISTENT TENSE

Underline the correct verb in each sentence.

1. When Ralph came home, he saw that his puppy had chewed the sofa pillows and (is, <u>was</u>) hiding under the bed.

2. I thought Abby had quit smoking, but when I went outside for my break, there she (stands, <u>stood</u>), smoking a cigarette.

3. The boat towed the skier to the far end of the lake, then (turns, <u>turned</u>) around and headed back toward the dock.

4. Every afternoon, the children play outside until their mother (<u>calls</u>, called) them in for dinner.

5. The cat was sleeping on the arm of a chair, but when the doorbell rang, he (darts, <u>darted</u>) under the sofa.

PRACTICE 2   CORRECTING UNNECESSARY TENSE SHIFTS

In each sentence, correct the unnecessary shift from past to present.

1. Valerie fills her gas tank on Monday, but by Friday it was empty again.

   Valerie filled *her gas tank* _____

2. Michael had been working all morning in the heat, and when he came in, he seems ill and unsteady.

   he seemed *ill and unsteady* _____

3. Lynn woke up in the middle of the night and could not go back to sleep, so she decides to clean out the refrigerator.

   she decided *to clean out the refrigerator* _____

4. The score was tied at the bottom of the ninth, and Michael Bourn comes up to bat amid the cheers of the fans.

   Michael Bourn came *up to bat* _____

5. Sylvester thought he no longer loved Carmen until he sees her at the laundromat on a Tuesday night in April.

   he saw *her at the laundromat* _____

✎ Active Voice and Passive Voice

mywritinglab

Visit MyWriting Lab for additional practice with active and passive voice.

Active voice means that the grammatical subject of a sentence performs the action described by the verb, as in the following sentence:

Before the game began, Cynthia sang the national anthem.

In this sentence, *Cynthia,* the grammatical subject, performs the action described by the verb *sang.*

Rewritten in **passive voice,** the sentence looks like this:

Before the game began, the national anthem was sung by Cynthia.

What has changed? Simply put, the grammatical subject of the sentence is not acting, but is acted upon. The subject *anthem* performs no action, but instead is acted upon by the person who sings it. Notice, too, another hallmark of the passive voice: The verb contains a helping verb that is a form of the verb *to be.* Though an active voice verb also may have a helping verb such as *is, was, were, have been, will be,* or another form of *to be,* a passive voice verb always does. Another hallmark of the passive voice is the "by" construction (*by Cynthia*) that sometimes tells who or what acted upon the subject.

Memory Jogger

In *active voice,* an action is done *by* the grammatical subject.
In *passive voice,* an action is done *to* the grammatical subject.

PRACTICE 3   EXAMINING ACTIVE VOICE AND PASSIVE VOICE

Answer the questions about each set of sentences. The first one is done for you.

Set 1

Active: The police arrested the suspected bank robbers on Thursday morning.

The subject of the verb is ___police___.

The verb that shows the action done *by* the subject is ___arrested___.

Passive: The suspected bank robbers were arrested by the police on Thursday morning.

The subject of the verb is ___robbers___.

The verb that shows the action done *to* the subject is ___were arrested___.

Set 2

Active: Samantha watered her house plants.

The subject of the verb is ___Samantha___.

The verb that shows the action done *by* the subject is ___watered___.

Passive: The house plants were watered by Samantha.

The subject of the verb is _____plants_____.

The verb that slows the action done *to* the subject is were watered.

Set 3

Active: Marcus caught the ball before it could reach the plate glass window.

The subject of the verb is _____Marcus_____.

The verb that shows the action done *by* the subject is _____caught_____.

Passive: The ball was caught by Marcus before it could reach the plate glass window.

The subject of the verb is _____ball_____.

The verb that shows the action done *to* the subject is _____was caught_____.

Set 4

Active: Claude took the mud-spattered Chevrolet to the car wash.

The subject of the verb is _____Claude_____.

The verb that shows the action done *by* the subject is _____took_____.

Passive: The mud-spattered Chevrolet was taken to the car wash by Claude.

The subject of the verb is _____Chevrolet_____.

The verb that shows the action done *to* the subject is _____was taken_____.

Set 5

Active: After the restaurant closes, the employees clean the tables and vacuum the carpet.

The subject of the verb is _____employees_____.

The verbs that show the actions done *by* the subject are _____clean and vacuum_____.

Passive: After the restaurant closes, tables are cleaned and the carpet is vacuumed.

In this sentence, the subjects of the verbs are _____tables_____ and carpet.

The verbs that show the actions done *to* the subjects are _____are cleaned_____ and _____is vacuumed_____.

Uses of Active Voice and Passive Voice

Active voice, with its directness and vitality, is stronger than passive voice and is preferred in most situations. Sometimes, however, passive voice is appropriate. For example, you would use passive voice in a sentence such as "The furniture will be delivered on Tuesday" because you don't care who delivers it; you just care that it arrives.

However, try to avoid awkward shifts between active and passive voice. Look at the following example:

active   passive

✗   The professor wished us luck, and at exactly 8:10, the tests were handed out.

active   active

✔   The professor wished us luck, and at exactly 8:10, he handed out the tests.

Writing Sentences in Active Voice and Passive Voice

To avoid unnecessary shifts between active and passive voice, you need to be able to recognize and write sentences in both voices.

Switching from Passive Voice to Active Voice

To switch from passive voice to active voice, determine *who* or *what* acts upon the subject of the sentence, and rewrite the sentence to make that actor the subject.

Examples of Switches from Passive Voice to Active Voice

Passive: The car was driven by Mario's brother.

To switch this passive voice sentence to active voice, look for the word or phrase that tells who performs the action described in the subject-verb sequence. In this sentence, look for a word or phrase that tells *who drove the car. Mario's brother* drove the car. To put the sentence into active voice, make *Mario's brother* the subject of the sentence and work from there.

Active: Mario's brother drove the car.

Sometimes, the *by* construction is omitted, and you need to mentally fill in the blank to put an actor into the sentence.

Passive: The prisoner was sentenced to life without parole.

The sentence does not say who sentenced the prisoner, but logic tells you that it must have been a judge. To rewrite the sentence in active voice, put a judge into the sentence.

Active: The judge sentenced the prisoner to life without parole.

PRACTICE 4   WRITING SENTENCES IN ACTIVE VOICE

Rewrite each of the following sentences in active voice. Answers will vary.

1. The pizza was delivered by a man with red hair.
    A man with red hair delivered the pizza.

2. Evidence was collected by two uniformed officers.
    Two uniformed officers collected evidence.

3. The concert was attended by a small, enthusiastic crowd.
    A small, enthusiastic crowd attended the concert.

4. After eight rings, the telephone was answered by a man who sounded as though he had been sleeping.
    After eight rings, a man who sounded as though he had been sleeping answered the telephone.

5. At the park's entrance, hot dogs were sold by a vendor.
    At the park's entrance, a vendor sold hot dogs.

Switching from Active Voice to Passive Voice

To switch from active voice to passive voice, reverse the position of the actor (the subject of the verb) and the recipient of the action (the object of the verb).

Examples of Switches from Active Voice to Passive Voice

Active: The technician expertly cleaned and repaired the old lawnmower.

The actor (the subject of the verb) is *the technician.* The recipient of the action is *the old lawnmower.* To convert the sentence to passive voice, switch the positions of the two.

Passive: The old lawnmower was expertly cleaned and repaired by the technician.

Here is a second example:

Active: The meteorologist predicted rain and temperatures in the seventies.

Passive: Rain and temperatures in the seventies were predicted by the meteorologist.

PRACTICE 5   WRITING SENTENCES IN PASSIVE VOICE

Rewrite each of the following sentences in passive voice. Answers will vary.

1. The dog ate the rest of the leftovers.
    The rest of the leftovers were eaten by the dog.

2. Hundreds of cattle ate the contaminated feed.
    The contaminated feed was eaten by hundreds of cattle.

3. The school board took a firm stand against the banning of books.
    A firm stand against the banning of books was taken by the school board.

4. The gardening expert gave a presentation on leaf mold.
    A presentation on leaf mold was given by the gardening expert.

5. The sound of his mother's voice calmed and reassured the child.
    The child was calmed and reassured by the sound of his mother's voice.

Correcting Shifts in Voice

When an unnecessary shift in voice occurs within a sentence, rewrite the sentence so that it is in one voice. Active voice is usually preferred.

Examples of Corrected Shifts in Voice

Unnecessary Shift:

                      active   passive

✘   Before Clayton took the test, his notes were reviewed quickly.

Corrected:

                      active   active

✔   Before Clayton took the test, he quickly reviewed his notes.

Unnecessary Shift:

             active   passive

✘   Camille lost her battered old umbrella, so a new one was purchased.

Corrected:

             active   active

✔   Camille lost her battered old umbrella, so she purchased a new one.

PRACTICE 6   CORRECTING SHIFTS IN VOICE

Each of the following sentences contains a shift in voice. Underline the passive-voice portion of each sentence. Then rewrite each sentence in active voice. Answers will vary.

1. After the newspaper <u>had been read by everyone in the family,</u> Cliff put it in the recycling bin.

    After everyone in the family had read the newspaper

2. Ramon was angry when he found out that <u>a trick had been played on him by his friends.</u>

    his friends had played a trick on him.

3. Connie wanted to monitor her food intake, so <u>everything she ate was written down.</u>

    she wrote down everything she ate.

4. After Nelson wrote a cover letter, <u>it was mailed along with his résumé.</u>

    he mailed it along with his résumés.

5. As if the instructor had not given us enough work, <u>an additional book was added to our reading list by her at midterm.</u>

    she added an additional book to our reading list at midterm.

Review Exercises

Complete the Review Exercises to find out how well you have learned the skills addressed in this chapter. As you work through the exercises, go back through the chapter to review any of the rules you do not understand completely.

REVIEW EXERCISE 1

The italicized portions of the following sentences contain unnecessary shifts in voice or tense or verbs that need to be shifted from the past to the past-perfect tense. For each sentence, circle *a, b,* or *c* to indicate the type of problem in the sentence. Then correct the problem in each sentence.

1. In the morning, Tom left his car at the dealership. When he returned at five-thirty, the mechanics *replaced the brake pads and tuned the engine.*

    The problem in this sentence is

    a. a shift in voice

    b. a shift between past and present tense

    (c.)   past-tense verbs that need to be further in the past (past perfect)

       had replaced the brake pads and tuned the engine.

2.   Marie's parents sat on the couch and *hold* hands as if they were teenagers. The problem in this sentence is

    a.   a shift in voice

    (**b.**)   a shift between past and present tense

    c.   a past-tense verb that needs to be further in the past (past perfect)

       held

3.   In the stands, baseball fans stood for the seventh-inning stretch while *hot dogs, soft drinks, and beer were sold by vendors.* The problem in this sentence is

    (**a.**)   a shift in voice

    b.   a shift between past and present tense

    c.   a past-tense verb that needs to be further in the past (past perfect)

       while vendors sold hot dogs, soft drinks, and beer

4.   In the shelter of the carport, the cats dismembered a small bird that *had been caught by them.* The problem in this sentence is

    (**a.**)   a shift in voice

    b.   a shift between past and present tense

    c.   a past-tense verb that needs to be further in the past (past perfect)

       they had caught

5.   When Adam reached his hotel room, he realized he *left* his toothbrush and toothpaste at home. The problem in this sentence is

    a.   a shift in voice

    b.   a shift between past and present tense

    (**c.**)   a past tense verb that needs to be further in the past (past perfect)

       had left

REVIEW EXERCISE 2

The italicized portions of the following sentences contain unnecessary shifts in voice or tense, or verbs that need to be shifted from the past to the past-perfect tense. Correct the problem in each sentence.

1.   The letter said Gary was a winner if *the winning number was held by him.*

    he held the winning number

2. When I saw Anita, *she says*, "Why weren't you at the meeting yesterday?"

   she said
   _____

3. Bonita asked Alan to join our study group, but he said *he studied already*.

   he had studied already
   _____

4. Hank shook the salesman's hand and said, "I'll let you know when *a decision has been reached by me*."

   I have reached a decision
   _____

5. In the computer store, Julia bought the new keyboard she needed, and just as she was ready to leave, she *decides* to get a mouse pad, too.

   decided
   _____

6. Since *bids were signaled by the buyers* with a nod or a slight hand movement, the auctioneer had to be alert.

   buyers signaled their bids
   _____

7. Rowe *already finished* his report and was ready to turn it in, so he was irritated when the instructor granted the class a last-minute extension.

   had already finished
   _____

8. Darrell and Ellie had just fallen asleep when *the baby starts crying*.

   the baby started crying
   _____

9. Bill held his burned finger under cold running water, and then *ice was applied*.

   he applied ice
   _____

10. Kim looked at the clock and realized she *worked* for half an hour.

    had worked
    _____

REVIEW EXERCISE 3

The italicized portions of the following sentences contain unnecessary shifts in voice or tense, or verbs that need to be shifted from the past to the past-perfect tense. For each sentence, circle *a*, *b*, or *c* to indicate the type of problem in the sentence. Then correct the problem in each sentence.

1. On the first day of class, the instructor handed each student a syllabus and *says*, "Everything you need to know about the course content, exams, and assignments is in this document."

   The problem in this sentence is

   a. a shift in voice

   (b.) a shift between past and present tense

   c.   a past-tense verb that needs to be further in the past (past perfect)

      said

2. When Ralph arrived at home, the mail carrier *left* a note, "Package on front porch."

      The problem in this sentence is

   a.   a shift in voice

   b.   a shift between past and present tense

   (c.) a past-tense verb that needs to be further in the past (past perfect)

      had left

3. When Stephanie fed Rover, the dog *eats* an entire can of food in one gulp.

      The problem in this sentence is

   a.   a shift in voice

   (b.) a shift between past and present tense

   c.   a past-tense verb that needs to be further in the past (past perfect)

      ate

4. Ray won the race today, *and another school record was set by him.*

      The problem in this sentence is

   (a.) a shift in voice

   b.   a shift between past and present tense

   c.   a past-tense verb that needs to be further in the past (past perfect)

      and he set another school record

5. After the exam, Carolyn walked into the hall and said she was certain *she did well.*

      The problem in this sentence is

   a.   a shift in voice

   b.   a shift between past and present tense

   (c.) a past-tense verb that needs to be further in the past (past perfect)

      she had done well

REVIEW EXERCISE 4

Underline the voice or tense problem in each sentence. Then write the correct voice or tense on the lines provided.

1. The heavy rains lasted for days, and soon every street <u>floods.</u>

     flooded

2. Jen was just about to hit the "save" button when the computer <u>crashes.</u>

     crashed

3. Elena was horrified when a man old enough to be her grandfather <u>asks</u> her out on a date.

   asked

4. Joe saw the light turn yellow, so <u>the brake pedal was pressed by him.</u>

   he pressed the brake pedal

5. The mountains were covered in snow, but the valley <u>is</u> sunny and green.

   was

6. When Jack reached the restaurant where he planned to meet Alice, she <u>left</u> already.

   had left

7. Rajit saw that he had a missed call and was disappointed there <u>isn't</u> a voicemail.

   wasn't

8. Jaime loved coffee, but after <u>four cups were drunk</u> on Tuesday afternoon, she felt sick.

   she drank four cups

9. Since the signature on the document was the defendant's, he had trouble denying that he <u>agreed</u> to the terms.

   had agreed

10. The day after the blizzard, Maria was furious with the city. <u>Her street wasn't plowed by the city</u> until after nightfall.

    The city didn't plow her street

REVIEW EXERCISE 5

Each sentence in the paragraph contains a voice or tense problem. First, underline the problem. Then correct it by rewriting the verb in past tense or past-perfect tense or by changing a passive voice construction to active voice. Answers may vary.

¹At my ten-year high school class reunion last week, I saw many people I <u>did not see</u> in years. ²One old classmate <u>seen by me</u> was Patrick, the class clown. ³<u>Many tricks had been played by him</u> on the teachers at Truman High School, but now he is a teacher himself. ⁴Another former classmate I saw was Heather, who <u>is</u> the homecoming queen ten years ago. ⁵Her bubbly personality <u>did not change</u> since high school. ⁶She remembered everyone's name and <u>greets</u> them with a hug and a warm hello. ⁷The person that

surprised everyone was Wanda, who in high school <u>is</u> a computer nerd. [8]Then she was quiet and shy, but today <u>a major software company is owned by her.</u> [9]Many of the guys probably wished they <u>paid</u> more attention to Wanda back then. [10]The reunion was fun; I <u>enjoy</u> myself and can't wait to see what changes the next ten years will bring.

1. had not seen
2. I saw
3. He had played many tricks
4. was
5. had not changed
6. greeted
7. was
8. she owns a major software company
9. had paid
10. I enjoyed myself

mywritinglab   For support in meeting this chapter's goal, log in to **www.mywritinglab.com** and select **Consistent Verb Tense and Active Voice**.

CHAPTER 15

Coordination and Subordination

> *✍ Chapter Goal:* Connect ideas and control emphasis through coordination and subordination.

Coordination required.

✍ Writing Effective Sentences

mywritinglab

Visit MyWriting Lab for additional practice combining sentences.
Imagine a world without choices. What if everyone were named John or Jane? What if everyone ate corn flakes for breakfast, wore purple clothing, and drove a white Ford? What if every sentence had to start with the subject and one verb and contain only one idea? Here's a paragraph from that strange and boring world:

> My name is Jane. I got up this morning. The sky was blue. The sun was shining. I put on my purple slacks. I put on my purple shirt. I put on my purple shoes. I ate corn flakes. I ate them for breakfast. I drove my white Ford. I drove it to work.

267

Fortunately, the real world is abundant with choices in names, food, cars, and sentence structure. Here's what it really looks like.

> Hi, I'm Michaela. When I got up this morning, I looked out on a sun-splashed world topped with a clear blue sky. I threw on a pair of faded jeans, a yellow shirt, and a pair of white athletic shoes. My stomach was rumbling, so I sliced a ripe peach into a bowl, poured milk over it, and ate it standing at the counter. Then I stepped into the sunlight, cranked up my silver Toyota, and headed to work.

When you learned to write, you started by expressing one idea per sentence. Now, your ideas are more complex. Your sentence structure, too, has become more sophisticated to handle those complex ideas. This chapter will help you polish your sentence structure with the tools of **coordination** and **subordination** and may even help you add a few new tricks to your repertoire.

Connecting Ideas through Coordination

Often, ideas expressed in short, simple sentences can be joined to make a more effective sentence. One way to connect sentences is called *coordination*. Coordination can be done in two ways: by using a comma and a FANBOYS conjunction, or by using a semicolon and a joining word.

Comma and FANBOYS

FANBOYS conjunctions, more commonly called *coordinating conjunctions,* are used with a comma to connect two independent clauses. Remember that a **clause** is a grammatical unit that contains a subject and a verb and that an **independent clause** can stand alone as a sentence. The acronym FANBOYS stands for all seven coordinating conjunctions: *for, and, nor, but, or, yet, so.*

This is the pattern used when a FANBOYS conjunction is used with a comma to connect two independent clauses. The comma goes before the FANBOYS conjunction.

Pattern: Independent clause, **and** independent clause.

Examples of Sentences Connected by a Comma and FANBOYS

Marcus scanned the crowded cafeteria. (independent clause)

He did not see his friend Hannah. (independent clause)

The preceding two independent clauses can be connected with a FANBOYS conjunction and a comma:

✔   Marcus scanned the crowded cafeteria, but he did not see his friend Hannah.

PRACTICE 1   CONNECTING SENTENCES WITH FANBOYS

Connect each of the following sentence pairs with a comma and a FANBOYS conjunction.

1. In the darkened theater, a cell phone began to ring.
    Someone quickly silenced it.

    In the darkened theater, a cell phone began to ring, but someone quickly silenced it.

2. David's girlfriend tells him that he is lazy.
    David says he's just an expert at conserving energy.

    David's girlfriend tells him that he is lazy, but David says he's just an expert at conserving energy.

3. The parking lot was crowded.
    The library was packed with students studying for finals.

    The parking lot was crowded, and the library was packed with students studying for finals.

4. Patricia loves her morning cup of coffee from the coffee shop.
    Rising coffee prices are not about to make her give it up.

    Patricia loves her morning cup of coffee from the coffee shop, and rising coffee prices are not about to make her give it up.

5. Alisha does not want to live with her parents for too much longer.
    She plans to find a roommate and rent an apartment.

    Alisha does not want to live with her parents for too much longer, so she plans to find a roommate and rent an apartment.

Semicolon and Joining Word

Another method of coordination is using a semicolon and a joining word. As with a comma and a FANBOYS conjunction, a complete sentence (an independent clause) will appear on both sides of the semicolon.

Pattern: <u>Independent clause</u>; **therefore,** <u>independent clause.</u>

Example of Sentences Connected by a Semicolon and a Joining Word

✔ Mary thought she would have extra money left over at the end of the month.

✔ She did not anticipate having to buy a new battery for her car.

The two separate sentences can be combined with a semicolon and a joining word.

✔ Mary thought she would have extra money left over at the end of the month; however, she did not anticipate having to buy a new battery for her car.

The joining words also function as transitional expressions, underscoring the relationship between the two clauses. A list of joining words commonly used with semicolons follows.

Joining Words Used with a Semicolon

accordingly	furthermore	meanwhile
also	however	nevertheless
as a result	in addition	of course
besides	in fact	on the other hand
finally	instead	therefore

PRACTICE 2   CONNECTING SENTENCES WITH A SEMICOLON AND A JOINING WORD

Connect each of the following sentence pairs with a semicolon, a joining word from the preceding list, and a comma.

1. Sunny knew she needed to study for the test.
    She resisted the temptation to go out for pizza with her friends.
    <u>Sunny knew she needed to study for the test; therefore, she resisted the temptation</u>
    <u>to go out for pizza with her friends.</u>

2. Tony agreed to help Felicia move.
    He did not realize she had so much furniture.
    <u>Tony agreed to help Felicia move; however, he did not realize she had so much</u>
    <u>furniture.</u>

3. The woman who sat next to Bart on the plane insisted on telling him her life's story.

He pretended to go to sleep to avoid her chatter.

The woman who sat next to Bart on the plane insisted on telling him her life's story; finally, he pretended to go to sleep to avoid her chatter.

4. Rain came down in torrents.
   Catherine could barely see to drive.

   Rain came down in torrents; as a result, Catherine could barely see to drive.

5. Julie tried desperately to start her stalled car.
   The driver behind her began to honk the horn repeatedly.

   Julie tried desperately to start her stalled car; meanwhile, the driver behind her began to honk the horn repeatedly.

Connecting Ideas through Subordination

Another way of connecting ideas is through **subordination**. Placing a **dependent word** such as *because, although, if, when,* or *after* in front of an independent clause makes it a **dependent** or **subordinate** clause, one that can no longer stand on its own as a sentence. It must be connected to another idea that is stated as a complete sentence. It will then depend on that sentence it is attached to and can no longer be separated from it.

Examples of Ideas Connected through Subordination

Rashida had no time to sit down for breakfast.
She picked up a banana and a granola bar and walked out the door.

If the dependent clause acts as an introductory clause, a comma follows it.

Pattern: Because dependent clause**,** independent clause.

✔ **Because** Rashida had no time to sit down for breakfast, she picked up a banana and a granola bar and walked out the door.

Cars were backed up for miles on the interstate.
A tractor-trailer truck had turned over, blocking two lanes.

Pattern: Independent clause **because** dependent clause.

✔ Cars were backed up for miles on the interstate because a tractor-trailer truck had turned over, blocking two lanes.

If the dependent clause comes second in the sentence, generally no comma is needed.

A list of dependent words follows.

Dependent Words

after	because	that	whenever
although	before	though	where
as	even though	unless	wherever
as if	if	until	which
as long	once	what	while
as soon as	since	whatever	who
as though	so that	when	

PRACTICE 3   CONNECTING SENTENCES WITH DEPENDENT WORDS

Choosing from the preceding list of dependent words, connect each sentence pair using the following pattern:

Dependent word dependent clause, independent clause.

1. Kyla said she could not afford to go to school.
   Her friend told her she could not afford not to.

   When Kyla said she could not afford to go to school, her friend told her she could

   not afford not to.

2. Movies and television shows have romanticized the pioneers' journey west.
   Pioneers traveled for four to six months in a small wagon with limited food and no baths.

   Though movies and television shows have romanticized the pioneers' journey west, pio-

   neers traveled for four to six months in a small wagon with limited food and no baths.

3. Johannes Gutenberg invented the printing press in the fifteenth century.
   He provided a way for books to be widely distributed in large numbers.

   When Johannes Gutenberg invented the printing press in the fifteenth century, he

   provided a way for books to be widely distributed in large numbers.

4. The forecast called for snow.
   The grocery store was crowded with people stocking up on food.

   Because the forecast called for snow, the grocery store was crowded with people

   stocking up on food.

5. Ken sat on an outdoor bench eating his lunch.

   A stray dog looked at him expectantly.

   As Ken sat on an outdoor bench eating his lunch, a stray dog looked at him
   expectantly.

PRACTICE 4 CONNECTING SENTENCES WITH DEPENDENT WORDS

Choosing from the preceding list of dependent words, connect each sentence pair
using the following pattern:

   Independent clause dependent word dependent clause.

1. State troopers were patrolling the highways.

   Heavy traffic was expected on the holiday weekend.

   State troopers were patrolling the highways because heavy traffic was expected on
   the holiday weekend.

2. Lucia had just fallen asleep.

   The telephone rang, startling her out of a dream.

   Lucia had just fallen asleep when the telephone rang, startling her out of a
   dream.

3. Glover gripped the steering wheel in frustration.

   Traffic on the interstate ground to a complete stop.

   Glover gripped the steering wheel in frustration as traffic on the interstate ground
   to a complete stop.

4. Brett's muscles were sore and tired.

   He had spent an entire day doing construction work.

   Brett's muscles were sore and tired because he had spent an entire day doing construction work.

5. Amelia enjoyed her nieces and nephews.

   She did not think she was ready to have children.

   Amelia enjoyed her nieces and nephews even though she did not think she was ready
   to have children.

Creating Emphasis through Subordination

Dependent words also act as transitional words, showing the relationship between the ideas. Using dependent clauses helps to downplay one idea while emphasizing another. Usually, the idea expressed in the independent clause is of greater importance, while the idea in the dependent clause is of lesser importance.

Examples of Creating Emphasis through Subordination

emphasis on the pay
✔ Although the work is dangerous, the job pays well.

emphasis on the danger
✔ Although the job pays well, the work is dangerous.

emphasis on the cheer
✔ A cheer went up from the crowd as the home team scored the winning run.

emphasis on the run
✔ The home team scored the winning run as a cheer went up from the crowd.

PRACTICE 5   USING DEPENDENT WORDS TO EMPHASIZE IDEAS

Choosing from the preceding list of dependent words, connect each sentence pair. The idea that is given less emphasis should be introduced by a dependent word. The first one is done for you.

1. Teresa needed the money.
   She agreed to work a second shift. ✔ *Emphasize this idea.*

   Because Teresa needed the money, she agreed to work a second shift

2. The entire day stretched invitingly ahead of Jenna.
   She had no idea what she wanted to do. ✔ *Emphasize this idea.*

   Though the entire day stretched invitingly ahead of Jenna, she had no idea what she wanted to do.

3. Lin Yao was excited by the trip. ✔ *Emphasize this idea.*
   She had never traveled by train.
   Lin Yao was excited by the trip because she had never traveled by train.

4. The bananas were soft and speckled with brown.   ✔ *Emphasize this idea.*
    Cameron had just bought them yesterday.

    The bananas were soft and speckled with brown although Cameron had just bought

    them yesterday.

5. Anna went to the electronics store to buy a new computer game.
    She could not find anything she wanted.   ✔ *Emphasize this idea.*

    Although Anna went to the electronics store to buy a new computer game, she could

    not find anything she wanted.

Review Exercises

Complete the Review Exercises to find out how well you have learned the skills addressed in this chapter. As you work through the exercises, go back through the chapter to review any of the rules you do not understand completely.

REVIEW EXERCISE 1

Connect each sentence pair using coordination. Use a comma and a FANBOYS conjunction, or use a semicolon, a joining word, and a comma.

1. Rahim created a new playlist on his computer.
    He listened to his favorite music as he wrote his research paper.

    Rahim created a new playlist on his computer, and he listened to his favorite music

    as he wrote his research paper.

2. Horace had expected that traffic would be heavy in Atlanta.
    He had not bargained for the drivers who were speeding, weaving in and out of traffic, and following an inch from his bumper.

    Horace had expected that traffic would be heavy in Atlanta, yet he had not bargained

    for the drivers who were speeding, weaving in and out of traffic, and following an

    inch from his bumper.

3. Economists tried to account for the sudden improvement in the economy.
    Politicians scrambled to take credit.

    Economists tried to account for the sudden improvement in the economy, and politi-

    cians scrambled to take credit.

4. Piano keys used to be made of ivory from elephant tusks.
    They are now made of plastic.

    Piano keys used to be made of ivory from elephant tusks; however, they are now made of plastic.

5. People used to have to wait for a daily paper or for the six o'clock news program for a news update.
    News is now available 24 hours a day on the Internet and on television.

    People used to have to wait for a daily paper or for the six o'clock news program for a news update, but news is now available 24 hours a day on the Internet and on television.

REVIEW EXERCISE 2

Connect each sentence pair using subordination. Answers will vary.

1. Tina does her grocery shopping after most people have gone to bed.
    The store is never crowded late at night.

    Tina does her grocery shopping after most people have gone to bed because the store is never crowded late at night.

2. Kim's children were bored.
    She took them to the miniature golf course on Saturday morning.

    Since Kim's children were bored, she took them to the miniature golf course on Saturday morning.

3. Sanjay carefully removed the casserole dish from the oven.
    It slipped from his fingers and shattered on the floor.

    As Sanjay carefully removed the casserole dish from the oven, it slipped from his fingers and shattered on the floor.

4. Nick had always wanted to try carpentry.
    He signed up for a woodworking class.

    Since Nick had always wanted to try carpentry, he signed up for a woodworking class.

5. The applicant seemed charming and capable at the job interview.
    She proved to be undependable and careless.

    Though the applicant seemed charming and capable at the job interview, she proved to be undependable and careless.

REVIEW EXERCISE 3

Connect each sentence pair using coordination or subordination. Answers will vary.

1. A little stress can enhance a person's ability to perform a task.
    Too much stress can impair performance.

    A little stress can enhance a person's ability to perform a task; however, too much

    stress can impair performance.

2. Most people go through life with the name their parents gave them.
    In Hong Kong, some people drop their given names and go by exotic names
    such as Komix, Zeus, Boogie, or Maverick.

    Most people go through life with the name their parents gave them, yet in Hong

    Kong, some people drop their given names and go by exotic names such as Komix,

    Zeus, Boogie, or Maverick.

3. The coffee was brewing.
    The pleasant aroma filled the kitchen.

    The coffee was brewing, and the pleasant aroma filled the kitchen.

4. Arlene came to work after a two-week vacation.
    She had 147 email messages waiting for her.

    When Arlene came to work after a two-week vacation, she had 147 email messages

    waiting for her.

5. Laney had trouble concentrating on her work.
    The room was too hot and muggy.

    Laney had trouble concentrating on her work because the room was too hot and

    muggy.

REVIEW EXERCISE 4

Connect each sentence pair using coordination or subordination. Answers will vary.

1. The line at the box office stretched around the theater.
    People shivered in the cold and waited for the line to move.

    The line at the box office stretched around the theater, and people shivered in the

    cold and waited for the line to move.

2. The wild cactus grew large and began to flower.
    The carefully planted azaleas withered and died.

    The wild cactus grew large and began to flower; however, the carefully planted

    azaleas withered and died.

3. Melva answered the phone and listened impatiently.
    Her cereal grew soggy on the kitchen table.

    Melva answered the phone and listened impatiently as her cereal grew soggy on the

    kitchen table.

4. The cat ran quickly away from the tree.
    An offended bluebird followed, screeching and flapping.

    As the cat ran quickly away from the tree, an offended bluebird followed, screeching

    and flapping.

5. Lightning heats the air that surrounds it to more than 50,000 degrees
    Fahrenheit.
    The superheated air rapidly expands, causing the sonic boom that we call
    thunder.

    Lightning heats the air that surrounds it to more than 50,000 degrees Fahrenheit, and

    the superheated air rapidly expands, causing the sonic boom that we call thunder.

REVIEW EXERCISE 5

Connect the twenty sentences in this paragraph using coordination and subordination, so that you have no more than ten sentences when you are through. Answers may vary.

[1]This semester, Teresa has cut back to part-time hours at her job. [2]She will attend school full time. [3]She does not want to struggle financially. [4]She is determined to closely monitor her spending. [5]Teresa begins each month by figuring out what her income will be. [6]Then she subtracts her necessary expenses, such as rent, gas, and tuition. [7]She considers the remaining money her spending money. [8]She still has to be careful with that money because it has to cover all her daily expenses. [9]To avoid unnecessary purchases, she writes a list before going shopping. [10]She has started bringing lunch to campus instead of buying it at the cafeteria. [11]Her friends suggest an expensive night out at the movies. [12]Teresa proposes that they rent something. [13]They

suggest dinner at a restaurant. [14]Teresa suggests a potluck party. [15] By the end of most months, Teresa is under budget. [16]She is able to save money. [17]Teresa plans to use her savings to support herself next semester when her work hours are further reduced. [18]Teresa's friends are impressed. [19]They are saving money too. [20]This month, Teresa is going to help several of them plan their budgets.

[1]This semester, Teresa has cut back to part-time hours at her job because she will attend school full time. [2]She does not want to struggle financially, so she is determined to closely monitor her spending. [3]Teresa begins each month by figuring out what her income will be and then subtracting her necessary expenses such as rent, gas, and tuition. [4]She considers the remaining money her spending money, but she still has to be careful with that money because it has to cover all her daily expenses. [5]To avoid unnecessary purchases, she writes a list before going shopping, and she has started bringing lunch to campus instead of buying it at the cafeteria. [6]When her friends suggest an expensive night out at the movies, Teresa proposes that they rent something. [7]When they suggest dinner at a restaurant, Teresa suggests a potluck party. [8]By the end of most months, Teresa is under budget and able to save money, which she plans to use to support herself next semester when her work hours are further reduced. [9]Teresa's friends are impressed because they are saving money, too. [10]This month, Teresa is going to help several of them plan their budgets.

mywritinglab™   For support in meeting this chapter's goal, log in to www.mywritinglab.com and select **Combining Sentences**.

CHAPTER 16

Run-on Sentences

> ✎ **Chapter Goal:** Identify and correct run-on sentences.

*If you know any reason why
these two should not be
joined in marriage, speak now
or forever hold your peace.*

The words above, from the traditional marriage ceremony, are intended
to prevent marriages between those who are not legally free to marry. In
movies, the words are often followed by a dramatic interruption as a long-lost
love returns to stop the marriage. In real life, people usually hold their peace.
But should you hold your peace when you see two sentences illegally joined
together? Of course not! Run-ons and comma splices are ungrammatical unions
of sentences that must be prevented.

✎ What Is a Run-on Sentence?

mywritinglab

Visit MyWritingLab
for additional prac-
tice identifying run-
on sentences.

A **run-on sentence** is not one sentence, but two or more, run together without
proper punctuation. The following sentence is a run-on.

✗ Tasha worked slowly and carefully she had trouble finishing tests on
time.

By examining the sentence, you can probably figure out where the first thought ends and the second begins: between *carefully* and *she*. Grammatically, too, you can figure out why the thoughts should be separate. Each has a subject and a verb and is an **independent clause**, a clause that can stand alone as a sentence or that can be combined with other clauses in specific patterns.

Another type of run-on is called a **comma splice** because two independent clauses are spliced, or joined, with a comma.

✗ Tasha worked slowly and carefully, she had trouble finishing tests on time.

The run-on can be corrected in a variety of ways. Here are two of them.

✔ Tasha worked slowly and carefully, so she had trouble finishing tests on time.

✔ Because Tasha worked slowly and carefully, she had trouble finishing tests on time.

The first step toward writing paragraphs and essays that are free of run-on sentences is to learn to recognize run-ons and comma splices. When you see a sentence that you believe is a run-on, test it. Read the first part. Is it a sentence that could stand alone? If your answer is "yes," read the second part, asking the same question. If your answer is again "yes," the sentence is probably a run-on.

PRACTICE 1 RECOGNIZING RUN-ONS AND COMMA SPLICES

In each sentence, underline the spot where the run-on or comma splice occurs. Mark RO in the blank to the left of the sentence if the sentence is a run-on, CS if it is a comma splice.

RO **1.** Harold had one claim to fame he could wiggle his ears without moving his face.

CS **2.** The renovated theater was beautiful, the plush seats and velvet curtains recalled a more elegant era.

RO **3.** Leonard was seasick he stayed in his cabin on the first evening of the cruise.

CS **4.** "All I do is work and go to school, I feel like I'm on an endless treadmill," said Angelica.

RO **5.** Kaya stopped at a convenience store for gas she also bought a cup of coffee and a doughnut.

✍ Correcting Run-ons

Five methods of correcting run-ons are presented in the following sections. The first three methods are simple; the final two are more complex. Learning all five methods will give you more than just ways to correct run-ons; it will give you a variety of sentence patterns and transitional words to use in your writing.

Method 1: Period and Capital Letter

Correcting a run-on with a period and a capital letter is the easiest method to use. The hard part is knowing when and how often to use it. Short, single-clause sentences can emphasize ideas by setting them apart. However, too many short sentences can make your writing seem choppy and disconnected.

> **Pattern:** Independent clause. Independent clause.

Put a period between the two sentences. Use a capital letter to begin the new sentence.

Example of a Run-On Corrected with a Period and a Capital Letter

✗   Leon looked glumly at the blank sheet of paper he could not think of a thing to write.

✔   Leon looked glumly at the blank sheet of paper. He could not think of a thing to write.

PRACTICE 2   CORRECTING RUN-ONS WITH A PERIOD AND A CAPITAL LETTER

In each sentence, underline the spot where each run-on or comma splice occurs. Write RO in the blank to the left of the sentence if it is a run-on, CS if it is a comma splice. Then correct each sentence using a period and a capital letter.

___RO___ 1. Carol plans to study audiology she wants to help people with hearing problems.

audiology. She _____

___RO___ 2. Sally and Layla have been friends for years now they plan to go into business together.

years. Now _____

___RO___ 3. Scientists have developed a new drug it can help grow new blood vessels.

drug. It _____

CS___ 4. The short-term memory holds only five to seven bits of <u>information, grouping</u> numbers or items together is one way of storing more information in short-tem memory.

information. Grouping

CS___ 5. The baby did not have hair <u>yet, a faint</u> peach fuzz covered her head.

yet. A faint

Method 2: Comma and FANBOYS Conjunction

Coordinating conjunctions, or FANBOYS conjunctions, are among the most useful and powerful connecting words in the English language. If you can remember the acronym FANBOYS, you can remember the seven coordinating conjunctions: *for, and, nor, but, or, yet, so.*

Pattern: <u>Independent clause</u>, and <u>independent clause</u>.

When a FANBOYS conjunction is used with a comma to separate two clauses, the comma goes *before* the FANBOYS conjunction.

Example of a Run-on Corrected Using a Comma and a FANBOYS Conjunction

✘ Greg had not eaten breakfast he cooked some instant oatmeal in the microwave.

✔ Greg had not eaten breakfast, so he cooked some instant oatmeal in the microwave.

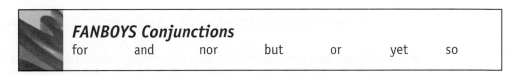

FANBOYS Conjunctions						
for	and	nor	but	or	yet	so

PRACTICE 3   CORRECTING RUN-ONS WITH A COMMA AND A FANBOYS CONJUNCTION

In each sentence, underline the spot where each run-on or comma splice occurs. Write RO in the blank to the left of the sentence if it is a run-on, CS if it is a comma splice. Correct each run-on or comma splice by using a comma and a FANBOYS conjunction. Answers will vary.

CS___ 1. The address label was shaped like a <u>teacup, the</u> sender's address was on the saucer.

teacup, and the

___RO___ 2. Victoria tried to tell Jim his plan would not <u>work he</u> did not want to hear her criticism.

work, but he
_____

___CS___ 3. Tyler's neighbors had three new cars and a recently installed hot <u>tub, they</u> each worked two jobs to pay for them.

tub, but they
_____

___CS___ 4. Sabrina felt stylish in her new <u>coat, there</u> was a little bounce in her walk.

coat, so there
_____

___RO___ 5. A cat rested on the porch <u>rail it</u> scampered away as a visitor approached.

rail, but it
_____

Method 3: Semicolon

Using a semicolon to join clauses works best with ideas that are closely connected and need no transitional word to explain the connection between them. The semicolon, as used here, is the grammatical equivalent of a period, but the first letter of the clause after the semicolon is *not* capitalized.

> **Pattern:** <u>Independent clause</u>; <u>independent clause</u>.

The semicolon goes between the two clauses.

Example of a Run-on Corrected with a Semicolon

✗ The book had been assigned for two weeks, Emily had not read a single page.

✔ The book had been assigned for two weeks; Emily had not read a single page.

PRACTICE 4 CORRECTING RUN-ONS WITH A SEMICOLON

In each sentence, underline the spot where each run-on or comma splice occurs. Write RO in the blank to the left of the sentence if it is a run-on, CS if it is a comma splice. Then correct the sentences using a semicolon alone.

___CS___ 1. The drama club held a car wash in a grocery store parking <u>lot, cars</u> lined up to take advantage of the low prices.

lot; cars
_____

RO   **2.** Bruce thought he was typing in the Internet address of a government <u>agency he</u> accessed a page of nude photographs instead.

agency; he

CS   **3.** Fashion trends exist in <u>language, new</u> words come into fashion as old ones go out.

language; new

CS   **4.** Valerie had several errands to <u>run, her</u> first was to go by the dry cleaners.

run; her

RO   **5.** The mailbox was filled with colorful sale flyers and <u>catalogs Terry</u> threw them in the trash.

catalogs; Terry

Method 4: Semicolon and Joining Word

A run-on sentence may also be corrected with a joining word. These joining words also function as transitional expressions, underscoring the relationship between the two clauses.

Pattern: <u>Independent clause</u>; therefore, <u>independent clause</u>.

A semicolon precedes the joining word, and a comma follows it. With the words *thus* and *then*, the comma is often omitted.

Example of a Run-on Corrected with a Semicolon and a Joining Word

✗ The bananas on the produce department's display were turning brown the lettuce looked wilted.

✔ The bananas on the produce department's display were turning brown; furthermore, the lettuce looked wilted.

Joining Words Used with a Semicolon

accordingly	furthermore	nevertheless
also	however	of course
as a result	in addition	on the other hand
besides	in fact	then
finally	instead	therefore
for example	meanwhile	thus
for instance	namely	

PRACTICE 5   CORRECTING RUN-ONS WITH A SEMICOLON AND A JOINING WORD

In each sentence, underline the spot where each run-on or comma splice occurs. Write RO in the blank to the left of the sentence if it is a run-on, CS if it is a comma splice. Then correct the sentence using a semicolon and an appropriate joining word. Answers will vary.

_**RO**_ **1.** The elevator did not <u>come Mina</u> pushed the button again.

come; therefore, Mina
_____

_**CS**_ **2.** The deli clerk was <u>daydreaming, he</u> cut nearly two pounds of meat instead of one.

daydreaming; as a result, he
_____

_**RO**_ **3.** Shane finally finished his phone call and returned to his <u>soup it</u> had gotten cold.

soup; of course, it
_____

_**CS**_ **4.** Sarah noticed a telephone number written inside the cover of her psychology <u>book, she</u> could not remember whose number it was.

book; however, she
_____

_**RO**_ **5.** The movie theater was <u>dark Michelle</u> almost sat on someone's lap.

dark; in fact, Michelle
_____

Method 5: Dependent Word

Placing a dependent word in front of an independent clause makes it a dependent clause, a clause that can no longer stand on its own as a sentence. It now *depends* on the sentence it is attached to and can no longer be separated from it.

Two variations of the dependent word method are shown below.

Examples of Run-ons Corrected with Dependent Words

✗   The restaurant was dark Martha could barely read her menu.

Pattern: Because <u>dependent clause</u>, <u>independent clause</u>.

When the dependent clause acts as an introductory clause, a comma follows it.

✔   Because the restaurant was dark, Martha could barely read her menu.

Pattern: <u>Independent clause</u> because <u>dependent clause</u>.

When the dependent clause comes last in the sentence, no comma is used.

✔ Martha could barely read her menu because the restaurant was dark.

Commonly Used Dependent Words

after	if	whatever
although	once	when
as	since	whenever
as if	so that	where
as long as	that	wherever
as soon as	though	which
as though	unless	while
because	until	who
before	what	whoever
even though		

PRACTICE 6   CORRECTING RUN-ONS WITH A DEPENDENT WORD

In each sentence, underline the spot where each run-on or comma splice occurs. Write RO in the blank to the left of the sentence if it is a run-on, CS if it is a comma splice. Correct each sentence using a dependent word. Answers will vary.

CS 1. Every computer in the lab was busy, Nelson put his name on the waiting list.

Because every computer in the lab was busy, Nelson

CS 2. The truck rumbled past, Veronica gripped the steering wheel of her small car.

rumbled past as Veronica

RO 3. Phil pumped gas into his car he noticed that the station across the street had lower prices.

As Phil pumped gas into his car, he

CS 4. Rita's week had been long and tiring, she did not feel like going out.

Since Rita's week had been long and tiring, she

RO 5. A little flag began to wave at the bottom of Joe's computer screen he knew he had email.

When a little flag began to wave at the bottom of Joe's computer screen,

he

Five Ways to Correct Run-on Sentences

Method 1: Period and Capital Letter

Pattern: Independent clause. Independent clause.

Method 2: Comma and FANBOYS Conjunction

Pattern: Independent clause, and independent clause.

A comma goes before the FANBOYS conjunction in this pattern.

FANBOYS Conjunctions

for   and   nor   but   or   yet   so

Method 3: Semicolon

Pattern: Independent clause; independent clause.

Method 4: Semicolon and Joining Word

Pattern: Independent clause; therefore, independent clause.

A semicolon goes before the joining word and a comma follows it. With the words *thus* and *then,* the comma is often omitted.

Joining Words Used with a Semicolon

also	however	of course
as a result	in addition	on the other hand
besides	in fact	then
finally	instead	therefore
for example	meanwhile	thus

Method 5: Dependent Word

Pattern 1: Although dependent clause, independent clause.

When a dependent word begins the sentence, a comma is used between the dependent and independent clause.

Pattern 2: Independent clause when dependent clause.

When the dependent clause ends the sentence, a dependent word separates the clauses.

Dependent Words

although	as though	once	unless	where
as	because	since	until	wherever
as if	before	so that	whatever	which
as long	even though	that	when	while
as soon as	if	though	whenever	who

Review Exercises

Complete the Review Exercises to find out how well you have learned the skills addressed in this chapter. As you work through the exercises, go back through the chapter to review any of the rules you do not understand completely.

REVIEW EXERCISE 1

In each sentence, underline the spot where the run-on or comma splice occurs. Then correct the ten run-on sentences, using each of the five methods at least once. Answers will vary.

1. The rain poured down in sheets Nell could barely see the road in front of her.
   sheets, and Nell

2. The edges of the wooden desk were once square and sharp now they are rounded from wear.
   sharp. Now

3. The lasagna was frozen solid, Linda knew it would take too long to reheat it.
   solid; Linda

4. Jemal tried to answer the telephone he dropped the receiver on the floor.
   When Jemal tried to answer the telephone, he

5. The delivery truck was behind schedule the hardware store employee said he did not think our order would be delivered today.
   schedule, and the hardware

6. Fred bit into a crisp toasted marshmallow, delicious white goo slid onto his tongue.
   marshmallow as delicious

7. Representatives from businesses and industries visited the campus today, students crowded around to sign up for interviews.
   today; students

8. Bootsie was due for her rabies shot, the vet sent a reminder in the mail.
   When Bootsie was due for her rabies shot, the

9. The loud pounding beat of the music in the aerobics room gave Jill a headache she wished someone would turn down the sound.
   headache. She

10. Brian fell asleep in front of the <u>television he</u> woke up at 2:00 A.M. with a crick in his neck.

television; as a result, he

REVIEW EXERCISE 2

In each sentence, underline the spot where the run-on or comma splice occurs. Then correct the ten run-on sentences, using each of the five methods at least once. Answers will vary.

1. Channing knew it was getting <u>late he</u> could not seem to stop playing his computer game.

late; however, he

2. The children visited the <u>museum some</u> of them petted a boa constrictor.

When the children visited the museum, some

3. Heather likes parties and <u>people her</u> husband prefers quiet evenings at home.

people; her

4. Jim bought highlighters, pens, index cards, and a <u>notebook he</u> still had trouble motivating himself to study.

notebook, but he

5. Vijay had his term paper stored on his USB <u>drive, however,</u> he could not find the drive.

drive; however, he

6. The lines were <u>long the</u> fast-food place was giving free fries to everyone.

long because the

7. The deli clerk asked how the customer wanted his bologna <u>sliced he</u> replied, "I want it so thin that I can read my newspaper through it."

sliced. He

8. Under the porch, a patch of flowers <u>grew apparently</u> the amount of sunlight was just right for them to thrive.

grew. Apparently

9. I saw Tom just a minute <u>ago, where</u> is he now?

ago. Where

10. A storm came through last <u>night two</u> trees were uprooted, and power lines were down.

When a storm came through last night, two

REVIEW EXERCISE 3

In the following exercise, underline the spot where each run-on or comma splice occurs. Then correct the two run-ons in each sentence group. Answers will vary.

1. Emily is training to run a 5K for her favorite <u>charity it supports</u> children with cancer. The race is in a <u>month Emily</u> plans to run after class every day.

charity; it supports

month. Emily

2. After his computer broke, Nathan called his <u>girlfriend she</u> is a computer science minor. She plans to get a job fixing computers this <u>summer after</u> graduation she wants to work for a major software company.

girlfriend; she

summer, and after

3. Alexandra saved her money all <u>year she</u> wanted to buy a new car. As she cruised down the highway on her way back from the dealership, she was thrilled with her <u>purchase, she</u> will never have to worry about bus schedules again.

year because she

purchase; she

4. Jonelle loves her job as a dental <u>assistant she</u> decided to go back to school for her hygienist's certificate. The hygienist at her office is retiring next <u>year, Jonelle</u> hopes to finish in time to get the hygienist position when it opens.

assistant, but she

year, and Jonelle

5. Faith's new job allows her to work from home once a <u>week without</u> her commute she has more time for her family and homework. She is thrilled with the new <u>arrangement, her</u> grades are better than ever.

week. Without

arrangement because her

REVIEW EXERCISE 4

In the following exercise, underline the spot where each run-on or comma splice occurs. Then correct the two run-ons in each sentence group. Answers will vary.

1. Marian browsed through the online film <u>selections the</u> latest releases didn't interest her. She decided to watch *Casablanca* one more <u>time, she</u> had always liked it.

   selections, but the latest

   time. She had

2. Fran rushed through the grocery <u>store, she</u> wished that the man in front of her would hurry. Then she noticed that the man was walking with a <u>cane, she</u> was ashamed of her impatience.

   As Fran rush through the grocery store, she

   cane, and she

3. The Gullah people are descendants of <u>slaves they</u> speak their own unique language. Their music incorporates the rhythms of clapping hands and stamping <u>feet, their</u> songs date back to the days of slavery.

   slaves, and they

   feet; furthermore, their

4. The Tomlinsons have just one <u>television, they</u> own two computers. They believe that their time is better spent on the <u>computer, watching</u> television does not engage their minds.

   television, but they

   computer because watching

5. At the barbecue place, Samuel ordered a quart of <u>barbecue then</u> he decided to add a rack of ribs to his order. He might be sorry <u>tomorrow, at</u> least he will eat well tonight.

   barbecue; then he

   tomorrow, but at least

REVIEW EXERCISE 5

In the following paragraph, underline the spot where each run-on or comma splice occurs. Then correct the ten run-on sentences or comma splices, using the five methods presented in this chapter. Try to use each method at least once. Answers will vary.

¹David woke up and squinted at the <u>clock, the</u> blue numbers on its face read 8:35. ²Immediately, he was filled with <u>panic he</u> had to be at work at nine. ³He leaped out of <u>bed then</u> he ran quickly to his son's room. ⁴"Get up, <u>Jason, it's</u> time for school, and Daddy's running late." he said. ⁵When David saw that his son was awake, he turned on the <u>shower as</u> the water warmed up, he thought of all the things he had to do. ⁶He would grab a shower and get <u>dressed, then</u> he would make sure Jason got ready for school. ⁷He would make a quick call to his office to say he would be a few minutes <u>late he</u> and Jason could take off, eating their breakfast in the car. ⁸After showering and dressing quickly, David went to check on <u>Jason his son</u> was still in his pajamas, eating Cheerios from the box and watching television. ⁹He stopped, astonished that his son was not getting ready for <u>school Jason</u> looked up at him and said, "Dad, it's Saturday." ¹⁰David laughed and flopped on the couch beside his <u>son "Pass</u> the Cheerios," he said.

1. When David woke up and squinted at the clock, the _____

2. panic because he _____

3. bed, and then _____

4. Jason. It's _____

5. shower. As the _____

6. get dressed, and then _____

7. late. Finally, he _____

8. Jason. His son _____

9. When he stopped, astonished that his son was not getting ready for school, Jason

10. son. "Pass _____

mywritinglab   For support in meeting this chapter's goal, log in to **www.mywritinglab.com** and select **Run-Ons**.

CHAPTER 17

Sentence Fragments

Chapter Goal: Identify and correct sentence fragments.

Has your sentence lost something?

Sentence fragments come in many varieties. Sometimes, all that is needed to correct a sentence fragment is the addition of a subject or a verb. Often, however, the sentence fragment can provide a logical beginning for the sentence that comes after it or a logical ending for the sentence that comes before it. Correcting a sentence fragment, then, becomes a matter of "lost and found." The fragment has lost its sentence, and your job is to find it and connect the two with proper punctuation.

What Is a Sentence Fragment?

mywritinglab
Visit MyWriting Lab for additional practice identifying sentence fragments.

✗ Susan finished reading the last section of the newspaper. *And dropped it on the floor beside her chair.*

✗ *When gasoline prices rise dramatically and stay high for a long time.* Automobile companies see a rise in the sale of smaller, more fuel-efficient cars.

The italicized word groups are **sentence fragments**: pieces of sentences that cannot stand alone. A sentence fragment is an incomplete sentence. It may be a dependent clause that cannot stand on its own, or it may lack a subject, a verb, or both. If you read a fragment by itself, without the other sentences that surround it, you will usually recognize that it does not express a complete thought. It is only a part, or fragment, of a sentence.

Dependent Clause Fragments

✗ *Because Javarez had missed the first bus.* He stood on the corner shivering and hoping that another one would come along soon.

✗ No one answered Alicia's knock. *Although someone was obviously at home.*

Each of the italicized fragments above is a **dependent clause fragment**. A dependent clause fragment always begins with a dependent word. To fix a dependent clause fragment, attach it to a complete sentence.

✔ Because Javarez had missed the first bus, he stood on the corner shivering and hoping that another one would come along soon.

✔ No one answered Alicia's knock although someone was obviously at home.

Dropping the dependent word or changing it to another type of transitional expression is an alternative to connecting the fragment to the sentence.

✔ Javarez had missed the first bus. He stood on the corner shivering and hoping that another one would come along soon.

✔ No one answered Alicia's knock. However, someone was obviously at home.

Punctuation Pointer

In general, use a comma to attach a dependent clause fragment at the beginning of a sentence.

Commonly Used Dependent Words

after	because	so that	when
although	before	that	whenever
as	even though	though	where
as if	how	unless	which
as long as	if	until	while
as soon as	once	what	who
as though	since	whatever	whoever

PRACTICE 1   CORRECTING DEPENDENT CLAUSE FRAGMENTS

Correct the dependent clause fragments by attaching them to an independent clause. Answers may vary.

1. While several of her friends planned to go out of town over the long weekend. Sarah preferred to stay at home, relax, and save her money.

    long weekend, Sarah preferred

2. Tyrell was put off by a salesman. Who placed an arm around his shoulder and greeted him like an old friend.

    salesman who placed

3. Because Mary slept through her alarm. She missed her 10:00 A.M. class.

    her alarm, she missed

4. As Dan unloaded the groceries from the car. He realized that the gallon of milk he had bought was not in the trunk.

    from the car, he realized

5. My grandparents say they have never considered divorce as a solution to their problems. Although Grandma says she has occasionally considered murder.

    their problems although Grandma

Verbal Phrase Fragments (*to, -ing,* and *-ed*)

✗ *To keep gasoline costs down.* Many people carpool to work or school.

✗ *Worrying about damage to his car.* Jonathan ran out into the hailstorm to pull it into the garage.

✗ *Curled in a protective ball in the corner of his cage.* Jo's hedgehog looked unhappy.

The previous examples are **verbal phrase fragments**. A verbal phrase fragment begins with a verb form that is not used as a main verb. Verbal phrase fragments include *to* fragments, *-ing* fragments, and *-ed/-en* fragments.

Correct verbal phrase fragments by attaching them to a complete sentence.

✔ To keep gasoline costs down, many people carpool to work or school.

✔ Worrying about damage to his car, Jonathan ran out into the hailstorm to pull the vehicle into the garage.

✔ Curled in a protective ball in the corner of his cage, Jo's hedgehog looked unhappy.

to Fragments

Correct the *to* fragments by connecting them to a sentence or by adding a subject and a verb.

Examples of *to* Fragments

✗ To keep her children entertained on the long trip home. Kayla challenged them to see who could spot the largest number of license plates from different states.

✔ To keep her children entertained on the long trip home, Kayla challenged them to see who could spot the largest number of license plates from different states.

✗ Last Friday, Ron invited his friends over. To help him celebrate his graduation from college.

✔ Last Friday, Ron invited his friends over to help him celebrate his graduation from college.

✗ Joann practiced for hours over the weekend. To make sure everything would go well during her interview on Monday.

✔ Joann practiced for hours over the weekend. She wanted to make sure everything would go well during her interview on Monday.

Punctuation Pointer

A *to* fragment attached to the beginning of a sentence is followed by a comma because it is an introductory phrase. A *to* fragment connected to the end of the sentence needs no comma.

PRACTICE 2   CORRECTING *TO* FRAGMENTS

Underline and correct the *to* fragments. Answers may vary.

1. <u>To strengthen her back and improve her posture.</u> Shauna began a weightlifting program.

   her posture, Shauna began

2. The cook used a wide metal spatula. <u>To turn the pancakes on the grill.</u>

   spatula to turn

3. <u>To give himself time to review for the exam.</u> Damon set his clock a half hour early.

   exam, Damon set his

4. The networks schedule popular movies and special shows. <u>To attract viewers during "sweeps week."</u>

   shows to attract

5. <u>To unwind at the end of the day.</u> Marcy took a walk and watched the sun set.

   the day, Marcy took

-ing Fragments

To correct an -*ing* fragment, connect it to the rest of the sentence with a comma. You may also correct it by adding a subject and a helping verb.

Examples of -ing Fragments

✗ Eating the hearty bean soup that he had made. Ed decided that he was becoming a good cook.

✔ Eating the hearty bean soup that he had made, Ed decided that he was becoming a good cook.

✗ The decorator stepped back from the paintings she had hung. Checking to make sure they were precisely aligned.

✔ The decorator stepped back from the paintings she had hung, checking to make sure they were precisely aligned.

✔ The decorator stepped back from the paintings she had hung. She was checking to make sure they were precisely aligned.

Punctuation Pointer

Usually, -*ing* fragments can be connected to the rest of the sentence with a comma.

PRACTICE 3   CORRECTING -ING FRAGMENTS

Underline and correct the -*ing* fragments. Answers may vary.

1. <u>Realizing that the high noise level could damage employees' hearing.</u> The factory's management required workers to wear earplugs.

   hearing, the factory's

2. <u>Hearing a commotion in the living room.</u> Rita wondered whether she should check on the children.

   room, Rita wondered

3. Samantha quickly locked the door and left. <u>Knowing she was probably going to be late for work.</u>

   door and left, knowing

4. <u>Swinging their bare feet and gazing down into the green water.</u> The two children amused themselves while their father fished from the dock.

   green water, the two

5. The police officer raised a white-gloved hand. <u>Stopping traffic to let a group of children cross the street.</u>

   hand, stopping traffic

-ed/-en fragments

Another kind of fragment begins with an *-ed* or *-en* verb form. If the verb is a regular verb, the verb form will end in *-ed*, like the verbs *walked, called,* or *plotted.* If the verb is irregular, then the verb form will end in *-en* or in another irregular ending. *Broken, grown, found, bought,* and *written* are some of these forms. These *-ed* and *-en* forms are called *past participles.* For other examples, see the list of irregular verbs in Chapter 12. This type of fragment can usually be corrected by connecting it to a complete sentence.

✘ Spaced evenly and set in rows. The desks seemed ready for the fall term.

✔ Spaced evenly and set in rows, the desks seemed ready for the fall term

✘ Everyone looked at the white rabbit. Held by the top-hatted magician.

✔ Everyone looked at the white rabbit held by the top-hatted magician.

✘ Caught with his car full of stolen property. The thief could only confess.

✔ Caught with his car full of stolen property, the thief could only confess.

Punctuation Pointer

Always connect *-ed/-en* fragments to the *beginning* of a sentence with a comma. An *-ed/en* fragment connected to the end of a sentence may sometimes require a comma, depending on usage. Those in this exercise will not require a comma.

PRACTICE 4   CORRECTING *-ED* SENTENCE FRAGMENTS

Underline and correct the *-ed /-en* fragments in the following exercise.

1. <u>Encouraged by her parents.</u> Dawn decided to apply for the scholarship.

   Encouraged by her parents, Dawn decided to apply for the scholarship.

   _____

2. Next week, students are invited to a career fair and resume workshop. <u>Presented by the college's career counseling office.</u>

   Next week, students are invited to a career fair and resume workshop presented by

   the college's career counseling office.

3. <u>Cleaned and pressed at the local cleaners.</u> Eldon's old sport coat looked like new.

   Cleaned and pressed at the local cleaners, Eldon's old sport coat looked like new.

   _____

4. <u>Drawn by the smell of food.</u> The dog decided to join our picnic.

   Drawn by the smell of food, the dog decided to join our picnic.

5. Kevin has kept his old model trains. <u>Stored on a shelf in a closet in his parents' house.</u>

   Kevin has kept his old model trains stored on a shelf in a closet in his parents'

   house.

Missing-Subject Fragments

Fragments beginning with a joining word such as *and, or, but,* or *then* followed by a verb are **missing-subject fragments**. The subject of the verb is usually in a previous sentence. Connect the fragment to the sentence or add a subject to begin a new sentence.

Examples of Missing-Subject Fragments

✗ The crowd grew silent when the player clutched his leg and fell. Then cheered as he was helped off the field.

✔ The crowd grew silent when the player clutched his leg and fell, then cheered as he was helped off the field.

✗ Kara mailed her telephone bill. But forgot to enclose a check.

✔ Kara mailed her telephone bill, but she forgot to enclose a check.

✔ Kara mailed her telephone bill. She forgot to enclose a check.

PRACTICE 5   CORRECTING MISSING-SUBJECT FRAGMENTS

Underline and correct the missing-subject fragments. Answers may vary.

1. Anthony started to fill out the questionnaire. <u>Then decided that it asked too many nosy questions.</u>

    questionnaire, then

2. The snow began to stick around 10:00 in the morning. <u>And was four inches deep by 5:00 in the afternoon.</u>

    morning and was

3. Tanisha longed for a double cheeseburger with a side order of fries. <u>But decided to have a plain chicken sandwich on whole wheat.</u>

    fries but decided

4. Narcissus was a mythological character who bent to look at himself in a pool of water. <u>And fell in love with his own image.</u>

    water and fell in

5. Beth jumped at a strange noise that seemed to come from her living room. <u>Then decided it was her imagination and turned back to her computer.</u>

    room. Then she decided

Real-World Writing: Is it okay to start a sentence with but?

Yes and no. Grammatically, it is correct to start a sentence with *but* or any other FANBOYS conjunction. However, your instructors may discourage the practice, for two good reasons.

1. Beginning a sentence with *but* is an informal technique. It may work in personal essays but should not be used in formal compositions such as research papers. (This text, you may have noticed, takes an informal, conversational approach, addressing you directly and occasionally using a FANBOYS conjunction to begin a sentence.)

2. Using *but* to begin a sentence can be addictive. *But* is the strongest contrast signal in our language, and it's easy to overuse.

The bottom line: Use conjunctions to begin sentences only if your instructor gives the green light, and then use them sparingly.

Example and Exception Fragments

Fragments often occur when a writer adds an example or notes an exception. Example fragments often begin with *such as, including, like, for example,* or *for instance.* Exception fragments often begin with *not, except, unless, without,* or *in spite of.* To fix the fragment, connect it to the sentence with which it logically belongs. If the fragment begins with *for example* or *for instance,* it is often best to make the fragment into a separate sentence.

Examples of Example and Exception Fragments

✗ Holly remained focused on the paper she was writing. In spite of her little brother's constant interruptions.

✔ Holly remained focused on the paper she was writing, in spite of her little brother's constant interruptions.

✗ Ed signed up for the Great American Smokeout, but he was not sure he could make it through the day. Without smoking a cigarette.

✔ Ed signed up for the Great American Smokeout, but he was not sure he could make it through the day without smoking a cigarette.

✗ Clayton says that there are many dishes he cooks well. For example, instant breakfasts and microwaveable dinners.

✔ Clayton says that there are many dishes he cooks well. For example, he does a great job with instant breakfasts and microwaveable dinners.

Punctuation Pointer

Usually, you can connect fragments beginning with *such as, including, not, especially,* and *in spite of* with a comma and fragments beginning with *except, unless, without,* and *like* with no comma.

A fragment beginning with *for example* or *for instance* may be attached with a comma if it immediately follows the idea it illustrates: **The chef enjoyed cooking with beans, for example, lima beans, garbanzo beans, and kidney beans.** If the idea that the example illustrates is expressed earlier in the sentence, place the example in a new sentence: **Beans are the specialty of the house at Rizzoli's Restaurant. For example, the chef makes delicious dishes from lima beans, garbanzo beans, and kidney beans.**

PRACTICE 6   CORRECTING EXAMPLE AND EXCEPTION FRAGMENTS

Underline and correct the example and exception fragments. Answers may vary.

1. Stacie says she never takes her children anywhere. <u>Without bringing along water, juice, and snacks.</u>

   anywhere without bringing

2. Kendrick complains that his wife has a few bad habits. <u>For example, never turning a light off when she leaves a room.</u>

   For example, she never turns

3. The dentist told Sharon she did not need to floss. <u>Unless she wanted to keep her teeth.</u>

   floss unless she

4. During the holidays, the department store where Amy works takes extra security measures. <u>Such as hiring store detectives who pose as shoppers.</u>

   measures, such as hiring

5. With a new pair of athletic shoes, a stationary bike, and a membership in a fitness center, Kyle had everything he needed. <u>Except willpower.</u>

   needed except willpower

Prepositional Phrase Fragments

A prepositional phrase, alone or within a series, cannot function as a sentence. Correct a prepositional phrase fragment by connecting it to a sentence with which it logically belongs.

Examples of Prepositional Phrase Fragments

✘   Kelsey rented a small, one-bedroom apartment. In a complex that offered a pool and other recreational facilities.

✔   Kelsey rented a small, one-bedroom apartment in a complex that offered a pool and other recreational facilities.

✘   On the day of his first political science test. Lee woke up with a pounding headache and a fever of 101 degrees.

✔   On the day of his first political science test, Lee woke up with a pounding headache and a fever of 101 degrees.

Punctuation Pointer

Use a comma after an introductory prepositional phrase. No punctuation is required to connect a prepositional phrase to the end of a sentence.

PRACTICE 7   CORRECTING PREPOSITIONAL PHRASE FRAGMENTS

Underline and correct each prepositional phrase fragment. Answers may vary.

1. <u>In the vacant lot beside the convenience store.</u> Someone had discarded an old recliner.

   store, someone had

2. It was such a pleasant day that we decided to study. <u>Under a tree beside the lake.</u>

   study under a tree

3. <u>Beneath the smooth-looking, freshly painted surface.</u> Hundreds of termites were gnawing at the wood.

   surface, hundreds of termites

4. Hassan thought he needed a car, but he decided against it after he checked prices. <u>In the classified ads on craigslist.</u>

   prices in the classified

5. <u>On a bus headed toward New Jersey.</u> Channa's woolen gloves, forgotten under the seat, traveled on without her.

   New Jersey, Channa's woolen

Review Exercises

Complete the Review Exercises to find out how well you have learned the skills addressed in this chapter. As you work through the exercises, go back through the chapter to review any of the rules you do not understand completely.

REVIEW EXERCISE 1

Underline and correct each fragment. Answers may vary.

1. A puzzled frown creased Martin's brow. <u>As he studied the recipe in front of him.</u>

   brow as he studied

2. When he investigated the strange lump on his bed. Walter found the cat curled up underneath the bedspread.

   bed, Walter found

3. During the storm, a rotting tree toppled. And lay across the road, blocking two lanes of traffic.

   toppled and lay

4. The police have set up a roadblock in front of the bridge. To catch drivers who don't have current tags or insurance.

   bridge to catch

5. With its arched doorways and intricate stained glass windows. The old church was a beautiful place to hold a wedding.

   windows, the old church

6. Speaking no English and with little savings. Kim's grandparents came to the United States to begin a new life.

   savings, Kim's

7. Eduardo and Maria built a successful business. And sent their five children to college.

   business and sent

8. Harry says that he never reads tabloids. Except when he is standing in line at the grocery store.

   tabloids except when he

9. Grover sat in line at the drive-through at the hamburger place for fifteen minutes. Wondering how fast food could be so slow.

   minutes, wondering how

10. As she looked at the clutter on top of her desk. Corinne wondered how she would ever sort it all out.

    desk, Corinne wondered

REVIEW EXERCISE 2

Underline and correct each fragment. Answers may vary.

1. Dave found his missing wallet. Even though he had been convinced it was stolen.

   wallet, even

2. Following in her older sister's footsteps. Natalie decided she would go into the medical field, too.

    footsteps, Natalie

3. After checking the weather forecast. Inez decided to bring an umbrella.

    forecast, Inez decided

4. Although the car's bumper sticker read "Have a Nice Day." The driver's angry gesture carried a different message.

    Day," the

5. Rushing to finish the grocery shopping and get home to make supper. Meghan forgot to buy the main ingredient.

    supper, Meghan

6. Sara tried Bright and Shiny Shampoo. After seeing her favorite celebrity rave about the shampoo in an interview.

    Shampoo after seeing

7. Emanuel called in sick from his job at the restaurant. To study for his exam.

    restaurant to study

8. Jessica's cell phone rang loudly. Interrupting her instructor during his lecture.

    loudly, interrupting

9. With lettuce, chicken breasts, tortillas, tomatoes, onions, and cheese in his cart. Mike hoped that he had everything he needed to make fajitas for supper.

    cart, Mike

10. Aline's patience ran out. Wondering if she would ever work her way up to the front of this line.

    Wondering if she would ever work her way up to the front of this line, Aline's

REVIEW EXERCISE 3

Underline and correct the two fragments in each numbered item. Answers may vary.

1. When Nora and A.J. returned from their vacation. They noticed a strange, unpleasant odor in the kitchen. They tried to find the source of the smell. And discovered a package of pita bread covered in dark green mold.

    vacation, they noticed

    smell and discovered

2. Antwan bought everything he needed for his backyard cookout. <u>Including three kinds of meat and two varieties of barbecue sauce.</u> He had thought of everything. <u>Except the possibility of rain.</u>

cookout, including three

everything except the possibility

3. Joseph spent many hours at his kitchen table. <u>Building and painting a delicate model ship.</u> When he was finally finished, he set it out to dry. <u>In a place that he hoped was too high for his three-year-old to reach.</u>

table, building and painting

dry in a place that he hoped

4. <u>Whenever she was almost finished with a task.</u> Such as reading a novel, writing a paper, or doing a set of math problems, Jennifer was anxious to get the job done. <u>Yet always put off reading the last few pages, writing the conclusion, or finishing the last few problems.</u>

task, such as reading

Yet she always put off

5. <u>Though Paul was an expert at many things, such as carpentry and music.</u> He had trouble functioning in daily life. He sometimes seemed unable to perform the simplest tasks. <u>Such as balancing his checkbook or remembering to fill his car with gas.</u>

music, he sometimes

living, such as balancing

REVIEW EXERCISE 4

Underline and correct the two fragments in each numbered item. Answers may vary.

1. Neil bought a small car a few years ago. <u>But kept his old pickup truck, too.</u> Neil is glad he kept the pickup. <u>Especially when he needs to transport a piece of furniture or some other large item.</u>

ago, but kept

pickup, especially

2. As the logs in the fireplace began to burn. Ebony realized she had forgotten to open the damper. When smoke started pouring into the living room. She began to cough.

burn, Ebony realized
_____

room, she began
_____

3. Maria had lived in the South all her life. But had never eaten grits. When she finally tried them. She said they tasted like buttered sand.

life but had never
_____

them, she said they
_____

4. Some drivers' behavior on the road would be funny. If it were not so dangerous. For example, some drivers put on makeup while driving. Or talk on a cell phone as if they are at home.

funny if it
_____

driving or talk
_____

5. In his glove compartment, Will found several items he had thought were lost. Such as an old address book and the good pen his grandmother had given him when he graduated from high school. But he did not find his license and registration. To give to the police officer who was standing patiently beside his car.

lost, such as an old
_____

registration to give to the police
_____

REVIEW EXERCISE 5

Underline and correct the ten fragments below. Answers may vary.

Jessie walked through the house, looking under chairs and behind sofa pillows. [1]And trying to find her cell phone. "When did you see it last?" her mother asked. Jessie said she had taken it with her the night before. [2]When she went out to walk Bruce, her big Newfoundland dog. [3]Then had thrown it into an armchair as she walked into the family room. Jessie and her mother searched every crevice of the armchair. [4]But did not find the phone. Jessie's brother suggested that she dial the cell phone's number. [5]Then locate the phone by its ringing. [6]When Jessie dialed the number. She heard the faint sound of music. Leaving the phone off the hook, Jessie walked into the family room. [7]Where Bruce was lying asleep in front of the fireplace. "It's under Bruce!" she called, trying to roll the dog over. Then she realized that the sound was not coming from underneath Bruce. [8]But from inside him. Her dog had somehow swallowed her cell phone. Immediately, she ran back to the kitchen and called the veterinarian. [9]As soon as the vet stopped laughing. He told Jessie not to worry. "Bruce is a big dog." he said. "The cell phone should pass through his system in a day or two." Jessie was relieved. [10]That her dog would be all right. She could get another cell phone, but Bruce was irreplaceable.

Jessie walked through the house, looking under chairs and behind sofa pillows for her cellular phone. "When did you see it last?" her mother asked. Jessie said she had taken it with her the night before when she went out to walk Bruce, her big Newfoundland dog. Then she had thrown it into an armchair as she walked into the family room. Jessie and her mother searched every crevice of the armchair but did not find the phone. Jessie's brother suggested that she dial the cell phone's number, then locate the phone by its ringing. When Jessie dialed the number, she heard the faint sound of music. Leaving the phone off the hook, Jessie walked into the family room where Bruce was lying asleep in front of the fireplace. "It's under Bruce!" she called, trying to roll the dog over. Then she realized that the sound was not coming from underneath Bruce but from inside him. Her dog had somehow swallowed her cell phone. Immediately, she ran back to the kitchen and called the veterinarian. As soon as the vet stopped laughing, he told Jessie not to worry. "Bruce is a big dog," he said. "The cell phone should pass through his system in a day or two." Jessie was relieved that her dog would be all right. She could get another cell phone, but Bruce was irreplaceable.

CHAPTER **18**

Pronoun Case

> ✎ **Chapter Goal:** Recognize subject, object, intensive, and reflexive pronouns and use them correctly.

I travel with a pronoun case;
I bring myself and I.
As you and he hop in my case,
Whoever waves goodbye.

We, them, himself, herself, and who
Pile in with she and him.
Someday I'd like to travel light;
The chances seem quite slim.

And when we reach the station,
All getting on the bus,
I look for fellow travelers,
But no one's here but us.

Pronouns are words that stand in for nouns or for other pronouns. They are useful words that keep writers and speakers from tediously repeating words. The rules that govern them are complex, however, and confusion over pronoun usage is common. If you have ever hesitated over "Carlton and me" or "Carlton and I" or wondered whether to say "between you and I" or "between you and me," this chapter will help you find the answers.

✎ Subject and Object Pronouns

mywritinglab

Visit MyWriting Lab for additional practice using pronouns correctly.

Personal pronouns (*I, we, you, he, she, it, they*) refer to specific people or things. These pronouns take different forms, called **cases,** as they perform various jobs in a sentence. Look at the example that follows to see how the first person pronoun *I* changes form as its role in a sentence changes.

✔ When *I* went to the post office to pick up *my* mail, the clerk said there was a package for *me.*

Subject pronouns (the subjective case) include pronouns such as *I, we, you, he, she, it,* and *they.*

✔ *They* were up until midnight trying to put up the wallpaper.

✔ *We* tried to call you, but your line was busy all evening.

✔ The winners were Bryan and *she.*

Object pronouns (the objective case) are pronouns such as *me, us, you, him, her, it,* and *them.*

✔ If you are through with the book, please pass it on to *me.*

✔ The cats are waiting for Hilary to feed *them.*

✔ I looked for the flashlight but could not find *it* in the dark.

Subject Pronouns

In most instances, you probably use the subject form of the pronoun correctly without thinking about it. You probably haven't said, "Me went to the park" since you were three. However, using the subject form becomes trickier when a *compound subject* is used. Is it "Tiffany and her went to the concert" or "Tiffany and she went to the concert"? Usually, trying the sentence with the pronoun alone helps you hear the correct answer. Without "Tiffany and" the sentence becomes clear. "*She* went to the concert" is correct, not "*Her* went to the concert."

Example of Pronouns in Compound Subjects

? *Her and Liz* worked in the same office.

Step 1: To determine if the sentence is correct, try the pronoun alone.

✗ *Her and Liz* worked in the same office.

✗ *Her* worked in the same office.

Step 2: If the pronoun alone sounds incorrect, try changing the form.

✔ She worked in the same office.

✔ She and Liz worked in the same office. (corrected sentence)

PRACTICE 1   USING SUBJECT PRONOUNS

Underline and correct the errors in each sentence. To determine the correct pronoun form, try the pronoun alone, without the compound element.

1. Joel and me took the afternoon off to go fishing.

    Joel and I

2. When I left for the day, Lynda and <u>them</u> were still working.
    <u>Lynda and they</u>

3. I heard that Monica and <u>him</u> made the two highest grades on the test.
    <u>Monica and he</u>

4. You and <u>me</u> should work on our grammar homework together.
    <u>You and I</u>

5. Have you and <u>him</u> known each other for very long?
    <u>you and he</u>

Subject Pronouns after Linking Verbs

"Hello?"
"May I speak to Tanisha Jones, please?"
<u>This</u> is <u>she</u>."
"Hello, Tanisha, this is Randall Groover from your biology class. I was wondering . . ."

This polite exchange is typical of the way many telephone conversations begin, and it illustrates a rule that many people use in telephone conversations but ignore otherwise: When a pronoun renames the subject (that is, when it is a *subject complement*) and follows the verb *to be* or any *linking verb*, that pronoun takes the subject form.

Examples of Subject Pronouns after Linking Verbs

Subject	linking verb	subject complement
✔ The <u>recipient</u> of the award	<u>will be</u>	<u>he</u>.

✔ *It* is *I*. (not *me*)

✔ I had not seen Sheldon since grade school, so I was not sure that *it* was *he*. (not *him*)

✔ If you want to see Ms. Long, *that* is *she* in the hat and sunglasses. (not *her*)

PRACTICE 2   USING SUBJECT PRONOUNS AFTER LINKING VERBS

Underline the correct pronoun in each sentence.

1. I enjoyed Dr. Barker's English 100 class, so when I found out the teacher for English 200 would be (<u>he</u>, him), I signed up.

2. For many years, my closest friend was (<u>she</u>, her).
3. The speaker at our club's luncheon will be (<u>he</u>, him).
4. As he answered the phone, Leon said "Who is this?" "It is (<u>I</u>, me)," said Pete.
5. If there is anyone who deserves a promotion, it is (<u>she</u>, her).

Object Pronouns

Object pronouns are used as objects of verbs and prepositions. As with subject pronouns, problems with object pronouns commonly occur in compound constructions. These problems can usually be resolved by isolating the pronoun.

Examples of Pronouns in Compound Objects

?   The instructor agreed to give *Tran and I* a makeup exam.

✗   The instructor agreed to give Tran and *I* a makeup exam.

✗   The instructor agreed to give *I* a makeup exam.

✔   The instructor agreed to give *me* a makeup exam.

Object Pronouns with *Between*

Object pronouns always follow the preposition *between*. Thus, it is always *between you and me, between us and them, between him and her, between Larry and him.*

> ### *Grammar Alert!*
>
> Pronouns are often misused with *between*. Remember to use the object form: between you and *me, him, her,* or *them*

Examples of Object Pronouns with *Between*

✗   Just between you and *I*, I think Sara is planning to quit school and work full time.

✔   Just between you and *me*, I think Sara is planning to quit school and work full time.

✗   The agreement was between Anita and *he*; I had nothing to do with it.

✔   The agreement was between Anita and him; I had nothing to do with it.

PRACTICE 3   USING OBJECT PRONOUNS

Underline the correct pronoun in each sentence.

1. The man behind the counter at the convenience store gave Yolanda and (I, me) directions, but we got lost anyway.
2. We aren't sure who will be elected president of the club, but the choice is between Calvin and (she, her).
3. The office barely had enough room for Leo and (he, him).
4. At the grocery store, an employee gave my husband and (I, me) a handful of coupons.
5. The table was small, but it was perfect for Tracy and (he, him).

Intensive and Reflexive Pronouns

Personal pronouns also take on forms known as *intensive* and *reflexive forms.* These pronouns are the *-self* pronouns: *myself, ourselves, yourself, himself, herself, itself,* and *themselves.*

Intensive Pronouns

Intensive pronouns are used for emphasis. They let a reader know that an action was performed by or directed toward *only* the person or thing that the pronoun refers to. It is easy to identify intensive pronouns. Since they are used strictly for emphasis, a sentence would make perfect sense and have the same meaning if the intensive pronoun were left out.

✔ The district attorney *himself* recommended that the charges be dropped.
✔ In spite of severe damage in outlying areas, the town *itself* was untouched by the tornado.
✔ Although the project was supposed to be a group effort, Sharon did every bit of the research *herself.*

Reflexive Pronouns

Reflexive pronouns show that an action was performed by someone on himself or herself (or by something on itself).

✔ Erica cut *herself* as she was slicing an onion.
✔ Brian forced *himself* to finish the job.
✔ The machine monitors *itself* for problems in functioning.

PRACTICE 4 RECOGNIZING INTENSIVE AND REFLEXIVE PRONOUNS

Underline the *-self* pronoun in each sentence below. Then, in the blank provided, write I if the pronoun is an intensive pronoun and R if it is a reflexive pronoun.

___I___ **1.** The president <u>himself</u> called to congratulate the soccer team.

___R___ **2.** Phyllis treated <u>herself</u> to dinner and a movie.

___I___ **3.** The building <u>itself</u> needs extensive repairs.

___R___ **4.** Hal bought <u>himself</u> a new car.

___I___ **5.** The instructor <u>herself</u> told Charles that the course was canceled.

Problems with Intensive and Reflexive Pronouns

Intensive and reflexive pronouns are often used incorrectly in compound subjects or objects. Look at the examples below.

> ### Grammar Alert!
> The *-self* pronouns are never used as subjects.

Example of Intensive and Reflexive Pronouns in Compound Subjects

✗ Jake and myself went to the auto parts store to pick up an oil filter.

When you leave out the compound element, the problem is easier to spot:

✗ *Myself* went to the auto parts store to pick up an oil filter.

A subject pronoun is needed to correct the sentence:

✔ *I* went to the auto parts store to pick up an oil filter.

✔ Jake and *I* went to the auto parts store to pick up an oil filter.

Example of Intensive and Reflexive Pronouns in Compound Objects

✗ "Janie makes *her mother and myself* very proud," said Mr. Smith.

✗ "Janie makes *myself* very proud," said Mr. Smith.

✔ "Janie makes *her mother and me* very proud," said Mr. Smith.

Grammar Alert!

Never use *hisself, theirself,* or *theirselves.* They are not recognized words. *Himself* and *themselves* are the proper forms.

PRACTICE 5   **AVOIDING ERRORS WITH *-SELF* PRONOUNS**

Underline the correct pronoun in each sentence.

1. The Andersons were proud because they had built the deck (them, <u>themselves</u>).

2. Brad and (<u>I</u>, me, myself) have agreed to meet at my house at 6:00 A.M. on Sunday.

3. When Roy looked at (him, <u>himself</u>) in the mirror, he realized he needed to comb his hair.

4. The supervisor assigned the task to Jondrea and (<u>me</u>, myself).

5. "If you do the job (you, <u>yourself</u>), you can save nearly five hundred dollars," said the contractor.

6. "Just between you and (I, <u>me</u>, myself)," said Brandon, "I did not study for the test at all."

7. Sandra decided to give (she, her, <u>herself</u>) a break from studying, so she took a walk.

8. "Would you like to go out to lunch with Natasha and (I, <u>me</u>, myself)?" said Gloria.

9. "No, thanks. I made lunch for (I, me, <u>myself</u>) before I left home," said Morgan.

10. The governor (he, him, <u>himself</u>) came over to shake Miguel's hand.

✍ Using *Who* and *Whom*

The use of *who* and *whom* poses difficulties for most people, partly because *whom* seems to be slowly disappearing from everyday speech. However, in academic writing, the distinction is still important.

While *who* and *whom* may seem intimidating, there is a shortcut to learning how to use these pronouns. It's called the *substitution method.* Once you have mastered this method, you will feel like an expert in the use of *who* and *whom.*

The Substitution Method for *Who* and *Whom*

The first step in the shortcut is a substitution. You have already seen in this chapter how natural it is—in most cases, anyway—to use the subject pronoun *he* and the object pronoun *him.* You rarely make mistakes with them because you use them all the time. Wouldn't it be nice if *who* and *whom* were as easy as *he* and *him?*

The good news is that they are—almost. *Who* is a subject pronoun, just like *he,* so we can temporarily equate the two, like this:

who (or whoever) = he

Whom is an object pronoun, so we can temporarily equate that with *him:*

whom (or whomever) = him

Now, look at a sentence to see how the system works.

No one knew (*who, whom*) had started the rumor.

> **Step 1:** Ignore everything that comes before *who* or *whom.*
>
> ~~No one knew~~ (*who, whom*) had started the rumor.

> **Step 2:** Substitute *he* for *who* and *him* for *whom,* and see which one makes sense.
>
> ✔ ~~Who~~ He had started the rumor.
> ~~Whom~~ Him had started the rumor.

Since "He had started the rumor" makes sense, you can now rewrite the sentence with confidence, using *who* in place of *he.*

✔ No one knew *who* had started the rumor.

PRACTICE 6 USING *WHO* AND *WHOM*

Use the substitution method to decide whether to use *who* or *whom* in the following sentences.

1. Anton was not sure (who, <u>whom</u>) to ask for advice.
2. Tawana could not remember (<u>who,</u> whom) had left the message.
3. The gems sparkled in the jeweler's case as Carlotta gazed at them, wondering (<u>who,</u> whom) could afford such expensive baubles.
4. The man (<u>who,</u> whom) donated the land for the new youth soccer field asked to remain anonymous.
5. Those of us (<u>who,</u> whom) had agreed to plan the party did not realize how much time and trouble it would take.

Who and *Whom* in Questions

Try another sentence, this time a question.

> Andrea needed a ride home from school, but (who, whom) could she ask?

Step 1: Ignore everything that comes before *who* or *whom*.

> ~~Andrea needed a ride home from school, but~~ (who, whom) could she ask?

Step 2: Substitute *he* for *who* and *him* for *whom*, and see which one makes sense.

> ✗ ~~Who~~ He could she ask.
> ✗ ~~Whom~~ Him could she ask.

Neither of these sounds natural, so the thing to do is shuffle them a bit.

> ✗ She could ask *he.*
> ✔ She could ask *him.*

Since "She could ask him" makes sense, you can now rewrite the sentence with confidence, using *whom.*

> ✔ Andrea needed a ride home from school, but whom could she ask?

PRACTICE 7 *WHO* AND *WHOM* IN QUESTIONS

Use the substitution method to decide whether to use *who* or *whom* in the following sentences:

1. (Who, Whom) ordered the veggie sandwich with hot peppers?
2. Have you heard (who, whom) is going to take over as CEO of the company?
3. (Who, Whom) tracked muddy footprints all over the white carpet?
4. (Who, whom) did you say was on the phone?
5. Do you know (who, whom) Ms. Smith is interviewing for the job?

Who and *Whom* after Prepositions

Sometimes, a preposition that comes before *who* or *whom* will need to be included in your sentence for it to make sense.

Brian was not sure to (*who, whom*) he should deliver the package.

Step 1: Ignore everything that comes before *who* or *whom*.

~~Brian was not sure to~~ (*who, whom*) he should deliver the package.

Step 2: Substitute *he* for *who* and *him* for *whom*, adding the preposition that comes in front of *who* or *whom*, and see which one makes sense.

Brian should deliver the package **to** *he*.
Brian should deliver the package **to** *him*.

Since "Brian should deliver the package to him" makes sense, you can now rewrite the sentence with confidence.

✔ Brian was not sure to whom he should deliver the package.

PRACTICE 8 *WHO* AND *WHOM* AFTER PREPOSITIONS

Use the substitution method to decide whether to use *who* or *whom* in the following sentences.

1. The suitcase had no tag, so the airline personnel did not know to (who, <u>whom</u>) it belonged.

2. Jill was not able to find the person to (who, <u>whom</u>) the lost dog belonged.

3. To (who, <u>whom</u>) should I write the check?

4. The person for (who, <u>whom</u>) the car was ordered backed out of the deal at the last minute.

5. Most parents want to know where their children are and with (who, <u>whom</u>) they are associating.

PRACTICE 9 USING *WHO* AND *WHOM*

Use the substitution method to decide whether to use *who* or *whom* in the following sentences.

1. Josh shrugged one shoulder slightly and said that his ex-girlfriend Andrea could date (whoever, <u>whomever</u>) she chose.

2. The shy young clerk's voice cracked as he asked his customers, "(Who, Whom) is next?"

3. Jesse's cat, (who, whom) had just caught an unsuspecting bird, gently laid the still prize at Jesse's feet.

4. The angry police chief promised that his force would never rest until they caught (whoever, whomever) had killed the young officer.

5. When Malcolm told Kimberly that he wanted a woman (who, whom) could cook, she told him he should try living at home with his mother.

PRACTICE 10   USING *WHO* AND *WHOM*

Use the substitution method to decide whether to use *who* or *whom* in the following sentences.

1. The student, (who, whom) high school counselors advised not to go to college, graduated from the university with honors.

2. As the paper plane glided silently onto his desk, the teacher looked across the top of his eyeglasses and asked, "To (who, whom) does this frivolous toy belong?"

3. Everyone (who, whom) plans to graduate this spring should fill out a form in the registrar's office.

4. One study showed that many people (who, whom) win large lottery jackpots find themselves broke ten years after the win.

5. Frank admitted that he couldn't remember to (who, whom) he had given the money.

Review Exercises

Complete the Review Exercises to find out how well you have learned the skills addressed in this chapter. As you work through the exercises, go back through the chapter to review any of the rules you do not understand completely.

REVIEW EXERCISE 1

Underline the correct pronoun in each sentence.

1. The teacher frowned at Steven, (who, whom) tried to sneak into class over 30 minutes late.

2. Emanuel bought (him, <u>himself</u>) a new parka at the spring clearance sale.

3. My friends and (<u>I</u>, me) have decided to go to the library for a study group Sunday night.

4. Rob and (<u>she</u>, her) found it difficult to choose a restaurant for their date because they like such different things.

5. When Vanessa picked up her friend at the airport, she met (he, <u>him</u>, himself) at the main entrance.

6. After winning second place in the league, Joe's soccer team treated (them, <u>themselves</u>) to pizzas and sundaes.

7. My mother and (me, <u>I</u>) meet for brunch every Sunday.

8. My father calls (<u>me</u>, I) every Saturday afternoon.

9. Daniel's basketball team needs two more players, so he wants (we, <u>us</u>) to join.

10. The coat in the lost and found bin belonged to (he, <u>him</u>).

REVIEW EXERCISE 2

Underline and correct the pronoun error in each sentence.

1. Rudy and <u>me</u> are going to take a walk if the rain has stopped.
   Rudy and I

2. Katrina said she had emailed both Teresa and <u>myself</u> about the meeting.
   Teresa and me

3. "May I speak to Mr. Smith?" asked the caller. "This is <u>him</u>," replied Andrew.
   This is he

4. Bruce showed Mary and <u>I</u> the hand-tied fishing flies his uncle had sent him.
   Mary and me

5. Mr. Jones and <u>her</u> said they would not mind working late on Thursday evening.
   Mr. Jones and she

6. Merrill and <u>myself</u> will stay with Aunt Beatrice when we visit New York.
   Merrill and I

7. Elaine wondered why the most trivial and boring jobs were always given to José and <u>she</u>.
   José and her

8. My little brother always wants me to take <u>he</u> and his friends to the mall on Saturdays.
   him and his friends

9. Amanda said that Morris and <u>her</u> had fixed the computer themselves.

Morris and she
_____

10. "I am glad that you and <u>me</u> are not fighting anymore," Al told his girlfriend.

you and I
_____

REVIEW EXERCISE 3

Underline and correct the two pronoun case errors in each sentence or sentence group.

1. Lonnie and <u>myself</u> went to the baseball game with Harold and <u>he</u>.

Lonnie and I
_____

Harold and him
_____

2. Please give the photographs to Anna and <u>they</u>, and be sure to say that they are from <u>myself</u>.

Anna and them
_____

from me
_____

3. "Can you pick the man who robbed you from the lineup?" asked the police officer. "Officer, it was <u>him!</u>" said Mr. Smith, pointing to a tall red-haired man. "He pulled a gun on the night manager and <u>I</u>."

it was he
_____

night manager and me
_____

4. Nicole's mailbox was stuffed with catalogs addressed to her husband and <u>she</u>. "We need to buy <u>us</u> a bigger mailbox," said Nicole.

her husband and her
_____

buy ourselves
_____

5. "Can you give Willie and <u>I</u> a ride?" asked Minardo. "<u>Him</u> and I will appreciate it."

Willie and me
_____

He and I
_____

REVIEW EXERCISE 4

Underline the correct pronoun in each sentence.

[1]Hiromi, a student from Japan, told me that (<u>she</u>, her, herself) and her family had been living in the United States for the past five

years. [2]When she first came here, she knew barely enough English to make (she, her, <u>herself</u>) understood. [3]After taking courses in English for several years, however, (<u>she</u>, her, herself) and her brother are excelling in their college classwork. [4]Hiromi says that for (she, <u>her</u>, herself) and her family, one of the biggest differences between living in Japan and living in the United States is the amount of space. [5]"Our house here is twice as big as the one (<u>we</u>, us, ourselves) had in Japan, and the streets here are far less crowded," she says. [6]She told (I, <u>me</u>, myself) that the Japanese politeness is born out of necessity. [7]"People are so crowded together in Japan that it would be hard for (they, <u>them</u>, themselves) to get along if they did not follow rules of etiquette," she said. [8]Another necessity in Japan is neatness—when people live in small spaces, (<u>they</u>, them, themselves) are forced to be tidy. [9]"I am not very neat (I, me, <u>myself</u>)," says Hiromi. [10]"Maybe living here in the United States has spoiled (I, <u>me</u>, myself)."

mywritinglab   For support in meeting this chapter's goal, log in to **www.mywritinglab.com** and select **Pronoun Case**.

CHAPTER 19

Pronoun Agreement, Reference, and Point of View

> ✎ **Chapter Goal:** Identify and correct problems in pronoun agreement, reference, and point of view.

Abbott: I'm telling you Who is on first.
Costello: Well, I'm asking YOU who's on first!
Abbott: That's the man's name.
Costello: That's who's name?
Abbott: Yes.
Costello: Well, go ahead and tell me.
Abbott: Who.
Costello: The guy on first.
Abbott: Who!

Abbott and Costello's classic comedy routine deliberately causes confusion through the use of pronouns. Sometimes, writers unintentionally cause confusion through errors in pronoun reference, agreement, and point of view. Each sentence that follows contains a pronoun error. Can you figure out why the pronouns in bold type are incorrect?

✘ The new grocery store closes on Christmas day, but **they** are open every other day of the year.

✘ Leo told Jim that **he** needed to clean up the work area.

✗   "I have looked everywhere," said Shelly, "but **you** just can't find an affordable apartment in this area."

Each of the sentences above contains a pronoun error that could confuse the reader. The first sentence contains an error in pronoun agreement. The pronoun *they* is plural, but the word it refers to is singular. The corrected sentence is shown below.

✔   The new grocery store closes on Christmas day, but **it** is open every other day of the year.

The second sentence contains an error in pronoun reference. The reader cannot be sure whether *he* refers to Leo or to Jim.

✔   Leo told Jim, "**I** need to clean up my work area."

The third sentence contains an error in pronoun point of view. The speaker switches from the first person (*I have looked*) to the second person (*you can't find*).

✔   "I have looked everywhere," said Shelly, "but **I** just can't find an affordable apartment in this area."

Keeping your writing free of errors in pronoun agreement, reference, and point of view helps your reader move through your work smoothly and without confusion.

Pronoun Agreement

mywritinglab

Visit MyWriting Lab for additional practice with pronoun agreement.

Pronoun agreement means that a pronoun agrees in number with the word it refers to. In other words, a singular pronoun can refer only to a singular noun or pronoun, and a plural pronoun can refer only to a plural noun or pronoun.

The word that a pronoun refers to is called its **antecedent**. An antecedent may be a noun such as *table* or *ideas,* a pronoun such as *everyone* or *they,* or even a compound construction such as *cars and buses* or *Ferdinand and Isabella.*

Examples of Pronoun Agreement

          singular antecedent   singular pronoun

✔   The dog caught the <u>Frisbee</u> in midair and brought <u>it</u> back to Julie.

In the sentence above, the singular pronoun *it* refers to one word in the sentence, the singular word *Frisbee.*

plural antecedent   plural pronoun

✔ Todd gathered up the <u>bills</u> he needed to mail and took <u>them</u> to the mailbox.

Here, the plural pronoun *them* refers to the plural antecedent *bills.*

plural antecedent   plural pronoun

✔ Todd gathered up the <u>bills and letters</u> he needed to mail and took <u>them</u> to the mailbox.

Above, the plural pronoun *them* refers to the compound antecedent *bills and letters.*

Problems in Pronoun Agreement

Errors in pronoun agreement occur when a singular pronoun is used to refer to a plural word or when a plural pronoun is used to refer to a singular word.

Examples of Problems in Pronoun Agreement

singular   plural

✘ Mary pulled into her bank's <u>drive-through</u>, but <u>they</u> had closed for the day.

singular   singular

✔ Mary pulled in to her bank's <u>drive-through</u>, but <u>it</u> had closed for the day.

singular   singular

✘ The teller was carrying several <u>rolls</u> of coins, but when she tripped, <u>it</u> flew out of her hands and spilled onto the floor.

plural   plural

✔ The teller was carrying several <u>rolls</u> of coins, but when she tripped, <u>they</u> flew out of her hands and spilled onto the floor.

PRACTICE 1   MAKING PRONOUNS AGREE

Underline the correct pronoun in each sentence.

1. The photographs on display were so striking that people lingered for a long time to look at (it, <u>them</u>).
2. As snow gathered on the branches of the tree, Harold watched the limbs sag under (<u>its</u>, their) weight.
3. Mr. Smith banks with First City Bank because (<u>it is</u>, they are) locally owned.

4. Every restaurant is required to display (<u>its</u>, their) health inspection certificate.

5. After the hailstorm, the dented cars on the dealership's lot had price reduction stickers on (its, <u>their</u>) windshields.

Singular Indefinite Pronouns

The following indefinite pronouns are always singular.

each	everybody	anyone	anything
either	somebody	everyone	everything
neither	nobody	someone	something
anybody	one	no one	nothing

Memory Jogger

Remember the singular indefinite pronouns more easily by grouping them:

each	either	neither
all the bodies	all the ones	all the things

Examples of Singular Indefinite Pronouns as Antecedents

      singular   plural

✗ <u>Somebody</u> called you, but <u>they</u> didn't leave a message.

      singular   singular

✔ *Somebody* called you, but *he* didn't leave a message.

      singular   plural

✗ <u>Each</u> of the team members has <u>their</u> own particular strength.

      singular   singular

✔ *Each* of the team members has *her* own particular strength.

PRACTICE 2   MAKING PRONOUNS AGREE WITH INDEFINITE PRONOUN SUBJECTS

Underline the correct pronoun in each sentence.

1. Somebody had parked (<u>his</u>, their) new car so that it took up two spaces in the parking lot.

2. Each of the treasured photographs had (<u>its</u>, their) own place of honor on the mantel.

3. Each of the children brought (<u>her</u>, their) lunch on the field trip.

4. Nobody in the room would admit that (<u>he</u>, they) had voted for the losing candidate.

5. When the hosts of the party began to argue loudly, everyone mumbled excuses and said that (they, <u>he</u>) had to go.

As you probably noticed when you did the previous practice exercise, the use of singular indefinite pronouns often raises a problem. Words like *everybody, somebody, anyone,* and *everyone* often designate both males and females. Saying "Each of the team members has *her* own particular strength" works only if you know that all team members are female. The use of indefinite pronouns raises not only the question of pronoun agreement but also the question of gender fairness.

Pronouns and Gender Fairness

Gender fairness means using gender-neutral terms such as *server, police officer,* and *firefighter*. It means not stereotyping professions: Gary Kubach is a *nurse,* not a *male nurse;* Sarita Gray is a *doctor,* not a *woman doctor.* Naturally, gender fairness also includes avoiding describing women solely in terms of their looks or men solely in terms of their bank accounts. Those things are fairly simple. The area of gender fairness and pronouns, however, requires more thought. Using *he or she* or *his or her* is often awkward, and constructions such as *he/she* or *(s)he* are downright ungraceful. How, then, can a writer's language be unbiased, graceful, and grammatically correct, all at the same time? There are several possible solutions.

Example of Correcting an Issue in Gender Fairness

✗   Nobody has received *their* grades from the last term yet.

This sentence contains an error in pronoun agreement. The singular indefinite pronoun *nobody* does not agree with the plural pronoun *their.* Below are several ways to correct pronoun agreement errors such as this one while remaining gender fair.

Solution 1: Choose a gender and stay with it throughout a single example or paragraph. Then, in your next example or paragraph, switch to the other gender.

✗   *Nobody* has received *their* grades from the last term yet.
✔   *Nobody* has received *his* grades from the last term yet.
✔   *Nobody* has received *her* grades from the last term yet.

Solution 2: Use a *his or her* construction. Because this solution is grammatically correct but stylistically awkward, use it in situations where you will not have to repeat the construction.

✘ *Nobody* has received *their* grades from the last term yet.

✔ *Nobody* has received *his or her* grades from the last term yet.

Solution 3: Use plural rather than singular constructions.

✘ *Nobody* has received *their* grades from the last term yet.

✔ The *students* have not received *their* grades from the last term yet.

Solution 4: Solve the pronoun agreement problem by removing the pronoun.

✘ *Nobody* has received *their* grades from the last term yet.

✔ *Nobody* has received grades from the last term yet.

PRACTICE 3   MAKING PRONOUNS AGREE

Underline and correct the pronoun agreement error in each sentence by using the solutions listed above. Answers may vary.

1. Each of the class members received a folder with their name on it.
    his or her name

2. The driver discovered that someone had left their camera on the tour bus.
    had left a camera

3. Has everyone in the class decided on their major?
    on a major

4. The table grew quiet as everyone began to enjoy their meal.
    enjoy the meal

5. No one in the apartment building where the murder occurred wanted to give their name or talk to reporters.
    No residents of . . . their names

6. Everybody is entitled to their own opinion.
    to an opinion

7. Each person in the discussion group was eager to express their ideas.
    Members of the discussion group were

8. "If one of those postal clerks puts <u>their</u> 'Next Window' sign up, I think I'll scream," said a woman carrying a bulky package.

   puts a 'Next Window' sign
   _____

9. When the driveway was poured, somebody put <u>their</u> handprint in the cement before it dried.

   his handprint
   _____

10. "I need to page someone. Would you call <u>their</u> name over the loudspeaker?" Anita asked the store clerk.

    her name
    _____

Pronoun Reference

mywritinglab

Visit MyWriting Lab for additional practice with pronoun reference.

If a sentence has problems with **pronoun reference,** then a pronoun has either no antecedent or more than one possible antecedent.

Pronoun Reference Problem: No Antecedent

If a pronoun has no antecedent, your reader may become confused.

Examples of Correcting a Pronoun Reference Problem

✗ When Melanie went to pick up her son's birthday cake, they told her it wasn't ready.

Who are *they?* Replacing the pronoun *they* with a more specific word makes the sentence's meaning clear.

✔ When Melanie went to pick up her son's birthday cake, the bakery clerk told her it wasn't ready.

✗ Because his brother is on the basketball team, Derrick wants to be one, too.

What does Derrick want to be? A brother? A basketball? A team? The word that should logically be the antecedent of *one*—the word *player*—appears nowhere in the sentence. The simplest way to correct the problem is to replace the word *one* with a more specific word.

✔ Because his brother is on the basketball team, Derrick wants to be a basketball player, too.

PRACTICE 4   CORRECTING PROBLEMS IN PRONOUN REFERENCE

Underline and correct the pronoun reference problems in each sentence.
Answers may vary.

1. The instructions said the form had to be filled out in ink, but Fred had not
   brought <u>one</u> with him.

   a pen

2. When Brett applied to the college, <u>they</u> told him he was exempt from physical
   education courses because he was a military veteran.

   the admissions clerk

3. When she arrived at her house, Andrea called the auto mechanic and told him
   <u>it</u> was still making a funny noise.

   her car

4. Eric applied for a car loan, but <u>they</u> told him he would need a cosigner since
   he had no credit history.

   the loan officer

5. Giselle said that from the time she first saw *The Nutcracker* as a child, she fell
   in love with ballet and knew she wanted to be <u>one</u>.

   a ballet dancer

Pronoun Reference Problems with *This*

The pronoun *this* is so often used incorrectly that you should check it every
time you see it in your writing.

When you see the pronoun *this* in a sentence, particularly if it begins the
sentence, ask the question, "This what?" If you cannot put your finger on a
noun that answers that question, then *this* probably has no antecedent.

Examples of Correcting Vague Uses of *This*

✗ In some neighborhoods, people are afraid to go out after dark. Increased
   police presence in high-crime neighborhoods could help to prevent *this*.

✗ In the twenty-first century, parents are spending more time at work, and
   children are increasingly involved in school, sports, and social activities.
   This means that families have less time to spend together.

There are two quick ways to fix the problem. The first is to place a noun
that answers the question "This what?" immediately after the word *this*.

✔ In some neighborhoods, people are afraid to go out after dark. Increased police presence in high-crime neighborhoods could help to prevent *this fear.*

✔ In the twenty-first century, parents are spending more time at work, and children are increasingly involved in school, sports, and social activities. *This increase in outside activity* means that families have less time to spend together.

The second solution is to take out the pronoun and replace it with an appropriate word or phrase. This solution takes a bit more time but is usually more graceful and exact.

✔ In some neighborhoods, people are afraid to go out after dark. Increased police presence in high-crime neighborhoods could help citizens feel safer.

✔ In the twenty-first century, parents are spending more time at work, and children are increasingly involved in school, sports, and social activities. As a result, families have less time to spend together.

PRACTICE 5   CORRECTING VAGUE USES OF *THIS*

Underline and correct the vague uses of *this.* Answers may vary.

1. Edward closed his math book and put his calculator aside with a sigh. "<u>This</u> makes no sense to me," he said.

   "These quadratic equations make

2. The courthouse, the oldest county building still in use and a local landmark, was burned down last year by a man who did not like the terms of his divorce. <u>This</u> saddened and outraged many people in the community.

   The arson

3. The lack of a traffic signal at the intersection of Wilroy Road and Broad Street creates a danger to drivers and pedestrians alike. Can't something be done about <u>this</u>?

   this dangerous situation

4. After gaining five pounds on the Chocolate Lover's Diet, Lisa tried counting calories and fat grams and exercising every day. <u>This</u> was more effective but not nearly as much fun.

   This method

5. Joe dug his toes into the warm sand and watched the waves roll in. "This is great," he said.

"This beach _____

Pronoun Point of View

It is important to avoid unnecessary shifts in **point of view,** that is, shifts from one person to another. The chart below shows common **first-, second-, and third-person** pronouns in their singular and plural forms.

Point of View	Singular	Plural
First person (the person speaking)	I	we
Second person (the person spoken to)	you	you
Third person (the person spoken about)	he, she, it singular indefinite pronouns (everybody, anybody, etc.)	they

Examples of Correcting Problems with Pronoun Point of View

    1st person   2nd person

✘ <u>I</u> enjoy going to auctions and flea markets because <u>you</u> can find bargains and unusual items.

The sentence contains an unnecessary shift in point of view. In this sentence, *you* do not find bargains and unusual items; *I* find them.

    1st person   1st person

✔ <u>I</u> enjoy going to auctions and flea markets because <u>I</u> can find bargains and unusual items.

    3rd person   1st person   1st person

✘ When <u>someone</u> studies all night for a test, <u>I</u> am disappointed if <u>I</u> don't make at least a B.

    1st person   1st person   1st person

✔ When <u>I</u> study all night for a test, <u>I</u> am disappointed if <u>I</u> don't make at least a B.

          3rd person   3rd person   3rd person

✔ When <u>someone</u> studies all night for a test, <u>he</u> is disappointed if <u>he</u> doesn't make at least a B.

PRACTICE 6 CORRECTING PROBLEMS IN PRONOUN POINT OF VIEW

Underline and correct the point of view problems in each sentence.
Answers may vary.

1. Dennis has decided to pursue a double major because <u>you</u> don't know what opportunities life will present.

   he doesn't know

2. You should always drive defensively because <u>I</u> see all sorts of crazy drivers on the road.

   Defensive driving is a good idea because of all the crazy drivers on the road.

3. People enjoy the Corner Café because it's a friendly place where <u>you</u> can always find someone to talk to.

   a friendly place where there is always someone to talk to.

4. Javarez likes many types of music, but he says that when he is feeling down, <u>you</u> might as well listen to the blues.

   he might as well listen

5. Kayla looked out the window and shivered; <u>you</u> could tell it was cold just by looking at the low, gray clouds and the white-frosted ground.

   she could tell it was cold

Review Exercises

Complete the Review Exercises to find out how well you have learned the skills addressed in this chapter. As you work through the exercises, go back through the chapter to review any of the rules you do not understand completely.

REVIEW EXERCISE 1

Underline the correct alternative in each sentence. Then in the blank to the left of the sentence, indicate whether the problem is one of *agreement* (singular with plural, plural with singular), *reference* (no clear antecedent), or *point of view* (shifts in person).

<u>point of view</u> 1. Claire begins her drive to work at 6:30 A.M. because (you miss, <u>she misses</u>) rush-hour traffic that way.

reference   **2.** At his job interview, (they, <u>the interviewer</u>) asked Richard to write a sample memo.

agreement   **3.** Neither of Kim's uncles is sure that (<u>he</u>, they) can fly in for her wedding.

reference   **4.** When Renee walked into the clothing store with her shopping bag, (they, <u>a store employee</u>) told her she would have to leave it at the customer service desk.

agreement   **5.** Each member of the women's bowling team brought (<u>her</u>, their) own ball and shoes to the tournament.

agreement   **6.** The Community Trust Bank has named Madeleine R. Bowen as (<u>its</u>, their) new president.

reference   **7.** Rick told Mr. Flanders (that the supplies he had ordered were ready for pickup, <u>"The supplies you ordered are ready for pickup."</u>)

reference   **8.** As he rubbed the clear liquid into his thinning hair, James said, "(They claim, <u>The company claims</u>) that this mixture will regrow hair in 70 percent of men. I hope I am one of the 70 percent."

reference   **9.** Glen stood over the crib making strange faces and funny noises because (this, <u>his clowning</u>) seemed to amuse the baby.

agreement   **10.** Roderick had a security system installed in his home because, as a firefighter, (<u>he has</u>, they have) to sleep at the fire station every other week.

REVIEW EXERCISE 2

Underline and correct the pronoun reference, agreement, or point of view error in each sentence. Answers may vary.

1. Joelle's favorite shows are back to back on Thursday night. She always makes time to watch <u>it</u>.

   to watch them.

2. Seth enjoys listening to sports radio when he is alone in the car. The commentators keep <u>you</u> company.

   keep him company.

3. Jessica told Angela that <u>she</u> should try out for the team.

   Angela, "You should _____

4. The pencils were worn down because Aline used <u>it</u> so much during the test.

   used them _____

5. Someone woke up the whole neighborhood when <u>their</u> car alarm sounded at 3:00 A.M.

   his or her _____

6. Each member of the team wore a special badge on <u>their</u> uniform.

   The team members wore special badges on their uniforms. _____

7. Despite summer weather, Katie brings a sweater to work because <u>you</u> often get cold in the air conditioned office.

   because she often gets _____

8. After Ryan filled his plate with hamburgers and hot dogs, he noticed <u>it</u> wasn't cooked thoroughly.

   noticed that they weren't _____

9. Studies show that many people suffer from lactose intolerance. <u>This</u> makes soy milk manufacturers anticipate growing profits.

   These studies make _____

10. John told Drew that <u>he</u> should sign up for intramural rugby.

    John told Drew, "You should _____

REVIEW EXERCISE 3

Underline and correct the errors in pronoun agreement, reference, or point of view in each numbered item. Answers may vary.

1. When Frank goes to the health club, <u>they</u> always ask him for his ID. But <u>you</u> don't always keep an ID in the pocket of <u>your</u> gym shorts.

   the receptionist always asks for _____

   But he doesn't always keep an ID in the pocket of his gym shorts _____

2. Karalyn does not drink, so when anyone offers <u>it</u> to her, she says, "No, thanks." If someone tries to pressure her, she tells <u>them</u> that she has to drive.

   offers her alcohol, she says, _____

   she says she has to drive _____

3. Everyone said <u>they</u> did not think the ventriloquist was very talented. <u>This</u> was evident in the way his lips moved when the dummy was supposed to be talking.

Audience members said
_____

His lips moved (omit "This was evident in the way")
_____

4. Noelle refuses to take money from her parents because she thinks she should be independent once <u>you</u> have a job. "Everyone eventually needs to take care of <u>themselves</u>," she says.

once she has a job
_____

to take care of herself
_____

5. Tyler told Dewayne that <u>his</u> car and <u>his</u> son's bicycle were blocking the driveway. "I'll move <u>it</u> right away," said Dewayne.

"Your car and your son's bicycle are blocking the driveway."
_____

move them right away
_____

REVIEW EXERCISE 4

Underline and correct the two errors in pronoun agreement, reference, or point of view in each numbered item. Answers may vary.

1. When the car's engine overheated, Andrew pushed <u>it</u> to the side of the road. He called a tow truck, but <u>they</u> did not come for two hours.

pushed the car
_____

it
_____

2. In my sociology class today, everyone said <u>they</u> had done the assigned reading. But <u>you</u> could tell that Professor Dunham suspected otherwise.

all of the students said they
_____

But I could tell
_____

3. When Paige received her first paycheck, she thought <u>they</u> had made a mistake. Then she realized how much money you <u>had</u> to pay toward taxes, insurance, and retirement benefits.

the payroll office had made
_____

how much money she had to pay
_____

4. When Dolores saw that <u>they</u> had brought her mail, she went eagerly to get it. But she came back with a frown on her face, asking "Why do <u>they</u> send me so many credit card offers?"

    that her mail had arrived
    _____

    Why do credit card companies send me so many offers?
    _____

5. As Paul drove past the dumpster, he noticed that someone had left a small, shivering puppy along with <u>their</u> bag of trash. <u>This</u> made him angry; he could not understand how people could be so cruel.

    with a bag of trash
    _____

    The sight made
    _____

REVIEW EXERCISE 5

Underline and correct the error in pronoun agreement, reference, or point of view in each numbered sentence.

[1]When I started college, <u>everybody</u> told me that registration would be difficult and time-consuming, but I did not believe them. [2]All <u>you</u> have to do is sign up for classes, I thought, and that can't be too difficult. [3]But registration turned out to be an all-day job that started when <u>you</u> walked onto the huge campus. [4]I tried asking for directions, but <u>everybody</u> was so new that they could not help me. [5]When I finally made it to orientation, <u>they</u> loaded me down with handouts and confusing information. [6]Finally, I was told to see an academic advisor in another building, but <u>this</u> turned out to be more difficult than I had anticipated. [7]I was herded into a big room with at least fifty other students, and it was half an hour before a harried secretary called my name and said <u>he</u> would see me. [8]When I had my prized class schedule in hand, I went to the business office where <u>you</u> had to stand in another line to pay. [9]Finally, <u>they</u> sent me to the bookstore to buy my books, an expensive and time-consuming process. [10]When I finally made it home, I decided that <u>they</u> were right: Registration was a big hassle.

1. other students told me
    _____

2. All I have to do
    _____

3. when I walked _____
4. but the students I asked were _____
5. I was loaded down _____
6. but seeing an advisor _____
7. and said an advisor would see _____
8. I had to stand _____
9. I was sent to _____
10. the other students _____

mywritinglab   For support in meeting this chapter's goal, log in to
www.mywritinglab.com and select **Pronoun Reference
and Point of View** and **Pronoun-Antecedent Agreement**.

CHAPTER 20

Adjectives, Adverbs, and Articles

> ✏ **Chapter Goal:** Use adjectives, adverbs, and articles effectively.

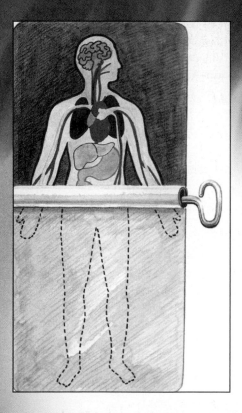

Verbs supply the muscle
That helps a sentence go,
And prepositions are the veins
That help control its flow.

Nouns and pronouns form the bones
That make it stand upright.
Conjunctions are the sinews
That help its parts unite.

But adjectives and adverbs
Are the flesh upon the bone.
They give each sentence its own face
And make its meaning known.

Nouns are the bones of a sentence and verbs are the muscles that move them, but adjectives and adverbs provide the flesh and the cartilage, the color and the texture. Without adjectives and adverbs, you could convey only the basics: what happened and to whom. You could not show how and why, how many and what kind. This chapter provides a brief overview of adjectives and adverbs and reviews three useful words called *articles*.

✐ Adjectives

mywritinglab
Visit MyWriting
Lab for additional
practice using
adjectives.

Adjectives are words that give information about nouns or pronouns. They answer the questions "What kind?" "How many?" and "Which one?" Usually, adjectives within a sentence come before the noun or pronoun they modify (*Fido nuzzled Horace's hand with his cold, clammy nose*) or after a verb that links them to the noun or pronoun (*Fido's nose was cold and clammy*).

Examples of Adjectives

A *scented* candle burned on the table.

The toffee was *smooth* and *creamy*.

Kasim looks *unhappy*.

Nick is the *smartest* person I know.

PRACTICE 1 FINDING ADJECTIVES AND THE NOUNS THEY MODIFY

Underline the two adjectives in each sentence and draw an arrow connecting each with the word it modifies.

1. The cookies were warm and delicious.

2. Holly wore a heavy coat and a pair of warm gloves.

3. The shivering dog huddled in a sheltered doorway.

4. Ben looked anxious and uncertain.

5. Comfortable benches had been placed alongside the winding pathway.

Adjective Forms: Positive, Comparative, and Superlative

Each adjective has three forms: the positive form, the comparative form, and the superlative form.

Positive

The positive form is the base form of the adjective. It is used when you are describing something but not comparing it to anything else.

Examples of Adjectives in Positive Form

The floor was *dirty*.

The ice cream tastes *good*.

Brenda was driving a *beautiful* car.

Comparative

The comparative form is used to compare two things or to compare one thing to a group of similar items.

Examples of Adjectives in Comparative Form

When the two children came in, Emily was *dirtier* than Leslie.

The ice cream tastes *better* than the yogurt.

Violet thought that France was even *more beautiful* than Italy.

Donna is *more efficient* than her coworkers.

Superlative

The superlative form is used to compare one thing with all others in its group.

Examples of Adjectives in Superlative Form

Ryan gave his grandmother a T-shirt that read, "World's *Best* Grandma."

Sam was the *least expensive* private detective we could find.

Chief was just a brown and white mutt, but to Jody, he was the *most beautiful* dog in the world.

Emily is the *most efficient* person in her office.

Adjective Forms

	Positive	Comparative	Superlative
One syllable		add -*er*	add -*est*
	cool	cooler	coolest
	smooth	smoother	smoothest
Two syllables ending in -*y*		change -*y* to -*i*, add -*er*	change -*y* to -*i*, add -*est*
	happy	happier	happiest
	tardy	tardier	tardiest

	Positive	**Comparative**	**Superlative**
Most words of two or more syllables		use *more* or *less*	use *most* or *least*
	solemn	more solemn	most solemn
	intense	more intense	most intense
	inventive	more inventive	most inventive
	slippery	more slippery	most slippery
	important	less important	least important
Irregular adjectives	good	better	best
	bad	worse	worst

PRACTICE 2   REVIEWING ADJECTIVE FORMS

Fill in the comparative and superlative forms of each adjective. Use the Adjective Forms chart as your guide.

	Positive	**Comparative**	**Superlative**
1.	full	fuller	fullest
2.	crisp	crisper	crispest
3.	pesky	peskier	peskiest
4.	trendy	trendier	trendiest
5.	toxic	more toxic	most toxic
6.	pleasant	more pleasant	most pleasant
7.	humorous	more humorous	most humorous
8.	colorful	more colorful	most colorful
9.	good	better	best
10.	bad	worse	worst

Grammar Alert!

Be sure to use *more* and *most* only in combination with base (positive) adjective forms, not with *-er* or *-est* forms. *More significant* is correct, but *more happier* or *most best* is not.

PRACTICE 3   USING ADJECTIVE FORMS

In each sentence below, decide whether the positive, comparative, or superlative form is needed. Then convert the adjective in parentheses to the proper form, using the Adjective Forms chart as your guide.

(careful)   1.   Elaine is a __more careful__ driver than her husband.

(big)   2.   The hotel was the __biggest__ that Chim had ever seen.

(attentive)   3.   The children, seated in a circle, watched the storyteller with __attentive__ faces.

(small)   4.   Maggie carried a __small__ notebook in her purse to jot down ideas and record her thoughts.

(brilliant)   5.   Few scientists are __more brilliant__ than Dr. Otto Schummer, but his work habits are erratic and his personality unconventional.

(tasty)   6.   As the server described the items on the dessert cart, each one sounded __tastier__ and more tempting than the last.

(ugly)   7.   "Frank, I do believe that is the __ugliest__ tie I have ever seen," said his wife.

(young)   8.   Glenn was the __youngest__ of the three brothers.

(old)   9.   Glenn was __older__ than his sister Jackie.

(good)   10.   Roberta has many good friends, but Ashley has been her __best__ friend since grade school.

Adverbs

mywritinglab

Visit MyWriting Lab for additional practice using adverbs.

Adverbs give information about verbs (skated *gracefully*), adjectives (*extremely* slippery), or other adverbs (*very* badly). Often, but not always, adverbs are *-ly* forms of the adjective. *Graceful* becomes *gracefully, bad* becomes *badly,* and *quick* becomes *quickly.* The easiest way to tell an adverb from an adjective is to see what question the word answers. An adjective tells *how many, what kind,* or *which one.* An adverb tells *how, when,* or *to what degree.*

Examples of Adverbs

After her run, Kerri was breathing *rapidly.* (how)

Don nodded *coldly* when he passed Al in the hall. (how)

The performance was *extremely* well done. (to what degree/how)

The check will be sent *immediately.* (when)

PRACTICE 4   RECOGNIZING ADVERBS

Underline the adverb in each sentence.

1. The turtle <u>slowly</u> made its way across the sandbar.
2. <u>Secretly</u>, the old man had taken fifty dollars from each check he received and <u>hidden</u> it under his mattress.
3. Geneva <u>artfully</u> braided her daughter's hair and tied a small bow at the end of each <u>braid</u>.
4. Arthur <u>seldom</u> had headaches, but the loud music in the nightclub made his head <u>pound</u>.
5. Samantha waited <u>anxiously</u> for the plane to arrive.

Adverb Forms

	Positive	**Comparative**	**Superlative**
Adverbs ending in -ly		use *more*	use *most*
	smoothly	more smoothly	most smoothly
	happily	more happily	most happily
	solemnly	more solemnly	most solemnly
	intensely	more intensely	most intensely
Irregular adverbs	well	better	best
	badly	worse	worst

> ### *Memory Jogger*
> **Adjectives** tell *how many, what kind,* or *which one.*
> **Adverbs** tell *how, when,* or *to what degree.*

PRACTICE 5   RECOGNIZING ADJECTIVES AND ADVERBS

Underline the correct word in each phrase. Decide whether the word tells *how many, what kind, which one, how, when,* or *to what degree,* and write your response in the first blank. In the second blank, write the part of speech: *adjective* or *adverb.* The first one is done for you.

1. sang (loud, <u>loudly</u>)
    The word tells <u>how</u> and is an <u>adverb</u>.
2. a (<u>beautiful</u>, beautifully) dress
    The word tells <u>what kind</u> and is an <u>adjective</u>.
3. walked (slow, <u>slowly</u>)
    The word tells <u>how</u> and is an <u>adverb</u>.
4. a (<u>slow</u>, slowly) dance
    The word tells <u>what kind</u> and is an <u>adjective</u>.
5. a (<u>complete</u>, completely) turnaround
    The word tells <u>what kind</u> and is an <u>adjective</u>.
6. turned around (complete, <u>completely</u>)
    The word tells <u>to what degree</u> and is an <u>adverb</u>.
7. (<u>several</u>, severally) reasons
    The word tells <u>how many</u> and is an <u>adjective</u>.
8. (happy, <u>happily</u>) agreed
    The word tells <u>how (in what manner)</u> and is an <u>adverb</u>.
9. (<u>responsible</u>, responsibly) behavior
    The word tells <u>what kind</u> and is an <u>adjective</u>.
10. behaved (responsible, <u>responsibly</u>)
    The word tells <u>how</u> and is an <u>adverb</u>.

PRACTICE 6   USING ADJECTIVES AND ADVERBS

Underline the correct word in each sentence.

1. Jason read the article (quick, <u>quickly</u>).
2. Mr. Smith made a (<u>quick</u>, quickly) trip to the grocery store.
3. The children had a (<u>good</u>, well) time at the museum.
4. "Please proceed (calm, <u>calmly</u>) to the exit," said the theater manager.
5. The coffee was (bare, <u>barely</u>) warm.
6. "Your presentation could not have gone more (smooth, <u>smoothly</u>)," Rick said.
7. Julia's (<u>helpful</u>, helpfully) attitude made everyone more cooperative.
8. The man was (<u>angry</u>, angrily).

9.   The man was (angry, <u>angrily</u>) gesturing at passing cars.

10. The card wished Kevin a (<u>speedy</u>, speedily) recovery.

Puzzling Pairs

Certain adjective and adverb pairs are confused more often than others. The next sections explain the differences between the pairs *good* and *well*, *bad* and *badly*, and *worse* and *worst*.

Good and *Well*, *Bad* and *Badly*

Good and *bad* are adjectives that tell *what kind*; *well* and *badly* are adverbs that tell *how*.

Examples of *Good* and *Well*, *Bad* and *Badly*

Since she has been using Mavis Beacon typing software, Clare has become a *good* typist. (adjective tells *what kind* of typist)

Since she has been using Mavis Beacon typing software, Clare has learned to type *well*. (adverb tells *how* she types)

Todd bought *good* tires that will perform *well* even in bad weather. (adjective tells *what kind* of tires and adverb tells *how* they perform)

Grammar Alert!

Well can be an adjective when it refers to health, as in "He is not a *well* man" or "I am not feeling *well*."

Ross had never been around children, and he was afraid he would

   adjective

be a *bad* parent. (adjective tells *what kind* of parent)

The dog was so timid that the animal shelter workers wondered if it

       adverb

had been treated *badly*. (adverb tells *how* it may have been treated)

     adverb   adjective

Helen slept *badly* after having a *bad* dream. (adverb tells how she slept and adjective tells what kind of dream)

PRACTICE 7   USING *GOOD* AND *WELL*, *BAD* AND *BADLY*

In each sentence, choose *good* or *well*, *bad* or *badly*.

1. Anita has a (good, well) job that pays her (good, well).
2. Because it was (bad, badly) prepared, the soufflé did not taste very (good, well).
3. Lev is not a (bad, badly) tennis player; in fact, he plays rather (good, well).
4. "(Good, Well) boy, Rex!" Mac told his dog. "Let's go to the vet so you can get (good, well)."
5. "I react (bad, badly) when I lose," said Franklin, "but I don't think that makes me a (bad, badly) person."

Worse and *Worst*

Worse and *worst* are both adjectives, but they are often confused. *Worse* is the comparative form, the form you use to compare one thing to another or one set of things to another set. *Worst* is the superlative form, used to compare one thing to all (or many) others in its class.

Examples of *Worse* and *Worst*

"I am disappointed in my grade," said Matt, "but I guess I could have done *worse*."

Matt is comparing two things: his actual grade and a hypothetical lower grade.

"This coffee tastes even *worse* with cream and sugar in it," said Kelly.

Kelly is comparing two things: the coffee before the addition of cream and sugar, and the same coffee after the flavorings were added.

Kelly made a face. "This is the *worst* cup of coffee I have ever drunk," she said.

Kelly is comparing the coffee she is drinking with all other cups of coffee she has drunk.

The *worst* meal I ever ate in a restaurant was at the No Way Café.

The meal is being compared with all others in its class.

PRACTICE 8   USING _WORSE_ AND _WORST_

Choose _worse_ or _worst_ in each sentence.

1. "I don't know which of them is (worse, worst)," said Kate, looking at her twin sons.
2. Not only did Adam lose the tennis match, but he probably turned in his (worse, worst) performance ever.
3. "I am your (worse, worst) nightmare," the drill sergeant snarled.
4. Nell's arthritis always gets (worse, worst) during rainy weather.
5. Meteorologists said that the hurricane was the (worse, worst) of the last century.

Articles

mywritinglab
Visit MyWriting
Lab for additional
practice using
articles.
The **articles** in the English language are _a, an,_ and _the._ Articles are small, easy-to-overlook words, but they are so widely used that it is important to use them correctly. When a writer uses the word _pen,_ for example, an article can reveal whether the writer is talking about a specific pen (_the_ pen) or any pen (_a_ pen).

Using _A_ and _An_

The most common mistake people make with articles stems from uncertainty over when to use _a_ and when to use _an._ Use _a_ before a **consonant sound**—that is, before any word that sounds as if it begins with anything other than _a, e, i, o,_ or _u._

_a_ bowl

_a_ peeled onion

_a_ youth

_a_ useful tool (_Useful_ begins with the sound of the consonant _y_—the _yoo_ sound. Therefore, the article _a_ is used.)

Use _an_ before a **vowel sound**—that is, before any word that sounds as if it begins with _a, e, i, o,_ or _u._

_an_ **u**nderstanding

_an_ **a**ble-bodied person

_an_ **o**melet

an **h**onor (*Honor* begins with the *ah* sound often associated with the vowels *o* and *a*. Therefore, the article *an* is used.)

PRACTICE 9 USING *A* AND *AN*

Put *a* in front of words that begin with a consonant sound. Put *an* in front of words that begin with a vowel sound.

1. _a_ calendar

2. _an_ eraser

3. _a_ hard-boiled egg

4. _a_ bottle of shampoo

5. _an_ orange T-shirt

PRACTICE 10 USING *A* AND *AN*

Put *a* or *an* in the blank in each sentence.

1. Gaby bought _a_ chocolate milk shake.

2. Cho went to the store for _a_ half gallon of orange juice.

3. _An_ orange mouse pad sat to the right of the computer keyboard.

4. Looking into his refrigerator, Esteban saw _an_ egg, a bottle of store-brand grape juice, and a four-day-old sandwich.

5. _An_ open container of gasoline can be dangerous.

6. Since it was warm, Stacie decided to wear _a_ short-sleeved shirt.

7. Peeling _an_ onion always makes Shika cry.

8. The pages of the calendar were held together by _a_ small plastic clip shaped like an airplane.

9. Jiro, do you have _an_ opinion on the subject?

10. When _a_ car pulled out in front of him, Erik blew the horn.

Review Exercises

Complete the Review Exercises to find out how well you have learned the skills addressed in this chapter. As you work through the exercises, go back through the chapter to review any of the rules you do not understand completely.

REVIEW EXERCISE 1

Underline the correct article in each sentence.

1. I had (a/an) pet goldfish as a child, but becoming (a/an) dog owner is a bigger responsibility.
2. Before signing her lease, Eliza sent (a/an) copy to her mother, who is (a/an) real estate agent.
3. (A/An) email probably is the fastest way to get (a/an) response from Kevin.
4. On this week's episode, the star dramatically demanded (a/an) honest answer, ending the season on (a/an) cliffhanger.
5. Prof. Jimenez promised his class (a/an) extra credit assignment to provide them with (a/an) boost for their grades.

REVIEW EXERCISE 2

In each sentence, decide whether the positive, comparative, or superlative form is needed. Then convert the adjective in parentheses to the proper form. Use the Adjective Forms chart in this chapter as your guide.

(bad)   1. Traffic is much ____worse____ than it was five years ago.

(large)   2. "I want the ___largest___ size that you have," Carl told the ice cream store clerk.

(sick)   3. When Tom woke up, he felt _____sick_____.

(small)   4. Although Tiffany is the older of the two children, she is the ___smaller___ of the two.

(cloudy)   5. The meteorologist said to expect a ____cloudy____ day.

(good)   6. Each of the ice cream flavors seemed ____better____ than the last.

(good)   7. Anya's grade on the final test was the ____best____ grade she had made.

(reliable) 8. Mr. Morton said that Ed was the __most reliable__ employee he had ever had.

(old)   9. Rosetta said that her house was ____older____ than she was.

(roomy)   10. When the company moved its office into the new building, the three supervisors bickered over who should get the ___roomiest___ office.

REVIEW EXERCISE 3

Underline the correct modifier (adjective or adverb) in each sentence.

1. Looking at the huge stone in Mrs. Smythe-Buffington's ring, Michelle wondered if it was a (<u>real</u>, really) diamond.

2. The blues musician said that before a person could (real, <u>really</u>) sing the blues, he had to live the blues.

3. The children tried to catch the squirrels, but the squirrels were too (<u>quick</u>, quickly) for them.

4. "If the appointment does not suit you," said the secretary, "we can reschedule at a (<u>more convenient</u>, most convenient) time."

5. Hajel was ambidextrous, but the writing he did with his left hand was (<u>neater</u>, more neatly) than the writing he did with his right hand.

6. The professor moved through the material so (rapid, <u>rapidly</u>) that the class was left confused.

7. Brendan ran so (quick, <u>quickly</u>) that his little brother found it hard to keep up.

8. The school bus driver said that she was (<u>grateful</u>, gratefully) for weekends and holidays.

9. One advantage of oil over coal is that oil burns (cleaner, <u>more cleanly</u>).

10. Hal's car always looks (<u>cleaner</u>, more cleanly) than mine.

REVIEW EXERCISE 4

Underline the correct modifier in each sentence.

1. Duncan reads very (quick, <u>quickly</u>), but he is a (<u>slow</u>, slowly) writer.

2. Looking at the CD his daughter had (recent, <u>recently</u>) bought, Jim asked if there was (real, <u>really</u>) a band called Bunnygrunt.

3. Though the critics agree that the movie is a (<u>good</u>, best) one, few would call it the (better, <u>best</u>) movie of the year.

4. Even though she did not do (bad, <u>badly</u>) on the exam, Rose knew she could have done (<u>better</u>, more better).

5. Real estate agents say it is a good idea to buy the (smaller, <u>smallest</u>) house in the (more, <u>most</u>) expensive neighborhood you can afford.

Underline and correct the errors in adjectives, adverbs, and articles. Each sentence contains one error.

[1]My friends envy me because I have an healthy bank account. [2]However, they could save money easy if they would just give up some of their wasteful spending habits. [3]My friend Abby, for instance, drinks only the most fanciest bottled water. [4]She says it is pure than tap water. [5]She may be right, but bottled water is also a expensive luxury she could probably do without. [6]Another friend, Jennifer, spends a great deal of money to dress fashionable. [7]If Jennifer waited for clothing to go on sale, then she could dress good for a lower price. [8]Toni, my best friend, is always complaining about her lack of money, but when she gets her paycheck, she heads for the bookstore for the most recently novels. [9]With an library card, Toni could read the latest bestsellers for free. [10]If I have more money than my friends, it is only because I spend more careful.

1. a healthy bank account

2. save money easily

3. the fanciest bottled water

4. purer than tap water

5. an expensive luxury

6. to dress fashionably

7. could dress well

8. most recent novels

9. a library card

10. spend more carefully

mywritinglab   For support in meeting this chapter's goal, log in to **www.mywritinglab.com** and select **Adjectives** and **Adverbs**.

CHAPTER 21

Parallel Structure

✍ **Chapter Goal:** Identify and revise constructions that are not parallel.

Parallel structure enhances this gate—and your sentences.

Choose the best answer to complete each sequence.

1. a, b, c,_____   a. t   b. z   c. d
2. ↘, ↗↗, ↘, ↗↗, _____   a. ↗   b. ↗↗   c. ↘
3. 20, 40, 60, _____   a. 10   b. 120   c. 80
4. ▶, ■, _____   a. •   b. □   c. ◉

I f you chose *c* each time, you are correct. Your mind was responding to the patterns you saw developing in each sequence. Patterns are pleasing to the human mind, and that is why parallel structure works.

In any famous speech, such as Abraham Lincoln's Gettysburg Address or Martin Luther King, Jr.'s, "I Have a Dream" speech, you will hear the regular,

354

memorable cadence of **parallel structure**—parallel words, parallel phrases, and parallel clauses. You will see it in good writing, too, lending elegance to ordinary sentences. Once you are used to seeing parallel structure, anything else will seem awkward. Look at the following lists to see examples of nonparallel and parallel structure.

✗ **Nonparallel:**
worrying about meeting expenses
to hold down two jobs
trying to pay bills on time

The phrase "to hold down two jobs" is not parallel with the *-ing* constructions of the other two phrases.

✔ **Parallel:**
worrying about meeting expenses
holding down two jobs
trying to pay bills on time

The phrases in the revised list have the same structure; that is, they are **parallel**.

✗ **Nonparallel:**
bright green
pale yellow
with a dull gray hue

✔ **Parallel:**
bright green
pale yellow
dull gray

✗ **Nonparallel:**
read two chapters in her sociology book
reviewed her notes for English class
working on a project for a health sciences class

✔ **Parallel:**
read two chapters in her sociology book
reviewed her notes for English class
worked on a project for a health sciences class

PRACTICE 1   USING PARALLEL STRUCTURE

Each of the following lists contains one item that is not parallel. Cross out the nonparallel item and reword it to make it parallel with the other items. Then write the reworded version on the line provided.

1. stopped for gas
    ~~buying stamps at the post office~~
    made a deposit at the bank
    bought stamps at the post office

4. polished floors
    ~~windows that gleam~~
    newly painted walls
    gleaming windows

2. friendly
    ~~was a very intelligent person~~
    funny
    intelligent

5. sitting on the patio
    grilling hamburgers
    ~~to swat at mosquitoes~~
    swatting at mosquitoes

3. ~~watching the sun rise~~
    to swim in the lake
    to eat freshly caught fish
    to watch the sun rise

In sentences, items given equal emphasis should be parallel in structure whenever possible. These items include words, phrases, or clauses in pairs or lists. Look at the following examples of nonparallel and parallel structure within sentences.

✗   The technician **tested** the battery and then **was checking** the connections.

✔   The technician tested the battery and then checked the connections.

✗   The dog **was looking** both ways, **waited** for a car to pass, and **crossed** the street.

✔   The dog **looked** both ways, **waited** for a car to pass, and **crossed** the street.

✗   The manager said he wanted to hire someone who was **courteous, dependable**, and **who was also hardworking.**

✔   The manager said he wanted to hire someone who was **courteous, dependable**, and **hardworking.**

PRACTICE 2   USING PARALLEL STRUCTURE

Each of the following sentences contains one item that is not parallel. Cross out the nonparallel item and reword it to make it parallel with the other items. Then write the reworded version on the line provided.

1. Watching football, reading, and ~~to work on his car~~ are my brother's favorite pastimes.
   working on his car

2. Alberto found a parking space, parked his car, and ~~was heading for class~~.
   headed for class

3. The chef chopped the garlic, ~~was grating the cheese~~, and sliced the tomatoes.
   grated the cheese

4. Mrs. Fabian told her doctor that she needed a medicine that was effective, inexpensive, and ~~that did not present any safety concerns~~.
   safe

5. Jason was proud of his old car because he had rebuilt the motor, ~~the upholstery had been replaced~~, and painted the body.
   replaced the upholstery

Review Exercises

Complete the Review Exercises to find out how well you have learned the skills addressed in this chapter. As you work through the exercises, go back through the chapter to review any of the rules you do not understand completely.

REVIEW EXERCISE 1

Each of the following lists contains one item that is not parallel. Cross out the nonparallel item and reword it to make it parallel with the other items. Then write the reworded version on the line provided. Answers will vary.

1. to rotate the tires
   ~~checking the tread~~
   to monitor the air pressure
   to check the tread

2. shiny
   new
   ~~costing a lot of money~~
   expensive

3. ~~with warmth from the sun~~
    nourished by the soil
    watered by the rain
    warmed by the sun
    _____

4. outstanding references
    a complete résumé
    ~~grades that were good~~
    good grades
    _____

5. that he had been speeding
    ~~running a red light~~
    that he had been intoxicated
    that he had run a red light
    _____

6. diving toward the ground
    flapping its wings
    ~~caws loudly~~
    cawing loudly
    _____

7. worn sneakers
    a ragged T-shirt
    ~~jeans with patches on them~~
    patched jeans
    _____

8. pine trees
    oak trees
    ~~trees in the aspen family~~
    aspen trees
    _____

9. happy
    wealthy
    ~~having good health~~
    healthy
    _____

10. turn on the computer
    bring up the Internet browser
    ~~you'll be typing in the URL~~
    type in the URL
    _____

REVIEW EXERCISE 2

In each of the following sentences, the italicized items should be parallel. Cross out the nonparallel item and reword it to make it parallel with the other items. Then write the reworded version on the line provided. Answers will vary.

1. By the time Friday evening came, all that Tybolt felt like doing was staying at home, *ordering a pizza, and* ~~*to watch a movie*~~.
    watching a movie
    _____

2. Many people own dogs because they want *companionship* and ~~*the dog also provides protection*~~.
    protection
    _____

3. Halogen bulbs *burn brighter*, ~~*are greater in cost*~~, and *last longer* than regular incandescent bulbs.
    cost more
    _____

4. The salesman was *polite,* ~~*had the quality of patience,*~~ *and persuasive*.
    patient
    _____

5. *Roller-skating servers, old-fashioned jukeboxes,* and ~~booths that are cozy~~ are the hallmarks of Bob's Deco Diner.

   cozy booths

6. Before leaving the house, Eric checked to make sure that he *had unplugged the coffeepot* and ~~the lights had been turned off~~.

   turned off the lights

7. Joanie hated working the late shift because she did not enjoy *losing sleep, driving in the dark,* and ~~the walk through a deserted parking lot to her apartment~~.

   walking through a deserted parking lot to her apartment

8. The boxer's *unfocused expression* and ~~eyes that were glazed~~ told the referee that it was time to stop the fight.

   glazed eyes

9. The construction project was plagued by ~~weather that was bad~~, *cost overruns,* and *labor problems.*

   bad weather

10. *Warm gloves,* ~~clothing that is put on in layers~~, and *waterproof boots* are necessities in cold, wet weather.

    layered clothing

REVIEW EXERCISE 3

Each of the following sentences contains one item that is not parallel. Cross out the nonparallel item and reword it to make it parallel with the other items. Then write the reworded version on the line provided.

1. A strong jawline and ~~a smile that dazzled~~ propelled the actor to fame.

   a dazzling smile

2. Anne spent her vacation doing errands and ~~caught up on school work~~.

   catching up on school work

3. Tony's morning routine includes walking the dog and ~~a hearty breakfast~~.

   eating a hearty breakfast

4. Because Melissa left her cell phone at home, her roomate worried and ~~was leaving numerous voicemails~~.

   left numerous voicemails

5. Studying, working, and ~~responsibility~~ were John's new daily habits.

   being responsible

6. As a sous chef, Jaime assisted the chefs and ~~was in charge of salad preparation~~.

    <u>prepared the salads</u>

7. ~~Laundry~~ and cleaning her bedroom are Jen's goals for today.

    <u>Doing laundry</u>

8. Because the sunsets were brighter and ~~beautiful~~, Pat scheduled the photo shoot for the summer.

    <u>more beautiful</u>

9. Losing weight, saving money, and ~~a promotion at work~~ are three of the most popular New Year's resolutions.

    <u>getting promoted at work</u>

10. Jacob's hobbies were reading books and ~~car repair~~.

    <u>repairing cars</u>

REVIEW EXERCISE 4

Each of the sentences in the following paragraph contains one item that is not parallel. Cross out the nonparallel item and reword it to make it parallel with the other items. Then write the reworded version on the lines provided.

¹Everyone experiences stress, regardless of gender, race, or ~~what age the person is~~. ²*Eustress* (from the Greek root *eu* meaning "good" or "well") is stress in response to a positive event such as going on vacation, ~~to win the lottery~~, or receiving a job promotion. ³Even positive events bring stress in the form of the need to act and ~~making decisions~~. ⁴Eustress is relatively easy to deal with: the decision whether to buy a Mercedes or ~~leasing a BMW~~ with lottery winnings may be tough, but most people can handle it. ⁵Distress, stress in response to negative events, is more serious and ~~causing~~ more harm. ⁶This type of stress is often in response to traumatic events such as the loss of a job, ~~a family member dying~~, or the end of a romance. ⁷Such stress can cause a person to feel anger, ~~having nightmares~~, or to gain or lose weight, among other responses. ⁸As if the stress itself is not bad enough, chronic stress is also said to contribute to illnesses such as heart disease, ~~becoming depressed~~, and cancer. ⁹But for most people, after a period of adjustment, stress and its symptoms fade and ~~are seen to disappear~~. ¹⁰Most stress is a normal response to the changes, good and ~~also the ones that are bad~~, in people's lives.

¹Everyone experiences stress, regardless of gender, race, or age. ²Eustress (from the Greek root *eu* meaning "good" or "well") is stress in response to a positive event such as going on vacation, winning the lottery, or receiving a job promotion. ³Even positive events bring stress in the form of the need to act and to make decisions. ⁴Eustress is relatively easy to deal with: the decision whether to buy a Mercedes or to lease a BMW with lottery winnings may be tough, but most people can handle it. ⁵Distress, stress in response to negative events, is more serious and causes more harm. ⁶This type of stress is often in response to traumatic events such as the loss of a job, the death of a family member, or the end of a romance. ⁷Such stress can cause a person to feel anger, to have nightmares, or to gain or lose weight, among other responses. ⁸As if the stress itself is not bad enough, chronic stress is also said to contribute to illnesses such as heart disease, depression, and cancer. ⁹But for most people, after a period of adjustment, stress and its symptoms fade and disappear. ¹⁰Most stress is a normal response to the changes, good and bad, in people's lives.

mywritinglab For support in meeting this chapter's goal, log in to **www.mywritinglab.com** and select **Parallelism**.

CHAPTER 22

Misplaced and Dangling Modifiers

> ✎ **Chapter Goal:** Identify and correct misplaced and dangling modifiers.

The Brush-off

The English major caught his eye,
He smelled her sweet perfume.
He said, "While dancing cheek to cheek,
Romance is sure to bloom."

She said, "To say romance can dance
Is silly from all angles,
And I could never love a man
Whose modifier dangles."

Although dangling and misplaced modifiers probably won't ruin your next romance, they may confuse your readers. That's reason enough to learn what they are and how to avoid them.

Look at the following sentences:

✗ **Hanging upside down from a tree,** Sarita saw a small brown bat.

✔ Sarita saw a small brown bat **hanging upside down from a tree.**

The words in bold type are **modifiers**. A **modifier** is a word, phrase, or clause that gives information about another word. In the preceding sentences, the placement of the phrase *hanging upside down from a tree* makes a great deal of difference. It is easy to imagine a bat hanging upside down from a tree, but the idea of Sarita hanging from a tree does not seem logical.

Although they are not always as obvious as the problem in this example, problems with modifiers are always problems in logic. If you approach this chapter—and your writing in general—with the idea that good writing should above all *make sense,* you will have an easier time spotting and correcting misplaced and dangling modifiers.

Misplaced Modifiers

mywritinglab

Visit MyWriting Lab for additional practice correcting misplaced or dangling modifiers.

Look at the following sentence:

✗ Covered in marinara sauce and sprinkled lightly with Romano cheese, Frank enjoyed spaghetti.

Do you see what is not logical about the sentence? Of course. Frank is not covered in marinara sauce and sprinkled lightly with Romano cheese. The spaghetti is. This type of modifier problem is called a **misplaced modifier**. The modifier *covered in marinara sauce and sprinkled lightly with Romano cheese* is misplaced to modify *Frank* instead of *spaghetti.* To fix a misplaced modifier, remember this principle: **A modifier should be placed as close as possible to the word it modifies.**

✔ Frank enjoyed spaghetti covered in marinara sauce and sprinkled lightly with Romano cheese.

Examples of Misplaced Modifiers

✗ The car was road-tested by the mechanic that had just had a tune-up.

The sentence seems to suggest that the mechanic had a tune-up. Putting the modifier *that had just had a tune-up* closer to *car,* the word it modifies, makes the meaning clear.

✔ The car that had just had a tune-up was road-tested by the mechanic.

Reconstructing the sentence is also a possibility.

✔ The mechanic road tested the car that had just had a tune-up.

✗ Stark and filled with angles, Paco said he did not like the abstract painting.

The sentence is worded as though Paco, not the painting, is stark and filled with angles.

✔ Paco said he did not like the abstract painting, which was stark and filled with angles.

✗ Old and battered, Glenda finally threw her calculator into the trash can.

Is Glenda old and battered, or is it her calculator?

✔ Glenda finally threw her old and battered calculator into the trash can.
✔ Because her calculator was old and battered, Glenda finally threw it into the trash can.

PRACTICE 1   CORRECTING MISPLACED MODIFIERS

Correct the misplaced modifiers in the following sentences. Answers may vary.

1. Brad found two abandoned puppies driving along the highway.
    Driving along the highway, Brad found two abandoned puppies.

2. Floating belly-up in the fish tank, Leonardo was afraid that his new angelfish was dead.
    Leonardo was afraid that his new angelfish, floating belly-up in the fish tank, was
    dead.

3. The customer complained to the server who had just found a fly in his soup.
    The customer who had just found a fly in his soup complained to the server.

4. Lakeisha replaced the light over the stove that had burned out.
    Lakeisha replaced the light that had burned out over the stove.

5. From a bench near the playground, a woman kept a close eye on her toddler who was reading the *Wall Street Journal*.
    From a bench near the playground, a woman who was reading the *Wall Street Journal*
    kept a close eye on her toddler.

Dangling Modifiers

Unlike a misplaced modifier, which needs to be moved closer to the word it modifies, a dangling modifier has no word to modify. Look at the following sentence:

✘   After sitting in front of the computer for two hours, Brian's head hurt.

The phrase *after sitting in front of the computer for two hours* has no word in the sentence to modify. Since a modifier needs a noun or pronoun to modify, the word *Brian's* will not work. The *'s* attached to it makes it a modifier itself—it acts as an adjective to modify the word *head. Head* is a noun, but Brian's head did not sit in front of the computer for two hours—at least not without the rest of him. Therefore, the sentence needs to be fixed in one of two ways. The easiest way to fix a dangling modifier is to give it a word to modify. Place the word immediately after the dangling modifier.

✔   After sitting in front of the computer for two hours, **Brian** had a headache.

The sentence may also be reconstructed.

✔   After Brian sat in front of the computer for two hours, his head hurt.
✔   After Brian sat in front of the computer for two hours, he had a headache.

Here is another example:

✘   Sitting in class, Antoinette's cell phone rang.

Obviously, it is Antoinette who is sitting in class, not her cell phone. The easiest way to fix the sentence is to put the word *Antoinette* (not the possessive form *Antoinette's*) immediately after the modifier.

✔   Sitting in class, Antoinette heard her cell phone ring.

But it is also permissible to reconstruct the sentence entirely.

✔   Antoinette's cell phone rang as she sat in class.
✔   As Antoinette sat in class, her cell phone rang.

Look at this example:

✘   By working cheerfully and conscientiously, an employer will be impressed.

It is not the employer who works cheerfully and conscientiously, but the employee trying to make a good impression. The sentence can be fixed by indicating, immediately after the modifier, who is working cheerfully.

✔ By working cheerfully and conscientiously, a worker can impress an employer.

The sentence can also be reworked entirely.

✔ Cheerful, conscientious workers are likely to impress their employers.

✔ An employer will be impressed by a cheerful and conscientious worker.

Here is another example:

✗ Bored and restless, the minutes seemed to crawl.

Who was bored and restless? (If the sentence does not say, the decision is yours.)

✔ Bored and restless, **Andre** felt the minutes crawl.

PRACTICE 2   CORRECTING DANGLING MODIFIERS

Underline and correct the dangling modifiers in the following sentences. Answers may vary.

1. <u>Hurrying down the steps</u>, a huge stack of books fell from Jerome's hands.

   A huge stack of books fell from Jerome's hands as he hurried down the steps.

2. <u>Swayed by the salesperson's smooth pitch</u>, Arlene's resolve weakened.

   Arlene's resolve weakened as the salesperson's smooth pitch swayed her.

3. <u>Embarrassed by the attention</u>, a bright red blush crept up Roy's neck and onto his cheeks.

   Because he was embarrassed by the attention, a bright red blush crept up Roy's neck and onto his cheeks.

4. <u>By planning projects carefully</u>, a last-minute rush can be avoided.

   By planning projects carefully, you can avoid a last-minute rush.

5. Dressed in a green satin ball <u>gown</u>, Brandy's father proudly led her onto the dance floor.

   Dressed in a green satin ball gown, Brandy was led onto the dance floor by her proud father.

Review Exercises

Complete the Review Exercises to find out how well you have learned the skills addressed in this chapter. As you work through the exercises, go back through the chapter to review any of the rules you do not understand completely.

REVIEW EXERCISE 1

Rewrite the sentences to correct the italicized misplaced or dangling modifiers. Answers may vary.

1. *Always a conscientious student*, the professor wasn't surprised to see Lynn during office hours the day before the exam.

   The professor wasn't surprised to see Lynn, always a conscientious student, during office hours the day before the exam.

2. Terrell found a twenty-dollar bill *searching in his coat pockets*.

   Searching in his coat pockets, Terrell found a twenty-dollar bill.

3. *Having been nervous and tense for weeks*, the relief didn't set in immediately when the problem was solved.

   Having been nervous and tense for weeks, Marcus did not feel immediate relief when the problem was solved.

4. The lovely cake made Mark's mouth water, *covered in chocolate frosting and topped with a cherry*.

   Covered in chocolate frosting and topped with a cherry, the lovely cake made Mark's mouth water.

5. *Smiling indulgently at her grandchild's mischievousness*, the prank didn't upset Joyce.

   Smiling indulgently at her grandchild's mischievousness, Joyce wasn't upset by the prank.

REVIEW EXERCISE 2

Correct the dangling and misplaced modifiers in the following sentences. Answers may vary.

1. Frozen solid and covered with snow, Kendra looked at the birdbath.

    Kendra looked at the birdbath, which was frozen solid and covered with snow.
    _____

2. Holding a sign that read "Will work for food," the well-dressed woman gave five dollars to a homeless man.

    The well-dressed woman gave five dollars to a homeless man holding a sign that

    read "Will work for food."

3. Filthy and flea-bitten, Doris gave the stray kitten a bath.

    Doris gave the filthy and flea-bitten stray kitten a bath.
    _____

4. Waxed and buffed, Daniel nearly slipped on the floor.

    Daniel nearly slipped on the waxed and buffed floor.
    _____

5. Pickled in brandy, the members of the garden club enjoyed the peaches.

    The members of the garden club enjoyed the peaches pickled in brandy.
    _____

6. Ben bought hot dogs for the children topped with mustard.

    Ben bought hot dogs topped with mustard for the children.
    _____

7. By advertising in the newspaper, Andrew's car was sold within a week.

    By advertising in the newspaper, Andrew sold his car within a week.
    _____

8. The red truck was driven by a tall man with four huge tires.

    The red truck with four huge tires was driven by a tall man.
    _____

9. Giving off a foul odor whenever the wind came from the east, the citizens complained that the landfill was too close to residential areas.

    The landfill gave off a foul odor whenever the wind came from the east, and the

    citizens complained that it was too close to residential areas.

10. Sanded and refinished, the worker looked with pride at the floor.
    The worker looked with pride at the sanded and refinished floor.

REVIEW EXERCISE 3

Underline and correct the two misplaced or dangling modifiers in each sentence group.

1. Thirty pizzas were brought into the student center at 5:00 P.M. by a delivery person covered with pepperoni and dripping with cheese. Hungry and eager for a treat, every last crumb was devoured by 6:00 P.M.
   Thirty pizzas, covered with pepperoni and dripping with cheese, were brought into the student center at 5:00 P.M. Hungry and eager for a treat, the students devoured every last crumb by 6:00 P.M.

2. Cathy saw a Bengal tiger visiting Safari Land on vacation. With a striped face and body and a long, graceful tail, Cathy thought the tiger was beautiful.
   Visiting Safari Land on vacation, Cathy saw a Bengal tiger. Cathy thought the tiger, with its striped face and body and a long, graceful tail, was beautiful.

3. Mitchell went to see the doctor with a bad cold and a sore throat. After describing his symptoms, the doctor prescribed medication, fluids, and plenty of rest.
   With a bad cold and a sore throat, Mitchell went to see the doctor. After Mitchell described his symptoms, the doctor prescribed medication, fluids, and plenty of rest.

4. Furry and cute, Andrew was captivated by the little puppy in the pet store window. As he went in to buy it, he rationalized that the puppy would be good for his children with floppy ears and big eyes.
   The furry and cute little puppy in the pet store window captivated Andrew. As he went in buy it, he rationalized that the puppy with floppy ears and big eyes would be good for his children.

5. Filled with air and tied off at the bottom, the balloon artist created objects from ordinary balloons. With great skill, a few colorful balloons were transformed into a hat.
   The balloon artist created objects from ordinary balloons, which were filled with air and tied off at the bottom. With great skill, the artist transformed a few colorful balloons into a hat.

REVIEW EXERCISE 4

Find and correct the misplaced and dangling modifiers in the following paragraph. Write your corrected sentences in the blanks provided. Answers may vary.

[1]Dirty and filled with old paint cans and forgotten garden implements, Griffin decided to clean the storage shed. [2]Determined to clean it at last, everything in the shed was removed. [3]Coughing at the dust, a broom was used to sweep dirt from the floor and cobwebs from the walls. [4]Squinting through dirty windows, a bottle of ammonia cleaner was needed to finish the cleaning. [5]Griffin then sorted through old paint cans, bent lawn chairs, and rusty tools with gloves on. [6]Useless and unusable, Griffin put most of the items in a junk pile to haul away later. [7]Tired from his efforts, the only task that remained was to put back all of the usable items and arrange them neatly on shelves. [8]Finally, surveying his clean shed with pride, the result had been worth the effort.

[1]Griffin decided to clean the storage shed because it was dirty and filled with old paint cans and forgotten garden implements. [2]Determined to clean it at last, Griffin removed everything in the shed. [3]Coughing at the dust, he used a broom to sweep dirt from the floor and cobwebs from the walls. [4]Squinting through dirty windows, Griffin needed a bottle of ammonia cleaner to finish the cleaning. [5]With gloves on, Griffin then sorted through old paint cans, bent lawn chairs, and rusty tools. [6]Griffin put most of the useless and unusable items in a junk pile to haul away later. [7]The only task that remained was to put back all of the usable items and arrange them neatly on shelves even though he was tired from his efforts. [8]Finally, Griffin surveyed his clean shed with pride and realized that the result had been worth the effort.

mywritinglab   For support in meeting this chapter's goal, log in to **www.mywritinglab.com** and select **Misplaced or Dangling Modifiers**.

CHAPTER **23**

Capital Letters

> ✍ **Chapter Goal:** Use capitalization appropriately.

ALL CAPS.

✍ Capital Letters to Begin Sentences

mywritinglab

Visit MyWriting Lab for additional practice with capitalization.

Capitalize the first word of a sentence or a direct quotation.

Examples of Capital Letters to Begin Sentences

- ✔ Pranav placed his coffee cup on the windowsill.
- ✔ On the roof of the house lay a lime-green Frisbee.
- ✔ "What time does the next bus come?" Frankie asked impatiently.

371

✐ Capitalization of Words Referring to Individuals

Names and the Pronoun *I*

Capitalize people's names and the pronoun *I*.

Examples of Capitalization of Names and the Pronoun *I*

May I have that last doughnut if you aren't going to eat it?

Mr. Bittenton gave Harold an old model train set.

Family Relationships

Family Designations Used in Place of a Name

Capitalize a word that designates a family relationship if it is used in place of a name. To make sure that the word is used as a name, try substituting a name for the word. If the word is used as a name, the substitution will sound natural.

Examples of Family Designations Used in Place of a Name

I took Grandma out to lunch at the mall.

I took Grandma Betty Smith out to lunch at the mall.

"I took Betty Smith out to lunch" sounds natural, so *Grandma* is correct.

Try your own substitution in the next sentence. If substituting a name for *Dad* sounds natural, the capitalization is correct.

This past fall, Dad enrolled in a college course to improve his thinking skills.

Family Designations Used with Possessives and Articles

When family designations such as *father, mother,* or *great-uncle Elmo* are preceded by a possessive pronoun (*my, her, his, their*), a possessive noun (*Ted's, Penny's*), or an article (*a, an,* or *the*), they are not capitalized. For additional proof, try directly substituting a name for the family designation. It will sound awkward.

Examples of Family Designations Used with Possessives and Articles

I took my grandma out to lunch at the mall.

I took my ~~grandma~~ Betty Smith out to lunch at the mall.

The phrase "my Betty Smith" sounds awkward, so *grandma* is correct.

Try substituting a name for *dad* in the next sentence, making sure to leave the pronoun *my* in the sentence. If the name does not sound natural, then the lowercase *dad* is correct.

"I am taking a course," my dad said, "because if I don't use my mind, I may lose it."

Professional Titles

Do not capitalize professional titles unless they are used immediately before a name.

- ✔ Pandita Gupta is the doctor on duty in the emergency room.
- ✔ The accident victims were treated by Dr. Pandita Gupta.
- ✔ James Solkowski is my English professor.
- ✔ I am taking American literature with Professor James Solkowski.

PRACTICE 1   CAPITALIZING WORDS REFERRING TO PEOPLE

Underline and correct the two capitalization mistakes in each sentence.

1. Uncle Ed took <u>grandpa</u> to the <u>Doctor</u> for a flu shot.
   Grandpa, doctor

2. My <u>Aunt</u> always said, "Experience is the best <u>Teacher</u>."
   aunt, teacher

3. Latrelle and <u>jason</u> are in <u>professor</u> Langley's Tuesday biology lab.
   Jason, Professor

4. Nathaniel, my <u>Cousin</u>, is an <u>Attorney</u> with the firm of Vogel and Krantz.
   cousin, attorney

5. Mr. <u>peabody</u> called his <u>Senator</u> to complain about taxes.
   Peabody, senator

Capitalization of Words Referring to Groups

Religions, Geographic Locations, Races, and Nationalities

Capitalize words that refer to specific religions, geographic locations, races, and nationalities.

Examples of Capitalization of Religions, Geographic Locations, Races, and Nationalities

✔ People of many races attend school with me. I have classmates who are Asian, Caucasian, African American, Latino, and Native American.

✔ Though Bjorn is originally from Sweden, he considers himself a Los Angeleno.

✔ Alan drives an American car, drinks German beer, and collects Mexican glassware.

✔ Rashid was brought up Baptist, but he converted to Islam when he was twenty-six.

Organizations, Businesses, and Agencies

Capitalize specific names of organizations, businesses, and government agencies.

Examples of Capitalization of Organizations, Businesses, and Agencies

✔ Harley belongs to the Meadow Community Chorus, the Spanish Club, and the Association of Nursing Students.

✔ Perry works at the Campbell Corporation and his wife works for Microsoft.

✔ After Lenore finished her accounting degree, she went to work for the Internal Revenue Service.

Do not capitalize nonspecific or generic organization names.

Examples of Lowercase Nonspecific Organization Names

✔ Clarissa is active in church and is also a member of the choir.

✔ As an executive in a large corporation, Simone travels often.

✔ After finishing college, Claud wants to work for the federal government.

PRACTICE 2 CAPITALIZING WORDS REFERRING TO GROUPS

Underline and correct the two capitalization mistakes in each sentence.

1. Janet went to the Library to find information on the american red cross.
   library, American Red Cross

2. The first methodist children's choir sold candy to benefit a charity called kids yule love.

    First Methodist Children's Choir, Kids Yule Love

3. When he began working for ford, Dwight joined the Union.

    Ford, union

4. One of the most active clubs at the College is the association of nontraditional students.

    college, Association of Nontraditional Students

5. I heard that our Company chairperson was offered a job at the federal trade commission.

    company, Federal Trade Commission

Capitalization of Words Referring to Time and Place

Months, Days, Holidays, and Seasons

Capitalize months of the year, days of the week, and names of holidays. Do *not* capitalize the names of the four seasons.

Examples of Capitalization of Months, Days, Holidays, and Seasons

✔ Thanksgiving Day is always celebrated on the last Thursday in November.

✔ October holidays include Halloween and Columbus Day.

✔ Marvin wants to take one last summer trip before his children go back to school in the fall.

Place Names

Capitalize specific place names.

Examples of Capitalization of Place Names

✔ On our trip to Orlando, we visited Disney World, Sea World, Universal Studios, and Wet 'n' Wild.

✔ We also ate at King Arthur's Feast.

✔ When Sandra attended Glendale Community College, she worked part-time at Pizza Hut.

✔ The robber ran out of the Kwickie Food Mart and tore down Lemon Street.

Do not capitalize *general*, *nonspecific* place names.

Examples of Lowercase Nonspecific Names

✔ On our trip to Orlando, we visited three theme parks and a water park.

✔ We also ate at two expensive and entertaining restaurants.

✔ When Sandra attended college, she worked for a pizza place.

✔ The robber ran out of the convenience store and tore down the street.

Do not capitalize compass points unless they refer to a specific geographical area.

Examples of Capitalization of Compass Points

✔ The car traveled north on the interstate before turning east toward the city.

✔ Having lived on the East Coast all her life, Deb found it hard to adjust to the mountainous West.

PRACTICE 3   CAPITALIZING WORDS REFERRING TO TIME AND PLACE

Underline and correct the two capitalization mistakes in each sentence.

1. Cathryn had always lived in the <u>south</u>, but when she was eighteen, she moved to <u>california</u>.
   South, California

2. The bus was headed <u>South</u> on <u>peachtree street</u>.
   south, Peachtree Street

3. People living in <u>new mexico</u> sometimes have trouble convincing people that they live in the <u>united states</u>.
   New Mexico, United States

4. Kim's family celebrates both <u>kwanzaa</u> and Christmas in the <u>Winter</u>.
   Kwanzaa, winter

5. The state of <u>north</u> Carolina is known for its beaches as well as its beautiful <u>blue ridge mountains</u>.
   North Carolina, Blue Ridge Mountains

Capitalization of Words Referring to Things and Activities

School Subjects

Do not capitalize subjects studied in school unless they are part of a *specific* course title.

Examples of Capitalization of School Subjects

✔ Sandro is taking physics, French, and sociology this term.

✔ Sandro is taking Physics 101, French 102, and Sociology 208 this term.

✔ Sandro is taking Principles of Physics, Intermediate French, and Social Problems this term.

Titles

In general, capitalize titles of novels, short stories, poems, newspapers, magazines, articles, works of art, television shows, movies, and songs and other musical works. There are exceptions to many rules in English, and this rule has more exceptions than most. Some newspapers and journals capitalize only the first word in the title of an article. Some writers, like e. e. cummings, do not follow the conventional rules of capitalization. When you write about an article, a poem, or any other piece of writing, preserve the title as it was published.

Otherwise, follow these rules: Capitalize the first word of a title. Do not capitalize articles (*a, an,* and *the*) or short prepositions (*to, of, from,* and similar short prepositions) unless they are the first word in a title. Capitalize all other words.

Examples of Capitalization of Titles

✔ Hisako read an article in *Sky and Telescope* called "Radio Astronomy in the 21st Century."

✔ Kelly's literature class read Anton Chekhov's play, *The Cherry Orchard.*

✔ Isabel wrote her paper on "Sorting Laundry" by Elisavietta Ritchie and "Snow White and the Seven Deadly Sins" by R. S. Gwynn.

✔ Myra tried to keep the children busy by teaching them to sing "Row, Row, Row Your Boat."

Consumer Products

For consumer products, capitalize the brand name but not the general product name.

Examples of Capitalization of Consumer Products

✔ At the college bookstore, Roger bought a Paper Mate highlighter, a roll of Scotch tape, a Bic pen, and a Mead notebook.

✔ A Toyota broke down in front of the drive-through at Burger King.

Abbreviations

Abbreviations of organizations, corporations, and professional designations are capitalized. Some examples include NBC, AFL-CIO, FBI, NAACP, CIA, UPS, CPA, M.D., Ph.D., D.D.S. The disease name AIDS is always written in all capitals.

PRACTICE 4   CAPITALIZING WORDS REFERRING TO THINGS AND ACTIVITIES

Underline and correct the two capitalization mistakes in each sentence.

1. Al pulled his <u>toyota</u> into the convenience store parking lot and ran over an empty Coke <u>Bottle</u>.

   Toyota, bottle

2. Mollie opened a can of <u>alpo</u> dog food, but when Taffy refused to eat it, she shared her <u>mcDonald's</u> cheeseburger with him.

   Alpo, McDonald's

3. Ann reads the *<u>miami herald</u>* or watches <u>cbs</u> to get the latest news.

   Miami Herald, CBS

4. Since he was out of Maxwell House <u>Coffee</u>, Ed decided to have some Lipton <u>Tea</u>.

   coffee, tea

5. Leshan read an article in *<u>new woman</u>* called "<u>how I lost fifty pounds.</u>"

   New Woman, "How I Lost Fifty Pounds."

Review Exercises

Complete the Review Exercises to find out how well you have learned the skills addressed in this chapter. As you work through the exercises, go back through the chapter to review any of the rules you do not understand completely.

REVIEW EXERCISE 1

Underline and correct the two capitalization mistakes in each sentence.

1. When Mimi couldn't find what she needed at <u>foodmax</u>, she went to <u>kroger</u>.

   Foodmax, Kroger

2. Alton bought a flower arrangement for his <u>Mother</u> to celebrate <u>mother's</u> day.

   mother, Mother's Day

3. When <u>grandpa</u> tried to cut the <u>thanksgiving</u> turkey, it slipped off the platter and shot across the table.

   Grandpa, Thanksgiving

4. When Randy went to his <u>High School</u> reunion, he borrowed a friend's <u>lexus</u> instead of driving his old <u>Chevy</u> truck.

   high school, Lexus

5. It was late <u>march</u> before Andrew received his letter of acceptance from the <u>College</u>.

   March, college

REVIEW EXERCISE 2

Underline and correct the two capitalization mistakes in each sentence.

1. Sonia wore her <u>mickey mouse</u> T-shirt and her <u>nike</u> shoes to the picnic.

   Mickey Mouse, Nike

2. The bus pulled into the town of <u>east point</u> at 6:00 A.M., then headed <u>West</u> on Route 27.

   East Point, west

3. Before the baseball game started, the crowd at <u>turner field</u> stood to sing "<u>the star-spangled banner</u>."

   Turner Field, "The Star Spangled Banner"

4. Kelsey munched on a bag of Frito's <u>Corn Chips</u> as she watched a rerun of *law and order*.

   corn chips, *Law and Order*

5. Some birds live in <u>north america</u> during the summer and migrate to <u>south america</u> in the winter.

   North America, South America

REVIEW EXERCISE 3

Underline and correct the two capitalization mistakes in each sentence.

1. Harry and his <u>Dad</u> went on a two-week fishing trip to Crystal Lake last <u>Spring</u>.
   dad, spring

2. Scientists who do <u>aids</u> research get a portion of their funding from the <u>Federal Government</u>.
   AIDS, federal government

3. Kim said, "<u>a</u> few years ago, I used to smoke Marlboro <u>Cigarettes</u>. Now my worst vice is Hostess Ho Hos."
   A, cigarettes

4. Kaya bought a half gallon of <u>breyer's</u> <u>Strawberry</u> frozen yogurt.
   Breyer's strawberry

5. Gary is from the <u>midwest</u>, but he has lived in <u>south</u> Carolina for three years.
   Midwest, South

REVIEW EXERCISE 4

Underline and correct the capitalization errors in the paragraph below.

[1]As a college student, with every new person I meet I face the same inevitable question, "<u>what</u> is your major?" [2]For many students, this may seem like a harmless question, but as an <u>english</u> major, I face blank stares and concerned expressions. [3]People often question the job prospects of students with degrees in the <u>Liberal Arts</u>. [4]Yet, many lucrative career fields reward a well-rounded <u>College</u> education. [5]For example, students can major in a myriad of fields before attending law school and becoming <u>Lawyers</u>. [6]After graduation, maybe I will write for the *<u>new york times</u>*. [7]I could possibly become an executive at a major <u>Corporation</u>. [8]It might even be rewarding to teach at my old <u>High School</u>. [9]My mentor, <u>professor</u> Calloway, says that students in the liberal arts learn to think and analyze. [10]<u>whatever</u> I decide to do, I feel confident that my degree is providing me with the balanced education I will need for success in the workplace.

1. What

2. English

3. liberal arts _____
4. college _____
5. lawyers _____
6. *New York Times* _____
7. corporation _____
8. high school _____
9. Professor _____
10. Whatever _____

mywritinglab For support in meeting this chapter's goal, log in to www.mywritinglab.com and select **Capitalization**.

CHAPTER 24

Words Commonly Confused

> 🎵 **Chapter Goal:** Choose the correct word when faced with commonly confused words such as *there* and *their*, *less* and *fewer*, or *to*, *too*, and *two*.

Red on black, venom lack;
Red on yellow, kill a fellow.

Is this snake a deadly North American coral snake, or one of the harmless varieties of striped snakes? Knowing the difference in these commonly confused snakes could save your life. Similarly, knowing the difference in commonly confused words can prevent deadly errors in a résumé or an email to a customer.

🎵 Words Commonly Confused

mywritinglab

Visit MyWriting Lab for additional practice working with commonly confused words.

a, an The article *a* is used before consonant sounds. The article *an* is used before vowel sounds. Thus you would write *a dog*, *a rocky shoreline*, *a patch of ice*, *an icy road*, *an oblong box*, *an office*. But you must base your choice on the consonant or vowel *sound*. Some words, such as those beginning with a silent *h* or with a *u* that is pronounced like *yoo*, require careful treatment: *an honest person*, but *a hat*; *an uncle*, but *a used car*.

382

✔ At the market, Trinh bought **an** eggplant, **a** large basket of crisp apples that came with **an** apple corer, and **a** few squash.

✔ The actor said that it was **an** honor to receive such **a** prestigious award.

accept, except   To *accept* is *to take* or *believe;* the word *except* means *but* or *with the exception of.*

✔ The company will **accept** applications, but **except** for a few clerical positions, no jobs are available.

advice, advise   *Advice* is a noun; one gives *advice* or asks for it. *Advise* is the verb form; one person may *advise* another.

✔ The psychic **advised** Abby to seek further **advice** at only $2.95 per minute.

affect, effect   *Affect* is the verb form. It means *to cause a change or variation. Effect* is the noun form. It means *outcome* or *result.*

✔ Jacob's illness does not seem to **affect** his mood.

✔ Even though Janice studied hard, the **effect** on her grades was not immediate.

all right, alright   *All right* is the only correct spelling. It is never all right to write *alright.*

✔ The computer was not working this morning, but it seems to be **all right** now.

a lot, alot, allot   *A lot* (never *alot*) is always written as two words when you mean *much* or *many,* but it's preferable to use a word such as *much, many, several,* or a specific amount instead of *a lot.* The word *allot* means *to allow or set aside* for a special purpose: Erica *allotted* fifty dollars per month to her vacation fund.

✔ **Acceptable:** It took **a lot** of work to make the old house livable.

✔ **Better:** It took **months** of work to make the old house livable.

among, between   *Among* is used with three or more persons or things; *between* is used with just two.

✔ At the banquet, Governor Albright was seated **between** the mayor and Senator Jones. Later, however, she walked **among** the tables, chatting with her constituents.

breath, breathe *Breath* is the noun form: a person can take a *breath* or be out of *breath*. *Breathe* is the verb form: someone may *breathe* heavily after exercising.

✔ "I can't take a vacation," said Pierre. "I am so busy I can't even take a **breath.**"

✔ "First, you need to learn how to **breathe,**" said the yoga instructor.

by, buy *By* means *beside* or *through*. *Buy* means *to purchase*.

✔ "If you go **by** the ice cream shop," said Brandon, "**buy** me a pint of strawberry."

fewer, less Use *fewer* when writing about things you count; *less* when writing about things you measure. Specifically, if you can put a number in front of a word (five dollars), use *fewer*. If you cannot put a number in front of a word (five money), use *less*. You would write *fewer rocks* but *less sand*, *fewer cookies* but *less flour*.

✔ Anita noticed that when she used **less** fertilizer, her plants produced **fewer** tomatoes.

good, well *Good* is an adjective that answers the question "What kind?" *Well* is an adverb that answers the question "How?" or "In what manner?" Therefore, a person writes a *good* essay. (*Good* answers the question, "What kind of essay?") But he writes it *well*. (*Well* answers the question, "How did he write it?")

✔ Carlisle has a **good** arm, but he does not pitch very **well** under pressure.

himself, ~~hisself~~ The word is always *himself*, never *hisself*.

✔ Rico was proud that he had done the repairs **himself.**

its, it's If you mean *it is* or *it has*, use *it's* (with the apostrophe). Otherwise, use *its*.

✔ The inchworm, bending double, then stretching full length, slowly made **its** way across the walkway.

✔ "**It's** a pleasure to drive my old Ford," said Daniel, "because **it's** been taken care of."

knew, new *Knew* is the past tense of *know*; *new* means *not old*.

✔ The owner of the small hardware store **knew** that he faced stiff competition from the **new** Handy Andy down the street.

know, no *Know* means *to understand; no* means *not any* or the opposite of *yes.*

✔ "I do not **know** why there are **no** gas stations along this stretch of highway," said Joan.

loose, lose *Loose* is the opposite of *tight; lose* is the opposite of *find.*

✔ Althea's clothes are getting **loose,** but she says she plans to **lose** more weight.

past, passed *Past* (an adjective) means *beyond* or *before now. Past* (a noun) means *a time before now. Passed* (a verb) means *went by.*

✔ The insurance company bases its rates on a client's **past** driving record.
✔ More and more, Aunt Emma seems to talk about the **past.**
✔ Every time Tammy **passed** a fast-food place, her son yelled, "Want fries!"

peace, piece *Peace* means *calm* or *tranquility; piece* means *a part.*

✔ Sam knew he would get no **peace** until he gave Cujo a **piece** of his hamburger.

plain, plane *Plain* means *clear* or *simple.* A *plane* is a form of air transportation, a carpenter's tool, or a geometric surface.

✔ Joseph's **plain,** simple office belied the fact that he had a company **plane** at his disposal.

principal, principle *Principal* means *chief* (principal reason) or *a person in charge of a school* (principal of Westmore High). A *principle* is a policy, a moral stand, or a rule.

✔ The **principal** said she hoped to encourage solid values and strong **principles** in her students.
✔ Pete's inability to get along with his coworkers was the **principal** reason he was fired.

quit, quite, quiet *Quit* means *to stop. Quite* means *entirely* or *very,* and *quiet* means *hushed.*

✔ "I am not **quite** through with my homework," Anna told her daughter. "If you will **quit** banging on that pot and be **quiet** for just a few minutes, I will play with you when I'm through."

regardless, ~~irregardless~~ Regardless of the number of times you may have seen it, *irregardless* is not a legitimate word. The word is *regardless*.

✔ **Regardless** of the setbacks and problems that Aldo had, his term paper turned out well.

themselves, ~~themself, theirself, theirselves~~ The word is always *themselves*.

✔ After they did their Saturday chores, Tina and Frank decided to give **themselves** a treat and order a pizza.

then, than *Then* is used to show time or cause and effect; *than* is used to compare.

✔ If you are going to the library tomorrow, maybe I will see you **then**.
✔ If Jerrald moves to the new apartment complex, **then** he will have a longer commute to work.
✔ The new copier takes up much less space **than** the old one did.

there, their, they're *There* is used to mean *in that place* or to start a sentence or clause. *Their* means *belonging to them,* and *they're* means *they are*.

✔ "**There** are not enough places in this mall to sit down," said Alberta.
✔ Valerie took her children to the health department for **their** school vaccinations.
✔ "**They're** not for you," Kim warned as the dog nosed the bag of sandwiches.

through, threw *Through* means *within, between,* or *finished. Threw* is the past tense of *throw*.

✔ After Jim was **through** with his newspaper, he **threw** it in the recycling bin and sat looking **through** the window.

two, too, to *Two* refers to the number two; *too* means *also* or indicates an excessive amount, as in the phrase *too much*. Any other use requires *to*.

✔ Alfredo said he wanted **to** go **to** the beach, **too,** but I told him we had **too** many people unless someone else agreed to drive so that we could take **two** cars.

weather, whether, rather *Weather* includes natural phenomena such as temperature, rainfall, and wind velocity. *Whether* means *if* and indicates the existence of two possibilities. It is often paired with *or not*. *Rather* indicates a preference.

- ✔ The **weather** is expected to turn warm after the weekend.
- ✔ We aren't sure **whether** we can afford a vacation this year.
- ✔ Would you **rather** have ice cream or frozen yogurt?

where, were *Where* rhymes with *air* and refers to *place*. *Were* rhymes with *fur* and is a past-tense form of *to be*.

- ✔ When Cari did not see you, she asked **where** you **were**.

Review Exercises

Complete the Review Exercises to find out how well you have learned the skills addressed in this chapter. As you work through the exercises, go back through the chapter to review any of the rules you do not understand completely.

REVIEW EXERCISE 1

Refer to the explanations in this chapter to choose the correct words in each sentence. Underline the correct choice.

1. I do not (<u>accept</u>, except) that all of the seats at the concert could be sold (accept, <u>except</u>) for those with obstructed views.
2. Could you offer some (<u>advice</u>, advise) for getting (<u>through</u>, threw) the final exam?
3. (<u>Regardless</u>, Irregardless) of the judge's decision, all of the competitors should be proud of (<u>themselves</u>, theirselves).
4. Students have said that (<u>they're</u>, their) concerned about getting to (there, <u>their</u>) classes on time with all of the construction on the highway.
5. If you like pizza better (<u>than</u>, then) steak, (than, <u>then</u>) we should go to Mario's for dinner.

REVIEW EXERCISE 2

Underline the correct words in each sentence.

1. After her children left for school in the morning, Monica enjoyed the (piece, <u>peace</u>) and (quite, <u>quiet</u>).

2. The singer flashed a (piece, <u>peace</u>) sign and said, "Everything is uptight, (alright, <u>all right</u>), and out of sight."

3. Lakeisha wore (<u>a</u>, an) caftan that was flowing and (<u>loose</u>, lose).

4. James could not (except, <u>accept</u>) Laurie's declaration that she was (<u>through</u>, threw) with him.

5. Aimee decided to take her conservative grandmother's (<u>advice</u>, advise) and print her résumé on (<u>plain</u>, plane) white paper instead of on hot pink paper.

REVIEW EXERCISE 3

Cross out the two word choice errors in each sentence. Then write the correct words on the line provided.

1. At the paint store, Marie found it hard to ~~chose between~~ the forty different shades of yellow.

   choose, among

2. "I used ~~too~~ wish I was smarter ~~then~~ my brother," said Joseph, "until I realized that I was."

   to, than

3. "The coffee tasted very ~~well~~," said Owen, "but I'm not sure ~~weather~~ I should have drunk it so late at night."

   good, whether

4. Dwight and Hakim reminded ~~theirselves~~ that they had meant ~~too~~ go to the library to study.

   themselves, to

5. Carol couldn't ~~except~~ our invitation because she had ~~alot~~ of work to do.

   accept, a lot

REVIEW EXERCISE 4

Cross out the two word choice errors in each sentence. Then write the correct words on the line provided.

1. Steve said that the ~~principle~~ reason he quit his job was that his supervisor asked him to falsify financial records. Dishonesty was against Steve's ~~principals~~.

   principal, principles

2. Ellen's goldfish was floating lifelessly in ~~it's~~ bowl Thursday morning. She wondered ~~weather~~ she had overfed it the night before.

   its, whether

3. Brian had told no one ~~accept~~ Courtney that he was planning to quit his job. He was surprised to find that all of his coworkers ~~new~~ about it.

   except, knew

4. When a wasp landed on her magazine, Susan held her ~~breathe~~. Then she quickly ~~through~~ the magazine over the porch railing.

   breath, threw

5. When Zack woke up screaming from his nightmare, his mother came to make sure he was ~~alright~~. Then she rocked him and sang to him until he was ~~quite~~.

   all right, quiet

REVIEW EXERCISE 5

Cross out the ten word choice errors in the paragraph below. Then correct them on the lines provided.

[1]One of the best things about technology is that it offers a host of ~~knew~~ excuses for not turning in assignments on time. [2]If you have a computer and a printer, you have access to excuses that almost any professor will ~~except~~. [3]Just before the class period when the assignment is due, run breathlessly into the professor's office and say that your printer cartridge ~~quite~~ printing just as you were trying to print your paper. [4]Or tell the instructor that your computer's hard drive crashed and made you ~~loose~~ all your files. [5]Even if you do not own a computer, technology still gives you ~~alot~~ of excuses. [6]If you need another day on your paper, call the professor, say you are sick, and ask if it is ~~alright~~ for your mother (or some other person) to email in the assignment. [7]The next day, take in your paper, apologize, and say that your mother kept getting disconnected because ~~their~~ was a downed cable wire in your neighborhood. [8]Another good excuse is that you tried to make ~~a~~ extra copy of your paper, but the copier had a paper jam as your paper went through. [9]If you feel bad about lying to your professor or think that he or she won't accept your excuse, ~~their~~ is another way. [10]You can take the safe, dull route and get ~~threw~~ with your paper in time to turn it in on the due date.

1. new
2. accept
3. quit
4. lose
5. a lot (or *many excuses*)

6. all right
7. there
8. an
9. there
10. through

mywritinglab   For support in meeting this chapter's goal, log in to **www.mywritinglab.com** and select **Easily Confused Words**.

CHAPTER 25

Word Choice

> 📝 **Chapter Goal:** Identify and eliminate slang, textspeak, clichés, wordiness, and conversational constructions in your writing.

Mike is interviewing for his first post-college job. When he is ushered into the office of the interviewer, what should he say?

a. "Yo! Got any jobs, man?"
b. "Allow me at this point in time to present and introduce myself to you."
c. "Good afternoon. I'm Mike Tan."
d. "If you're looking for the cream of the crop, it's as plain as the nose on your face that I am a cut above the rest."

If you answered *c* to the question in the box above, you have shown good judgment in word choice. But when you write, word choice is not always so clear-cut. This chapter helps you to fine-tune your judgment and to recognize categories of word choice that are generally not appropriate for college writing: slang, textspeak, clichés, and wordiness.

✎ Slang and Textspeak

mywritinglab

Visit MyWriting Lab for additional practice with standard and non-standard English.

People enjoy using **slang** because it is informal, up to the minute, and fun. **Textspeak** or **"txtspk"** is the abbreviated language that people use to send text messages on cell phones or online in chat rooms. Just as a common language is a bond among those who speak it, so is slang or textspeak a bond among the members of the groups that use it. Yet the very things that make slang and textspeak appealing make these types of language unsuitable for writing to a broad audience.

Writing requires a common language and is usually more formal than conversation. In addition, no writer wants to use words that may be out of date when an audience reads them years later. Slang expressions such as *the bee's knees, hunky-dory*, and *groovy* may have sounded up-to-the-minute decades ago, but now they are relics of another time.

Textspeak is a relatively new form of abbreviated written language that is mainly used in text messages and sometimes in emails, online posts, and chat rooms. Textspeak often contains acronyms, words formed from the first letter of each word in an expression. Thus, *laughing out loud* becomes *LOL.* Single letters can stand in for words: *See* becomes *c*, and *you* becomes *u*. Sometimes, numbers are used as part of a word, and *later* becomes *l8r*, or *anyone* becomes *ne1*. Vowels are also omitted from words to shorten them; the word *vowels*, for instance, might be shortened to *vwls*.

Group Exercise 1 Discussing Slang Terms and Textpeak ✎

Form small groups. Try to include both sexes and as many different ages and ethnic groups as possible. (The more diverse the group, the more likely that it will generate a variety of slang and texting terms.) Each group member should write down five slang terms and five textspeak terms and then share the list with other group members. Are there any expressions that not all group members are familiar with? What conclusions can the group draw about the use of slang and textspeak? Choose one spokesperson to report the group's findings, along with a few of the most interesting terms, to the class.

PRACTICE 1   AVOIDING SLANG EXPRESSIONS

Replace the italicized slang expressions in each sentence with more formal word choices. Answers will vary.

1.   Vince was wearing a *cool* new pair of *shades* with round lenses.

     stylish

     sunglasses

2. Shara *flipped out* when she *eyeballed* the scratch on her car door.

   became upset

   saw

3. Dolores went on a huge shopping spree and *maxed out* her *plastic*.

   reached the limit on

   credit cards

4. Instead of studying, Frank decided to *chill* in front of the *tube* for a few hours.

   relax

   television

5. Lucinda's brother is going with her to buy her car because he thinks she is so *clueless* that she would probably be *ripped off*.

   naive

   cheated

PRACTICE 2   AVOIDING TEXTSPEAK

Underline the two textspeak expressions in each sentence; then substitute more formal word choices.

1. Nayana was <u>ROFL</u> at something her friend whispered to her, so she missed the <u>411</u> about tomorrow's quiz.

   rolling on the floor laughing; information

2. <u>IDK</u> when I'll have <u>enuf</u> time to start my term paper.

   I don't know; enough

3. If <u>u</u> decide to go to that movie, <u>b</u> sure to call me.

   you; be

4. Our professor told us <u>2</u> review our notes every day so we would not have to study so much <u>b4</u> the test.

   to; before

5. Does <u>ne1</u> want to hear a <u>gr8</u> joke?

   anyone; great

Clirés Clichés

While slang is fresh and new, **clichés** are expressions used so often for so long that they have become worn out. The cliché *burn the midnight oil,* for instance, is a relic of a time when working until midnight meant lighting an oil lamp to illuminate the workspace during the hours of darkness. Because they are easy to remember and widely used, clichés are often the first expressions that come to mind. It takes a deliberate effort to recognize them and eliminate them from your writing.

Look at the following list of clichés. Can you think of others?

apple of my eye	dead as a doornail	live and let live
as good as gold	easy as pie	once in a blue moon
as old as Methuselah	flat as a pancake	pretty as a picture
at the drop of a hat	in the lap of luxury	raining cats and dogs
cream of the crop	light as a feather	sick as a dog

PRACTICE 3   AVOIDING CLICHÉS

Rewrite each sentence to eliminate the two italicized clichés. Answers will vary.

1. The job bagging groceries was as *easy as pie,* but Tom was fired because he was *slow as molasses.*

   easy
   _____

   a slow worker
   _____

2. During the interview, Sally looked *as cool as a cucumber,* but inside she was *shaking like a leaf.*

   calm
   _____

   nervous
   _____

3. Keisha says her job keeps her *as busy as a bee* and that she gets a vacation *once in a blue moon.*

   busy
   _____

   very rarely
   _____

4. Because Kevin has *worn so many hats* at Acme Tool and Die, he knows the company *like the back of his hand.*

   worked at so many different jobs
   _____

   well
   _____

5. My next-door neighbor is *as old as Methuselah,* but he seems to be *fit as a fiddle.*
in his eighties

physically fit

 # Wordiness

Wordiness sometimes happens when writers do not take the time to make their writing concise. The shortest and simplest way of expressing an idea is usually the best way.

The words and phrases below contribute to wordiness and can usually be omitted.

basically	*basically* performs no function in most sentences
definitely	is *definitely* a space-waster
in my opinion	usually weakens a sentence *in my opinion*
the fact is that	*The fact is that* facts, like opinions, can usually be stated without preamble.
totally	usually *totally* unnecessary
very	can *very* often be omitted

The following phrases are wordy and can usually be shortened and strengthened.

Wordy	Concise
at the present time	now, today
due to the fact that	because, since
for the reason that	because, since
in point of fact	in fact
in today's society	today
long in length	long

Examples of Wordiness

✗ I dreaded taking the course, but *in point of fact*, I needed a course in the *basic fundamentals* of English.

✔ I dreaded taking the course, but in fact, I needed a course in the fundamentals of English.

✗ *Due to the fact that at this point in time* I don't have a car, I ride the bus every day.

✔ Because I don't have a car now, I ride the bus every day.

PRACTICE 4   ELIMINATING WORDINESS

Each sentence contains two italicized wordy expressions. Rewrite the sentences to eliminate wordiness. Answers will vary.

1. I stayed awake until *1:00 A.M. in the morning* to watch the *lunar eclipse of the moon.*

   1:00 A.M
   _____

   lunar eclipse
   _____

2. Because of the high crime rate *in today's society,* many people are *basically* distrustful of other people.

   today
   _____

   (omit)
   _____

3. *Annually each year,* an employees' picnic is held to reward the workers for the hard work they do *each and every day.*

   Each year
   _____

   every day or each day (omit "each and" or "and every")
   _____

4. *In my opinion, I think* that *financial decision making about money matters* should be taught in high school.

   (omit)
   _____

   personal finance
   _____

5. James was *totally and completely dedicated* to *the best on-the-job performance he could deliver to his employer in the workplace.*

   dedicated
   _____

   doing his job well
   _____

Group Exercise 2 Eliminating Slang, Clichés and Wordiness

In small groups, "translate" the sentences written here in slang, clichés, or wordy language. Then rewrite the same thought in clear, concise language. Answers will vary.

Sentence Group 1

Slang: Leo had the pedal to the metal, but he thought his radar detector would keep him from being busted by the fuzz.

Wordiness: Leo was definitely exceeding the speed limit posted upon the signs beside the road, but he thought having a radar detector in his car to alert him to police presence would prevent the authorities from detecting or stopping him.

Your revision: Leo was speeding, but he thought his radar detector would keep him from getting caught.

Sentence Group 2

Slang: Catherine flipped out when she saw her main squeeze hanging out with another woman.

Cliché: When Catherine saw the apple of her eye with another woman, she hit the ceiling.

Your revision: When Catherine saw her boyfriend with another woman, she screamed that she never wanted to see him again.

Sentence Group 3

Cliché: Joanna eats like a horse, but she is still as thin as a rail.

Wordiness: Joanna eats a great deal of food of all kinds and types, but she somehow manages to maintain a thin slenderness of body that is surprising.

Your revision: Joanna eats anything she wants and still remains slender.

Sentence Group 4

Slang: Jake really dug his new ride to the max.

Wordiness: Jake received a great deal of enjoyment and pleasure from his Nissan automobile, which was red in color.

Your revision: Jake loved his new red Nissan.

Sentence Group 5

Slang: I pulled out my plastic, but the clerk said I had to lay some Benjamins on him.

Wordiness: I retrieved my Visa credit card from its place within my wallet, but the store clerk in the convenience store said that the store accepted only cash money, not a Visa credit card, or for that matter, a MasterCard or American Express credit card.

Your revision: I pulled out my credit card, but the clerk said I had to pay cash.

Review Exercises

Complete the Review Exercises to find out how well you have learned the skills addressed in this chapter. As you work through the exercises, go back through the chapter to review any of the rules you do not understand completely.

In the blank to the left of each sentence, indicate whether the italicized expression is slang (*S*), a cliché (*C*), or a wordy expression (*W*). Then replace the italicized words to correct the problem in word choice.

___S___ **1.** Ben *freaked out* when he saw the parking ticket on his windshield.
became angry

___C___ **2.** It was *raining cats and dogs* by the time Tasha got out of her political science class.
raining hard

___W___ **3.** *In point of fact,* trees prevent soil erosion, produce oxygen, and provide cooling shade.
(omit)

___W___ **4.** Because he had *prearranged plans that he had made at an earlier time to attend a conference,* the professor canceled Friday's class.
planned to attend a conference

___C___ **5.** Samantha was *born with a silver spoon in her mouth* and has lived *in the lap of luxury* all her life.
born to wealthy parents, comfortably

___S___ **6.** Professor Adams was *ticked off* because the class did so poorly on the last test.
angry

____W____ **7.** Because it was raining, the game was *postponed until a later time.*

postponed
_____

____S____ **8.** At the restaurant, we *pigged out* on hamburgers and fries, so we were too full to order dessert.

gorged
_____

____C____ **9.** Without her friends from high school, Amy felt *like a fish out of water* during her first few months at college.

out of place
_____

____W____ **10.** The speaker *concluded his speech with a wrap-up that summarized* his major points.

ended by reviewing
_____

REVIEW EXERCISE 2

Underline and correct the two word choice problems in each sentence.

1. Because Hal has a <u>heart of gold</u>, he agreed to take care of his sister's two <u>rug rats</u> while she was out of town.

good heart
_____

children
_____

2. Rollo thought he would <u>cop some z's</u> during class, but the professor became angry and <u>threw him out on his ear.</u>

nap
_____

threw him out
_____

3. When the strange noise <u>persisted in continuing</u>, Alissa put on her bedroom slippers, grabbed a flashlight, and went outdoors <u>to examine the outside exterior of the house.</u>

persisted
_____

to investigate
_____

4. Since Anna has <u>wheels</u>, I asked her if we could ride with her, and she said <u>she was cool with that.</u>

a car
_____

it was fine with her
_____

5. Laurie is basically tired of Sam, but she is definitely interested in Paul.
    (omit both)

    _____

    _____

REVIEW EXERCISE 3

Some slang expressions have alternative meanings that are not slang. For each sentence pair, choose the expression from the word list that best fits both sentences. Then write the slang meaning and the standard meaning of the expression in the blanks provided. Answers will vary.

Word list: cool, bust, bug, shaft, gross

1. Sentence pair 1

    a. Jason's mother bought a gelatin mold in the shape of a human brain. She thought it was ___gross___, but she knew Jason would love it.

    b. The store manager was sorry he had ordered a ___gross___ of glow-in-the-dark yo-yos. In six months, he sold just 10 and had 134 left in stock.

    Slang meaning: unappetizing

    Standard meaning: 144

2. Sentence pair 2

    a. "Don't ___bug___ me, squirt," Al said to his little brother.

    b. Ever since a ___bug___ crawled into his shoe one night, Bobby shakes out both shoes before putting them on in the morning.

    Slang meaning: bother

    Standard meaning: insect

3. Sentence pair 3

    a. The drug dealer peddled his wares from a bench in the park, seemingly unafraid of a police ___bust___.

    b. On the piano, Mr. Schoenmeyer had a small ___bust___ of Mozart.

    Slang meaning: arrest

    Standard meaning: statue of head and shoulders

4. Sentence pair 4

    a. After his divorce, Raymond's favorite song was "She Got the Gold Mine,
       I Got the ___Shaft___."

    b. Through a high window, a single ___shaft___ of sunlight fell into the
       cheerless room.

    Slang meaning: unfair treatment

    Standard meaning: narrow bar

5. Sentence pair 5

    a. The candy, called Boogers, came in a plastic nose. "___Cool___!" said the
       delighted twins.

    b. When the rest of us are comfortable, Pat always shivers and says it is too
       ___cool___.

    Slang meaning: great

    Standard meaning: chilly

REVIEW EXERCISE 4

Underline and correct the two word choice problems in each sentence.

1. The Chinese tea was <u>pale green in color</u> and deliciously <u>fruity in taste</u>.

    green

    fruity

2. Arthur was <u>as mad as a wet hen</u> because the car's battery was <u>as dead as a
   doornail</u>.

    mad

    dead

3. The <u>dude</u> in the <u>gross-looking</u> work boots is my cousin Malcolm.

    guy

    dirty

4. <u>Due to the fact that</u> she had not found a job, Luanne was <u>basically</u> broke.

    Because

    (omit)

5. Reginald <u>was hip to the fact</u> that the exam would be <u>a bummer.</u>
knew
_____

difficult
_____

REVIEW EXERCISE 5

Rewrite the letter below, correcting the errors in word choice in the salutation, body, and close of the letter. Answers will vary.

[1]Yo, Professor Smith,

[2]What a major bummer it was to miss the midterm exam in your class yesterday. [3]I know that your syllabus definitely states that you basically do not give make-up exams. [4]However, I am absolutely certain beyond a shadow of a doubt that in my case you will see fit to make an exception to this policy. [5]You see, I became as sick as a dog after a late-night study session with some friends over at the Keg and Barrel.

[6]I know that we have had our differences, but aside from the unfortunate incident of the fake vomit, you have to admit that I have been as good as gold in your class. [7]I swear I am as innocent as a lamb in the matter of the stolen exam key.

[8]Let me say prior to concluding this letter that in my opinion, I think you are one of the best and most fair-minded professors on this campus. [9]I hope that you will forgive and forget, let bygones be bygones, and allow me to make up the exam.

[10]Later, Teach!

Desmond Kruger

[1]Dear Professor Smith,[2]What a disappointment it was to miss the midterm exam in your class yesterday.[3]I know that your syllabus states that you do not give make-up exams.[4]However, I am certain that in my case you will make an exception to this policy.[5]You see, I became ill after a late-night study session with some friends over at the Keg and Barrel.[6]I know that we have had our differences, but aside from the unfortunate incident of the fake vomit, I have

been a good student in your class.[7]I am innocent in the matter of the stolen exam key.[8]I think you are one of the best and most fair-minded professors on this campus.[9]I hope that you will allow me to make up the exam.[10]Sincerely, Desmond Kruger

mywritinglab   For support in meeting this chapter's goal, log in to **www.mywritinglab.com** and select **Standard and Nonstandard English**.

CHAPTER 26

Commas

> ✍ **Chapter Goal:** Use commas correctly.

Unreliable Rules

"When in doubt, leave it out."

"Put a comma where there is a natural pause."

"Sprinkle them sparingly, like salt."

There are so many comma rules that, in desperation, people often resort to makeshift rules like the ones above. Unfortunately, these blanket statements don't always work. When it comes to commas, rules—and exceptions—abound. The rules presented in this chapter will help you cope with the complexities of comma usage.

Commas to Set Off Introductory Words, Phrases, and Clauses

mywritinglab

Visit MyWriting
Lab for additional
practice using
commas.

Use commas after an introductory word, phrase, or clause.

Examples of Commas to Set Off Introductory Words, Phrases, and Clauses

✔ Later, we walked on the beach and watched the sun set.

✔ In the long run, getting an education pays.

✔ When Ethan saw the giraffe, he laughed and clapped his hands.

✔ In the spaces between the keys on her keyboard, Kim could see dust.

PRACTICE 1   USING COMMAS AFTER INTRODUCTORY ELEMENTS

Insert commas after introductory words, phrases, and clauses.

1. Painfully the man rose to his feet and walked toward us.
   Painfully, the
   _____

2. To Arlene's irritation a little sports car slipped into the parking place she had been waiting for.
   To Arlene's irritation, a
   _____

3. By the time the pizza arrived it was cold.
   By the time the pizza arrived, it
   _____

4. Without apology or explanation Eric strolled in two hours late.
   Without apology or explanation, Eric
   _____

5. After Mary's coupons were deducted her grocery bill came to $34.95.
   After Mary's coupons were deducted, her
   _____

Commas to Join Items in a Series

When a series of three or more words, phrases, or clauses is connected with *and*, *or*, or *nor*, place a comma after each item except the last one. The final comma will come before *and*, *or*, or *nor*.

Real-World Writing

In journalism, it is becoming customary to omit the comma before *and, or,* or *nor.* Academic usage is more traditional and favors keeping the final comma.

Examples of Commas to Join Items in a Series

✔ Ferrell said his car needed a wash, a wax job, and an oil change.

✔ Apples, oranges, and bananas filled a wooden bowl on the kitchen counter.

✔ Nell said she would consider herself successful if she graduated from college, opened her own business, and had a happy family.

✔ Ellie said she knew Brett was smart because he was a good Scrabble player, he read a lot, and he had a good sense of humor.

If only two items appear in the series, no comma is used.

✔ The old farmer said he had cut his livestock to just a few cows and three dozen pigs.

✔ The toll collector said that there was a traffic tie-up in the tunnel and a wreck near the downtown connector.

✔ On his new diet, Uncle Frank said he was hungry just twice a day: when he was awake and when he was asleep.

PRACTICE 2   USING COMMAS TO JOIN ITEMS IN A SERIES

Insert commas to join words, phrases, and clauses in a series of three or more. One sentence has only two items in the series and does not require a comma.

1. Jason's summer job with a lawn maintenance firm helped him learn that he hates grass dirt and heat.

   grass, dirt, and heat

   _____

2. Mom makes her special orange cookies only at Christmas because of the cost and the labor involved in making the cookies.

   correct

   _____

3. The receptionist said that Dr. Brantley was booked solid during June July and August.

   June, July, and August

4. The white-hatted chef pulled the soufflé from the oven set it on the counter and watched as it slowly deflated.

   pulled the soufflé from the oven, set it on the counter, and watched as it slowly

   deflated

5. At the opening of the ice-skating rink, skaters leaped twirled wobbled or fell, according to their level of expertise.

   leaped, twirled, wobbled, or fell

🖌 Commas to Join Independent Clauses

Use a comma with a FANBOYS conjunction (*for, and, nor, but, or, yet, so*) to join independent clauses. Recall that an independent clause has a subject and a verb and can stand alone as a complete sentence.

Examples of Commas to Join Independent Clauses

✔ Evelyn needed to go to the post office, so she left the house twenty minutes early.

✔ Thad felt an uncomfortable twinge in his right ankle, but he kept running anyway.

✔ The temperature is expected to drop, and snow is predicted.

Do not use a comma if the FANBOYS connects a verb to a clause rather than a clause to a clause. That is, do not use a comma unless there is a complete sentence (subject *and* verb) on both sides of the FANBOYS.

subject verb   verb
Carrie put her tea in the microwave and made a tomato sandwich.

✔ The dog stood by the door and waited for Vince to come out.

✔ Fernando can take a new job at lower pay or stay with the old job he hates.

PRACTICE 3   **USING COMMAS WITH *FANBOYS* CONJUNCTIONS TO JOIN INDEPENDENT CLAUSES**

Place commas before FANBOYS conjunctions that join two independent clauses. One sentence contains a compound verb, not two clauses, and does not need a comma.

1. Grass and weeds grew tall around the unpainted house and shutters hung haphazardly from its windows.

   house, and shutters

2. The sun was hot but a cool breeze occasionally brought relief.

   hot, but a

3. A police car circled the block several times but did not stop.

   correct

4. Laurie woke up early so she decided to work on her term paper.

   early, so

5. Ralph thought he could fix the sink easily but it took him most of the afternoon.

   easily, but it

Commas around Interrupters

An **interrupter** is a word, phrase, or clause inserted into a sentence to give more information about some element within the sentence. An interrupter is never essential to the structure of the sentence. If you took the interrupter out, the sentence would still make perfect sense.

Examples of Commas around Interrupters

✔ The road, freshly paved, was no longer pitted with dangerous potholes.
✔ The bag, crumpled and stuffed under a bench, held the remains of someone's lunch.

PRACTICE 4   **USING COMMAS AROUND INTERRUPTERS**

Insert commas around interrupters in the following sentences.

1. The song one of Bryan's favorites was first recorded over thirty years ago.

   song, one of Bryan's favorites,

2. Mr. Cartwright the building's custodian retired because of poor health.

   Cartwright, the building's custodian,

3. The child sulking unhappily picked up his toys.

   child, sulking unhappily,

4. The container of cottage cheese still sealed was two months past its expiration date.

   cottage cheese, still sealed,

5. The highway long and lonely stretched through the trees and over the hill.

   The highway, long and lonely,

Commas with Direct Quotations

A **direct quotation** is an exact repetition of the words that someone speaks or thinks. When a comma is used with a direct quotation, the comma is always placed in front of the quotation mark.

1. When a direct quotation is followed by a **tag** (such as *he said*), a comma goes after the quoted words and *in front of* the closing quotation mark:

   "I would like to go on a cruise ship someday," said Maria.

2. When a tag leads into a direct quotation, a comma goes after the tag and *in front of* the opening quotation mark:

   Spencer asked, "Where is the best place to buy a used car?"

3. When a sentence is written as a split quotation, commas are placed *in front of* the closing quotation mark of the first part and *in front of* the opening quotation mark of the second part:

   "If our dog had not awakened us," the woman told the reporter, "we might have died in the fire."

PRACTICE 5   USING COMMAS WITH DIRECT QUOTATIONS

Insert commas to set off direct quotations in the following sentences.

1. Tiffany asked "Which bus will take me to the library?"

   Tiffany asked, "Which

2. "Since I started walking every day" said Dee "I feel like a different person."
   day," said Dee, "I feel
   _____

3. "Can someone help me? I have locked my keys in the car" said Nando.
   car," said
   _____

4. "If I could choose the color of grass" said the child "I would pick purple."
   grass," said the child, "I
   _____

5. Oscar Wilde said "I can resist everything except temptation."
   said, "I can
   _____

Commas in Names and Dates

When a professional title follows a name, it is set off with commas.

✔ The clerk's name tag read, "Betty, Associate."
✔ Samuel Spencer, M.D., is the Holtons' family doctor.

When you write the month, day, and year, a comma goes between the day and year.

✔ The Declaration of Independence was signed on July 4, 1776.

When you write just the month and year, no comma is used.

✔ The Declaration of Independence was signed in July 1776.

PRACTICE 6   USING COMMAS IN NAMES AND DATES

Insert commas as needed in the following sentences. One sentence needs no comma.

1. The letter was dated September 1 2011.
   September 1, 2011
   _____

2. Stephanie Bascomb D.V.M. did the surgery on Sparky's paw.
   Bascomb, D.V.M., did
   _____

3. Kwame was born in May 1990.
   correct
   _____

4. Burton Fellstone C.P.A. has opened an office on Grant Street.

Fellstone, C.P.A., has _____

5. The sign on the door read Anne Grossman M.D.

Grossman, M.D. _____

Review Exercises

Complete the Review Exercises to find out how well you have learned the skills addressed in this chapter. As you work through the exercises, go back through the chapter to review any of the rules you do not understand completely.

Insert commas where they are needed in each sentence.

1. With camera in hand Dana began her nature walk.

With camera in hand, Dana _____

2. Rob will never forget the day his wife agreed to marry him: June 28 2009.

June 28, 2009 _____

3. The profile had led Lauren to expect a tall man so she was surprised when Roy approached her.

man, so she _____

4. Streamers confetti and banners decorated the living room for the party.

Streamers, confetti, and banners _____

5. When the pizza delivery car pulled into the driveway the children stampeded to the door.

driveway, the children _____

Review Exercise 2

Insert commas where they are needed in each sentence.

1. Before leaving his car in the stadium's huge parking lot Ron tied a bright orange flag to the antenna.

lot, Ron _____

2. Elmont Morrison M.D. sleepily fumbled for the ringing telephone.

    Elmont Morrison, M.D., sleepily

3. Muttering angrily under her breath Juanita retrieved her soggy newspaper from the puddle where it lay.

    her breath, Juanita

4. The well-dressed woman unaware of the store detective's presence slipped the silver necklace into her handbag.

    woman, unaware of the store detective's presence, slipped

5. In the basement dusty jars of Grandma's vegetables and preserves lined the shelves.

    basement, dusty

6. After the hurricane residents slowly emerged to assess the damage to houses and cars.

    hurricane, residents

7. The bookstore's comfortable chairs were filled with people reading chatting or even sleeping.

    reading, chatting, or even sleeping.

8. The directory on the wall beside the elevator said that Carl Smith D.D.S. was in Suite 205.

    Smith, D.D.S., was

9. Andrew saw billboards advertising motels restaurants and nightclubs.

    motels, restaurants, and nightclubs

10. With a powerful leap the cat lunged after the bird.

    leap, the cat

REVIEW EXERCISE 3

Insert commas where they are needed in each sentence. Each numbered item contains two problems that can be fixed with the addition of a comma or commas.

1. When she tried to unlock the door with her arms full of groceries Leslie dropped her keys into the bushes beside the front steps. She set the groceries on a chair took a flashlight from her purse and hunted through the bushes for her keys.

    groceries, Leslie

    set the groceries on a chair, took a flashlight from her purse, and

2. Even though he was tired Joshua tried to stay up to watch the movie. However he soon fell asleep on the couch.

   tired, Joshua
   _____

   However, he
   _____

3. A stuffy head a runny nose and a sore throat told Ashley that she was coming down with a cold. She decided to stop at the drugstore on the way home for tissues cough drops and decongestant tablets.

   A stuffy head, runny nose, and
   _____

   tissues, cough drops, and
   _____

4. Pretending to read a newspaper the detective sat outside the apartment complex for an hour and watched the door. "I never thought this would be such a boring line of work" he thought.

   newspaper, the
   _____

   work," he
   _____

5. The date on the letter was April 13 1932. "This letter was written by my great-grandfather" said Michael.

   April 13, 1932
   _____

   great-grandfather," said
   _____

REVIEW EXERCISE 4

Insert commas where they are needed in each sentence.

1. The T-shirt was old ragged and stained with paint. "It's still too good to throw away" Mia said.

   old, ragged, and
   _____

   away," Mia
   _____

2. Containers on a table beside the hot dog stand held ketchup relish and even chopped onions. However there was not a drop of mustard.

   ketchup, relish, and
   _____

   However, there
   _____

3. Jeff made just one New Year's resolution but it was one he wanted to keep. He said "I want to pay off all my credit card debt."

   resolution, but
   _____

   said, "I
   _____

4. Tacked to the bulletin board were several old receipts two greeting cards and a yellowed newspaper article. On the desk a calendar was still turned to July 2003.

   several old receipts, two greeting cards, and

   desk, a

5. Arthur wearing only his bathrobe and his underwear slipped out of the house to get his newspaper. Halfway down the driveway he realized he had accidentally locked himself out.

   Arthur, wearing only his bathrobe and his underwear, slipped

   driveway, he

REVIEW EXERCISE 5

Insert commas where they are needed in the following paragraph. Each sentence contains one comma problem.

[1]Stephanie who used to share my apartment with me likes to hoard things. [2]When she was living with me we never had an empty closet or cabinet. [3]In the kitchen cabinet Stephanie would store all the items she had bought on sale. [4]The cabinet under the counter was jammed with bricks of coffee five-pound bags of sugar and rolls of paper towels that had been too good a bargain to resist. [5]Under the bathroom sink Stephanie stored the many boxes of toothpaste and bars of soap she had purchased at bargain prices. [6]"You'll be old enough to wear dentures before you use all that toothpaste" I told her once. [7]Stephanie however paid no attention to my teasing. [8]She said "It makes me feel secure to have enough of everything." [9]When Stephanie moved to another city she packed up all her carefully hoarded items to take with her. [10]I was sorry to see her go but I'm glad to have a little more room to store things now.

1. Stephanie, who used to share my apartment with me,

2. me, we

3. cabinet, Stephanie

4. bricks of coffee, five-pound bags of sugar, and

5. sink, Stephanie

6. toothpaste," I _____

7. Stephanie, however, _____

8. said, "It _____

9. city, she _____

10. go, but _____

mywritinglab   For support in meeting this chapter's goal, log in to
www.mywritinglab.com and select **Commas**.

CHAPTER 27

Other Punctuation

> 🐾 **Chapter Goal:** Use periods, exclamation points, quotation marks, semicolons, colons, dashes, and parentheses correctly.

Why we need semicolons, colons, and parentheses

Punctuation marks other than the comma are useful not only for making emoticons but also for punctuating sentences to convey grammatical relationships and shades of meaning. Some of these punctuation marks, such as the period and the question mark, are familiar. Others, such as the dash and the colon, seem more exotic and are less often used. This chapter reinforces the familiar marks of punctuation and introduces the less familiar.

End Punctuation: Period, Question Mark, and Exclamation Point

mywritinglab
Visit MyWriting
Lab for additional
practice using final
punctuation.

The period, the question mark, and the exclamation point are all forms of **end punctuation;** that is, they signal the end of a sentence.

The Period

The **period** is used to mark the end of a sentence that makes a statement.

Examples of Periods at the End of Sentences

✔ The car was less than two years old, but it already had nearly 35,000 miles on the odometer.

✔ The peacock unfurled its tail in a colorful display of blue and green.

Periods are also used to signal an appropriate abbreviation. Except for abbreviations in courtesy titles, such as *Mr., Ms., Dr.,* or *Rev.* used before proper names, spell out words in your paragraphs and essays. Most abbreviations should be reserved for only the most informal usage, such as your class notes or email to a friend.

Examples of Periods in Abbreviations

✘ Marg. is going to Fla. with her bro. in Apr. of next yr.

✔ Margaret is going to Florida with her brother in April of next year.

✔ Ms. O'Neill refuses to take Dr. Moore's advice.

The Question Mark

A **question mark** is used at the end of a direct question.

Examples of Question Marks at the End of Direct Questions

✔ Who borrowed my stapler?

✔ Does the tan Hyundai belong to you?

No question mark is used with an indirect question.

✔ "I wonder if animals dream, too," said Jamie.

✔ Judge Gronsky asked if anyone objected to postponement of the hearing.

The Exclamation Point

Exclamation points are used to show extreme excitement or surprise and are seldom needed in college writing. Unless you are quoting someone who has just discovered that the building is on fire, there will be few opportunities to use an exclamation point. Interjections such as "Ouch!" or "Yikes!" are followed by exclamation points but are seldom needed for college writing. Use exclamation points when you quote someone who is shouting or speaking excitedly. Otherwise, let your words, not your punctuation, carry the excitement of your essay.

Examples of Exclamation Points

✗ Samantha noticed smoke streaming from under the hood of her car! She realized her engine was on fire!

✔ Samantha noticed smoke streaming from under the hood of her car. She realized her engine was on fire.

✗ She pulled to the side of the road! Now she could see flames coming from under the hood!

✔ She pulled to the side of the road. Now she could see flames coming from under the hood.

✔ She heard a bystander yell, "Get away from the car!"

PRACTICE 1   USING ABBREVIATIONS AND END PUNCTUATION

In each sentence, correct an inappropriate abbreviation or place a period after an appropriate abbreviation. Then place end punctuation (period, question mark, or exclamation point) where needed.

1. Janice asked, "Do you know why the door to the study <u>rm.</u> is <u>locked</u>"

    room _____

    locked?" _____

2. I asked the <u>dr.</u> if she would prescribe something for my <u>cold</u>

    doctor _____

    cold. _____

3. <u>Dr</u> Miller told me that if she prescribed medication, my cold would be gone in two weeks. Without medication, it would take fourteen <u>days</u>

    Dr. _____

    days. _____

4. Aunt Rachel wants to know if you will come to her <u>Sun.</u> morning <u>breakfast</u>

    Sunday
    _____

    breakfast.

5. "Come <u>back</u>" Jason yelled, as the dog ran off with his <u>Oct.</u> paycheck.

    back!"
    _____

    October

 # The Semicolon

Semicolon to Join Independent Clauses

mywritinglab

Visit MyWriting Lab for additional practice using semicolons, colons, dashes, and parentheses.

A **semicolon** may be used with a transitional expression between independent clauses or alone between independent clauses that are closely related. (For a more detailed discussion of this use of the semicolon, see Chapter 15, "Coordination and Subordination," and Chapter 16, "Run-on Sentences.")

Examples of Semicolons Joining Independent Clauses

✔ The copier was out of order this morning; it seems to be working now, though.

✔ The smart phone was convenient and fun to use; however, the monthly fees were high.

Semicolon to Join Items in a List

Ordinarily, items in a list are joined by commas. However, if the items themselves contain commas, avoid confusion by using semicolons to join the items.

Examples of Semicolons Joining Items in a List

✔ Arlene has relatives in Richmond, Virginia; Atlanta, Georgia; and Houston, Texas.

✔ The new book on heart-healthy eating was written by James Hobson; Carletta Berry, Ph.D.; and Lazarus Salter, M.D.

PRACTICE 2   USING SEMICOLONS

Use semicolons in the following sentences to join independent clauses or items in a series.

1. The coffee was too strong Karla felt jittery throughout the morning.
   strong; Karla
   _____

2. Andrew says he rejects his parents' materialistic values he would rather serve others than enrich his bank account.
   values; he
   _____

3. Michael's three children were born on April 1, 1995 May 3, 1997 and July 29, 1999.
   April 1, 1995; May 3, 1997; and July 29, 1999
   _____

4. Our city's tap water is of high quality in fact, it tastes better than most bottled water.
   quality; in fact
   _____

5. At its first meeting, the club elected the following officers: Amy Gray, President Juanita Gonzales, President-elect Perry Malden, Treasurer and Kim Park, Recorder.
   Amy Gray, President; Juanita Gonzales, President-elect; Perry Malden, Treasurer; and
   Kim Park, Recorder

Colons and Dashes: Formal and Informal Punctuation

The Colon

The **colon** is used to introduce a list, a restatement, or a clarification. The most important thing to remember when you use a colon is that the words that come before the colon must always be a complete sentence.

1. A colon is sometimes used to introduce a list. A complete sentence must come before the colon.

Examples of Colons Introducing Lists

✗ On his overnight trip, Jamal carried only: a toothbrush, a change of clothes, and a good book.

✔ On his overnight trip, Jamal carried only the necessities: a toothbrush, a change of clothes, and a good book.

It is also correct—and sometimes simpler—to integrate a list into a sentence without using a colon.

✔ On his overnight trip, Jamal carried only a toothbrush, a change of clothes, and a good book.

2. A colon is used to introduce a restatement or clarification of an idea. A complete sentence must come before the colon.

Examples of Colons Introducing Clarifications

✔ Ed says there are two reasons he stays broke: Visa and MasterCard.

The words *Visa and MasterCard,* preceded by a colon, restate and clarify the "two reasons" that Ed stays broke.

✔ Vera was never out of her family's reach: she carried a cell phone wherever she went.

The colon introduces a clarification of the idea "never out of her family's reach."

The Dash

While the colon is a formal mark of punctuation, the **dash** is an informal mark. The first two uses of a dash are exactly like those of the colon: (1) to introduce a list, a restatement, or a clarification; and (2) to set off material that a writer wants to emphasize.

1. A dash introduces a list or restatement. When used in this way, a dash must be preceded by a complete sentence. A dash is typed as two hyphens, with no spaces before or after.

Examples of Using Dashes to Introduce a List and to Restate or Clarify

In the first example, the dash introduces a list.

✔ On his overnight trip, Jamal carried only the necessities—a toothbrush, a change of clothes, and a good book.

In the next example, the dash is used to introduce a restatement and clarification of reasons Ed stays broke.

✔ Ed says there are two reasons he stays broke—Visa and MasterCard.

2. A dash is used to set off material that the writer wants to emphasize.

Examples of Using Dashes to Emphasize

✔ It was his easygoing personality—not his money—that made him popular.

A more formal way of punctuating the previous sentence would be to use commas to set off the interrupter: *It was his easygoing personality, not his money, that made him popular.*

✔ There was so much to do—bills to pay, errands to run, and yard work to finish—that Tom did not know where to begin.

One way of expressing the idea in the previous sentence more formally would be to use two sentences: *There was so much to do that Tom did not know where to begin. He had bills to pay, errands to run, and yard work to finish.*

Parentheses: Tools of Understatement

While dashes emphasize, **parentheses** downplay. Parentheses are used to enclose material that a reader could skip over without missing the more important ideas.

Examples of Parentheses

✔ Miss Clara, my elderly neighbor, says there is no better way to spend a Sunday afternoon than listening to Handel (her favorite composer) and drinking a cup of tea.

✔ Harlan told the salesman he loved driving the car. He liked the color (maroon) and he loved the interior (a rich, tan leather). But he hated the price.

PRACTICE 3 USING COLONS, DASHES, AND PARENTHESES

Rewrite each sentence as indicated, punctuating the italicized portion of the sentence with a colon, a dash (or dashes), or parentheses.

1. Analida says that staying sane on rainy weekends at home with her children requires just three things. It requires *plenty of patience, a good supply of games and songs, and a pair of heavy-duty earplugs.*

Directions: Rewrite as one sentence, with a colon introducing the list. Remove words as needed.

three things: plenty of patience

2. The professor said that the price of the hardback dictionary, *just eighteen dollars,* was small, considering all the words we would get for our money.

    Directions: Rewrite so that the price of the dictionary is de-emphasized. You will need to remove the commas.

    dictionary (just eighteen dollars) was

3. Allan says if his house were on fire and he could save just one possession, the choice would be easy: *his computer.*

    Directions: Rewrite so that the restatement is set off in an informal way rather than a formal way.

    easy—his computer

4. Dad's shoes (*tan loafers he has had since his college days*) are so old they are coming apart at the seams.

    Directions: Rewrite so that the parenthetical material is emphasized. Assume that the sentence can be written informally.

    shoes—tan loafers he has had since his college days—are

5. The half-gallon carton contained three flavors of ice cream: *chocolate, vanilla, and strawberry.*

    Directions: Rewrite so that the list is introduced in an informal way.

    ice cream—chocolate

Review Exercises

Complete the Review Exercises to find out how well you have learned the skills addressed in this chapter. As you work through the exercises, go back through the chapter to review any of the rules you do not understand completely.

REVIEW EXERCISE 1

Look at the punctuation printed in color in each sentence; then briefly explain the rule that justifies its use. The first one is done for you.

1. After the unexpected frost, the plants on Mrs. Kowalski's porch turned brown and died.

    A period is used to end a sentence that makes a statement.

2. Gary asked whether I had ever been to Disney World.

    A period is used to end a sentence that makes a statement.

3. The scientist revealed his formula for success: perseverance, hard work, and a little luck.

    A colon is used to introduce a list. It must be used after a complete thought.

4. The movie (which has set box-office records) contains scenes of extreme violence: two explosions, a hanging, and seventeen deaths by shooting.

    Parentheses are used around material that is to be de-emphasized.

5. The salesperson—who must have been in a bad mood that day—was surly and unhelpful.

    Dashes are used informally to set off interrupters.

6. Traffic was backed up for miles on the interstate; hundreds of cars and trucks had slowed to a crawl.

    A semicolon is used to join independent clauses.

7. "Hey! Watch out for that open manhole!" the worker called to the pedestrian.

    Exclamation points are used at the end of a sentence when someone is speaking excitedly.

8. The company had offices in Seattle, Washington; London, England; and Tokyo, Japan.

    Semicolons are used to join items in a list when those items themselves contain commas.

9. The mailbox contained only two pieces of mail—a drugstore flyer and a credit card offer.

    A dash is used informally to set off a phrase that elaborates the word or phrase immediately before it.

10. At 5:00 A.M., a garbage truck rumbled past Ed's house; Ed woke suddenly, wondering if he had remembered to take the trash to the curb.

    A semicolon is used to join independent clauses.

REVIEW EXERCISE 2

In each sentence, add a period, question mark, exclamation point, semicolon, colon, dash (or dashes), or parentheses.

1. "Could you repeat the fourteen flavors of ice cream again" Millie asked the server.

    again?" Millie

2. The Simmonses were devastated when the house their first home together burned to the ground.

    house—their first home together—burned

3. "Come out with your hands on your head" the police officer yelled.

    head!" the police

4. The headline read, "Con Artists Foiled in Aluminum Siding Scam"

    Scam."

5. William's parents told him he had two choices go to school or get a job.

    choices: go to school

REVIEW EXERCISE 3

Fill the blank(s) in each sentence with a period, question mark, exclamation point, semicolon, colon, dash (or dashes), or parentheses. On some questions, more than one answer may be possible. Be sure you can justify the answer you choose.

1. Dawn slammed on the brakes when the dog __—__ a slow-moving basset hound __—__ lumbered into the road.

    dashes to emphasize or parentheses to de-emphasize

2. Steve could not remember the accident that had totaled his car and put him in the hospital, but he was sure of one thing __:__ he was lucky to be alive.

    colon (formal) or dash (informal)

3. "Call 911 __!__ " yelled Andrea as she ran past the door.

    exclamation point

4. The lease states that any resident who has a pet __(__ either a dog or a cat __)__ must pay a nonrefundable pet deposit of two hundred dollars.

    dashes to emphasize or parentheses to de-emphasize

5. "Do you mind if I cut in line __?__ I have only two items," the woman said.

    question mark to end a direct question

6. The company's employees will be off on Thursday, November 27 _;_ Friday, November 28 _;_ Thursday, December 26 _;_ and Friday, December 27.

   semicolons to join a list that contains commas

7. After Tiana loaded a new program _—_ a virus scanner _—_ on her computer, she felt safer downloading material from the Internet.

   dashes to emphasize or parentheses to de-emphasize

8. "I won _!_ I won _!_ " the red-haired woman yelled, waving her Bingo card in the air.

   exclamation points

9. The company vice president said that three things would kill a job candidate's chances _:_ late arrival, poor language skills, and a sloppy appearance.

   colon to introduce a list or a dash to introduce a list informally

10. The woman rolled down her window and handed something _(_ probably a dollar bill _)_ to the man standing at the interstate exit.

    dashes to emphasize or parentheses to de-emphasize

REVIEW EXERCISE 4

Fill in the blanks with the correct punctuation.

[1]When he twisted his knee playing softball, Jack made his own diagnosis _—_ just a muscle pull. [2]There was a sharp pain as he slid into second _;_ when he tried to get up, he could not. [3]"We need help here _!_ " the second baseman called, and his teammates came running to help him off the field. [4]"Do you want me to take you to the emergency room _?_ " his coach asked. [5]But Jack insisted that all he needed was an ice pack and a good night's sleep _._ [6]The next morning, Jack's knee was a rainbow of colors _—_ mostly black, blue, and yellow _—_ and was swollen to the size of a grapefruit. [7]He called a friend _—_ his softball buddy Levon _—_ to drive him to the doctor's office. [8]His doctor said nothing was broken but told Jack his softball days were over _—_ at least for a while. [9]Now, Jack walks with the help of crutches _._ [10]Jack won't be sliding into second for a while, but he will be at every game to support his teammates _._

mywritinglab   For support in meeting this chapter's goal, log in to **www.mywritinglab.com** and select **Final Punctuation** and **Semicolons, Colons, Dashes, and Parentheses**.

CHAPTER 28

Apostrophes

> ✍ **Chapter Goal:** Use apostrophes correctly.

Apostrophe on a stick? It's true that when it comes to apostrophes, people are often not sure where to, well, *stick* them. In possessives, do they go before the *s*? After the *s*? This chapter will help you decide. In the meantime, be careful with that apostrophe-on-a-stick—you could put an eye out with that thing.

✍ Apostrophes in Contractions

mywritinglab

Visit MyWriting Lab for additional practice with apostrophes.

Contractions are informal or conversational shortenings of words: *doesn't* for *does not*, *won't* for *will not*, and *it's* for *it is* or *it has*. Contractions are used in informal writing, but are generally inappropriate for formal or scholarly writing. You will find them in some journalistic writing, in some textbooks, in works of fiction, and in informal essays. However, contractions are considered inappropriate in academic research papers or in legal documents.

Your instructor will specify the level of formality you should use in your essays and other writings.

To form a contraction, replace omitted letters with a single apostrophe. Close any spaces between words.

Examples of Contractions

couldn't = could not

don't = do not

hasn't = has not

isn't = is not

won't = will not (*Won't* is an irregular contraction: The *i* in *will* changes to an *o*.)

wouldn't = would not

PRACTICE 1   FORMING CONTRACTIONS

Make a contraction of each expression. Be sure to place an apostrophe where letters are omitted, not in the space between the words.

1. she is   she's
2. I am   I'm
3. would not   wouldn't
4. does not   doesn't
5. he is   he's

6. it is   it's
7. we are   we're
8. I will   I'll
9. they are   they're
10. cannot   can't

PRACTICE 2   USING CONTRACTIONS

Underline the error in each sentence. Then supply the missing apostrophe in the contraction and write the contraction in the blank provided.

she's   **1.** Mariko says <u>shes</u> well enough to play in the hockey game next week.

isn't   **2.** It <u>isnt</u> unusual for Tabitha to bring home dead birds and mice.

I've   **3.** "After <u>Ive</u> found a job," said Roberta, "I have to worry about paying back my student loan."

couldn't   **4.** Art had no money, but he <u>couldnt</u> resist visiting the electronics store in the mall.

don't   **5.** The children <u>dont</u> like couscous; they want hamburgers instead.

〰️Apostrophes to Show Possession

If you could not use apostrophes to show **possession**, you would have to rely on long, tedious constructions such as "I drove the car of my father to the house of Ray to study for the test of tomorrow," instead of "I drove my father's car to Ray's house to study for tomorrow's test."

Making Nouns Possessive

There are two rules for making nouns possessive.

Rule 1:

Add an apostrophe and *s* (*'s*) to form the possessive of singular nouns and of plurals that do not end in *s*.

Examples of Possessives of Nouns That *Do Not* End in *s*

the dish that belongs to the dog = the *dog's* dish

the pages of the magazine = the *magazine's* pages

the work of a day = a *day's* work

the flower garden belonging to Carlton = *Carlton's* flower garden

the toys that belong to the children = the *children's* toys

the office of my boss = my *boss's* office

PRACTICE 3   FORMING POSSESSIVES OF SINGULAR NOUNS

Convert the five expressions to possessives using *'s*.

1. the glow of the flashlight = the flashlight's glow
2. the blue shirt belonging to Charlie = Charlie's blue shirt
3. the office of Dr. Bell = Dr. Bell's office
4. the career of the pianist = the pianist's career
5. the schedule of next week = next week's schedule

Rule 2:

If a plural noun already ends in *s*, add an apostrophe after the *s* to make it possessive.

Examples of Possessives of Nouns That End in *s*

the lawn belonging to the Smiths = the *Smiths'* lawn

the brightness of the stars = the *stars'* brightness

PRACTICE 4   FORMING POSSESSIVES OF PLURAL NOUNS

Convert the ten expressions to possessives using an apostrophe.

1. the jobs of my sisters = <u>my sisters' jobs</u>
2. the leashes of the dogs = <u>the dogs' leashes</u>
3. the energy of the dancers = <u>the dancers' energy</u>
4. the determination of the athletes = <u>the athletes' determination</u>
5. the appearance of the cupcakes = <u>the cupcakes' appearance</u>
6. the test grades of two classes = <u>the two classes' test grades</u>
7. the keyboards of the computers = <u>the computers' keyboards</u>
8. the overseas trip of the Joneses = <u>the Joneses' overseas trip</u>
9. the barking of the dogs = <u>the dogs' barking</u>
10. the movements of the actors = <u>the actors' movements</u>

PRACTICE 5   FORMING POSSESSIVES OF SINGULAR AND PLURAL NOUNS

Convert the ten expressions to possessives by adding *'s* or by adding an apostrophe after the *s*.

1. the whir of the ceiling fan = <u>the ceiling fan's whir</u>
2. the tick of the clock = <u>the clock's tick</u>
3. the smiles of the children = <u>the children's smiles</u>
4. the sale of Sports World = <u>Sports World's sale</u>
5. the disgust of Mrs. Bliss = <u>Mrs. Bliss's disgust</u>
6. the impact of the suggestion = <u>the suggestion's impact</u>
7. the hairstyles of the women = <u>the women's hairstyles</u>
8. the strong belief of Gina Terrino = <u>Gina Terrino's strong belief</u>

9.   the glow of the streetlights = <u>the streetlights' glow</u>

10.   the Web site of the college = <u>the college's Web site</u>

Distinguishing Possessives from Simple Plurals

To use apostrophes correctly, it is important to distinguish between possessives and simple plurals ending in *s*. A plural may be followed by a verb, a prepositional phrase, or by nothing at all. Words that show possession are immediately followed by something that is possessed, as in "Mom's *homemade chicken and dumplings*" or "*the* horse's *mane.*"

Possessive (apostrophe used)	Plural (no apostrophe used)
a computer's hard drive	computers used in class
a day's work	days in a month
Mother's Day	Mothers Against Drunk Driving
a king's ransom	kings in the seventeenth century
the turtles' habitat	the mating habits of turtles
the tornadoes' fury	several tornadoes
the washer's spin cycle	the broken washers

PRACTICE 6   DISTINGUISHING POSSESSIVES FROM PLURALS

In each sentence, underline the noun that ends in *s'* or *'s*. If the noun is possessive, write *possessive* in the blank provided. If the noun is simply a plural, remove the apostrophe and write the corrected plural form in the blank. The first one is done for you.

<u>parents</u>   1.   Sometimes I think my <u>parents'</u> are hopelessly old-fashioned.

<u>possessive</u>   2.   The <u>dog's</u> expression was mournful.

<u>possessive</u>   3.   The <u>speaker's</u> voice was so soothing that Kim nearly fell asleep.

<u>schools</u>   4.   Anthony visited several <u>schools'</u> before making his decision.

<u>typewriters</u>   5.   Many years ago, most offices had <u>typewriters'</u> instead of computers.

<u>possessive</u>   6.   Amy had never liked the <u>carpet's</u> color.

<u>Smiths</u>   7.   The <u>Smith's</u> host a neighborhood party every Fourth of July.

years	8.	The youngest employee in the library is thirty <u>year's</u> old.
possessive	9.	The <u>manatee's</u> large gray body moves gracefully in the water.
benefits	10.	The <u>benefit's</u> of a good breakfast include increased alertness and improved mental function during the morning hours.

Possessive Forms of Pronouns

Personal pronouns (*I, we, you, he, she, it,* and *they*) have their own possessive forms that never require an apostrophe. These forms include *my, mine, our, ours, your, yours, his, her, hers, its, their,* and *theirs.*

The pronoun that is the focus of the most confusion is *its.* Since the possessive form of a pronoun never takes an apostrophe, *its* is the possessive form, meaning *belonging to it. It's,* the form with the apostrophe, always means *it is* or *it has.*

Examples of *Its* and *It's* Used Correctly

The lawnmower seems to have lost *its* pep. (belonging to it)

It's too hot to mow, anyway. (it is)

That old paring knife has outlived *its* usefulness. (belonging to it)

It's time to buy a replacement. (it is)

PRACTICE 7   CORRECTING APOSTROPHE ERRORS WITH *ITS* AND *IT'S*

Underline and correct the apostrophe errors in the following sentences. Write *Correct* in the blanks beneath the two sentences that have no errors.

1. "<u>Its</u> essential that you come to class every day," Professor Vanta told the class.
   It's

2. The house was old, and <u>its</u> owner had not painted or repaired it for many years.
   Correct

3. Ted is committed to getting in shape; <u>it's</u> his first priority.
   Correct

4. The salmon swiftly made <u>it's</u> way upstream.
   its

5. Because Lindsay has not had time to finish her report, <u>its</u> sitting unfinished on her desk.

it's

Proofreading for Apostrophe Errors

Apostrophes Incorrectly Omitted from Possessives

To find apostrophes incorrectly omitted from possessives, check each noun ending in *s* to see if it is followed by something it possesses.

✘ The *cars brakes* made a squealing sound whenever Vashti came to a stop.

Cars is followed by the word *brakes*. Do *brakes* belong to *cars?* Yes. But does the apostrophe go before or after the *s?* Look for clues to whether the original word (before it was made possessive) was intended to be singular or plural. The main clue in this sentence lies in the words *whenever Vashti came to a stop.* There is one driver, therefore also one car.

Brakes is followed by *made,* a verb, so it is plural, not *possessive.*

✔ The car's brakes made a squealing sound whenever Vashti came to a stop.

✘ The *employees paychecks* were small, but their work was strenuous.

Does anything belong to *employees?* Yes, *paychecks* belong to *employees,* but does the apostrophe go before or after the *s?* Since there is more than one paycheck, and since the pronoun *their* is used to refer to *employees,* the word *employees* is clearly plural. Therefore, the apostrophe goes after the *s.*

Does anything belong to *paychecks?* No, a verb follows the word, so *paychecks* is simply a plural.

✔ The employees' paychecks were small, but their work was strenuous.

PRACTICE 8 CORRECTING APOSTROPHE ERRORS

Underline and correct the missing-apostrophe errors in the following sentences.

1. The <u>driveways</u> concrete surface had cracked in several places.

driveway's

2. The <u>speakers</u> voice could not be heard clearly in the back of the auditorium.
   speaker's
   _____

3. The <u>books</u> ending was disappointing to many of its readers.
   book's
   _____

4. Sam and Elaine said they spent two <u>weeks</u> salary in one weekend.
   weeks'
   _____

5. The doctor said <u>Elizabeths</u> shoulder should begin to feel better in about two weeks.
   Elizabeth's
   _____

Apostrophes Placed Incorrectly in Possessives

An incorrectly placed apostrophe is usually a confusion of singular and plural. As you proofread, target words ending in 's or s' and look for clues that tell you whether the word is singular or plural.

✘   For the landowner, the *tree's* beauty outweighed their value as lumber.

The pronoun *their* suggests more than one tree.

✔   For the landowner, the *trees'* beauty outweighed their value as lumber.

✘   The *buildings'* roof leaked and was in need of repair.

Only one roof is mentioned, so there is just one building.

✔   The *building's* roof leaked and was in need of repair.

PRACTICE 9   CORRECTING APOSTROPHE ERRORS

Underline and correct the apostrophe errors in the following sentences.

1. The <u>airplanes'</u> wings glinted in the sunlight as it flew overhead.
   airplane's
   _____

2. The <u>twin's</u> grade point averages are nearly identical.
   twins'
   _____

3. Andre swept a <u>days'</u> accumulation of litter and cigarette butts from the sidewalk in front of the restaurant.
   day's
   _____

4. At her <u>husbands'</u> urging, Valerie decided to enroll in college.
   husband's
   _____

5. As the tennis <u>player's</u> skills improved, they enjoyed the game more.
   players'
   _____

Review Exercises

Complete the Review Exercises to find out how well you have learned the skills addressed in this chapter. As you work through the exercises, go back through the chapter to review any of the rules you do not understand completely.

REVIEW EXERCISE 1

Convert the five expressions in the exercise to possessives using 's or an apostrophe.

1. the beam of the searchlight = the searchlight's beam
2. the covers of the books = the books' covers
3. the weed trimmer belonging to Jacob = Jacob's weed trimmer
4. a rest of three days = three days' rest
5. the voice of Ms. Bradshaw = Ms. Bradshaw's voice

REVIEW EXERCISE 2

Each sentence has an omitted apostrophe in a contraction or a possessive form. Underline the error; then, in the blank, write the word with the apostrophe placed correctly.

couldn't
1. After turning his ankle, Allen <u>couldnt</u> complete his run.

restaurant's
2. The <u>restaurants</u> lunch menu featured a variety of homemade soups.

Ronita's
3. Using an ice pack helped to ease the pain in <u>Ronitas</u> knee.

tabloid's
4. The <u>tabloids</u> headline read, "I Married a Space Alien!"

river's
5. Amin stood on a dock at the <u>rivers</u> edge and watched the sun set.

it's
6. "Work is important," said Dana. "But <u>its</u> my family that really matters."

__desk's__	7. Memos, notes, and papers entirely covered the <u>desks</u> surface.
__building's__	8. The office <u>buildings</u> immense lobby was obviously created to impress visitors.
__Fred's__	9. The letter said that <u>Freds</u> car payment was overdue.
__pirate's__	10. A <u>pirates</u> treasure was said to be buried on one of the small islands.

REVIEW EXERCISE 3

Each sentence contains two omitted apostrophes. Underline the errors; then, in the blank, write the words with the apostrophes placed correctly.

1. Rosalia <u>couldnt</u> believe her <u>brother's</u> luck; her parents always let Alejandro and Luis borrow the car.
   couldn't, brothers'

2. According to the popular busines<u>spersons</u> adage, it's not what you know; <u>its</u> who you know.
   businessperson's, it's

3. Two <u>Brothers</u> Pizzeria is <u>Cass'</u> favorite restaurant.
   Brothers', Cass's

4. The true sports <u>fans</u> favorite hobby is discussing their <u>teams</u> chances at victory.
   fans', teams'

5. Despite his fog-misted glasses, <u>Harrys</u> vision was clear enough to spot his <u>sisters'</u> pink umbrella as she searched the parking lot for him.
   Harry's, sister's

REVIEW EXERCISE 4

Each numbered item contains two apostrophe errors, one omitted apostrophe in a contraction or a possessive form and one misplaced or unnecessary apostrophe. Underline each error; then write the correct form of each word below.

1. <u>Lees</u> garage is piled high with tools and <u>bag's</u> of fertilizer.
   Lee's, bags

2. "Its been warm for October," said Max. "Usually, temperature's are in the fifties by now."

   It's, temperatures
   _____

3. An old sofa and several bundles of clothes' sat on the porch, awaiting the Goodwill trucks arrival.

   clothes, truck's
   _____

4. The cough remedys price was high, but it's performance was disappointing.

   remedy's, its
   _____

5. Tom said his DVD players feature's include a remote control and a prepro-gramming feature that he has never learned how to use.

   player's features
   _____

REVIEW EXERCISE 5

Underline and correct the ten apostrophe errors in the restaurant review, writing your answers in the numbered spaces. Each numbered section of the review contains one error. Apostrophes may be misplaced, missing, or unnecessary.

[1]Restaurant Review: Eds R. K. Café [2]When I told a friend I was reviewing Ed's R. K. Café on Interstate Drive, he whispered, "No! Havent you heard the rumors about how Ed gets his meat?" [3]I told my friend that rumor's were common in small towns, and I offered to treat him to dinner and put those rumors to rest. [4]There were no line's on Monday night at Ed's, and as we sat down, Ed himself came in with a large cloth sack. [5]He looked surprised to see customers but said, "Youre lucky. I was just bringing in some groceries." [6]I decided on Steak Michelin, which I assumed to be a French dish, and ordered "Sunday Drivers Stew" for my friend, who had suddenly excused himself from the table. [7]When it came, the Steak Michelin, pounded very flat with some sort of tool that left an attractive zigzag pattern on it's surface, met all my expectations. [8]My friends' stew smelled delicious and looked as if it contained several kinds of meat, but he said he was not feeling well and that he could not eat. [9]In any case, its a pleasure to recommend Ed's, which is close enough to the highway to be convenient for everyone. [10]Service is slow, but worth the wait, and the meat taste's wonderfully fresh.

1. Ed's
2. Haven't
3. rumors
4. lines
5. You're

6. Driver's or Drivers'
7. its
8. friend's
9. it's
10. tastes

mywritinglab   For support in meeting this chapter's goal, log in to
www.mywritinglab.com and select **Apostrophes**.

CHAPTER 29

Quotation Marks

> ✐ **Chapter Goal:** Identify direct quotations, indirect quotations, and titles appropriately in your writing.

"May I quote you?"

Quotation marks are visual signals that give a reader information that would otherwise have to be conveyed in words. They are a kind of academic shorthand that says, "Someone else wrote, said, or thought these words" or "These words are the title of a short work." Underlining and italics say, "These words are the title of a long work." Learning to use quotation marks, underlining, and italics adds another dimension to your ability to communicate within the academic world.

✐ Quotation Marks to Signal Quotations

Direct Quotations

mywritinglab
Visit MyWriting Lab for additional practice with quotation marks.

Quotation marks are used to signal a **direct quotation**; that is, they are placed around the exact words that someone speaks, writes, or thinks. As you look at the examples, notice that when a comma or a period comes at the end of a quotation, it is always placed *before* the closing quotation mark. When a direct question is quoted, the question mark also goes *before* the closing quotation mark.

Examples of Direct Quotations

"I'll pick up the dry cleaning on my way home," said Pat.

Keiko said, "I don't need to go to the gym. I stay in shape lugging all these books around the campus."

The child asked, "Why don't people have wings?"

"Did you bring the doughnuts?" asked David.

PRACTICE 1   Using Quotation Marks with Direct Quotations

Place quotation marks around direct quotations.

1. I am sorry I'm late, said Al.
    "I am sorry I'm late," said Al.

2. Is this something we need to know for the test? Karen asked the professor.
    "Is this something we need to know for the test?" Karen asked the professor.

3. The bumper sticker said, If you can read this, thank a teacher.
    The bumper sticker said, "If you can read this, thank a teacher."

4. Alicia said, I think there's a gas station at the next exit.
    Alicia said, "I think there's a gas station at the next exit."

5. I get a headache whenever it rains, complained Rosa.
    "I get a headache whenever it rains," complained Rosa.

Split Quotations

Some direct quotations are **split quotations**. Here are two rules for splitting quotations.

1. When you split a sentence, use commas to set off the *tag* (such as *she said*) that tells who said, thought, or wrote the words you are quoting.

"When you come through the door," Raven told her son, "please try not to slam it."

2. When there is a complete sentence before and a complete sentence after the tag, put a comma after the first sentence and a period after the tag.

"I couldn't turn in my paper yesterday," Alex told the professor. "I wasn't here."

PRACTICE 2   USING QUOTATION MARKS AND COMMAS WITH DIRECT QUOTATIONS

Place quotation marks around direct quotations, and add commas where they are needed.

1. Your stock clerks need to be more careful the customer told the manager. This milk was expired when I bought it.

   "Your stock clerks need to be more careful," the customer told the manager. "This milk was expired when I bought it."

2. My job as a human cannonball is great said the circus performer. Business is booming.

   "My job as a human cannonball is great," said the circus performer. "Business is booming."

3. If you can't say something nice Aunt Dolly said come over here and talk to me.

   "If you can't say something nice," Aunt Dolly said, "come over here and talk to me."

4. You have won third prize in a beauty contest the Monopoly card read. Collect $10.

   "You have won third prize in a beauty contest," the Monopoly card read. "Collect $10."

5. For Mother's Day this year Charlotte told her husband I'd like a day of peace and quiet.

   "For Mother's Day this year," Charlotte told her husband, "I'd like a day of peace and quiet."

PRACTICE 3   USING QUOTATION MARKS AND COMMAS WITH DIRECT QUOTATIONS

Place quotation marks around direct quotations, and add commas or question marks as needed.

1. Are you new to this area the real estate agent asked.

"Are you new to this area?" the real estate agent asked.

2. I hate roller coasters said Anthony. I am afraid of heights.
    "I hate roller coasters," said Anthony. "I am afraid of heights."

3. Spreading his arms wide, the singer shouted Hello, Philadelphia!
    Spreading his arms wide, the singer shouted, "Hello, Philadelphia!"

4. I know you love your hunting dogs Janice told her husband but do we have to take them on vacation with us?
    "I know you love your hunting dogs," Janice told her husband, "but do we have to take them on vacation with us?"

5. You have been preapproved for a $10,000 line of credit the letter began.
    "You have been preapproved for a $10,000 line of credit," the letter began.

Indirect Quotations

An **indirect quotation** is a paraphrase. It repeats the essence of what a person said. It may repeat some or all of the words, but it is not a word-for-word quotation. The word *that* is either stated or implied before an indirect quotation. An indirect quotation is not set off by quotation marks.

Examples of Indirect Quotations

Ashley said that she needed a vacation.

Ashley said she needed a vacation.

The two examples above are indirect quotations. They do not repeat Ashley's exact words (Ashley did not use the word *she*). The word *that* is stated in the first example and implied in the second. Therefore, no quotation marks are used.

PRACTICE 4   IDENTIFYING DIRECT AND INDIRECT QUOTATIONS

On the line provided, label each quotation as direct (*D*) or indirect (*I*).

_D__ 1. Ellen said, "I would have caught the ball if the sun had not been in my eyes."

___I___ 2. Ellen said that she would have caught the ball if the sun had not been in her eyes.

___I___ 3. The customer in the drive-through said he wanted extra ketchup.

___D___ 4. Jan asked, "Has anyone watered the fern?"

___I___ 5. Jan asked if anyone had watered the fern.

PRACTICE 5 WORKING WITH DIRECT AND INDIRECT QUOTATIONS

On the line provided, label each quotation as direct (*D*) or indirect (*I*). Place quotation marks around direct quotations, and leave indirect quotations as they are.

___D___ 1. Ray said, Mr. Bartlett, I can work nights but not weekends.
Ray said, "Mr. Bartlett, I can work nights but not weekends."

___I___ 2. Ray told Mr. Bartlett that he could work nights but not weekends.
Indirect

___D___ 3. The headline read, Too Few Americans Exercise.
The headline read, "Too Few Americans Exercise."

___I___ 4. Two out of three people surveyed said they were better off financially than they had been last year.
Indirect

___D___ 5. Perry said, I wish I could afford a new truck.
Perry said, "I wish I could afford a new truck."

___I___ 6. The article said Americans receive fewer vacation days than Europeans do.
Indirect

___I___ 7. The child said she knew nothing about the broken cookie jar.
Indirect

___D___ 8. I'm not in the mood to watch a movie, said Theo.
"I'm not in the mood to watch a movie," said Theo.

___D___ 9. Would you like dessert? asked the server.
"Would you like dessert?" asked the server.

___I___ 10. The salesperson said that she could order any color we wanted.
Indirect

Quotation Marks, Italics, and Underlining to Set Off Titles

Quotation marks, italics, and underlining act as academic shorthand to signal a title. **Quotation marks** are used around titles of short works or works that are contained within other works. The following types of titles are set off by quotation marks:

1. Chapter title (short works contained within a longer work)
    "Subject-Verb Agreement"
    "Sentence Variety"

2. Essays
    "Barbie Madness"
    "Action Hero"

3. Individual episodes of a TV series (short works contained within the longer series)
    "The Fuzzy Boots Corollary" (an episode of *The Big Bang Theory*)
    "The Slicer" (an episode of *Seinfeld*)

4. Song titles (short works, often contained within a longer album of works)
    "The Star-Spangled Banner"
    "Georgia on My Mind"

5. Newspaper articles
    "NFL Injury List Grows"
    "Hungry for housing"

6. Poems
    "I Wandered Lonely as a Cloud"
    "Fern Hill"

7. Short stories
    "Sonny's Blues"
    "The Ones Who Walk Away from Omelas"

Grammar Alert!

When you write *about* an essay, place the title of the essay within quotation marks. When you type the title of *your* essay on a cover sheet or at the head of the essay, do not use quotation marks.

Italics and underlining are used to set off the title of a long work, a continuing work (such as a comic strip or television series), or a complete published work (such as a pamphlet or brochure). Use italics in computer-generated papers and underlining in handwritten papers with the following types of titles:

1. Books

    The Color Purple or The Color Purple

    The Curious Incident of the Dog in the Night-time or The Curious Incident of the Dog in the Night-time

2. Comic strips (a series containing individual daily or weekly strips)

    Dilbert or Dilbert

    Jumpstart or Jumpstart

3. Newspapers

    The New York Times or The New York Times

    The Telegraph or The Telegraph

4. Anthologies (collections) of poetry or short stories

    The Poem: An Anthology or The Poem: An Anthology

    Discovering Literature: Stories, Poems, Plays or Discovering Literature: Stories, Poems, Plays

5. Music Albums

    Amar La Trama or Amar La Trama

    Born This Way or Born This Way

6. Television programs

    NCIS: Los Angeles or NCIS: Los Angeles

    American Idol or American Idol

7. Movies

    Pirates of the Caribbean: On Stranger Tides or Pirates of the Caribbean: On Stranger Tides

    The Girl with the Dragon Tattoo or The Girl with the Dragon Tattoo

Grammar Alert!

Italics are used instead of underlining in published or computer-generated materials.

PRACTICE 6   USING QUOTATION MARKS AND UNDERLINING WITH TITLES

In each sentence, use quotation marks and underlining to set off titles.

1. Tonight's episode of Wild Discovery is entitled Cheetah.

    Tonight's episode of <u>Wild Discovery</u> is entitled "Cheetah."

    _____

2. For next week, the professor assigned a chapter called Using Critical Thinking Skills in the book College Success.

    For next week, the professor assigned a chapter called "Using Critical Thinking Skills"

    in the book <u>College Success</u>.

3. Rita's favorite song on Sorry for Party Rocking is Party Rock Anthem.

    Rita's favorite song on <u>Sorry for Party Rocking</u> is "Party Rock Anthem."

    _____

4. From a book called Poetry: An Introduction, the class read The Ballad of Birmingham by Dudley Randall.

    From a book called <u>Poetry: An Introduction</u>, the class read "The Ballad of Birmingham"

    by Dudley Randall.

5. The headline in the Wall Street Journal read Economy on the right track, but Sam did not feel any richer.

    The headline in the <u>Wall Street Journal</u> read "Economy on the right track," but Sam

    did not feel any richer.

Review Exercises

Complete the Review Exercises to find out how well you have learned the skills addressed in this chapter. As you work through the exercises, go back through the chapter to review any of the rules you do not understand completely.

REVIEW EXERCISE 1

Rewrite the following sentences, placing quotation marks around direct quotations.

1. I wish I didn't have to work on Saturday complained Ted.

"I wish I didn't have to work on Saturday," complained Ted.

2. I can't believe you came! exclaimed Stella. I'm so excited to see you!

   "I can't believe you came!" exclaimed Stella. "I'm so excited to see you!"

3. We hold these truths to be self-evident, begins the Declaration of Independence.

   "We hold these truths to be self-evident," begins the Declaration of Independence.

4. Frustrated with her lack of progress, Liz groaned I'll never get through all of this homework.

   Frustrated with her lack of progress, Liz groaned, "I'll never get through all of this homework."

5. As Nicole desperately clicked the Save button, the computer screen read Not responding.

   As Nicole desperately clicked the Save button, the computer screen read, "Not responding."

REVIEW EXERCISE 2

Rewrite the following sentences, placing quotation marks around direct quotations. Four of the sentences are indirect quotations that do not require quotation marks.

1. The loan officer told Brad and Lexie that she hoped they hadn't had to wait too long.

   Indirect

2. Why are your paws so wet? Alfreda asked her dog.

   "Why are your paws so wet?" Alfreda asked her dog.

3. If he could have talked, Alfreda's dog might have said that he had walked through a puddle on the way home.

   Indirect

4. When she came back from the All-Night Moonlight Sale-a-Thon, Bernice said, Never again.

   When she came back from the All-Night Moonlight Sale-a-Thon, Bernice said, "Never again."

5. What is this disgusting-looking bug? asked Phillip.

   "What is this disgusting-looking bug?" asked Phillip.

6. Patrick said he had already finished his paper.

   Indirect

7. If I have to eat spaghetti one more time, said Nick, I'll turn into a meatball.

   "If I have to eat spaghetti one more time," said Nick, "I'll turn into a meatball."

8. Too late, said his wife.

   "Too late," said his wife.

9. I've got it, said the worker as he grabbed one end of the sofa.

   "I've got it," said the worker as he grabbed one end of the sofa.

10. The disk jockey said that he would play audience requests for the next two hours.

    Indirect

REVIEW EXERCISE 3

Correct the following sentences, using underlining or quotation marks to set off titles.

1. Wendy took out a library book called Cold Mountain.

   Wendy took out a library book called <u>Cold Mountain</u>.

2. Before Chet turned on his video game console, his wife said she would leave him if he beat her in Guitar Hero again.

   Before Chet turned on his video game console, his wife said she would leave him if he beat her in <u>Guitar Hero</u> again.

3. Chapter 10, Taking Care of Yourself, discusses stress and nutrition.

   Chapter 10, "Taking Care of Yourself," discusses stress and nutrition.

4. Meghan's Irish grandfather believes there's no sweeter sound than Danny Boy sung by an Irish tenor.

   Meghan's Irish grandfather believes there's no sweeter sound than "Danny Boy"

   sung by an Irish tenor.

5. Luis bought an album by Los Fabulosos Cadillacs called Fabulosos Calavera.

   Luis bought an album by Los Fabulosos Cadillacs called <u>Fabulosos Calavera</u>.

6. Derek swears there is a country song called If My Nose Were Full of Nickels, I'd Blow It All on You.

   Derek swears there is a country song called "If My Nose Were Full of Nickels, I'd

   Blow It All on You."

7. The Complete Works of Shakespeare, Bjorn's text for English 210, must weigh at least ten pounds.

   <u>The Complete Works of Shakespeare</u>, Bjorn's text for English 210, must weigh at

   least ten pounds.

8. After new special effects were added to the 1970s movie Star Wars, it was brought out again for a new generation.

   After new special effects were added to the 1970s movie <u>Star Wars</u>, it was brought

   out again for a new generation.

9. When it was released, the movie Titanic broke box-office records.

   When it was released, the movie <u>Titanic</u> broke box-office records.

10. A small headline at the top of the page said No clues in hit and run.

    A small headline at the top of the page said "No clues in hit and run."

Grammar Review: Five Editing Exercises

EDITING EXERCISE 1   **WORDS COMMONLY CONFUSED, FRAGMENTS, RUN-ONS, AND SUBJECT-VERB AGREEMENT**

Find and correct the ten sentence errors in the paragraph below. In the blanks provided, write the number of the sentence in which you find each error, followed by your correction. Two of the sentences are correct. Answers may vary slightly.

2 errors in words commonly confused

2 sentence fragments

2 run-on sentences

4 subject-verb agreement errors

¹I read an article not long ago that claimed that the weather effects the human body. ²Since I can link both my headaches and my moods to the weather. ³I can support the claim made by the author of the article. ⁴My headaches begins with the drop in barometric pressure that precedes a storm. ⁵The clouds roll in a throbbing pain that no aspirin can completely relieve begins on one side of my head. ⁶As soon as the clouds dissipate. ⁷My headache slips away like a forgotten memory. ⁸Additionally, winter affect my state of mind like no other season. ⁹With the falling of the leaves, my generally upbeat attitude begins to fall as well I slide into a gloomy mood. ¹⁰According to the article, the changes in my mood is symptomatic of a condition called Seasonal Affective Disorder, or SAD. ¹¹Plenty of sunshine eventually lift my spirits. ¹²The whether does play an important role in my well-being.

1. affects
2. to the weather, I can support
3. correct
4. begin
5. in; a throbbing pain
6. clouds dissipate, my headache
7. correct
8. affects
9. to fall as well, and I slide

10. are
_____

11. lifts
_____

12. weather
_____

EDITING EXERCISE 2   **COMMAS, WORDS COMMONLY CONFUSED, AND COMMA SPLICES**

Find and correct the ten sentence errors in the paragraph below. Each sentence contains an error. Answers may vary slightly.

1 comma omitted after introductory element

2 commas omitted in a series of three items

3 errors in words commonly confused

4 comma splices

[1]When I look back over the jobs I've held none of them taught me more about responsibility and hard work than my summer job at Tossi's Bakery. [2]My principle responsibility was to arrive at the bakery at 5:20 every morning and prepare the machines and the ingredients for the baker. [3]One Saturday morning, I turned off the alarm rolled over for just one more minute under the covers, and drifted back to sleep. [4]On that day, disappointed customers did not get there fresh bread and breakfast rolls when the bakery opened at 7:00. [5]Ashamed of my irresponsibility, I promised Mr. Tossi that I would never be late again, I never was. [6]I also learned too perform hard physical work. [7]I hauled huge sacks of flour, sugar and other ingredients from the storehouse in the back of the bakery to a platform near the large machines that blended the ingredients into dough. [8]At first, I dragged myself home each day and barely moved until the next morning, however, I soon adjusted to the hard work. [9]The huge bags of flour seemed lighter, the workday no longer seemed to last forever. [10]My job at the bakery lasted just one summer, it helped mold me into the responsible person that I am today.

1. I've held, none of them
_____

2. principal
_____

3. alarm, rolled
_____

4. their
_____

5. <u>again, and I never</u>

6. <u>to</u>

7. <u>sugar, and other</u>

8. <u>morning; however, I</u>

9. <u>lighter, and the</u>

10. <u>summer, but it</u>

EDITING EXERCISE 3   **APOSTROPHES, COMMAS, SUBJECT-VERB AGREEMENT**

Find and correct the ten sentence errors in the paragraph below. Each sentence contains an error. Answers may vary slightly.

1 apostrophe error

3 commas omitted after introductory element

6 subject-verb agreement errors

[1]At one time, seasonal displays and products appeared on <u>retailers shelves</u> near their actual season. [2]Halloween costumes and candy, for example, <u>was</u> placed on shelves a month or so before pint-sized ghosts and witches canvassed the neighborhood in search of as much sugar as they could carry. [3]In mid-<u>January Valentine</u> candy would appear, allowing sufficient time for children to purchase boxes of pastel conversation hearts and for adults to buy heart-shaped boxes of chocolate. [4]<u>Traditionally Christmas</u> displays appeared only after the Thanksgiving turkey had been digested. [5]Lately, however, stores <u>seems</u> to have lost their sense of time. [6]Halloween costumes and candy <u>is</u> on display from Labor Day through the end of October. [7]Christmas catalogs and advertisements <u>begins</u> to arrive in mailboxes in September. [8]By October, Christmas merchandise slowly <u>appear</u> on store shelves. [9]When Christmas items are removed in late December, the red hearts of Valentine's Day <u>appears</u>. [10]For <u>retailers every</u> day is a holiday.

1. <u>retailers'</u>

2. <u>were</u>

3. <u>January, Valentine</u>

4. <u>Traditionally, Christmas</u>

5. seem
6. are
7. begin
8. appears
9. appear
10. retailers, every

| EDITING EXERCISE 4 | PRONOUN POINT OF VIEW, PRONOUN AGREEMENT, SUBJECT-VERB AGREEMENT, PRONOUN CASE |

Find and correct the ten sentence errors in the paragraph below. Each sentence contains an error. Answers may vary slightly.

2 shifts in pronoun point of view

3 pronoun agreement errors

4 subject-verb agreement errors

1 pronoun case error

^{1}As an intern for a television station, I see firsthand how strangely some people behave when <u>you</u> point a camera at them. ^{2}Once, when I accompanied the camera crew to a local mall, we had trouble interviewing the manager because of all the teenagers who stood behind him, waving, grinning, and yelling out comments as if <u>he or she</u> were the reason the cameras were there. ^{3}Among my favorite assignments <u>is</u> street interviews. ^{4}When the interviewer tries to stop someone on the street to ask <u>them</u> a question, some people just shake their heads and walk on. ^{5}Other people look at their shoes and <u>mumbles</u> the briefest possible answer. ^{6}There is always at least one star-quality interviewee who looks directly into the camera and gives a polished answer that sounds as if <u>they</u> have rehearsed it for hours. ^{7}But the strangest people of all are the ones who act as if they <u>has</u> something to hide. ^{8}Once, when the camera operator and <u>me</u> were setting up the camera for the shot, a man covered his face with his jacket and actually ran from us. ^{9}Other camera-shy people cross the street to avoid <u>you</u>, as if they are afraid of being recognized on TV. ^{10}If there is one thing I have learned during my internship, it is that the sight of a TV crew and cameras <u>make</u> some people behave strangely.

1. I _____

2. they _____

3. are _____

4. omit the word "them" _____

5. mumble _____

6. he or she has _____

7. have _____

8. I _____

9. me _____

10. makes _____

EDITING EXERCISE 5 **CAPITALIZATION, VERB SHIFTS, SUBJECT-VERB AGREEMENT, WORDS COMMONLY CONFUSED, ADJECTIVES AND ADVERBS, COMMA SPLICES, RUN-ONS, FRAGMENTS**

Find and correct the ten sentence errors in the paragraph below. Two of the sentences are correct. Answers may vary slightly.

1 capitalization error

1 verb shift from past to present

1 subject-verb agreement error

2 errors in words commonly confused

1 confusion of adjective and adverb

1 comma splice

1 run-on sentence

2 sentence fragments

[1]Greek mythology shows that ancient <u>greek</u> gods took terrible revenge on those who opposed or displeased them. [2]When Tantalus, son of Zeus, displeased the gods, he was condemned to float for eternity in a <u>beautifully</u> lake. [3]If he bent to drink from the clear, sparkling water, it <u>recedes</u> from him. [4]<u>If he reached for the luscious grapes hanging overhead.</u> [5]They stayed just out of reach. [6]Sisyphus displeased the gods by telling their <u>secrets he</u> was taught the meaning of frustration. [7]His task for all the years of eternity <u>were</u> to roll a huge, heavy rock up a steep hill. [8]When he had almost

reached the top, the rock would invariably break loose and roll to the <u>bottom, poor</u> Sisyphus had to start again. [9]Arachne bragged that she could weave more skillfully than the gods <u>theirselves</u>. [10]She was sentenced to spend eternity spinning beautiful webs as <u>a</u> eight-legged spider. [11]<u>With gods so cruel and imaginative.</u> [12]It is a wonder that even mythological characters dared to oppose them.

1. Greek
2. beautiful
3. receded
4. hanging overhead, they stayed
5. Correct
6. When Sisyphus . . . secrets, he
7. was
8. bottom; poor
9. themselves
10. an
11. cruel and imaginative, it is a wonder
12. Correct

Action Hero

Rulon Openshaw

Everyone treated him like a hero. It was easy to get used to . . . maybe a little too easy.

1 A few years ago, I stopped at a neighborhood market for some late-night ice cream. As I got out of my car, a young man hailed me from across the street. He was college-aged and dressed to the nines: expensive pullover, dress shirt and slacks so sharply creased they could have cut frozen fish. I thought he wanted directions; he had that urgent late-for-a-party look. When he reached me, he pulled up his sweater and smoothly drew a pistol from inside his waistband. "Get in the car," he ordered.

2 My brain went into hyperspeed. I remembered watching a personal-security expert on a talk show advise victims not to stare at an assailant's face. His reasoning was that if a robber thinks you cannot identify him, he's less likely to kill you. No one asked how much less likely. Given its importance to my future, I focused instead on his weapon—a .38 Smith & Wesson revolver, blued steel, short barrel. I'd fired others like it at pistol ranges. This was no mouse gun. Nervously, I directed my gaze lower. His shoes were highly polished. Strange as it sounds, I admired his sense of style.

3 The click of the revolver's hammer being cocked snapped my head up eye to eye with his. So much for not looking at his face. Contrary to the belief that when death appears imminent, a person's entire life passes before him, I was completely focused on the moment. Instinct told me that a car trip with this guy would turn out to be a one-way journey for me. I held out my keys. "Take my car," I said in a tone I prayed would inspire calmness and reason. "I'm not getting in."

4 He hesitated, then ignoring my proffered keys, thrust out a hand and yanked off my shoulder bag. In it were my wallet and a couple of rented videos. He took a step back, his gun still aimed at me. Neither of us spoke.

5 Laughter broke the silence, making us both turn. Several couples were leaving a Chinese restaurant on the opposite corner. The gunman gave them a fast scan, then lowered his revolver. Holding it against his thigh to conceal it, he began to stride quickly across the almost-trafficless street, my bag clutched under his arm.

6 Incredibly, I took off after him. "Hey," I shouted to the people in front of the restaurant. "This guy just robbed me." I was halfway across the street when I realized my would-be posse was not mounting up. The gunman, now aware of my proximity, pivoted in my direction. As I watched him raise his gun, everything

went into slow motion. A tongue of flame flashed from the snub-nosed barrel, followed by a loud crack.

I lost my balance. I felt no pain, but when I looked down, I saw my left leg 7 flopped out sideways at my shin. A half-dollar-sized spot of blood stained my jeans. When I looked up, my assailant was sprinting down a dark side street.

Later that night at a nearby hospital, I was told that the bullet had fractured 8 my tibia and fibula, the two bones connecting the knee and ankle. Doctors insert-ed a steel rod secured by four screws into my leg. They also gave me a "prosthesis alert" card to show security personnel if the rod set off a metal detector.

But a remarkable thing began to happen—my popularity soared. When friends in- 9 troduced me as "the guy who got shot," women who a moment before had no interest in me came after me like groupies. Men wanted to buy me drinks—they considered me "brave" for running after the gunman. I'm reminded of war movies in which the green infantrymen behave reverentially around the grizzled vets who have seen action.

I found it difficult to forgive myself for what I considered an act of colossal 10 folly. Sometimes, I thought I had chased the kid out of anger at being victimized; other times, I attributed my actions to an adrenaline rush that needed a physical outlet. Whatever the reason, I knew it had nothing to do with bravery.

Clearly, I was being given credit for something I didn't deserve, yet I was 11 reluctant to give up my newly acquired status. After all, it wasn't as if I were taking an active part in any deception, I was merely allowing people to come to whatever conclusions they wished. I finally rationalized my decision to maintain the status quo: I considered any misperception to be my compensation for having gone through a horrible situation.

Things went well until the day I was approached by a panhandler. On a whim, I 12 told him I had no money because I'd been unable to work since being shot in a rob-bery. His eyes grew large, and it was obvious that the information impressed him. "That's heavy," he said, then leaned closer, conspiratorially. "Did you get caught?"

Building Vocabulary

For each question, choose the meaning that most closely defines the italicized word or phrase as it is used in the essay.

1. The phrase *dressed to the nines* most nearly means
   a. well dressed.
   b. carelessly dressed.
   c. oddly dressed.
   d. shabbily dressed.

2. The word *hyperspeed* most nearly means
   a. slow motion.
   b. top speed.

    c. full stop.

    d. normal speed.

3. The word *reverentially* most nearly means

    a. boastfully.

    b. quietly.

    c. bravely.

    (d.) worshipfully.

4. The word *folly* most nearly means

    a. bravery.

    b. wisdom.

    (c.) foolishness.

    d. anger.

5. The phrase *the status quo* most nearly means

    a. the way things used to be.

    b. the rationalization.

    c. the plan for the future.

    (d.) the current situation.

Understanding the Essay

1. The person who robbed the author at gunpoint

    a. looked like a desperate criminal.

    b. was a homeless person.

    (c.) looked like a well-dressed college student.

    d. had a police record.

2. The robber was distracted and ran away when

    a. a police car slowly drove by.

    b. the author refused to get into the car with him and instead offered his keys.

    (c.) some people came out of a nearby restaurant.

    d. Bruno, the author's Rottweiler, lunged for the robber's throat.

3. The pattern of development in this essay is mainly

    a. definition.

    b. cause-effect.

    (c.) narrative.

    d. description.

4. The author implies that the main reason he accepted being treated as a hero was that

    a. he enjoyed the attention he received from women.

    b. his popularity soared and he always had a funny story to tell at parties.

    c. he had been through so much that he felt he deserved the attention.

    d. he knew that chasing the robber was a heroic action.

5. Which of the following familiar sayings is best supported by the essay?

    a. Clothes make the man.

    b. Honesty is the best policy.

    c. Crime does not pay.

    d. You can't judge a book by its cover.

Writing in the Margins

These questions encourage you to think not just about the essay but about the issues it raises. Your instructor may ask you to write down your answers, to discuss them in groups, or simply to think about them for class discussion.

1. This essay revolves around misperception. How many instances do you see in the essay where people see things as they are not? How do you account for these misperceptions?

2. It has been said that "perception is everything." What do you think the statement means? Is it true?

3. If this story were a fable or a folktale, it would have a moral. If there is a moral to this story, what is it?

4. To what extent do we rely on appearance when we judge people? What are the benefits and dangers of using appearance to judge others?

5. Is society more dangerous or less dangerous than it was when your parents or grandparents were growing up? How do you know?

Topics for Writing

Assignment 1: Facing Danger

Paragraph or Journal Entry

Have you ever faced a dangerous or potentially dangerous situation? How did you react? Did your reaction surprise you? Write a narrative journal entry or paragraph describing the situation and your reaction to it.

Assignment 2: Judgments and Misjudgments

Paragraph

Has someone ever given you more credit than you deserved or suspected you of something you did not do? Write a narrative paragraph describing the incident. Alternatively, have you ever misjudged another person? Write a narrative paragraph describing that incident.

Assignment 3: Types of Stereotypes

Paragraph or Essay

Sometimes, entire groups of people are routinely misjudged. This kind of misjudgment is called *stereotyping*—attributing positive or negative characteristics to people simply because they are of a particular age, gender, religion, race, or socioeconomic group. Write a classification paragraph or essay in which you discuss three common stereotypes about one particular group. Give specific examples of each stereotype you discuss.

Assignment 4: Protection against Crime

Paragraph or Essay

What steps can people take to protect themselves against crime? Explain in a process paragraph or essay.

A Generation of Slackers? Not So Much

Catherine Rampell

Is the latest generation the laziest generation?

1   You'd think there would be a little sympathy. This month, college graduates are jumping into the job market, only to land on their parents' couches: the unemployment rate for 16- to 24-year-olds is a whopping 17.6 percent.

2   The reaction from many older Americans? This generation had it coming.

3   Generation Y—or Millennials, the Facebook Generation or whatever you want to call today's cohort of young people—has been accused of being the laziest generation ever. They feel entitled and are coddled, disrespectful, narcissistic and impatient, say authors of books like *The Dumbest Generation* and *Generation Me*.

4   And three in four Americans believe that today's youth are less virtuous and industrious than their elders, a 2009 survey by the Pew Research Center found.

5   In a sign of humility or docility, young people agree. In that 2009 Pew survey, two-thirds of millennials said older adults were superior to the younger generation when it came to moral values and work ethic.

6   After all, if there's a young person today who's walked 10 miles barefoot through the snow to school, it was probably on an iPhone app.

7   So is this the Laziest Generation? There are signs that its members benefit from lower standards. Technology has certainly made life easier. But there may also be a generation gap; the way young adults work is simply different.

8   It's worth remembering that to some extent, these accusations of laziness and narcissism in "kids these days" are nothing new—they've been levied against Generation X, Baby Boomers and many generations before them. Even Aristotle and Plato were said to have expressed similar feelings about the slacker youth of their times.

But this generation has had it easy in some ways.

9

They can access just about any resource, product or service anywhere from a mere 10
tap on a touch screen. And as many critics have noted, it's also easier to get A's. The
typical grade-point average in college rose to about 3.11 by the middle of the last
decade, from 2.52 in the 1950s, according to a recent study by Stuart Rojstaczer,
professor emeritus at Duke, and Christopher Healy of Furman University.

College students also spend fewer hours studying each week than did their coun- 11
terparts in 1961, according to a new working paper by Philip S. Babcock of the University of California, Santa Barbara, and Mindy Marks of the University of California,
Riverside. That doesn't mean all this leftover time is spent on PlayStation 3's.

There is <u>ample</u> evidence that young people today are hard-working and pro- 12
ductive. The share of college students working full time generally grew from 1985
onward—until the Great Recession knocked many millennials out of the labor
force, according to the Labor Department.

And while many college students today—like those of yesterday—get 13
financial help from their parents, 44 percent of students today say that work
or personal savings helped finance their higher educations, according to a
survey of recent graduates by Rutgers University.

"I don't think this is a generation of slackers," said Carl Van Horn, a labor 14
economist at Rutgers. "This image of the kid who goes off and skis in Colorado,
I don't think that's the correct image. Today's young people are very focused on
trying to work hard and to get ahead."

Defying the narcissism stereotype, community service among young people 15
has exploded.

Between 1989 and 2006, the share of teenagers who were volunteering dou- 16
bled, to 26.4 percent from 13.4 percent, according to a report by the Corporation
for National and Community Service. And the share of incoming college freshmen
who say they plan to volunteer is at a record high of 32.1 percent, too, U.C.L.A.'s
annual incoming freshman survey found.

Perhaps most important, many of the behaviors that older generations inter- 17
pret as laziness may actually enhance young people's productivity, say researchers
who study Generation Y.

Members of Gen Y, for example, are significantly more likely than Gen X'ers 18
and boomers to say they are more productive working in teams than on their own,
according to Don Tapscott, author of *Grown Up Digital: How the Net Generation is
Changing Your World*, a book based on interviews with 11,000 millennials.

To older workers, wanting help looks like laziness; to younger workers, the 19
gains that come from teamwork have been learned from the collaborative nature
of their childhood activities, which included social networks, crowd-sourcing and
even video games like *World of Warcraft* that "emphasize cooperative rather than
individual competition," Mr. Tapscott says.

Employers also complain about millennials checking *Facebook* and *Twitter* on 20
the job, or working with their ear buds in.

Older workers have a strong sense of separate spheres for work and play: the cubicle is for work, and home is for fun. But to millennials, the boundaries between work and play are fuzzier, said Michael D. Hais, co-author of *Millennial Makeover: MySpace, YouTube, and the Future of American Politics*. 21

Think of the corporate cultures at prototypical Gen Y employers like Facebook and Google, he says, where football, volleyball courts and subsidized massages are office fixtures. 22

The prevailing millennial attitude is that taking breaks for fun at work makes people more, not less, productive. Likewise, they accept that their work will bleed into evenings and weekends. 23

Some experts also believe that today's young people are better at quickly switching from one task to another, given their exposure to so many stimuli during their childhood and adolescence, said John Della Volpe, the director of polling at Harvard's Institute of Politics. (The jury is still out on that one.) 24

Of course, these explanations may be unconvincing to older bosses, co-workers and teachers on the other side of this culture clash. But at least they can take comfort in one fact: someday, millennials will have their own new generation of know-it-all ne'er-do-wells to deal with. 25

Building Vocabulary

For each question, choose the meaning that most closely defines the italicized word or phrase as it is used in the essay.

1. The word *cohort* most nearly means
   a. a rowdy group.
   b. a personal friend.
   c. the group in which a person belongs for statistical purposes.
   d. a cooperative group within the workplace.

2. The word *narcissistic* most nearly means
   a. altruistic; putting others first.
   b. addicted to narcotics.
   c. flower-like.
   d. self-admiring, self-centered.

3. The word *humility* most nearly means
   a. thinking too highly of oneself.
   b. modesty.
   c. percentage of moisture saturation in the air.
   d. the state of being human.

4. The word *ample* most nearly means
   a. little.
   b. faked.
   c. abundant.
   d. dubious.

5. The word *prototypical* most nearly means
   a. making a model for those who come after.
   b. sterotypical.
   c. characteristic and not out of the ordinary.
   d. professional.

Understanding the Essay

1. The author's purpose in writing the essay is
   a. to describe the millennial geneneration and its characteristics.
   b. to convince the reader that the millennial generation is lazy and narcissistic.
   c. to argue that the millennial generation is as hard-working as any previous generation.
   d. to explain why the millennual generation "had it coming" when jobs became difficult to find.

2. The existence of books such as *The Dumbest Generation* and *Generation Me* suggests that
   a. previous generations are afraid their jobs will be taken by millennials.
   b. an organized conspiracy against millennials exists.
   c. some writers doubt that the millennial generation will measure up.
   d. people look only for the bad in others.

3. According to the essay, which of the following is *not* a way that the millennial generation has it easier than previous generations?
   a. It's easier to get an A.
   b. Computer touch screens connect them to nearly limitless resources.
   c. It is easier to get a job.
   d. They spend less time studying.

4. According to the essay, what are some of the new ways of working that may keep older generations from understanding millennials?
   a. They combine work and play.
   b. They like working in groups or teams.

c. They are better at task switching.

(d.) All of the above

5. The author implies that the idea that the younger generation is lazy and self-centered

a. will be proven wrong as younger workers are trained to follow the methods of older workers.

b. will not matter when workplaces begin to model their corporate culture after those of Facebook and Google.

(c.) is an idea that recurs as each new generation comes along.

d. is untrue because studies show that millennials are actually more dedicated and hard-working than other generations.

Writing in the Margins

These questions encourage you to think not just about the essay but about the issues it raises. Your instructor may ask you to write down your answers, to discuss them in groups, or simply to think about them for class discussion.

1. The essay suggests that each generation comes to believe that the younger generation is filled with coddled, unmotivated slackers. How do you explain this negative view of each upcoming generation?

2. Statistics show that Americans are taking fewer and fewer vacations and that when they do, they are still in touch with the office via cell phones and text messages. The article suggests that many people integrate work and play, by getting their exercise in the company gym, for instance. Do you prefer to separate work and play or to intermingle them? How do you feel about working on job-related projects at home? What effect might these trends have on family life?

Topics for Writing

Assignment 1: Community Service

Paragraph or Journal Entry

Describe a community service that you have performed, including a description of the benefits of that work to you and to others. If you have never performed community service work, describe the kind of community service that you would like to perform, including a description of how that work benefits you and others.

Assignment 2: Passing It Down

Paragraph or Essay

Members of different generations often clash because their values differ, but there are also values that are worth preserving and passing down to the next generation. Identify and discuss three values that your parents or grandparents have passed on to you that you think are worthy of passing on to the generation that comes after you.

Assignment 3: Work Perks

Paragraph or Essay

The essay mentions some of the perks (shortened form of the word *perquisite*—look it up!) that Facebook and Google employees have, including basketball courts, foosball games, and massages that are at least partially paid for by the employer. Below is a list of perks offered by some companies. Some are subsidized (that is, the employer pays in part), and some are completely furnished by the employer. Choose your three favorites, or come up with your own, and discuss why you would like your employer to offer these perks.

Subsidized child care

Subsidized meals in company cafeterias

Onsite company gyms for employee use

Housecleaning services

Use of company vehicles for the commute to work and back

Flextime

Employee discounts

Up to two weeks off to participate in volunteer work in the community

Assignment 4: Generational Work Styles

Paragraph or Essay

Do you notice that members of another generation work differently from the way members of your generation do? List some of the differences that you notice, and then write a paragraph or essay contrasting the way members of your generation work with the way members of another generation work. Before you write, decide whether you are going to contrast objectively, without making any judgment about whose methods are preferable, or whether you will try to make a case that one generation's methods are preferable over the other's.

Setting Boundaries

Cara DiMarco

Setting boundaries is an act of self-esteem and a way to protect yourself and your emotions. In this essay, Cara DiMarco tells why and how to set boundaries.

What exactly is a boundary? Boundaries can be physically or psychologically based. A physical boundary is determined by how much you want to allow or limit access to your physical self. A mental or emotional boundary is the psychological line you draw around yourself that says this is where you end and other people begin. How <u>sturdy</u> and definite your boundaries are depends on many factors. It largely depends on how much you were taught as a child that you had a right to your own separateness and distinctness, or how much you were expected to allow others access to your mental and emotional inner life. Some families allow each member a great deal of psychological privacy and separateness. Other families function in an <u>enmeshed environment</u>, where individuals aren't allowed private thoughts and feelings, and everything is considered open. This can make functioning in the world a confusing and frightening process if you aren't certain how to set clear boundaries that others understand and respect. 1

Creating firm, clear boundaries is important because it helps you stay safe in the world and allows you to decide how much you want to let someone into your emotional space. I encountered a good description of boundary setting in a counselor training class, where an instructor represented boundary setting as the difference between having an internal versus an external zipper. Picture that you have a zipper running from beneath your chin down to your belly button. The zipper allows or denies access to your emotions. An external zipper has the pull tab on the outside of your body, while an internal zipper has the pull tab on the inside. With an external zipper, anyone you meet can potentially grab the pull tab and open it as far as they want, allowing themselves access to whatever amount of your private emotional life or personal details that they want. An internal zipper, on the other hand, allows you to control how much emotional access a person has to your feelings and thoughts. When you meet someone, you can decide how safe and trusting you feel and determine how far you want to lower your zipper and whether you want to let that individual in. 2

Many people have a preset level to which they automatically lower their zipper when they meet new people. It is their way of assuming that people are trustworthy until they prove otherwise, and also of making certain that they allow people access to only some of their emotional lives until they determine if they want to become more emotionally intimate. 3

Setting boundaries with people requires <u>assertiveness</u> skills. . . . Part of what 4
makes boundary setting so challenging is that no one likes to have limits placed
on them or hear "No, you can't have access to that part of me." If you experience
difficulties saying "no," continue to practice in small ways, remembering that you
get good at what you practice.

Some relationships allow you to set boundaries in a relatively comfortable, 5
easy way because that person's sense of boundaries will naturally mesh with your
own. Others will have very different ideas about what is appropriate, and you may
need to agree to disagree on your <u>respective</u> viewpoints. Despite someone's reaction, you never need to apologize for wanting to keep parts of your life private.

Maintaining boundaries is often even more difficult because many people 6
want to test the limits, thinking that if you make an exception for them, it
indicates their special status and importance. Let's say you told a friend not
to call you between 5:00 and 7:00 P.M. because you are busy with the kids and
dinner. You've set that boundary clearly; your friend adheres to it for a time,
but eventually she starts calling during those hours. This is where you make a
decision about what is the most important thing: Is your friend going through
a difficult time and needing extra support from you, or do you need to reassert
your boundaries?

To maintain a boundary, <u>reiterate</u> your stand. If your boundary continues to 7
be violated, state the consequences to the other person. Either the boundary is
honored or you will spend less time with that person. Sometimes it may not be
possible to continue even an important relationship with someone who refuses to
respect your boundaries.

By not allowing others more access to your sense of self than you want, you 8
also honor your own preferences and desires, which in itself is an act of self-
esteem. People with low self-esteem have a difficult time believing that they
are worthy enough to say no to other people. They believe that others are more
important than they are, so how dare they say, "This part of me is important, and
I'm keeping it private." Setting and maintaining boundaries states that what you
want, feel, and are comfortable with is important, you choose to honor that, and
you expect others to do the same. And if you'd like, you can visualize boundaries
as the fence around the garden of your self-esteem, with your boundaries protect-
ing all of the precious aspects that you've been cultivating and nurturing in your
developing self-esteem.

Building Vocabulary

For each question, choose the meaning that most closely defines the italicized
word or phrase as it is used in the essay.

1. The word *sturdy* most nearly means
   a. special.
   b. indefinite.

       c. intellectual.

       (d.) strong.

2. The phrase *enmeshed environment* most nearly means

       a. an environment in which people are free to do as they please.

       (b.) an environment in which people are closely emotionally linked.

       c. an environment in which people keep emotions hidden.

       d. an environment in which everyone has strong boundaries.

3. The word *assertiveness* most nearly means

       a. diffidence.

       (b.) straightforwardness.

       c. shyness.

       d. bullying.

4. The word *respective* most nearly means

       a. shared.

       b. respectful.

       (c.) individual.

       d. steady.

5. The word *reiterate* most nearly means

       a. assess.

       b. show interest in.

       c. abandon.

       (d.) repeat.

Understanding the Essay

1. The main idea of this essay is that

       a. setting boundaries requires assertiveness skills.

       b. how strong a person's boundaries are can depend on factors established in childhood.

       c. a friend who repeatedly calls during a time when she has been asked not to call is violating boundaries.

       (d.) setting firm boundaries is necessary for self-protection and self-esteem.

2. Families that are most likely to foster the setting of strong boundaries are those that

       (a.) allow the most privacy and individuality.

       b. are the most honest and open about emotional issues.

       c. are the happiest.

       d. provide an enmeshed environment.

3. Is it better to have a boundary that works like an internal zipper or one that works like an external zipper?

    a. external, because it shows that you are open and have no secrets

    b. internal, because it allows you to be completely cut off emotionally

    c. external, because it lets people decide how intimately they want to know you

    (d.) internal, because it allows you to control how much emotional access others have

4. Paragraph 5 implies that boundaries

    a. will automatically be respected by friends and family members.

    (b.) are flexible and can be temporarily changed in special situations.

    c. should be maintained no matter what the circumstances.

    d. are too much trouble to maintain.

5. People with low self-esteem may have trouble maintaining boundaries because

    a. they don't mind revealing their emotional life.

    (b.) they have trouble telling people no.

    c. they are eager for people to find out who they really are.

    d. they feel flattered when others want to know their intimate secrets.

Writing in the Margins

These questions encourage you to think not just about the essay but about the issues it raises. Your instructor may ask you to write down your answers, to discuss them in groups, or simply to think about them for class discussion.

1. DiMarco discusses more than one kind of boundary. She talks about emotional boundaries that help people to keep parts of themselves private. She discusses boundaries of time, for example, the family time a person might set aside as a time for no outside intrusion. What other kinds of boundaries do people set? Are they generally helpful or harmful?

2. Do modern conveniences such as cell phones, email, instant messaging, and answering machines make it easier or harder to set boundaries? Can you think of examples?

Topics for Writing

Assignment 1: Your Childhood Boundaries

Paragraph or Journal Entry

As a child, were you allowed or encouraged to set boundaries? How has your upbringing affected your ability to set boundaries as an adult?

Assignment 2: Encouraging Children to Set Boundaries

Paragraph

Should parents encourage children to set boundaries? If so, what kinds of boundaries should be encouraged, and how should parents encourage the setting of these boundaries?

Assignment 3: On Call

Paragraph or Essay

Write a paragraph or essay explaining how modern technological conveniences such as cell phones, email, instant messaging, and answering machines affect your ability to set boundaries.

Assignment 4: Types of Boundaries

Paragraph or Essay

Write a paragraph or essay describing different kinds of boundaries that people set to protect their time, their emotions, or some other important aspect of themselves.

How's the Day Treating You? Your Teller Wants to Know

Ann Bancroft

Maybe we don't want to be treated like family.

1 Before there were self-serve checkout counters, Internet shopping and punching "the following menu" to be placed on 20 minutes of musical hold, before we did most of our shopping online, all business and commerce was conducted between live human beings.

2 You'd hand your cash to a clerk at a store, your check to a bank teller (unobstructed by a bullet-proof shield) or you'd ask a person on the phone why you seem to have been charged $3,760 for your monthly electric bill. These human-to-human transactions were begun and ended with simple, polite phrases.

3 "How may I help you?" the person serving the customer would say. Or simply, "May I help you?"

4 "Yes (or No) thank you," the customer would say.

5 Business was cordial, but chitchat strictly limited to non-specific greetings. Only polite, non-specific answers were required.

6 "How are you?" begs no details. It allows a response of "Fine, thanks," regardless of actual circumstances. The question speaks only to the moment, in which the customer is at least "fine" enough to be standing there, buying something. If he just got fired or his wife ran off with their kid's soccer coach, a simple, "How are you?" doesn't corner him into lying or divulging these things.

7 What's happened to these short, civil, non-intrusive interactions? Why must we now tell our bank tellers and grocery clerks our weekend plans?

8 I'm "fine" with shopping online, with ordering prescriptions by number, with ATMs and pressing 0 to talk to a representative. But I don't get why our few remaining human-to-human business transactions now require faux social conversation.

9 I suspect there have been Meetings, where men in brown suits and yellow ties sat all the employees of the world in semi-circles, each facing the same flip chart. These Meetings were held while you were waiting 15 minutes at the butcher counter for someone, anyone, to show up.

10 "Be Your Customer's Friend," the flip chart instructed. "How are you?" was crossed out and replaced by, "How's the day treating you so far?"

"Ask About the Weekend," the next page advised.   11

"Monday-Tuesday: 'Did you do anything fun over the weekend?' Wednesday: 12
'What's on tap for the rest of the afternoon?'

"Friday: 'So, any big plans for the weekend?'"   13

Now it's not enough to wait in line to deposit a check, you must also wait for   14
everyone ahead of you to be asked, with robotic consistency, their game plan for
a fun time in the hours and days ahead.

Don't get me wrong. Some days, I'm chatty and happy to converse in the gro-   15
cery store or bank about the weather, the World Series or the great recipe I have
for these Brussels sprouts I'm buying. Some days. Some moments on some days.

Life is ever changing and, even-keeled as we may be, it goes up and it goes   16
down and then up and then down again, swells rising and falling from ecstasy to
grief as the current carries you along. Inevitably, we experience moments that are
not nice, wonderful, fantastic or fun. Often, we like to keep such moments to ourselves. Our plans for the weekend may be hot and private, unspeakably mundane,
or the weekend may loom with dread.

Sometimes it is all we can do to just get ourselves into the bank and hand the   17
piece of paper to the teller without falling apart.

Such was the quality of the moment for my friend recently when she had to   18
conduct a sad piece of business. Rain was sheeting outside, but she entered the
bank with dark glasses, removing them to reveal her puffy eyes only when she
reached the teller's window.

"How's the day going for ya?" the teller chirped.   19

"I'm getting through it," my friend said.   20

"Got anything fun planned for the weekend?"   21

My friend paused for a moment, feeling put upon to make something up, but   22
then told the truth.

"My husband just died."   23

You see how a simple, how are you/fine, thanks interaction would have been   24
more kind? How isolated and uncared for, in fact, the enforced chattiness made
my friend feel?

Memo to the men in brown suits and yellow ties, to employers all over the   25
world: Smiley-faced efforts to be your customer's pal do not compensate for longer lines or poor service. Phony attempts at familiarity do not take customers back
to the day when the folks down at the corner store or the one bank in town knew
who you were and what your kids were up to.

In all but a few places, places where most people do not live, those days are gone. 26

Face it. If you want to connect with your customers, do so with your eyes,   27
your genuine (not giddy) smile, and then just do the transaction.

Thank the customer for her business. Look forward to seeing that customer   28
again. But please, don't demand that she experience the moment as nice, great,
fantastic or wonderful. Some moments are, some aren't, no matter what you wish
them to be. It's just a human condition thing.

And customers? If what you've got on tap for the weekend is nothing you care   29
to discuss, try this as a response:

"Oh, you know me!"   30

Building Vocabulary

For each question, choose the meaning that most closely defines the italicized word or phrase as it is used in the essay.

1. The word *cordial* most nearly means
   a. pleasant.
   b. carefully scripted.
   c. familiar.
   d. casual.

2. The word *divulging* most nearly means
   a. diverting.
   b. indulging.
   c. revealing.
   d. hiding.

3. The word *faux* most nearly means
   a. simple.
   b. complex.
   c. genuine.
   d. false.

4. The word *inevitably* most nearly means
   a. unavoidably.
   b. dramatically.
   c. enviably.
   d. viably.

5. The word *mundane* most nearly means
   a. unusual.
   b. routine.
   c. horrid.
   d. unspeakable.

Understanding the Essay

1. Which statement best expresses the main idea of the essay?
   a. Customer relations is a field in which friendliness is required.
   b. The new custom of asking customers specific questions about their days and weekends is much preferable to the vague inquiries used in the past.

    c. The new custom of asking customers specific questions about their days and weekends is intended to be friendly.

    (d.) The new custom of asking customers specific questions about their days and weekends is overly intrusive and unnecessary.

2. The phrase "with robotic consistency" in paragraph 14 suggests that
    a. a robot could do a bank teller's job.
    b. scripted greetings ensure that customers are treated equally.
    (c.) scripted greetings can become tiresome.
    d. the author does not like her bank.

3. According to the essay, what are "smiley-faced attempts to be [the] customer's pal" incapable of doing?
    a. making customers happy.
    b. making customers spend more money.
    (c.) compensating for poor service and longer lines.
    d. compensating for the bad day the customer may be having.

4. From the example of the woman whose husband had just died, you may infer that
    a. the bank teller was simply following company policy.
    b. the encounter was painful for the customer.
    c. the bank teller did not intend to hurt the customer.
    (d.) all of the above.

5. The overall tone of the essay is
    (a.) humorous.
    b. serious.
    c. informative.
    d. objective.

Writing in the Margins

These questions encourage you to think not just about the essay but about the issues it raises. Your instructor may ask you to write down your answers, to discuss them in groups, or simply to think about them for class discussion.

1. Have you ever worked in a customer service position? Were there certain phrases or sentences that you were expected to say? How did you feel about that requirement?

2. From your perspective as a customer, do you agree with the author that a simple "How are you?" before proceeding to the business at hand is better than asking about plans for the weekend? What are your experiences with customer service workers?

Assignment 1: Worst Customer Service Experience

Paragraph or Journal Entry

Write a narrative paragraph or journal entry abut the worst customer service experience you have ever had. This experience can be written from your perspective as a customer or from your perspective as a customer service representative. As you write the narrative, try to analyze what went wrong, and, at the end of the narrative, include a sentence or two about how the experience could have been made better.

Assignment 2: You're in Charge!

Paragraph

Imagine that you are the owner of a shop or business (the type is up to you). What rules and guidelines would you make for greeting and assisting customers? Why?

Assignment 3: The Future of Customer Service

Paragraph or Essay

The field of customer service has changed greatly over the last few decades. Many customer service positions, such as the telephone operator, elevator operator, and milk deliverer, have been eliminated entirely. Other customer service positions have been created. Fifty years ago there were no patient representatives in hospitals, no professional organizers, and certainly no "live chat" representatives for online firms.

Fifty years from now, what new services would you predict, or would you like to see available?

Assignment 4: Secret Shopper

Paragraph or Essay

If you are writing an essay, visit three places as a customer. These can be places that you often visit or that you have never been to before. They can be places that are similar to each other (for example, three bookstores) or places that are different from one another (a bookstore, a restaurant, a clothing store). Before you go into the place, on the basis of the type of place it is, decide what your expectations are. For instance, if you go into a small shop, you might expect to be greeted immediately. If you go into a large, bustling store, you might not expect a greeting at all.

After your visit, write down you impressions. Were you treated well? Was the way you were treated in line with your expectaions? If you were managing the place of business, would you change your instructions to the employees?

Next, write an essay describing your experience, expectations, and recommendations for each place you visited.

For a paragraph-length composition, choose just one place to visit and follow the procedure outlined in the essay assignment.

Barbie Madness

Cynthia Tucker

Since the 1950s, Barbie has been a part of the American culture. But critics say that Barbie is just one of the cultural influences that encourage young girls to pursue an impossible standard of physical beauty. Should parents worry? Cynthia Tucker explores the issue.

When I was 9 or 10, I was steeped in Barbie madness. So much so that I joined the Barbie fan club. My mother still has the membership document displaying my careful cursive writing alongside the scrawled block letters of a younger sister. 1

Too old to play with baby dolls, I was developing a vicarious interest in high fashion—a world to which Barbie allowed me access. Her overpriced collection of clothes included everything from bridal gowns to swimsuits, all accented by stiletto heels. In fact, her feet were permanently arched so that she could not wear sensible shoes. 2

She wore sheath dresses, capri pants, long gowns. She never got dirty; she never burst a seam (she never bent, of course); she never tripped over those heels. 3

Nor did she ever cause me to believe I would see many real women in the real world who looked or dressed like that. I had never seen a grown woman on the beach in high heels, and if I had—even at 10—I would have thought her nuts. Barbie was fantasy, one of the joyous escapes offered by childhood. My Barbie, white and brunette, never symbolized what I thought anyone ought to look like. 4

After nearly four decades of building a doll with a figure that, by one estimate, gives her measurements of 38-18-34, Mattel is preparing to release a new Barbie of less fantastic proportions. Many parents are breathing a sigh of relief that their daughters will no longer be subjected to such an unrealistic—and possibly damaging—cultural icon. Well, I have good news and bad news for those parents. 5

The bad news is, there will always be damaging cultural icons, plenty of unrealistic representations of women that emphasize youth and a weird voluptuousness/thinness, the combination of which defies physiology. If you think Barbie is the last of them, check out the *Sports Illustrated* swimsuit issue. Check out *Baywatch*. (The syndicated show sells well around the world. Sexism needs little translation.) 6

Now, for the good news: Parents will always have more influence over their children than any doll, any model, any magazine, any movie. Perhaps even more than their children's peers. Don't take my word for it—scientific research has confirmed it. 7

A recent study found that no matter a teenager's economic background, a   8
close-knit family helps prevent risky behavior and encourages educational excellence. Might not attentive parents also provide protection against the sexist
influences that permeate the culture?

Children learn not just from their parents' rhetoric, but also from their behav-   9
ior. When a father leaves his family for a younger and more glamorous trophy wife,
he gives his children a much more profound lesson about the value of women than
Barbie ever could. So does the mother who constantly applauds her adolescent
daughter's popularity with boys.

Years ago, Barbie's wardrobe evolved beyond *haute couture* to include profes-   10
sional attire. She also became more ethnically diverse. Now, the doll will get a
little nip-and-tuck that widens her waist and de-emphasizes her chest (a bit).

But no matter what she looks like, Barbie will never be as important a role   11
model as Mom and Dad are. When Dad coaches his daughter's soccer team or helps
her build a treehouse, he gives her a measure of her worth that overshadows even
Barbie's bustline.

Building Vocabulary

For each question, choose the meaning that most closely defines the italicized
word or phrase as it is used in the essay.

1. The word *steeped* most nearly means
   a. drenched.
   b. made vertical.
   c. forced.
   d. indifferent.

2. The phrase *a vicarious interest* most nearly means
   a. an obsession that excludes everything else.
   b. a lukewarm interest.
   c. something that is enjoyed indirectly, through another person or thing.
   d. a dangerous interest.

3. The word *fantastic* most nearly means
   a. unreal.
   b. wonderful.
   c. damaging.
   d. beautiful.

4. The word *icon* most nearly means
   a. ambassador.
   b. god.

     (c) symbol.

     d. destroyer.

5. The word *rhetoric* most nearly means

     (a.) words.

     b. actions.

     c. parents.

     d. behavior.

Understanding the Essay

1. The main idea of "Barbie Madness" is that

     a. Barbie is damaging to the self-image of young girls and should be banned.

     b. toys are just toys and nothing more.

     (c) the influence of Barbie and other cultural icons is outweighed by the influence of parents on a child's self-image.

     d. there is nothing unrealistic about Barbie.

2. When she had a Barbie of her own, the author

     a. considered herself too young to play with dolls.

     (b.) realized that Barbie was a toy, not a role model.

     c. wanted to be just like Barbie when she grew up.

     d. joined a fan club only because her little sister did.

3. If the author wanted to subscribe to the magazine least likely to show unrealistic images of women, which of the following would she choose?

     a. *Sports Illustrated*

     (b.) *Bloomberg Businessweek*

     c. *Vogue*

     d. *Cosmopolitan*

4. How does Tucker support her statement that parents have more influence than the surrounding culture?

     a. She provides examples from her own life.

     b. She provides no support because her statement is obviously true.

     (c) She cites scientific research and gives examples.

     d. She includes interviews with child psychologists.

5. The author would probably agree that a mother who wanted her daughter to be successful and well-rounded would

     a. forbid the child to play with dolls.

     b. teach her to use feminine wiles to get along in a man's world.

   c. insist that she go into a traditionally "male" field such as engineering.

   (d.) praise her daughter for her achievements and not for her looks.

Writing in the Margins

These questions encourage you to think not just about the essay but about the issues it raises. Your instructor may ask you to write down your answers, to discuss them in groups, or simply to think about them for class discussion.

1. In what ways does Barbie present an unrealistic image of women? Are there also toys that present an unrealistic image of men? Do you think these toys can harm the self-image of young girls or boys?

2. Tucker says that the messages that parents send with their own words and behavior overshadow any messages a toy could send. What example does Tucker give of a positive parental message? Which of her examples shows a negative parental message? Can you think of your own examples, both positive and negative?

3. In paragraph 9, Tucker uses the term *trophy wife.* Think about the meaning of the term *trophy,* and then write a sentence defining the term *trophy wife.* What does the term imply about a man's reasons for choosing the woman he marries?

4. Who are some of our cultural icons? What does each say about the things we value as a society?

Topics for Writing

Assignment 1: A Favorite Toy

Paragraph or Journal Entry

What was your favorite toy when you were a child? Write a paragraph or journal entry explaining what made it so special. This task will involve not just a description of the toy, but a description of how it made you feel. Did it capture your imagination, encourage one of your special talents, or take you to a fantasy world? Discuss.

Assignment 2: A Child's Self-Worth

Paragraph

What specific steps would you take as a parent to ensure that your child grew up with a healthy sense of self-worth? Write a paragraph outlining and explaining each step.

Assignment 3: Making Barbie Realistic

Paragraph or Essay

If Barbie's beauty, her fashionable wardrobe, and her dream house and car present an unrealistic image, then what would a reality-based Barbie be like? In a paragraph or essay, describe what her appearance, clothing, and accessories would be like if she were truly realistic.

Assignment 4: Stereotypes

Paragraph or Essay

A *stereotype* is a kind of misjudgment that attributes negative (and occasionally, positive) characteristics to a group of people simply because they are of a particular age, gender, religion, race, or socioeconomic group. Can you think of a television show, toy, video game, music video, or advertisement that presents a certain group of people (women, men, teenagers, members of a particular ethnic group, members of a particular profession) in a way that is narrow, stereotypical, or damaging? Write a paragraph or essay describing three of these stereotyped shows, toys, or advertisements.

Living at Warp Speed

Michael Ashcraft

With all of the labor-saving devices we have, why is it that we still don't get any rest? Michael Ashcraft explores the issue.

1   It's a given these days that practically everyone on the planet is way too busy for his or her own good. We set up unreal expectations of what we can accomplish in any twenty-four-hour period, then beat ourselves up and stress out about not getting it all done.

2   It's become almost a badge of honor to be busier than is humanly possible. To express a desire to slow down is blasphemy—like the ravings of some sort of sluggard, obviously an underachiever.

3   Is this the fruit of our success? I thought the whole idea of the technological revolution was for machines to work faster and more efficiently so that we could work less, or at least less frantically. And then we'd use this extra time for leisure and life enrichment.

4   But just the opposite seems to have happened. We've worked our ethics into a frenzy. Whenever machines buy us time, we don't save the time for living. Instead, we spend it trying to get more work out of it, leaving us even less room to live than before.

5   And somehow, this overachieving mindset is seen as socially acceptable. In fact, some companies now offer employees the alleged "benefit" of services that will buy greeting cards, gifts and other personally thoughtful items for alleged "loved" ones, so that employees can keep right on working—free from the distractions of spouses and kids.

6   Granted, many secretaries have been doing this sort of thing for years for male executives who couldn't pick their kids out of a lineup. But now the busy-busy mindset is not limited by gender.

7   You don't even have to be employed. People outside the paid workforce also are feeling the pressure to overbook their daily flights.

8   You see it in stay-at-home mothers racing to find the right size of plastic foam for the school project on the way to soccer practice in between church meetings, all the while working out, making supper and remodeling the kitchen.

9   We're not only doing this to our adult selves, mind you. By perpetually screaming "GET IN THE CAR WE'RE LATE FOR . . . ," we're also programming this warp speed into our children.

Here's perhaps the most alarming sign of just how far the infection has spread: 10
Some of the busiest, most overbooked people I know are "retired."

And the sad thing is, I don't think most people are happy about the break-   11
neck pace at which we live. You can see it in a subtle shift in what was once an
innocuous social exchange.

Go ahead. Ask someone, "How are you today?"   12

It used to be, people would say something like, "I'm fine, thank you," even if   13
that wasn't exactly true. But now, at best, the answer you often get is a hesitant,
"Well, I'm keeping up."

And too many times what you get is someone going on and on about how   14
busy he or she is—as though anyone really wants to hear all the stuff someone
else has to do.

And even if you did want to hear about someone else's impossibly hectic   15
schedule, who on earth would have the time to listen?

Building Vocabulary

For each question, choose the meaning that most closely defines the italicized
word or phrase as it is used in the essay.

1. The word *blasphemy* most nearly means
   a. irreverence.
   b. natural.
   c. honorable.
   d. an everyday occurrence.

2. The word *sluggard* most nearly means
   a. a lazy person.
   b. a crazy person.
   c. an energetic person.
   d. an argumentative person.

3. The word *alleged* most nearly means
   a. social.
   b. useful.
   c. recalled.
   d. so-called.

4. The word *innocuous* most nearly means
   a. formal.
   b. harmless.
   c. meaningful.
   d. impressive.

5. The word *hectic* most nearly means
   a. impossible.
   b. rigid.
   c. busy.
   d. serene.

Understanding the Essay

1. A good alternative title for the essay would be
   a. "The Modern Search for Serenity."
   b. "The Hectic Pace of Modern Life."
   c. "How to Live a More Balanced Life."
   d. "The Effects of Technology on Modern Life."

2. According to Ashcraft, the technological revolution
   a. has been beneficial because it has increased productivity.
   b. has freed Americans with labor-saving devices and allowed them more leisure.
   c. has enabled Americans to use their minds instead of their hands.
   d. has led to less leisure instead of more.

3. From the statement "Some companies now offer employees the alleged 'benefit' of services that will buy greeting cards, gifts, and other personally thoughtful items for alleged 'loved' ones" (paragraph 5), you can infer that the author believes
   a. companies have come a long way from the oppressive working conditions that existed during the early Industrial Revolution.
   b. buying services for employees is an example of corporate generosity toward employees.
   c. the service benefits the company more than it does the employee, and besides, loved ones deserve a personally selected gift.
   d. the modern world is changing, and employees may as well change with it.

4. According to the essay, the symptoms of the modern time crunch affect
   a. those who are employed.
   b. retired people, stay-at-home-mothers, and children.
   c. senior citizens and parents.
   d. all of the above.

5. According to the author, how do people feel about the hectic pace of life?
   a. Most people are unhappy about it.
   b. Most people view it as a necessary evil and try not to let it bother them.

    c. People who are motivated view it as a challenge to be met.

    d. A fast pace is so much a part of modern life that no one notices it anymore.

Writing in the Margins

These questions encourage you to think not just about the essay but about the issues it raises. Your instructor may ask you to write down your answers, to discuss them in groups, or simply to think about them for class discussion.

1. Are full-time college students more pressured or less pressured than people who hold full-time jobs? Why?

2. List some factors that make modern life hectic. What changes would need to occur in the workplace and in society to slow down the pace?

3. Discuss some of the "labor-saving devices" that modern Americans take for granted. What kind of labor, specifically, does each device save us?

4. Ashcraft suggests that labor-saving devices cause feelings of guilt. Do you believe that most Americans share a work ethic that drives them to more work and longer hours? Can you think of specific examples?

Topics for Writing

Assignment 1: Handling Stress

Paragraph or Journal Entry

Write a paragraph or journal entry discussing the ways that you handle stress. Alternatively, write a paper giving your reader advice on how to handle stress.

Assignment 2: Out of the Rat Race?

Paragraph

Some people long for the simple life. They envision themselves and their families living on a small plot of land, growing their own vegetables, and living free of the rat race. Is the simple life a part of your dream, or do you prefer the rat race? Write a paragraph giving reasons for your preference.

Assignment 3: Technology Rationing

Paragraph or Essay

The twentieth century put within the reach of most Americans many labor-saving devices and other technologies that we now take for granted: telephones, computers, coffee makers, washing machines, televisions, CD players, and automobiles, to name a few. If you could keep only one of your modern conveniences, which would it be? Write a paragraph or essay giving your reasons.

Assignment 4: A Day in the Life . . .

Paragraph or Essay

Does your typical day unfold in a leisurely manner, or are you on an endless treadmill of activity? Write a narrative paragraph or essay describing a typical day in your life.

Recipe for a Sick Society

Donna Britt

How can we foil those pesky do-gooders and make kids violent in the process? Donna Britt has some answers.

1 Just for laughs, let's pretend. Say we wanted to create, in a relatively peaceful society, a nation of youthful killers or just millions of aggressive young jerks. How could we do it?

2 We'd have to start young. Analyzing infants, we'd realize their desperate need for love and intimacy. We would also note that a baby's only real job is to study, digest and mimic everything he or she encounters.

3 Then we'd go to work.

4 We'd create an economy where in most families, both parents needed to work outside the home to survive. Soon after birth, babies would be placed with caregivers who would tend to their basic needs.

5 Working moms and dads would remain on the job for ever-increasing hours. Their "free" time at home would be eaten up by paying bills, cooking, cleaning, helping with homework and finishing work uncompleted at the job. Relaxed time with kids? Rare to nonexistent.

6 Even so, many children would still receive considerable love and attention, especially at home. To minimize that, we could design, say, an electronic box that beamed seductive, violent images—fistfights, beatings, rapes and murders into every dwelling.

7 A few troublesome kids would realize such images are fiction. So we would invent "news shows" highlighting real-life mayhem from local, national and even international sources. The box could also provide "talk shows" on which real people aired their problems before slapping, kicking and otherwise attacking one another as audiences cheered.

8 But this might fail to make enough kids violent. So what if we invented strikingly realistic visual "games" for use on the box? Using the games, children could shoot, impale or beat to death lifelike images of people and monsters.

9 Some pesky parents would, of course, limit their kids' exposure to the box and the games. To deal with that, we could create public living rooms. Here, kids could share with strangers the thrill of experiencing—on gigantic screens complete with sophisticated sound systems—vivid moving images of stabbings, garrotings, explosions and dismemberments. No one killed would be

mourned for more than a minute; every death would be as choreographed as a ballet. Killjoys might try to keep small children from seeing these images, but we'd get around that by making versions of the images available to be seen later on the box.

In certain parts of the country, rural and urban, we could glorify guns, make   10 folks think they can't live without firearms. Then we could make it relatively easy for anyone, even kids, to get them.

Still not enough? What if we did something with music? We could somehow   11 attach violent, materialistic or overtly sexualized images to music. We could per-suade certain music-makers to celebrate guns, greed and irresponsible sex in their songs! They, too, could provide images for the box—of threatening-looking men and barely dressed women, all singing about the glories of instant, consequence-free gratification of every urge.

In schools, we could avoid offering any classes in conflict resolution, rela-   12 tionship building or tolerance. We could stage "sporting events" in which young athletes' viciousness is accepted, even encouraged.

To be sure kids got the pro-violence message, we adults could pretend to   13 abhor brutishness. We could bemoan violence ceaselessly in the media, and feign astonishment each time a youngster assaulted or killed someone. "How could this happen?" we'd wail after each brutality.

With straight faces, we could present shows on the box about "Children Who   14 Kill," write shocked editorials, swear to "get to the bottom" of the problem. Then, *we wouldn't change a thing*.

So. If a society actually did those crazy things, would kids—not every kid, but   15 way too many of them—behave in frighteningly aggressive ways?

Maybe. But what intelligent, caring culture could be that stupid?   16

Building Vocabulary

For each question, choose the meaning that most closely defines the italicized word or phrase as it is used in the essay.

1. The word *seductive* most nearly means
   a. alluring.
   b. repulsive.
   c. simple.
   d. sexual.

2. The word *mayhem* most nearly means
   a. maybe.
   b. violence.
   c. politics.
   d. news.

3. The word *choreographed* most nearly means
   a. gruesome.
   b. peaceful.
   c. spontaneous.
   (d.) planned.

4. The word *materialistic* most nearly means
   (a.) dealing with the things money can buy.
   b. having to do with matters of the heart.
   c. spiritual.
   d. realistic.

5. The word *gratification* most nearly means
   (a.) satisfaction.
   b. denial.
   c. punishment.
   d. longing.

Understanding the Essay

1. Britt's *stated* purpose (not her implied purpose) is
   a. to prevent violence.
   (b.) to tell the reader how to create a nation of aggressive youth.
   c. to show how the media corrupt youth.
   d. to describe a peaceful society.

2. Which statement best expresses the *implied* main idea of the essay?
   a. Our society is relatively peaceful and is likely to remain that way.
   b. By following a few simple steps, we can create a society of violent youth.
   (c.) Inadequate parental attention and violence on television, in movies, and in video games is fostering violence in young people.
   d. Serious problems in the economic structure of the United States are leading to the breakdown of the family.

3. The economy that Britt describes in paragraphs 4 and 5 is
   a. an entirely fictional example.
   b. the economy of the United States in the 1950s.
   (c.) the economy of the United States today.
   d. the economy of a country less prosperous than the United States.

4. According to the essay, "troublesome kids" are the ones who
   (a.) can tell the difference between television and real life.
   b. perform violent acts and sometimes even kill.

   c. do not take school seriously enough.

   d. play violent video games.

5. In paragraph 14, the author implies that those who write editorials and swear to get to the bottom of the problem of youth violence are
    a. misguided, because violence is natural.
    b. sincere and well-meaning.
    c. effective, because they make people think.
    d. hypocritical, because no action is taken.

Writing in the Margins

These questions encourage you to think not just about the essay but about the issues it raises. Your instructor may ask you to write down your answers, to discuss them in groups, or simply to think about them for class discussion.

1. Britt's essay is a form of *satire.* Satire is a type of writing that seeks to change society by holding its practices and customs up to ridicule. Notice, too, how Britt poses as an outsider to society, pretending to come up with ideas that are already an ingrained part of our culture. What customs does Britt invite her readers to see as ridiculous? What changes do you think she would like to see in society?

2. Do you believe that violence on television, in video games, and in music videos can encourage violent behavior in young people?

3. How big a problem is violence in American society? What can be done to stop it?

Topics for Writing

Assignment 1: Close to Home

Paragraph or Journal Entry

Write a paragraph or journal entry telling how violence has touched your life or the life of someone you know.

Assignment 2: Violence Czar

Paragraph

You have just been appointed violence czar. Your budget is unlimited, and you have complete freedom to devise a plan and try it out for a year. You may call on any advisers and use any resources you wish, and you may try anything as long as it is within the law and does not violate the Constitution of the United States. Whom would you consult? What would you do? How would you reduce violence in the United States? Write a paragraph describing the steps you would take if you were the violence czar.

Assignment 3: Seeds of Violence

Paragraph or Essay

In a paragraph or essay, discuss some of the causes of violence in American society.

Assignment 4: A Satire

Paragraph or Essay

Write a satire modeled after Britt's. Take the position of outsider and write a paragraph or essay about a problem that exists in your school, in your workplace, in your city, or in society in general. If you wish, use Britt's method and give a recipe for homelessness, racism, apathy, or whatever problem you choose to discuss.

Don't Blame Me! The New "Culture of Victimization"

John J. Macionis

Is America becoming a nation of people who refuse to take responsibility? Sociologist John J. Macionis weighs the evidence.

A New York man recently leaped in front of a moving subway train; lucky enough to survive, he sued the city, claiming the train failed to stop in time to prevent his serious injuries. (A court awarded him $650,000.) In Washington, D.C., after realizing that he had been videotaped smoking crack cocaine in a hotel room, the city's mayor blamed his woman companion for "setting him up" and charged that the police were racially motivated in arresting him. After more than a dozen women accused former Senator Bob Packwood of sexual harassment, he tried to defuse the scandal by checking into an alcohol treatment center. In the most celebrated case of its kind, Dan White, who gunned down the mayor of San Francisco and a city council member, blamed this violent episode on insanity caused by having eaten too much junk food (the so-called Twinkie defense). In each of these cases, someone denies personal responsibility for an action, claiming to be a victim. Rather than taking the blame for our mishaps and misdeeds, in other words, more and more members of our society are pointing the finger elsewhere. Such behavior has prompted sociologist Irving Horowitz to announce a developing "culture of victimization" in which "everyone is a victim" and "no one accepts responsibility for anything." 1

One indication of this cultural trend is the proliferation of "addictions," a term that people once associated only with uncontrollable drug use. We now hear about gambling addicts, compulsive overeaters, sex addicts, and even people who excuse mounting credit-card debts as shopping addiction. Bookstores overflow with manuals to help people come to terms with numerous new medical or psychological conditions ranging from "The Cinderella Complex" to "The Casanova Complex" and even "Soap Opera Syndrome." And the U.S. courts are ever more clogged by lawsuits driven by the need to blame someone—and often to collect big money—for the kind of misfortune that we used to accept as part of life. 2

What's going on here? Is U.S. culture changing? Historically, our way of life has been based on a culture of "rugged individualism," the notion that people are responsible for whatever triumph or tragedy befalls them. But this value has been eroded by a number of factors. First, everyone is more aware (partly through 3 the work of sociologists) of how society shapes our lives. This knowledge has expanded the categories of people claiming to be victims well beyond those who have suffered historical disadvantages (such as African Americans and women) to include even well-off people. On college campuses, moreover, a sense that "everybody gets special treatment but us" is prompting white males to view themselves as the latest "victims."

Second, since they began advertising their services in 1977, lawyers have encouraged a sense of injustice among clients they hope to shepherd into court. The number of million-dollar lawsuit awards has risen more than twenty-five-fold in the last twenty-five years.   4

Third, there has been a proliferation of "rights groups" that promote what Amitai Etzioni calls "rights inflation." Beyond the traditional constitutional liberties are many newly claimed rights, including those of hunters (as well as those of animals), the rights of smokers (and nonsmokers), the right of women to control their bodies (and the rights of the unborn), the right to own a gun (and the right to be safe from violence). Expanding and competing claims for unmet rights, then, generate victims (and victimizers) on all sides.   5

Does this shift signal a fundamental realignment in our culture? Perhaps, but the new popularity of being a victim also springs from some well-established cultural forces. For example, the claim to victimization depends on a long-standing belief that everyone has the right to life, liberty, and the pursuit of happiness. Yet this new explosion of "rights" does more than alert us to clear cases of injustice; it threatens to erode our sense of responsibility as members of a larger society.   6

Building Vocabulary

For each question, choose the meaning that most closely defines the italicized word or phrase as it is used in the essay.

1. The word *defuse* most nearly means
   a. inflame.
   b. detonate.
   c. worsen.
   d. ease.

2. The word *celebrated* most nearly means
   a. condemned.
   b. publicized.
   c. suppressed.
   d. cheered.

3. The word *shepherd* most nearly means
   a. graze.
   b. farm.

    (c.) guide.

    d. fleece.

4. The phrase *more than twenty-five-fold* most nearly means

    a. twenty-five.

    b. more than twenty-five.

    (c.) more than the original number times twenty-five.

    d. less than twenty-five.

5. The word *proliferation* most nearly means

    (a.) rapid growth.

    b. profit.

    c. decrease.

    d. fantasy.

Understanding the Essay

1. Which statement most nearly expresses the main idea of the essay?

    a. People in our society no longer allow their rights to be trampled on by others.

    b. People often claim to be addicts or victims of disease rather than blaming themselves for their troubles.

    (c.) Increasingly, people are avoiding responsibility by blaming their woes on outside factors.

    d. People who eat junk food are apt to commit violent crimes.

2. The "culture of victimization" is characterized by

    a. refusal to accept responsibility.

    b. a prevalence of "addictions."

    c. lawsuits.

    (d.) all of the above.

3. The author implies that African Americans and women

    a. are among the most vocal in claiming their rights.

    (b.) have more reason to call themselves victims than some other groups.

    c. are the only groups that have any right to claim they are victims.

    d. are less likely to think of themselves as victims than other groups.

4. A driver runs a red light while talking on a cell phone and hits a pedestrian. If the driver were a "rugged individualist," what would he say to the pedestrian?

    a. "Get up, Pilgrim; it's only a scratch."

    b. "I will take full responsibility for your hospital bills as soon as I sue my cell phone company."

c. "What are *you* whining about? As a color-blind male, I am discriminated against by the red light/green light traffic signal system. Good
thing I have this cell phone to call my lawyer."

(d.) "I'm sorry. It was my fault."

5. The author believes that the "rights explosion"

a. signals a shift in our cultural ideals.

b. has roots that stretch back as far as the Declaration of Independence.

c. is a threat to our sense of responsibility.

(d.) all of the above.

Writing in the Margins

These questions encourage you to think not just about the essay but about the
issues it raises. Your instructor may ask you to write down your answers, to discuss them in groups, or simply to think about them for class discussion.

1. Do you see evidence of the "rights explosion" that the author discusses?
What are some of the advantages and disadvantages of the focus on individual rights?

2. Many people criticize the explosion of frivolous lawsuits and astronomical
monetary awards in our society. Do you agree that this kind of problem
has increased? To what do you attribute the problem?

3. When applied to behavior, are the words *addiction, complex,* and *syndrome*
likely to increase or decrease an individual's sense of responsibility? Why?

Topics for Writing

Assignment 1: Rabbit or Coyote?

Paragraph or Journal Entry

What are the advantages and disadvantages of seeing oneself as a victim? As a
"rugged individualist"? Explain in a paragraph or journal entry.

Assignment 2: The Rights Explosion

Paragraph

Do you believe the "rights explosion" has gotten out of hand? Write a paragraph
giving specific examples to support your answer.

Assignment 3: Rights and Responsibilities

Paragraph or Essay

It has been said that every right we gain brings with it a corresponding responsibility. Following are some rights that citizens of the United States take for granted.

In a paragraph or essay, discuss one of these rights and the corresponding responsibilities that go along with it.

having children	attending school
driving	expressing an opinion
choosing a career	choosing where to live
voting	choosing a mate

Assignment 4: "Certain Unalienable Rights"

Paragraph or Essay

In the Declaration of Independence, Thomas Jefferson wrote that, simply by virtue of being born, everyone has "certain unalienable rights"—that is, rights that cannot simply be taken away at the whim of government. Jefferson listed "life, liberty, and the pursuit of happiness" among those rights. What right or rights do you believe every human being should have? Write a paragraph or essay explaining your choice(s).

Assignment 5: Judgment Day

Paragraph, Journal Entry, or Essay

Macionis points out that lawsuits are common in our society. Imagine that you are a judge appointed to decide one of the following lawsuits. As a judge, you must approach each objectively, without assuming they are "frivolous lawsuits" of the kind Macionis discusses. Like any collection of lawsuits, some of the examples will have more merit than others. Pick any of the four cases and write a paragraph, journal entry, or essay giving your decision as a judge and your reasons for the decision.

Lawsuit A: The Case of the Nonsinging Server

A woman takes a job as a server in a restaurant. After she accepts the job, she finds that if a customer is celebrating a birthday, all servers are required to gather around the table and sing. She explains to her manager that her religion does not celebrate holidays or birthdays, and she does not feel right about singing to celebrate a customer's birthday. The manager understands and excuses her from the requirement, but when a new shift manager is hired six months later, the employee is told she will be fired if she does not join in the songs. She refuses to sing and is fired. She sues, claiming she has been discriminated against on the basis of her religion. The restaurant's lawyers argue that like any other employee, she is subject to firing if she cannot perform all the duties of the job.

Lawsuit B: The Case of the Harassed Designer

Shortly after earning his degree in graphic arts design, Dan is hired by an advertising agency. His boss takes him under her wing, giving him plum projects, a corner office, and special attention. But one evening, as they are working late, the attention becomes a bit *too* special. When Dan tells his boss he is not interested in a sexual relationship, she immediately apologizes for stepping over the line. Though his boss never again approaches him sexually, one year later, Dan's office is a converted janitor's closet, and he is working on routine jobs usually assigned to administrative assistants rather than graphic designers. In a year when average raises are 7 percent, Dan's raise is 1 percent. Dan files a sexual harassment lawsuit for one million dollars. The company's lawyers say that since the boss apologized and since Dan still has his job, his complaint is not valid.

Lawsuit C: The Case of the Bungled Burglary

A family goes on vacation, and Tom, a burglar, attempts to break in. Sturdy burglar bars cover the window, and the house is wired with an alarm system. But Tom goes up on the roof, intending to let himself in through a skylight. Instead, he falls off the roof and breaks several bones. Tom later files a lawsuit for $500,000 for medical expenses and pain and suffering. The lawyer for the vacationing homeowner argues that since the injuries were sustained during an attempted felony, the burglar is entitled to nothing.

Lawsuit D: The Case of the Overweight Achiever

Sally, president of the Math Club and a member of the Debate Team at the small college she attends, has finished all of her academic course work with a 4.0 average and has passed two physical education classes: bowling and first aid, with a C and an A. However, she has failed a third required course, jogging and fitness, three times. No matter how hard she tries, her weight will not allow her to do enough pushups and situps or jog a mile quickly enough to pass the "basic physical requirement" section of the course. After unsuccessful appeals to the head of the Physical Education Department and the college's administration to allow her to fulfill the course requirements in some other way, Sally sues the college for five million dollars. Her lawyer argues that the college's rigid physical education policies discriminate against people who have a genetic tendency toward obesity. However, Sally says that she is not really interested in the money. She is willing to settle for the right to fulfill the requirements of the course in another way so that she can complete her degree. The college's lawyers argue that Sally is simply being asked to fulfill the same requirements as all other students and that if she cannot complete those requirements, she should not be awarded a degree.

One for the Books

Rheta Grimsley Johnson

Some predict that as computers become more prevalent, books will gradually disappear. Rheta Grimsley Johnson weighs the issue.

In 1875 the folks at Remington asked Mark Twain to write a <u>testimonial</u> for their new typewriter. Here's how he answered: 1

"Please do not use my name in any way. Please do not even divulge the fact that I own a machine. I have entirely stopped using the Type Writer for the reason that I never could write a letter with it to anybody without receiving a request by return mail that I would not only describe the machine but state what progress I had made in the use of it. . . . I don't like to write letters, and so I don't want people to know that I own this curiosity breeding little joker." 2

Twain's main complaint was that the typewriter's novelty caused people to ignore the content of his letters. Technology overshadowed genius. The "curiosity breeding little joker" had become more important than the dictation of one of the great brains of the last century. 3

I found that <u>anecdote</u> in a paperback called *The Typewriter Legend,* on sale for a pittance at my local library. 4

It was an ink smudge of a February day, dark and messy, and so I trotted on down to the book sale. Cheap books call out to me like "Night Train" to a wino. I love the feel of used volumes, the esoteric titles that inevitably end up in card-board boxes labeled "SALE BOOKS." 5

In all, I bought about one thousand pages of words for ten dollars. That's a lot of pages, a lot of words. I got Robert Penn Warren's long poem, "Chief Joseph of the Nez Perce," and a book of Herblock cartoons and a stack of children's books for my niece and nephews. All the way home I congratulated myself for enterprise and frugality. 6

If you believe the <u>shibboleths</u> of today's high-tech boosters, the screen has replaced the book as the symbol, the literal repository, the ultimate source of most knowledge. After centuries of use, the book's spine and pages have been replaced with electronic scrolls. 7

But you cannot do with a screen what I've been doing the past few days with Jacki Lyden's memoir, *Daughter of the Queen of Sheba.* At least not without a lot of trouble and miles of extension cord. 8

Sheba has gone to bed with me, and to Pollard's Drive-In, where I sat at the raggedy lunch counter and alternated turning pages and eating turnip greens. I read a few pages while soaking in a hot tub. 9

The typewriter—this according to my new, old book on the machine—became   10
truly important only after becoming so <u>ubiquitous</u> that it was invisible. That will have
to happen to computers, too. Otherwise, <u>novelty</u> will continue to overwhelm content.
We'll all be doing things on computers not because we need to, but because we can.

I studied my fellow booklovers at the library sale. We didn't look special, or en-   11
dangered. There were noisy children, out of school for Presidents Day. There was a
retired man, searching for books on the Civil War. There was a skinny teenager, checking out the hobby section. A tough-looking woman in jeans picked up a book called
Filing for Divorce in Georgia and said to her son, "I wish I'd had this a few years ago."

All of us could have gone into the next room and surfed the Net for free, I   12
suppose, but we wouldn't have left with a satisfying sack, a collection of cover-
less volumes branded with other owners' names and stamped at the back with ink
from the pad of some efficient librarian. "DISCARD," they say.

Not yet. Not quite yet.   13

Building Vocabulary

For each question, choose the meaning that most closely defines the word or
phrase as it is used in the essay.

1. The word *testimonial* most nearly means
    a. recommendation.
    b. description.
    c. book.
    d. last will and testament.

2. The word *anecdote* most nearly means
    a. antidote.
    b. story that makes a point.
    c. story that rambles.
    d. page.

3. The word *shibboleths* most nearly means
    a. expensive computers.
    b. widely held ideas.
    c. books.
    d. symbols.

4. The word *ubiquitous* most nearly means
    a. widespread.
    b. transparent.
    c. scarce.
    d. cheap.

5. The word *novelty* most nearly means
   a. thoughtfulness.
   b. anything relating to a book.
   c. computer programming.
   d. the attraction of something new.

Understanding the Essay

1. Which statement best expresses the main idea of the essay?
   a. According to computer experts, computers are becoming a replacement for books.
   b. Inexpensive books can often be found at library book sales.
   c. Computers are useful tools, but—at least so far—they cannot replace books.
   d. Mark Twain was one of the first to use a typewriter, but he did not want to give a testimonial for it.

2. Johnson includes the story about Mark Twain because
   a. Twain is a much-beloved American author.
   b. Twain was one of the first well-known people to use a typewriter.
   c. she sees similarities in people's reactions to typewriters in Twain's day and to computers today.
   d. she knows that typewriters and computers serve similar functions in writing.

3. When Johnson writes "cheap books call out to me like 'Night Train' to a wino" (paragraph 5), she means that
   a. winos are often well-read individuals.
   b. she enjoys feeding her addiction to books without spending much money.
   c. Night Train is her beverage of choice when she reads books.
   d. she does not have enough money to pay full price for books.

4. Which of the following is *not* mentioned as something the author could do with a book but not with a computer?
   a. take it to bed
   b. turn down the pages to mark her place
   c. visit a restaurant
   d. relax in a hot tub

5. The people at the book sale Johnson went to were
   a. all ages and of diverse interests.
   b. mostly older people on limited incomes.

    c. children out of school for Presidents Day.

    d. people who were not likely to be computer literate.

Writing in the Margins

These questions encourage you to think not just about the essay but about the issues it raises. Your instructor may ask you to write down your answers, to discuss them in groups, or simply to think about them for class discussion.

1. Do you see any evidence that computers are taking the place of books, magazines, and newspapers? If so, what is the evidence? On the other hand, is there evidence that books, magazines, and newspapers are flourishing despite computers?

2. What are some of the ways that computers have changed libraries?

3. Is there a place in education (and in the lives of most Americans) for both books and computers? How are their functions separate? How do they overlap?

Topics for Writing

Assignment 1: Autobiography of a Reader

Paragraph or Journal Entry

Write a paragraph or journal entry detailing your lifelong experience with books and reading. Since you can't do justice to your entire reading life in a paragraph, try describing a typical memory about reading, an incident that involved reading, or your reading habits in three different stages of your life.

Assignment 2: Computers for Research

Paragraph

Write a paragraph discussing the advantages and disadvantages of using a computer for research instead of relying on traditional printed matter.

Assignment 3: Bargain Basement

Paragraph or Essay

For the author of "One for the Books," part of the thrill of the library sale was getting a bargain. Do you enjoy shopping at flea markets, secondhand stores, or yard sales? Write a paragraph or essay telling why or why not.

Assignment 4: "Paging" Yourself

Paragraph or Essay

What kinds of reading material do you prefer? Why? Answer in a paragraph or essay.

Civil Rites

Caroline Miller

Are good manners dead in the modern world, or will the next generation chart a new course for etiquette? Maybe there's hope, says Caroline Miller.

1 I was taking my kids to school not long ago when I had one of those experiences particular to parents—a moment that nobody else notices, but that we replay over and over because in it we see something new about our children.

2 On this morning the bus was standing-room-only as we squeezed on at our regular stop. Several blocks later my son, Nick, found a free seat halfway back on one side of the bus and his little sister, Elizabeth, and I took seats on the other.

3 I was listening to Lizzie chatter on about something when I was surprised to see Nick get up. I watched as he said something quietly to an older, not quite grandmotherly woman who didn't look familiar to me. Suddenly I understood: He was offering her his seat.

4 A little thing, but still I was flooded with gratitude. For all the times we have talked about what to do and what not to do on the bus—say "Excuse me," cover your mouth when you cough, don't point, don't stare at people who are unusual looking—this wasn't something I had trained him to do. It was a small act of gallantry, and it was entirely his idea.

5 For all we try to show our kids and tell them how we believe people should act, how we hope *they* will act, it still comes as a shock and a pleasure—a relief, frankly—when they do something that suggests they understand. All the more so because in the world in which Nick is growing up, the rules that govern social interaction are so much more ambiguous than they were when we were his age. Kids are exposed to a free-for-all of competing signals about what's acceptable, let alone what's admirable. It's a world, after all, in which *in your face* is the style of the moment. Civility has become a more or less elusive proposition.

6 I was reminded of this incident on the train the other day, on another crowded morning, as I watched a young man in an expensive suit slip into an open seat without so much as losing his place in the *New York Times,* smoothly beating out a silver-haired gentleman and a gaggle of young women in spike heels.

7 My first thought was that his mother would be ashamed of him. And then I thought, with some amusement, that I am hopelessly behind the times. For all I know, the older man would've been insulted to be offered a seat by someone two or three decades his junior. And the women, I suppose, might consider chivalry a

sexist custom. Besides, our young executive or investment banker probably had to compete with women for the job that's keeping him in Italian loafers; why would he want to offer a potential competitor a seat?

Of course, this sort of confusion is about much more than etiquette on public transportation. It's about what we should do for each other, and expect of each other, now that our roles are no longer closely dictated by whether we are male or female, young or old. 8

Not for a minute do I mourn the demise of the social contract that gave men most of the power and opportunity, and women most of the seats on the bus. But operating without a contract can be uncomfortable, too. It's as if nobody quite knows how to behave anymore; the lack of predictability on all fronts has left all our nerve endings exposed. And the confusion extends to everything from deciding who goes through the door first to who initiates sex. 9

Under the circumstances, civility requires a good deal more imagination than it once did, if only because it's so much harder to know what the person sitting across from you—whether stranger or spouse—expects, needs, wants from you. When you don't have an official rulebook, you have to listen harder, be more sensitive, be ready to improvise. 10

But of course improvising is just what Americans do best. And unlike the European model, our particular form of civility here in the former colonies aims to be democratic, to bridge our diverse histories with empathy and respect. At a moment when so many people are clamoring for attention, and so many others are nursing their wounds, the need for empathy and respect is rather acute. 11

And so, as we encourage our children to define themselves actively, to express themselves with confidence, we hope they will also learn to be generous—with those they don't know, as well as with those they love. And we hope they will care enough, and be observant enough, to be able to tell when someone else needs a seat more than they do. 12

Building Vocabulary

For each question, choose the meaning that most closely defines the italicized word or phrase as it is used in the essay.

1. The word *gallantry* most nearly means
   a. love.
   b. defiance.
   c. courtesy.
   d. pettiness.

2. The word *ambiguous* most nearly means
   a. certain.
   b. demanding.

c. unclear.

d. competitive.

3. The word *demise* most nearly means

   a. death.

   b. establishment.

   c. understanding.

   d. law.

4. The word *improvise* most nearly means

   a. progress.

   b. follow a rigid code of conduct.

   c. conform.

   d. invent new solutions.

5. The word *acute* most nearly means

   a. urgent.

   b. accurate.

   c. charming.

   d. small.

Understanding the Essay

1. Miller's purpose in writing the essay is

   a. to impress the need for manners on a new generation.

   b. to compare the manners of a former age with those of today.

   c. to show how proud she is of her son.

   d. to point out that etiquette is more complex than it used to be.

2. On the bus, Miller's son Nick

   a. covers his mouth when he coughs.

   b. refuses to sit with Miller and her daughter.

   c. makes her ashamed.

   d. does something Miller had not trained him to do.

3. The author implies in paragraph 7 that the young man in the expensive suit

   a. may have been in tune with modern etiquette.

   b. was inexcusably rude.

   c. needed the seat more than the older man or the young women did.

   d. may have had a hidden disability.

4. According to the author, people in the modern world must

   a. look out for themselves and forget about etiquette.

   b. avoid being polite to competitors.

    c. be flexible and consider others' needs.

    d. return to the good manners of an earlier age.

5. Which of the following is *not* mentioned as a factor in the confusion over manners?

    a. Women's roles in society have changed.

    b. Parents do not adequately train their children.

    c. The modern style is "in your face."

    d. People find it harder to know what others want.

Writing in the Margins

These questions encourage you to think not just about the essay but about the issues it raises. Your instructor may ask you to write down your answers, to discuss them in groups, or simply to think about them for class discussion.

1. Are manners still important in the modern world?

2. Miller suggests that some older forms of etiquette might actually be offensive. Can you think of examples of etiquette you would find offensive, that would make you uncomfortable, or that are simply no longer useful?

3. One area of etiquette that is changing is dating etiquette. As recently as the 1960s and 1970s, for instance, asking for a date was usually the male's prerogative, as was paying for it. It would not be unlikely that he would hold the car door for his date, pull out her chair in the restaurant, and perhaps even order for her. Now, customs have changed, and the rules are less clear. Whose job do you believe it is to ask for the date? To pay for it? What is dating etiquette like today?

Topics for Writing

Assignment 1: Are Manners Obsolete?

Paragraph or Journal Entry

Are manners still necessary? Write a paragraph or journal entry explaining why or why not.

Assignment 2: Interview Etiquette

Paragraph

Write a paragraph describing the rules of etiquette a job candidate should follow to impress the interviewer.

Assignment 3: The Dating Game

Paragraph or Essay

If you could write the rules of etiquette for dating, what would they be, and why? Write a paragraph or essay discussing the most important rules and the reasons behind them.

Assignment 4: Classroom Manners

Paragraph or Essay

Write an example paragraph or essay classifying the types of mannerly or unmannerly behavior you observe in your college classes. (For help in constructing a classification paper, see Chapter 8.)

Conversational Ballgames

Nancy Masterton Sakamoto

For the author, conversing in English was easy, but Japanese conversation was a whole different ballgame.

After I was married and had lived in Japan for a while, my Japanese gradually improved to the point where I could take part in simple conversations with my husband and his friends and family. And I began to notice that often, when I joined in, the others would look startled, and the conversational topic would come to a halt. After this happened several times, it became clear to me that I was doing something wrong. But for a long time, I didn't know what it was.   1

Finally, after listening carefully to many Japanese conversations, I discovered what my problem was. Even though I was speaking Japanese, I was handling the conversation in a Western way.   2

Japanese-style conversations develop quite differently from Western-style conversations. And the difference isn't only in the languages. I realized that just as I kept trying to hold Western-style conversations even when I was speaking Japanese, so my English students kept trying to hold Japanese-style conversations even when they were speaking English. We were unconsciously playing entirely different conversational ballgames.   3

A Western-style conversation between two people is like a game of tennis. If I introduce a topic, a conversational ball, I expect you to hit it back. If you agree with me, I don't expect you simply to agree and do nothing more. I expect you to add something—a reason for agreeing, another example, or an elaboration to carry the idea further. But I don't expect you always to agree. I am just as happy if you question me, or challenge me, or completely disagree with me. Whether you agree or disagree, your response will return the ball to me.   4

And then it is my turn again. I don't serve a new ball from my original starting line. I hit your ball back again from where it has bounced. I carry your idea further, or answer your questions or objections, or challenge or question you. And so the ball goes back and forth, with each of us doing our best to give it a new twist, an original spin, or a powerful smash.   5

And the more vigorous the action, the more interesting and exciting the game. Of course, if one of us gets angry, it spoils the conversation, just as it spoils a tennis game. But getting excited is not at all the same as getting angry. After all, we are not trying to hit each other. We are trying to hit the ball. So long as we attack only each other's opinions, and do not attack each other   6 personally, we don't expect anyone to get hurt. A good conversation is supposed to be interesting and exciting.

If there are more than two people in the conversation, then it is like doubles in tennis or like volleyball. There's no waiting in line. Whoever is nearest and quickest hits the ball, and if you step back, someone else will hit it. No one stops the game to give you a turn. You're responsible for taking your own turn. 7

But whether it's two players or a group, everyone does his best to keep the ball going, and no one person has the ball for very long. 8

A Japanese-style conversation, however, is not at all like tennis or volleyball. It's like bowling. You wait for your turn. And you always know your place in line. It depends on such things as whether you are older or younger, a close friend or a relative stranger to the previous speaker, in a senior or junior position, and so on. 9

When your turn comes, you step up to the starting line with your bowling ball, and carefully bowl it. Everyone else stands back and watches politely, murmuring encouragement. Everyone waits until the ball has reached the end of the alley, and watches to see if it knocks down all the pins, or only some of them, or none of them. There is a pause, while everyone registers your score. 10

Then, after everyone is sure that you have completely finished your turn, the next person in line steps up to the same starting line, with a different ball. He doesn't return your ball, and he does not begin from where your ball stopped. There is no back and forth at all. All the balls run parallel. And there is always a suitable pause between turns. There is no rush, no excitement, no scramble for the ball. 11

No wonder everyone looked startled when I took part in Japanese conversations. I paid no attention to whose turn it was, and kept snatching the ball halfway down the alley and throwing it back at the bowler. Of course the conversation died. I was playing the wrong game. 12

This explains why it is almost impossible to get a Western-style conversation or discussion going with English students in Japan. I used to think that the problem was their lack of English language ability. But I finally came to realize that the biggest problem is that they, too, are playing the wrong game. 13

Whenever I serve a volleyball, everyone just stands back and watches it fall, with occasional murmurs of encouragement. No one hits it back. Everyone waits until I call on someone to take a turn. And when that person speaks, he doesn't hit my ball back. He serves a new ball. Again, everyone just watches it fall. 14

So I call on someone else. This person does not refer to what the previous speaker has said. He also serves a new ball. Nobody seems to have paid any attention to what anyone else has said. Everyone begins again from the same starting line, and all the balls run parallel. There is never any back and forth. Everyone is trying to bowl with a volleyball. 15

And if I try a simpler conversation, with only two of us, then the other person tries to bowl with my tennis ball. No wonder foreign English teachers in Japan get discouraged. 16

Now that you know about the difference in the conversational ballgames, you **17** may think that all your troubles are over. But if you have been trained all your life to play one game, it is no simple matter to switch to another, even if you know the rules. Knowing the rules is not at all the same thing as playing the game.

Even now, during a conversation in Japanese I will notice a startled reaction, **18** and belatedly realize that once again I have rudely interrupted by instinctively trying to hit back the other person's bowling ball. It is no easier for me to "just listen" during a conversation, than it is for my Japanese students to "just relax" when speaking with foreigners. Now I can truly sympathize with how hard they must find it to try to carry on a Western-style conversation. If I have not yet learned to do conversational bowling in Japanese, at least I have figured out one thing that puzzled me for a long time. After his first trip to America, my husband complained that Americans asked him so many questions and made him talk so much at the dinner table that he never had a chance to eat. When I asked him why he couldn't talk and eat at the same time, he said that Japanese do not customarily think that dinner, especially on fairly formal occasions, is a suitable time for extended conversation.

Since Westerners think that conversation is an indispensable part of dining, **19** and indeed would consider it impolite not to converse with one's dinner partner, I found this Japanese custom rather strange. Still, I could accept it as a cultural difference even though I didn't really understand it. But when my husband added, in explanation, that Japanese consider it extremely rude to talk with one's mouth full, I got confused. Talking with one's mouth full is certainly not an American custom. We think it very rude, too. Yet we still manage to talk a lot and eat at the same time. How do we do it?

For a long time, I couldn't explain it, and it bothered me. But after I dis- **20** covered the conversational ballgames, I finally found the answer. Of course! In a Western-style conversation, you hit the ball, and while someone else is hitting it back, you take a bite, chew, and swallow. Then you hit the ball again, and then eat some more. The more people there are in the conversation, the more chances you have to eat.

But even with only two of you talking, you still have plenty of chances to eat. **21**

Maybe that's why polite conversation at the dinner table has never been a **22** traditional part of Japanese etiquette. Your turn to talk would last so long without interruption that you'd never get a chance to eat.

Building Vocabulary

For each question, choose the meaning that most closely defines the italicized word or phrase as it is used in the essay.

1. The word *elaboration* most nearly means
   a. explanation.
   b. challenge.

   c. refusal to comment.

   d. simple agreement.

2. The word *previous* most nearly means

   a. later.

   b. earlier.

   c. effective.

   d. relative.

3. The word *registers* most nearly means

   a. specifies.

   b. votes on.

   c. writes down.

   d. takes in.

4. The word *instinctively* most nearly means

   a. automatically.

   b. rudely.

   c. deliberately.

   d. belatedly.

5. The word *indispensable* most nearly means

   a. needless.

   b. unpleasant.

   c. impolite.

   d. necessary.

Understanding the Essay

1. A good alternative title for this essay would be

   a. "Take Me Out to the Ballgame."

   b. "Japanese Conversational Style."

   c. "Two Cultures, Two Conversational Styles."

   d. "American Talk."

2. Which of the following statements best describes Sakamoto's occupation?

   a. She taught English to Japanese students.

   b. She was the athletic director at a Japanese school.

   c. She taught Japanese to English-speaking students.

   d. She was a student taking courses in Japan.

3. The primary pattern of development in this essay is

   a. cause-effect.

   b. definition.

     c. narration.

     (d.) comparison-contrast.

4. If Western conversation is like a tennis game, Japanese conversation is like

     a. volleyball.

     b. mixed doubles.

     (c.) bowling.

     d. baseball.

5. The author implies all of the following *except*

     a. her Japanese friends and in-laws were startled by her conversational style.

     b. knowing a language may not be enough to ensure good communication.

     c. rudeness may unintentionally result if one violates a culture's conversational style.

     (d.) American conversational style is superior because it is more lively.

Writing in the Margins

These questions encourage you to think not just about the essay but about the issues it raises. Your instructor may ask you to write down your answers, to discuss them in groups, or simply to think about them for class discussion.

1. In looking at the Japanese and American conversational styles, what do you see as the advantages and disadvantages of each?

2. From time to time, someone proposes a "universal language" that would enable people from different cultures to communicate more effectively. For example, Esperanto, a made-up language that is a blend of several languages, including Spanish and English, has been proposed as a language that would bridge all cultures if everyone would only learn it. What are the barriers that stand in the way of successfully carrying out such a proposal? If those barriers could be overcome, is a "universal second language" a good idea? What are some of its advantages and disadvantages?

Group Exercise 3

Form groups of three, four, or five and discuss the rules of a Japanese-style conversation as you understand them from the essay. Then, with the members of your group, try to hold a Japanese-style conversation. Then discuss the following questions as a class: Was it easy or difficult? Did anyone break the rules? What was difficult? What was fun? What seemed strange to you?

    A possible alternative activity is to have four or five volunteers from the class sit in a semicircle in front of the class and converse, Japanese-style, while the rest of the class observes. Be sure to outline the rules that the group will follow before the conversation starts.

Topics for Writing

Assignment 1: Communicating across Cultures

Paragraph or Journal Entry

Have you ever needed to communicate with someone whose language you could not speak or someone whose language you could speak only in a limited way? Write a paragraph or journal entry describing the barriers to communication and telling how you overcame (or tried to overcome) those barriers.

Assignment 2: Your Conversational Style

Paragraph

Conversational styles differ among individuals as well as cultures. Write a paragraph discussing the characteristics of your personal conversational style. Give specific supporting examples.

Assignment 3: Classifying Conversationalists

Paragraph or Essay

Write a paragraph or essay classifying people's conversational styles. Think of your own terms of classification or use some of the following terms. Be sure to explain or give examples of each particular style.

the steamroller	the egotist
the butterfly	the comedian
the echo	the snoop
the naysayer	the whiner

Assignment 4: Shocked by Your Style

Paragraph or Essay

Sakamoto describes the startled expressions on the faces of her Japanese friends when she interrupted a conversation. Have you ever met someone whose style—the way they spoke, looked, or acted—originally shocked you or put you off, but whom you later came to like and understand? Write a paragraph or essay about that person. Be sure to include an account of your first meeting; then tell what happened to change your mind about the person.

Alternatively, was one of your friends put off by your style at first? Describe your friend's initial reaction as well as the reasons for his or her change of heart.

I Wonder: Was It Me or Was It My Sari?

Shoba Narayan

The author had always tried to fit into the American way of life. Now, it was America's turn to adjust to her.

A sari for a month. It shouldn't have been a big deal but it was. After all, I had   1
grown up around sari-clad women in India. My mother even slept in one.

In India, saris are adult attire. After I turned 18, I occasionally wore a sari   2
for weddings and holidays and to the temple. But wearing a sequined silk sari to
an Indian party was one thing. Deciding to wear a sari every day while living in
New York, especially after 10 years in Western clothes, sounded outrageous, even
to me.

The sari is six yards of fabric folded into a graceful yet cumbersome garment.   3
Like a soufflé, it is fragile and can fall apart at any moment. When worn right, it
is supremely elegant and unabashedly feminine. However, it requires sacrifices.

No longer could I sprint across the street just before the light changed. The   4
sari forced me to shorten my strides. I couldn't squeeze into a crowded subway
car for fear that someone would accidentally pull and unravel my sari. I couldn't
balance four grocery bags in one hand and pull out my house keys from a convenient pocket with the other. By the end of the first week, I was lumbering around
my apartment, feeling clumsy and angry with myself. What was I trying to prove?

The notion of wearing a sari every day was relatively new for me. During my   5
college years—the age when most girls in India begin wearing saris regularly—I
was studying in America. As an art student at Mount Holyoke, I hung out with
purple-haired painters and rabble-rousing feminists wearing ink-stained khakis
and cut-off T-shirts. During a languid post-graduation summer in Boston, when
I sailed a boat and volunteered for an environmental organization, I wore politi-
cally correct, recycled Salvation Army clothes. After getting married, I became a
Connecticut housewife experimenting with clothes from Jones New York and Ann
Taylor. Through it all, I tried to pick up the accent, learn the jargon and affect
the posture of the Americans around me.

Then I moved to New York and became a mother. I wanted to teach my   6
3-year-old daughter Indian values and traditions because I knew she would be
profoundly different from her preschool classmates in religion (we are Hindus),

eating habits (we are vegetarians) and the festivals we celebrated. Wearing a sari every day was my way of showing her that she could melt into the pot while retaining her individual flavor.

It wasn't just for my daughter's sake that I decided to wear a sari. I was tired of trying to fit in. Natalie Cole had never spoken to me as eloquently as M.S., a venerable Indian singer. I couldn't sing the lyrics of Ricky Martin as easily as I could sing my favorite Hindi or Tamil songs. Much as I enjoyed American cuisine, I couldn't last four days without Indian food. It was time to flaunt my ethnicity with a sari and a bright red bindi on my forehead. I was going to be an immigrant, but on my own terms. It was America's turn to adjust to me.   **7**

Slowly, I eased into wearing the garment. Strangers stared at me as I sashayed across a crowded bookstore. Some of them caught my eye and smiled. At first, I resented being an exhibit. Then I wondered: perhaps I reminded them of a wonderful holiday in India or a favorite Indian cookbook. Grocery clerks enunciated their words when they spoke to me. Everywhere, I was stopped with questions about India as if wearing a sari had made me an authority. One Japanese lady near Columbus Circle asked to have her picture taken with me. A tourist had thought that I was one, too, just steps from my home.   **8**

But there were unexpected advantages. Indian cabdrivers raced across lanes and screeched to a halt in front of me when I stepped into the street to hail a taxi. When my daughter climbed high up the Jungle-Gym in Central Park, I gathered my sari and prepared to follow, hoping it wouldn't balloon out like Marilyn Monroe's dress. One of the dads standing nearby watched my plight and volunteered to climb after her. Chivalry in New York? Was it me or was it my sari?   **9**

Best of all, my family approved. My husband complimented me, my parents were proud of me. My daughter oohed and aahed when I pulled out my colorful saris. When I cuddled her in my arms, scents from the vetiver sachets that I used to freshen my sari at night escaped from the folds of cloth and soothed her to sleep. I felt part of a long line of Indian mothers who had rocked their babies this way.   **10**

Soon, the month was over. My self-imposed regimen was coming to an end. Instead of feeling liberated, I felt a twinge of unease. I had started enjoying my sari.   **11**

Saris were impractical for America, I told myself. I would continue to wear them, but not every day. It was time to revert to my sensible khakis. It was time to become American again.   **12**

Building Vocabulary

For each question, choose the meaning that most closely defines the italicized word or phrase as it is used in the essay.

1. The word *outrageous* most nearly means
   a. angry.
   b. wild and crazy.

    c. sensible.

    d. out of style.

2. The word *cumbersome* most nearly means

    (a.) hard to manage.

    b. easy to wear.

    c. beautiful.

    d. charming.

3. The word *lumbering* most nearly means

    a. hauling wood.

    b. dancing.

    c. moving gracefully.

    (d.) moving clumsily.

4. The word *affect* most nearly means

    a. influence.

    (b.) imitate.

    c. infect.

    d. reject.

5. The word *profoundly* most nearly means

    (a.) thoroughly.

    b. superficially.

    c. partly.

    d. slightly.

Understanding the Essay

1. As stated in the essay, one of the main reasons the author decides to wear a sari for a month is

    a. to get back in touch with her cultural identity.

    b. to enjoy the comfort and freedom of movement that a sari provides.

    c. to add variety and cultural flair to her wardrobe.

    (d.) to show her daughter that it's possible to be different and still fit in.

2. In India, what is the custom for wearing a sari?

    a. Saris are worn on special occasions such as weddings, parties, and visits to the temple.

    b. Women and female children wear saris for everyday events such as school, work, and play.

    (c.) Adult females may wear saris for everyday events, special occasions, and even sleeping.

    d. Men and women wear saris on special occasions.

3. Which of the following is *not* mentioned as a disadvantage of wearing a sari in New York?

   a. Strangers stare at her.

   b. She is unable to sprint across the street.

   (c.) She finds it difficult to hail a cab.

   d. She can't ride in a crowded subway.

4. In the years before she decided to wear a sari for a month, the author tended to

   a. not worry at all about what she wore.

   b. dress conservatively so that no one would notice her.

   c. wear expensive designer clothing.

   (d.) dress to fit in with the people she associated with.

5. The advantages of wearing the sari include all but which of the following?

   a. Receiving unexpected courtesies from strangers.

   b. Feeling connected to her heritage.

   (c.) Being able to run, jump, and move freely.

   d. Enjoying her family's approval.

Writing in the Margins

These questions encourage you to think not only about the essay but about the issues it raises. Your instructor may ask you to write down your answers, to discuss them in groups, or simply to think about them for class discussion.

1. The author writes at the end of paragraph 7, "It was America's turn to adjust to me." What is the background of this statement? How do you imagine the author feels about her decision to let America adjust to her?

2. What message does clothing send to others? Give at least one example of specific attire and the message it sends. What message do you think Shoba Narayan's sari sent to the people around her?

Topics for Writing

Assignment 1: Someone Else's Turn to Adjust

Paragraph or Journal Entry

The author writes, "It was America's turn to adjust to me." After trying to fit into American life, she is ready to stand out and let other people adjust to her. Have you ever been in a situation where you were no longer willing to fit in with someone else's views about how you should be? Although you may not have put it in exactly the same words, it was time for that person (or group) to adjust to you.

Write a paragraph or journal entry about your experience of deciding to let someone else adjust to you.

Assignment 2: You Are What You Wear

Paragraph

The old saying "Clothes make the man," implies that people will take a person for what he or she appears to be. Can you describe a time when people treated you differently because of your attire? Write a paragraph describing such an incident and the effect that it had on you.

Assignment 3: Your Cultural Heritage

Paragraph or Essay

In the United States, most families originally came from somewhere else. Some, like the author of the essay you just read, try to stay in close touch with their heritage. As generations pass, however, many families grow away from their original culture and become "just Americans." What is your family's cultural heritage? Do you and your family celebrate that culture in any way? Answer in a paragraph or essay.

Assignment 4: The Fabric of Your Life

Paragraph or Essay

Many people undergo similar metamorphoses as their lives change, as they change, as their circumstances change. Think of the various ways you have dressed and the various images you have projected over the past several years (or whatever period of time you wish to include). Then, in a paragraph or essay, write a brief history of the changes in the way you dress. Include a description of the clothing you typically wore, the image you believe it projected, and your reason for choosing the styles you did.

Credits

Michael Ashcraft, "Living at Warp Speed." Originally published in *The Dispatch*, Moline, Illinois, March 27, 1996, under the headline "How Are We Today? Too Busy!" Reprinted with permission of Michael Ashcraft.

Ann Bancroft, "How Is the Day Treating You? Your Bank Teller Wants to Know," in *Open Salon Online*, March 28, 2011, http://open.salon.com/blog/annban/2011/03/28/hows_the_day_treating_you_your_teller_wants_to_know. Reprinted by permission of the author.

Donna Britt, "Young Monsters R U.S." from *The Washington Post*, March 27, 1998. © 1998 by The Washington Post. All rights reserved. Used by permission and protected by the Copyright Laws of the United States. The printing, copying, redistribution, or retransmission of the Material without express written permission is prohibited. www.washingtonpost.com.

Angie Cannon, "National Park Service Collects, Stores Items Left Along the Vietnam Veterans Memorial Wall," *Knight Ridder/Tribune News Service*, May 23, 1997. © by McClatchy-Tribune Information Services. All Rights Reserved. Reprinted with permission.

Cara DiMarco, "Setting Boundaries" from *Moving Through Life Transitions with Power and Purpose*, 2nd edition, by Cara DiMarco. © 2000. Reprinted by permission of Pearson Education, Inc., Upper Saddle River, NJ.

Susanne Goldstein, "Graduated? Seven Tips for College Graduates" from *Christian Science Monitor*, May 13, 2011. Susanne Goldstein is the author of *Carry a Paintbrush: How to Be the Artistic Director of Your Own Career*. You can learn more at www.carryapaintbrush.com. Reprinted with permission of the author.

John J. Macionis, "Don't Blame Me! The New 'Culture of Victimization'" *Sociology*, 6th edition. © 1997, pp. 72–73. Reprinted by permission of Pearson Education, Inc., Upper Saddle River, NJ.

Cynthia Miller, "Civil Rites," from *Lear's* (August 1993). Reprinted by permission of Caroline Miller.

Photo Credits

Index